MICHAEL JACKSON'S
Complete Guide to
SINGLE MALT SCOTCH

MICHAEL JACKSON'S
Complete Guide to
SINGLE MALT SCOTCH

UPDATED BY DOMINIC ROSKROW,
GAVIN D. SMITH, AND
WILLIAM C. MEYERS

LONDON • NEW YORK • MUNICH • MELBOURNE • DELHI

Produced for Dorling Kindersley by
Thameside Media
www.thamesidemedia.com

Photography   Michael Ellis, Ian O'Leary

For Dorling Kindersley
Project Editor   Robert Sharman
Designer   Kathryn Wilding
Managing Editor   Dawn Henderson
Managing Art Editor   Christine Keilty
Production Editor   Ben Marcus
Production Controller   Seyhan Esen
Creative Technical Support   Sonia Charbonnier
US Editor   Chuck Wills

MD364—03/2010

First American edition published by Running Press, 1989
Revised 6th edition first published 2010
Published in the United States by
DK Publishing
375 Hudson Street
New York, New York 10014

10 11 12   10 9 8 7 6 5 4 3 2 1

ISBN 978-0-7566-5898-4

DK books are available at special discounts when purchased in bulk for sales
promotions, premiums, fund-raising, or educational use. For details, contact:
DK Publishing Special Markets, 375 Hudson Street, New York, New York 10014
or SpecialSales@dk.com.

Color reproduction by Media Development Printing Ltd.
Printed and bound in China by Leo Paper Group

Discover more at
www.dk.com

CONTENTS

INTRODUCTION
MICHAEL JACKSON'S LEGACY

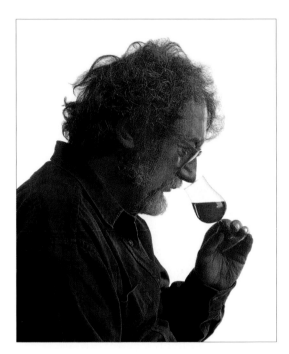

WHEN MICHAEL JACKSON DIED in 2008, he took a special part of the whisky industry with him. Across the world, thousands were saddened by his sudden death. Many of them had never met him or had spoken to him only fleetingly; nevertheless he had touched their lives. Why? Because the characteristics that best defined him were imbued in his writing.

The whisky industry is full of wonderful characters whose talents are matched only by their modesty. Michael, as unpretentious and unassuming as the characters he met and interviewed, was the perfect person to bring their talents to a wider audience. He built bridges within the industry, linking whisky makers and whisky devotees around the world. He gave us access to the world's great distilleries and the people who create great whisky within them. For that we owe him a huge debt of gratitude.

At heart, Michael was a traditionalist. His values harked back to a time when the pace of life was slower and more considered, and he fought with quiet determination to preserve the things he loved and saw as under threat. He wrote for *Slowfood* magazine, eschewed marketing terms such as "brand" and "product," and had little time for the insincerity and disposability of modern consumerism.

Honorable as this approach might be, it could be frustrating on occasion. At tasting competitions, for instance, he refused to be rushed and often a room full of judges would be forced to wait for him as he hunched over a sample long after everyone else had finished and their glasses had been collected. His attitude was simple: if someone had gone to the trouble to create a drink and mature it for several years, the least it deserved was due consideration before judgment was meted out.

It was a similar case with distillery visits. Michael would be at the front of any group, old-fashioned reporters' notebook in hand, asking question after question of the poor guide entrusted with his presence. On one distillery tour, he was asked why he had so many questions when he had visited the distillery several times before. "There's always something new to learn," he said simply.

Which brings us to another of Michael's endearing traits. He was respectful and careful about what he said and how he said it. He held the view that there are very few bad malt whiskies and sought to find something positive about all of them, or to say nothing at all. He set about his tasting notes with almost scientific precision, describing the flavors he encountered while avoiding subjective indulgences.

Over the last 18 months since we were asked to update this book we have spent more time with Michael's writings than most people normally do and we have become increasingly conscious of how these traits—old-fashioned values, modesty, and positivity—define his writing. They are what his many admirers picked up on and loved him for. The closer we have come to his work, the more we have come to admire his precision and astuteness. And as a result, attempting to do justice to Michael and this legacy has been an awesome but ultimately rewarding challenge.

The *Complete Guide to Single Malt Scotch* was last revised more than five years ago, and much has happened since then. Distilleries have reopened, expanded, or changed ownership, new markets have developed for malt, and a whole new malt category has blossomed. Most of all, there has been a proliferation of new expressions. All in all, we have removed more than 500 whiskies from the last edition, as they are no longer available, and replaced them with in excess of 300 new distillery bottlings and more than 200 independent bottlings.

About two-thirds of all the tasting notes are new, but our intention was always to leave as much of Michael's book intact as possible. The opening chapters are largely unchanged, for example, and the introductory pieces for the individual distillery entries have only been updated as necessary. That said, new chapters have been added to reflect the biggest changes in the world of whisky during the last five years, specifically the large growth in malt whisky from non-traditional countries across the world, and the emergence of blended (or vatted) malts as a category in their own right.

We have also tried to be as true to Michael's precise and frugal writing style as possible, and to score whiskies in the same way as he did. This hasn't been easy because scoring is highly subjective and each of us found malts in the old editions that we would have scored differently to Michael. When scoring other malts from the same distillery, were we to give them the score we felt they justified, or align them with Michael's other scores? We went with the latter approach.

Michael also scored most malts in a very tight band. With some notable exceptions, he rarely scored below 60 or above 85. The scoring must therefore be seen in this context. Where other writers often score whiskies over 90, and even 95, this book does so only rarely. And while other books pass judgment on malts, both good and bad, we have sought to do what Michael did and merely describe their properties.

The way to approach this book is to accept that if a malt has been included at all, we consider that it is of sufficient quality to justify being sought after and tasted. A score of 65 suggests a good, decent, but unexceptional whisky. A score of 75 represents a Grade A malt. A score of 85 is a Grade A with distinction, and a whisky that is warmly recommended by the authors. Anything above that is in an elite class of the very finest malts.

Finally, in recognition of Michael's special affection for The Macallan, we have left his extensive work on the distillery's malts as he wrote it, adding in the more recent Fine Oak range but removing virtually nothing from the chapter.

In updating this book we have been helped by countless people within the industry, and we would particularly like to thank those who went to the trouble of expressing support for what we were doing. Hopefully we have repaid their faith by producing a book that still represents Michael and all that he stood for, a book in which the joins don't show and in which Michael's personality and values shine bright.

This *Complete Guide to Single Malt Scotch* is very much Michael Jackson's book, and may it always remain so.

Dominic Roskrow
Gavin D. Smith
William Meyers

March 2010

WHY MALTS?

AN INSTANT GUIDE TO THE PLEASURES OF THE PURSUIT

AT ITS SIMPLEST, MALT WHISKY HAS A STARTLING PURITY. The snow melts on the mountains, filters through rock for decades, perhaps even centuries, bubbles out of a spring, then tumbles down a hillside, until it finds land flat enough and warm enough to grow barley. The water irrigates the barley in the field; persuades it to germinate in the maltings; infuses its natural sugars in the mash tun; becomes beer when the yeast is added; vaporizes in the still; becomes liquid once more in the condenser; enters the cask as spirit, and leaves it as whisky.

THE FLAVOR of malted barley is always present to a degree, clean, sweet, and restorative, but there are many other elements. The rock from which the water rises will influence the character of the whisky. The vegetation over which it flows can also be an influence. In the process of malting, the partially germinated grain is dried, sometimes over a peat fire, and this will impart smokiness. The yeasts used in fermentation can create fruity, spicy flavors. Similar characteristics can be influenced by the size and shape of the stills, which also affect the richness and weight of the spirit. Further aromas and flavors are assumed during maturation in the cask, from the wood used, its previous contents, and the atmosphere it breathes (*see pp. 62–3*).

For people who enjoy a spirit with flavor, malt whisky at its most robust is a world champion. The flavors in a blended Scotch are usually more restrained, as they might be in a cognac. Those who suffer from fear of flavor might feel safer with white rums or vodkas.

THE INDIVIDUALITY of malts is what makes each so different. Naturally enough, they appeal to people who are individualists. A smoky, earthy, seaweedy, medicinal malt from the coasts or islands of Scotland is a spirit of unrivalled power on the palate. A Speysider may be sherryish, honeyed, flowery, and often very complex. Lowlanders are few, but they can be appetizingly grassy and herbal.

Glasses from a distillery tasting session
Tasting glasses after a master class at Bruichladdich. Malt lovers like to learn—classes, tastings, and whisky festivals are popular. Finding flavors and aromas is a sensuous activity.

THE MOMENT for a malt may simply be the occasion for a sociable drink, but some pleasures are more particular: the restorative after a walk in the country or a game of golf; the aperitif; even, occasionally, the malt with a meal; the digestif; the malt with a cigar, or with a book at bedtime.

Martine's cuisine
Writer Martine Nouet conducts classes in cooking with whisky. She drinks whisky with her meals.

THE MEAL Although malt whiskies are more commonly served before or after a meal, as an aperitif or digestif, they very happily accompany some dishes, most obviously sushi. Some malt-loving chefs also like to use their favorite spirit as an ingredient.

THE EXPLORATION Malt drinkers rarely stick to one distillery. They enjoy comparing malts from different regions, and familiarizing themselves with the aromas and flavors of each. To do this is to explore Scotland by nosing-glass. This armchair exploration often leads on to the real thing.

THE DISTILLERIES are often in beautiful locations. Some have their own distinctive architecture. Most are quite small, and it is not unknown for visiting malt lovers to strike up long-term friendships with distillery managers or workers.

THE VISIT Malt lovers often become passionate about Scotland itself. Whisky tourism extends beyond visits to distilleries. The principal whisky regions (the Highlands, especially Speyside; and the Islands, especially Islay) are set in countryside offering outstanding opportunities for hiking, climbing, bird-watching, and fishing. Islay has a festival of whisky and folk music in late May; Speyside has festivals in spring and autumn; and the distilling town of Pitlochry has a summer theater festival.

THE CONNOISSEUR Just as wine enthusiasts progress from comparing vineyards or châteaux to assessing vintages, so malt lovers develop their own connoisseurship. A single distillery may offer malts of different ages, vintage-dated malts, a variety of strengths, and a diversity of wood finishes. As new bottlings are constantly being released, there is no end to this pleasure.

THE COLLECTOR Every lover of malt whiskies sooner or later becomes, to some extent, a collector. It may not be a conscious decision. It can just happen. A few casual purchases, the odd gift. For the collector's friends, birthdays and Christmas are suddenly easy. Some collectors have backgrounds in the trade. Some buy two of every bottle: one to drink, the other to keep. Such collectors pour scorn on those who do not drink any of their whisky. The most serious collections are often found in countries with a nostalgia for the Britain of gentlemen's clubs, leather-upholstered Bentleys, and rugby union. There are famous collectors in Brazil, Italy, and Japan.

Sukhinder's stash
In London, Sukhinder Singh started collecting miniatures. Now he has 2500 bottles in his private collection, and is a whisky merchant and bottler.

Even if it was not bought for that purpose, a collection soon begins to represent a valuable asset. Collections that began after World War II started to come up for sale in the 1980s, and ever since then the size of the whisky auction market has grown and grown.

In 2009 it reached unprecedented heights when McTear's expanded its stand-alone whisky auctions to four a year. At the same time, Bonhams recruited former McTear's auction expert Martin Green and also began to hold whisky auctions quarterly. With the financial markets in turmoil, whisky has attracted a new breed of investor—one who is more interested in pecuniary gain than any love of malt. Whisky may change hands for thousands of pounds, and the possibility of a bottle selling for $120,000 (£100,000) is considered realistic. There are a handful of "grand cru" distilleries and rare bottles from distilleries such as Ardbeg, Springbank, The Macallan, and The Dalmore that will always attract big investments.

If you are considering developing a collection of your own, you might want to think about a theme, based on a specific distillery or geographical region; or you might want to opt for limited edition bottlings. Though whisky is more robust than wine, high temperatures and direct sunlight should be avoided, and bottles should be stored upright, not lying down, as with wine.

THE ORIGINS OF
MALT WHISKY

WHILE GRAPE VINES HAVE their roots in prehistory, barley staked out the beginning of civilization. As hunter-gatherers, human beings picked wild fruits such as grapes, but this source of refreshment and nutrition had a short season and a propensity to rot (or spontaneously ferment) into wines. Fruits take up rainfall from the soil and turn it into highly fermentable, sugary juice. Wild yeasts trigger fermentation, and this process creates alcohol. Perhaps the hunter-gatherers enjoyed the effect, but wine did not provide them with any much needed protein.

When human beings ceased to be nomadic and settled in organized societies they did so in order to cultivate crops. The earliest evidence of this, between 13000 and 8000 years ago, occurs at several sites in the fertile crescent of the Middle East. The first crop was a prototype barley, and the first explanation of its use is a depiction in Sumerian clay tablets of beer making. This is sometimes described as the world's first recipe of any kind.

HALF-WAY TO WHISKY

To grow barley, transform it into malt and then into beer, is half-way towards the making of whisky. While it is easy to obtain the sugars from fruit—peel me a grape, take a bite from an apple—grain is less yielding. The first step toward the unlocking of the sugars in barley and several other grains is the process of malting. This means that the grain is steeped in water, partially germinated, and then dried. The Sumerian civilization was on land that is today Iraq. It may be that malting occurred naturally while the barley was still in the field, as the water rose and fell in the flood plains of this land. This is described poetically on clay tablets in "A Hymn to Ninkasi" *(see p. 16).*

It seems likely that at this stage the Sumerians had no more precise aim than to make grain edible. They did so in the form of beer, though pictograms and relics suggest a grainy, porridgey beverage consumed through straws. This depiction bears a startling resemblance to the "traditional" beer still brewed in villages in some parts of Africa.

Road to the Isles
A few miles from the Bushmills distillery in Ireland, this remarkable rock formation heads for Fingal's Cave, Staffa, and Mull. The first whisky road ... or the first whisky legend?

WHEN YOU POUR OUT THE FILTERED
BEER OF THE COLLECTOR VAT,
IT IS [LIKE] THE ONRUSH OF TIGRIS AND EUPHRATES.
NINKASI, YOU ARE THE ONE WHO POURS OUT THE
FILTERED BEER OF THE COLLECTOR VAT,
IT IS [LIKE] THE ONRUSH OF TIGRIS AND EUPHRATES.

Grain and water meet ...

... in the "Hymn to Ninkasi" (c. 1800bc), found on tablets at several sites in Iraq.
Translated in 1964, by Miguel Civil, of the Oriental Institute of the University of Chicago.
The first evidence of malting?

If the cultivation of grain originally radiated from the first civilization of the Ancient World, the crop itself varied from place to place. To the east, the Chinese and Japanese grow rice, which is fermented to produce saké. To the north, the Russians use rye to make kvass. To the west, barley is brewed. The words "brewed" and "bread" have the same etymology, and, in Germany, beer is sometimes known as "liquid bread."

The soft, sensuous, delicate, capricious grape and the tall, spiky, resilient grain compete to make the world's greatest drinks: fermented and distilled. The weather divides temperate Europe into wine and beer belts. Wine is made in the grape-growing south: Greece, Italy, France, Iberia. Beer belongs to the grainy north: the Czech Republic, Germany, Belgium, and the British Isles. All of these countries also produce distilled counterparts, but the real emphasis on spirits is in the colder countries. The spirits belt links Russia, Poland, the Baltic and Nordic states, and Scotland.

Modern-day Iraq is due south of Armenia, and the Greek historian Herodotus tells us that the Armenians made "barley water." So perhaps the brewing of barley malt spread by way of Armenia, Georgia, and the Ukraine. The Greeks also called all "strangers" Celts. The Romans called them Gallic people, and a part of Turkey is known as Galatia. The term "Galatian" was also used by the Roman author Columella to describe the two-row "race" of barley, preferred today by many brewers.

Sites that were Celtic settlements are even today known for the brewing of beer, notably sites in Bohemia, Bavaria, and Belgium. Many of these sites later gave rise to abbeys, with breweries. Most of the early brewing sites in England, Scotland, and Ireland are on the locations of former abbeys. So are the distilling towns of Cork and Midleton in Ireland. The northeast of Ireland and the western isles of Scotland have associations with St. Columba, who urged his community of Iona to grow barley. In 1494, Friar Cor, of Lindores Abbey in Fife, placed on record in the rolls of the Scottish Exchequer the purchase of malt "to make *aqua vitae*." He probably wasn't the first malt distiller, but he left us the first evidence.

THE ART OF DISTILLATION

It is easy to see how spontaneous fermentation provides a natural model for the first brewers. Evaporation and condensation occur in nature, too, but it is not clear when, or where, distillation was first practised. To distill is to boil the water, wine, or beer, collect the steam, and condense it back into liquid. This drives off certain substances (for example, the salt in water) and concentrates others (such as the alcohol in wine or beer). The process was used by Phoenician sailors to render sea water drinkable, by alchemists, by makers of perfumes and, eventually, in the production of medicines and alcoholic drinks.

One theory has the Phoenicians bringing distillation to Western Europe, via the Mediterranean and Spain, whence it crossed the sea again to Ireland. Another theory has the art spreading by way of Russia and the Nordic countries to Scotland.

The fermented raw material—wine or beer—is boiled to make steam, which, being wraith-like, may have given rise to the English word "spirit" or to the German "*Geist*" (ghost), especially since condensation brings it back to life in a restored (and restorative) form. The "water of life" they call it: vodka, a diminutive form, in Slavic countries; aquavit, in various spellings, in Nordic lands; *eau-de-vie* in French; and *usquebaugh*, in various spellings, in Gaelic. This last became *usky*, then whisky, in English. All of these terms at first simply indicated a distillate, made from whatever was local.

All spirit drinks were originally made in a batch process in a vessel that superficially resembles a kettle or cooking pot, and malt whisky is still made in this way today. But this "pot still" was an inefficient purification vessel, and, in the early days, if the spirit emerged with flavors that were considered disagreeable, they were masked with spices, berries, and fruits.

"PLAIN MALT"

In the mid-1700s, a distinction was made in Scotland between flavored spirits and "plain malt." As the first industrial nation, Britain shaped its beer and whisky with the early technologies of the Industrial Revolution: England's "bright beer" was a copper-colored pale ale, rather than the more "evolved" golden lager of Continental Europe, which was made using more advanced techniques. Scotland's whisky remained a pot-still product, with its own inherent flavors, turned to an attractive complexity.

Most of the northern European countries use a generic term such as "schnapps" for a spirit, and offer both plain and flavored examples. More specific flavorings include caraway and dill, traditional in the aquavit of Scandinavia; and juniper, together with botanical flavorings such as iris root and citrus peel, in the gins of northern Germany, the Low Countries, northern France, and England. Flavored or not, many grain-based spirits outside Britain employ a column still, and most are not aged.

The elements that go to make up a Scottish malt whisky are the local water; a grist comprising malted barley only; traditionally, a degree of peat; pot stills, usually designed and built in Scotland; and aging in oak casks. The last of these elements gradually became more significant from the late 1700s onward.

BLENDED SCOTCH

Like most drinks production, the distilling of malt whisky in Scotland was originally a sideline for farmers. In the coastal coves and Highland glens, illicit distillation was rife. Legislation in 1824 to regulate this activity began the shaping of today's industry. That process was largely finished by the legislation of 1909–15, which initially arose from a trading standards case in the London borough of Islington.

For the farmer-distiller, a few casks of malt whisky might be a hedge against a rainy day. A farm distillery would not have a bottling line. The casks could be sold directly to wealthy householders, to hotels or pubs, or to a licensed grocer, a Scottish institution similar to an

Blending the bottles
The "medicine bottles" on Richard Patterson's workbench contain the latest samples taken from casks of malt whiskies normally included in Whyte and Mackay's blended Scotch. Every cask is slightly different. Patterson checks color, nose, palate—and adjusts accordingly.

American country store. (The outstanding example of such a shop, and still active, is Gordon & MacPhail of Elgin.) One or two renowned distillers might sell their whisky to a wine merchant, sometimes as far away as Edinburgh or London.

Each farmer's whisky would vary from one year to the next, and supply would be irregular. So rather than run out of farmer McSporran's fine dram, the licensed grocers would vat the malts and sell the result under their own label. Some became famous: names such as Chivas Brothers, Johnnie Walker, and George Ballantine. Among the wine merchants known for their bottlings, two in London are still active: Justerini & Brooks and Berry Brothers & Rudd.

Vatting turned to blending when, in the mid-1800s, the column-shaped continuous still was patented. This type of still, operated on an industrial scale, can produce whisky that is lighter in flavor and body. It can also produce whisky more quickly, at a lower cost, and in larger quantities than a pot still. Column-still whisky provides the bulk of a blend, while a combination of pot-still malt whiskies add character and individuality. The volume afforded by blended Scotches, and their less challenging style, helped them become the world's most popular spirits at a time when much of the globe was embraced by the British Empire.

Mountainous Scotland, with its long coastline, had provided mariners, explorers, engineers, teachers, soldiers, and administrators for the empire. Each turned out also to be a propagandist for the virtues of his country's greatest product.

BORN-AGAIN MALTS

More than 90 percent of malt whisky still goes into blends. Scotland has about 100 malt distilleries, of which about two thirds are working at any one time. All but a handful are owned by international drinks companies whose products include blended Scotches. A blend can contain anything from six or seven malts to 30 or 40. The drinks companies like to own the distilleries whose malt whiskies are vital to their blends. They also exchange malts with one another.

The big drinks companies have been growing through mergers since the 1920s. A round of mergers after World War War II left the handful of remaining independent distillers feeling vulnerable. William Grant & Sons, producers of Glenfiddich and Balvenie, decided they no longer wished to rely on supplying blenders, but to actively market their whisky as a single malt. The industry view was that single malts belonged to the past, and that the dominant position of the blends could not be challenged. Happily, Grant's were not dissuaded.

ABERLOUR

ESTD 1879

WAREHOUSE №1

SINGLE CASK SELECTION

SPEYSIDE MALT SCOTCH WHISKY

AGED 11 YEARS

BOURBON CASK MATURED

┌─────────── FILL DETAILS ───────────┐

☑ 1ST   ☑ 2ND   ☐ REFILL

CASK NUMBER...._LL122_........................

FILLED INTO CASK ...._03/12/1998_....

BOTTLE NUMBER..._PRESELECTION_

└────────────────────────────────────┘

70cl   HAND FILLED AT ABERLOUR DISTILLERY   57.2 %
THE ABERLOUR GLENLIVET DISTILLERY CO. LTD.
ABERLOUR ~ SPEYSIDE ~ SCOTLAND

THE WORDS USED ON
THE LABEL

C ONTROVERSY was aroused in 2003 when Cardhu single malt was relaunched as a pure malt. What is the difference, and why did it matter? This book is primarily concerned with malt whisky, but also looks briefly at grain whisky. The main body of the book, the A–Z section, is devoted only to single malt Scotches, but a section at the back deals with products from other countries—these are malt whiskies, but not Scotches. All of these overlapping terms are employed in labeling. What do they say about the liquid in the bottle?

MALT Cereal grain that has been partially sprouted—in preparation for the release of its fermentable sugars—then dried in a kiln. The grains look drier and slightly darker after being malted for distillation. The grain is always barley if the end result is to be malt whisky in the Scottish or Irish style. Other grains can be malted and used in other whiskies, as in the case of rye.

For the beer brewer or whisky distiller, the process of malting in part parallels the crush in wine making or brandy distilling. The premises in which it takes place is called a maltings. The grains are first steeped in water, to encourage their sprouting (or partial germination). Traditionally, the sprouting continues with the grains spread on a stone floor. They are constantly raked, or turned with a shovel, to keep them aerated. Floor malting requires a lot of space and is labor-intensive, but is felt by many to produce the most delicious result. There are several other methods, including ventilated boxes and rotating drums.

Just as grapes are also eaten or used to provide juice, so malted barley is used, either as whole grains or milled, in breads, cakes, and milk shakes. A syrupy, water-based extract of malt sugars is sold as a tonic. An ever-evolving series of barley varieties is used for malting. These are required to produce plump kernels and clean, sweet malt sugars. The farmer distinguishes between malting barley and feed barley for cattle.

Almost all types of whisky employ a proportion of malt. Those that employ no other grain are known as malt whisky. Single malt whiskies are often referred to simply as "malts."

Detailed dram
Malt lovers like to know what they are drinking, and Aberlour provides every last detail when you make your own vatting and bottling at the distillery's visitor center.

Mountain men?
These pot-bellied creatures are the whisky stills at Ben Nevis. The pot-still shape is more evident when the whole vessel is visible.

WHISK(E)Y A spirit drink originating from Scotland and Ireland—but produced in a variety of styles in other countries—distilled from malted barley and other grains, and matured in oak. Its complex aromas and flavors originate from the raw materials, manufacturing process, and maturation. These distinguish whiskies from the more neutral grain spirits in the schnapps and vodka families.

There is a misunderstanding that there are British and American spellings of this term. However, it is not the nationality of the writer, or the country of publication, that should determine the spelling. It is the type of whisk(e)y: thus Scottish and Canadian "whisky," but Irish "whiskey." American styles, such as Kentucky Bourbon and Tennessee whiskey, generally favor the "e", but some labels dissent.

MALT WHISKY Whisky made only from malted barley. Typically distilled in a batch process, in a copper vessel resembling a kettle or cooking pot.

SINGLE MALT WHISKY Malt whisky produced in a single distillery, and not vatted or blended with whisky made in any other distillery. Scotland has by far the most malt distilleries: in the region of a hundred, of which between 80 and 90 percent are operating at any one time. Ireland has one distillery that can produce only malt whiskey, namely Bushmills. Malt whiskies are also distilled on a more limited scale at Cooley and Midleton in Ireland, though both of these distilleries also produce a range of other styles of whiskey. Some very serious malt whiskies are made in Japan, which has seven malt-producing distilleries, and a scattering elsewhere in the world.

SCOTCH WHISKY This term can be applied only to a whisky made in Scotland, and matured for at least three years. No other nation can call a product "Scotch," although any nation can call a product whisky.

Scotland's status is not widely understood beyond its borders. It is not a region but a nation, and has been for almost 1000 years. For the past 300 years, it has been part of a union, and this was not altered by the recent restoration of the Scottish Parliament. Scotland, England, and Wales share an island called Great Britain. These three nations combine with Northern Ireland (a six-county province) to form the United Kingdom.

SINGLE MALT SCOTCH WHISKY Single malt whisky made in Scotland.

SINGLE CASK A bottling made from just one cask.

VATTED MALT If malt whiskies from different distilleries are combined, the result will be called a vatted malt. This might be done to create a desired character, perhaps the flavor of a region. This term assumes that all the whiskies in the vatting are malts.

BLENDED MALT Exactly the same as a vatted malt, this is the term adopted by the whisky industry. It is not the same as a blended Scotch whisky or a blended whisky because there is no grain whisky in a blended malt. Some whisky makers persist with the old terminology, insisting the term blended malt is confusing. You be the judge.

BLENDED SCOTCH WHISKY A stroke of Scottish genius, devised in the Victorian era. Craft producers, mainly in the Highlands and Islands, make small quantities of flavorsome malt whisky. Much larger, more industrial distilleries, mainly in the Midlands and the south, produce large quantities of more neutral grain whiskies to add volume to the malt. The result is a blended Scotch.

GRAIN WHISKY These may be produced from corn (maize), wheat, or raw barley. A small amount of malted barley is required to provide the enzymes needed in fermentation, in a continuous process, in a column-shaped still. Grain whiskies are light in body and flavor, but not neutral, and are matured for a minimum of three years in oak.

SINGLE GRAIN WHISKY There have been attempts to market single grain whisky as a more interesting alternative to vodka, or perhaps as a Scottish "grappa"? Occasional independent bottlings are also of interest to collectors.

FURTHER LABEL TERMS

PEATING When maltsters kilned their grains over open fires, the fuel was whatever could easily be found. In Poland, a style of beer was made from oak-smoked malt. In Franconia, in Germany, beechwood was favored. In Scotland, whisky malt was traditionally kilned over peat fires. The peat gave an especially distinct smokiness to Scotch whisky, and has to varying degrees been retained. Serious whisky lovers have come to cherish peatiness, and demand more, as many of the popular malts have become less smoky to appease consumers who fear flavor. Within the industry, the peat-smoke character is measured in parts per million (ppm) of phenol. The figures do not tell the whole story, however, as the smokiness can be accentuated or softened by the design, shape, and configuration of the stills, the woods used in aging, and so on.

DOUBLE/TRIPLE DISTILLATION Most Scottish malt whisky is run through a pair of stills, but a handful of distilleries have over the years used a system of three linked stills (*see* Springbank). Triple distillation was once traditional in the Lowlands of Scotland (*see* Auchentoshan). It is also favored in Ireland. In theory, the more thorough the distillation, the lighter and cleaner the spirit. Triple should be more exhaustive than double. While this is broadly true, the still's influence on flavor is not completely understood.

BOURBON AGING Why the name bourbon? The French helped the Americans in the War of Independence, and the Americans acknowledged this by naming towns and counties after the French royal family. Bourbon County, in Kentucky, was known for shipping whiskey down the Ohio and Mississippi rivers to New Orleans and other big cities. (Whiskey had been introduced to the United States by Northern Irish immigrants of Scottish origin.)

Local corn is always used to make bourbon, along with rye or wheat, and the bourbon is then matured in a fresh oak barrel. The inside of the barrel is charred to help the whiskey permeate the wood. After only one use in Kentucky, the barrel may be sent to Scotland and used to mature Scottish whisky. It will still retain enough of its typical vanilla-like flavors to impart some of these to the first fill of this whisky; and along with the vanilla, there may be caramel-toffee flavors, dessert apple, and a touch of tannin. There will still be some lively flavor contribution in a second fill. By the third fill the barrel may be relatively neutral. Some barrels are recharred in Scotland.

SHERRY AGING The word "sherry" derives from English attempts to pronounce the Spanish place name Jerez. The wine makers of the Jerez area, in the southwest, near Cadiz and Seville, have a long relationship with the British Isles. Large quantities of their fortified Jerez wines were for a long time shipped to Cork, Bristol (the nearest English port), and Leith (the port that adjoins Edinburgh). Instead of being shipped empty back to Spain, the drained butts and hogsheads were snapped up by whisky distillers. Today, this wine is bottled in Spain, and sherry wood is expensive. Nonetheless some distillers feel that its influence is important. They make the investment (*see pp. 60–1*), and are precise in their requirements. Most sherry is made from the Palomino grape. There are several styles—fino: dry, delicate and fresh; manzanilla: a saltier coastal cousin; amontillado: darker and nuttier; palo cortado: aromatic, complex, and cookie-like; oloroso: rich, creamy, and fruity; Pedro Ximénez (made with the grape of the same name, and not the Palomino): intensely raisiny, syrupy and dark.

CASK STRENGTH A spirit enjoys a number of potencies on its way to the bottle. When it is first distilled it will have a strength in the low 70s or high 60s percentage ABV. It is sometimes reduced with water to a casking strength of about 63% ABV because distillers feel this is the ideal strength to open the spirit up for maturation.

During the maturation process in Scotland and some other countries, a proportion of the spirit's strength is lost through evaporation. This is known as the "angels' share." The amount of loss depends on a number of factors, including the position of the cask in the warehouse, the type of warehouse, the ambient temperature and humidity, the size of cask, and the length of maturation.

At the end of maturation the whisky will be considerably stronger than the common bottling strength of 40–46% ABV. Water is normally added to the whisky to bring it down to this strength. However, the bottler may choose to bottle the whisky at the strength it came out of the cask, in which case it is known as a cask strength whisky.

UNCHILLFILTERED When whisky is chilled some of the proteins, fats and congeners effectively solidify and make the whisky cloudy. To avoid this and keep the whisky in the bottle bright and clear, many distillers chill the whisky and filter out the compounds. But it is increasingly common to leave them in, because it is thought they include flavor compounds. This is what is referred to by "unchillfiltered" or "non chill-filtered" on the label.

FLAVORS

THE INFLUENCE OF THE LANDSCAPE

THE UNIVERSE OF SPIRITS BEGAN to change when the word "designer," having become an adjective, attached itself to the word "vodka." Then, some of the most famous names in the world of distillation became better known for their "ready-to-drink" confections, misleadingly known in the United States as "malternatives." Now a new generation of consumers faces a choice between drinks that come from nowhere, taste of nothing much, and have a logo for a name; and drinks that come from somewhere, have complex aromas and flavors, and may have a name that is hard to pronounce.

Such drinks reflect their place of origin. They have evolved. They have a story to tell. They are good company, and they require something of the drinker in return: that he or she experiences the pleasure of learning to drink. Real, evolved drinks begin as the gift of God. They are grown, whether from grapes, grain, sugar cane, or, for example, the agave plant. They arise from their own *terroir*: geology, soil, vegetation, topography, weather, water, and air. To what extent they are influenced by each of these elements is a matter for debate, often passionate. People care about real drinks.

The most sophisticated of real drinks are the brandies of France and the whiskies of the British Isles. The most complex brandies are the cognacs and armagnacs. The most complex whiskies are those of Scotland and Ireland.

Within these two duopolies, cognac and Scotch are the best known. In Cognac, the regions of production are contiguous, stretch about 90 miles (144 kilometers) from one end to the other, and are all in flat countryside. The whisky distilleries of Scotland, on the other hand, are spread over an area of about 280 miles (448 kilometers) from one end of the country to the other, from the Lowlands in the south to the northern Highlands, from mountain to shore, and from the Hebrides in the west to Orkney in the northeast. Theirs is surely the greater complexity.

Under the volcano
Scotland's landscape can be silent and still, yet the evidence of eruptions, glaciations, and rocky collisions is everywhere. The dews and frosts, the marine plants and mountain forests—each valley or island has its own flavor. Arran, left, has extinct volcanoes and a newish distillery.

Whisky is a real drink. A single malt is as real as it gets. There are many potential influences on its character, and much dispute as to the relative importance—if any—of each. The Macallan distillery receives what might seem disproportionate attention in the following pages because it takes what might aptly be termed single-minded positions on almost every issue: the variety of barley; the strains of yeast; the size of still; and the provenance of the casks.

On these and other issues ever more research is carried out, but an apparent insight into one stage of the whisky-making process may raise new questions about the next. In production, if a procedure is changed, the result may not be apparent until the whisky is mature, perhaps 10 years hence.

THE WHISKY COUNTRIES

Scotland and Ireland can be cool and rainy, but their climates are temperate. The conditions are very favorable for the growing of barley, though excessive damp and wind can occasionally be a problem.

The windy main island of the Orkney islands still cultivates bere, a precursor to barley, but grown today for local bakers rather than distillers. It was used in whisky making in the past, and its importance was such that a dispute over taxes on beer even threatened the Act of Union in 1707.

Today, just as different wine regions champion their own grapes, so there are debates in Europe as to the merits of "continental" barleys, such as those grown in Moravia, Bohemia, and Bavaria, versus the "maritime" examples of Denmark, Scotland, England, and Ireland.

The blood of ...
... *John Barleycorn was spilled by Robert Burns, a Lowlander but from the West. This field of barley is in the East, near the Lowland distillery, Glenkinchie.*

Supporters of the continental barleys say they provide a sweeter, nuttier flavor. Protagonists for the maritime varieties argue that they have a clean, "sea-breeze" character.

Naturally, the Scots prefer their own barley. Depending upon the harvest, and their own needs, they have on occasion exported, but in other periods they have augmented their own malt with "imports" from England. Their second choice would be Denmark, and then elsewhere. Purists would prefer that the Scots used only their own barley. The Scots could argue that they are simply victims of their own success in selling so much of their whisky.

It is because barley is more resilient that it has a broader belt of cultivation, and can be more easily transported, than the grapes that make wine and brandy. Scotland's main growing regions are on the more sheltered eastern side of the country: on the shores of the Moray firth (The Black Isle and The Laich of Moray), Aberdeenshire, and the Borders. Ireland's are in the southeast, behind an imaginary line on the map, which runs from the border city of Dundalk (with a history of brewing) in County Louth, to the sailing (and gastronomic) resort of Kinsale, County Cork. Both countries might wish for more cultivable land; Scotland is mountainous, and Ireland boggy.

TASTING THE *TERROIR*

Scotland seems like a machine for the making of whisky: a nation on a small island, awaiting the vapors of the sea; providing summits to unlock their precipitation, which then filters through a diversity of rock, via springs and mountain streams, over peat and heather, to the fields of barley and the distilleries.

Scotland's heather-clad hillsides, its peaty moorlands, and its seaweed-fringed islands all contribute to the character of its national drink. To sample some of the more pungent malts is to taste the *terroir*. But to what extent are the aromas and flavors carried by the mountain streams or burns that feed the distilleries? Is the greater influence in the peat that is used to dry the malt? Then there is the question of the atmosphere in the damp, earth-floored warehouses, and its influence on the whisky.

Heather, peat, and seaweed are not unique to Scotland, but the country is unusually rich in all three. Their local variations, their proportion, their juxtaposition, and their relationship with the rest of the landscape are unique. Every landscape is. The color of a person's hair or eyes, or the shape of a nose or jawline, are not unique, but the face is, and it derives from them all.

On the map, Scotland presents a weatherbeaten face. The outline—the coast—is penetrated by endless inlets from the sea. These inlets are variously known as "sea lochs" or "firths"; the latter word has the same roots as the Norwegian "fjord."

"SCANDINAVIAN SCOTLAND"

In its topography, its use of Viking words, its Protestant rigor (with some ambivalence toward alcohol), Scotland can resemble Norway, the nearest of the Scandinavian countries. Scotland seems to reach northward, higher into the spirits belt, while its Celtic cousin Ireland (more especially the Republic) appears to lean south, toward the Roman Catholic countries of mainland Europe.

Scotland is bigger in both land area and population than Ireland. It also has 20 or 30 times as many distilleries. At one stage, for a brief period, the numbers of stills in each of the countries were close, but Ireland's industry spent decades in decline before rediscovering itself in recent years. Whichever country "discovered" the barley distillate, and this is contentious, Scotland is today's pre-eminent "Land of Whisky."

Only whisky made there can be called Scotch. For many years, the industry repeated this without making clear its meaning. Were their spokesmen simply repeating an appellation? Or did they mean that no other country could make a comparable product? Scotch whiskies all taste of their homeland to varying degrees, but in many the taste is so subtle as to be scarcely evident, while in others the aromas of peat and seaweed, for example, are wonderfully shocking.

The handful of malt whiskies (as opposed to the "pot-still Irish" type) made at Bushmills and Cooley in Ireland are similar in style to their Scottish counterparts; as are the handful of Japanese malts, though some have distinct local features. But a whisky cannot taste of Scotland if it is made in Ireland or Japan, however similar the *terroir*. The most characterful whiskies taste of the *terroir*, wherever it is. They are real drinks.

ROCK

Geology as a discipline began in Scotland—with the book *Theory of the Earth*, published in 1788. The author, Dr. James Hutton, was a Scot, inspired in part by the natural landscape of his homeland. The geology of Scotland is more varied than that of any country of a similar size. Much of this diversity arises from a spectacular collision 400–500 million years ago. The part of the earth's crust that is now Scotland was at that time attached to North America. It was in

Rosebank
Roses once bloomed at Rosebank. Now rosebay willowherb has taken over. The whisky tastes of camomile … or carboniferous rock.

collision with a European plate that included England, Wales, and Ireland. The fault line where the two plates met was more or less followed a few million years later by Hadrian's Wall, and the border between England and Scotland has rarely strayed more than a few miles from this line since. The geological turbulence continued, with everything from volcanoes to glaciers, until 20,000 years ago.

Thus not only did geology begin with Scotland, but Scotland began with geology: with the thrusts, intrusions, eruptions, and glaciations. It came to rest, semantically, as a Gaelic-language landscape, with "corries" (hollows in the mountainside); "lochans" (small lakes) and "lochs" in a wide range of sizes (sometimes stretching for many miles, and possibly with a small opening to the sea); "straths" (broad valleys); and the "glens" (or narrower valleys) that appear on every other label. *This* is the whisky-making machine.

In 1990, geologists Stephen Cribb and Julie Davison made a study of rock formations in Scotland's whisky regions, and compared them with tasting notes in books on the drink, including this one. Their findings suggested that the similar tastes in certain whiskies produced near each other might in part be due to the similar rock from which the water rose. For example, in the Lowlands, the crisp, dry Glenkinchie and Rosebank share the same carboniferous rock. The oldest rock is that which supplies water to the Bowmore and Bruichladdich distilleries on Islay, off the west coast of Scotland; it was formed about 600–800 million years ago, and seems to contribute an iron-like flavor.

For many years, whisky makers always spoke of granite. Being so hard, granite does not donate minerals to the water. Thus hard rock means soft water, and vice versa. Granite is the principal rock of the

Grampians, the group of mountains and sub-ranges that dominates the Highlands, and from which the Spey River flows. Every Speyside distiller seemed to claim that he had soft water, "rising from granite and flowing over peat." In looking at the Grampians, the Cribbs' book *Whisky on the Rocks* identified Ben Rinnes and the Conval Hills as sources of the typical Speyside water, feeding distilleries such as Glenfarclas, Aberlour, and Craigellachie. The study went on to point out that the region's geology is diverse, embracing substantial areas of limestone and sandstone. One distillery that has, sensibly, made a virtue of its sandstone water source is Glenmorangie, located in the northern Highlands.

Mineral flavors—and textures—are familiar from bottled waters, and also seem evident in some malt whiskies. Water is used to steep the grain at maltings (though only a handful of these are attached to distilleries). It is employed in the mash tun at every distillery to extract the sugars from the malted barley. It is used to reduce the strength of spirit in the cask to aid maturation. It is also used to reduce mature whisky to bottling strength. For this last stage the local water is influential only in the handful of distilleries that bottle on site, and in those cases, it is very influential indeed.

SNOW

Vodka marketeers love to promote their products with suggestions of snowy purity, whether they are distilled in St. Petersburg, Poznan, or in Peoria, Illinois. Some vodkas are distilled in one place and rectified in another. Others have Slavic origins, but are produced under license in North America or elsewhere.

Snow on the Spey
The Spey River rises south of the Dalwhinnie distillery, one of Scotland's highest. Clearly whisky made from snowmelt, but also with some peaty complexity. Absolut Scotland ...

Snow-melt is more reliably found in Scottish malt whisky. There is typically snow on Scotland's highest mountain, Ben Nevis (measuring 4410 feet or 1344 meters high), for six to seven months of the year, and occasionally for longer: perhaps from September to May, or even all year. The same can be true in the Grampians, though three or four months is more common.

At sea level, especially in the drier east, Scotland may have less than 32 inches (800 millimeters) of rain and snow a year. In the mountains, that figure can more than triple. Once the snow melts, it descends by a variety of routes, filtering through fissures in the rock, emerging from springs, swelling streams or burns, or gushing into rivers like the Spey, Livet, and Fiddich.

High in the hills, distilleries like Dalwhinnie or Braeval might regard their water as snow-melt. By the time it has swollen the Spey, then been tapped by Tamdhu, it is regarded as river water. If it filters through the Conval Hills in search of Glenfiddich, Balvenie, or Kininvie, it emerges as the spring water of Robbie Dubh. Every distillery knows where it collects its water, and protects its source as a critical asset. Distillers know where their water arrives, but it may be impossible to say whence it came, or how long its journey was, except that it was once rain or snow.

WATER

The worry over water concerns not only quality, but also quantity. A great deal is required, not only for the steeps at the maltings and the mash tun at the distillery, but also to cool the condensers or worm tubs, to wash vessels, and to reduce the strength of the spirit in the cask or the mature whisky at bottling.

Unlike brewers of beer, the distillers of whisky do not add or remove salts to change the composition of their water. Not only must water for malting and mashing be available in volume, it must also be consistent in character. If a source threatens to run dry in the summer, the distillery may stop production and devote a few weeks' "silent season" to annual maintenance and vacations. If the water runs unusually slowly, or quickly, it may become muddy or sandy. If the water source is endangered by a project in the next county upstream, that could be a critical problem. And it is certainly critical if the distillery's production is outstripping the water source. Even the most sophisticated of distillery companies has been known to hire a water diviner to find an additional nearby source. Every effort will be made to match the character of the principal water used.

The issue of soft water versus hard goes beyond the flavor of any salts naturally occurring in the water. Calcium, for example, increases the extract of malt sugars in the mash tun, and may also make for a cleaner, drier whisky. Whether it does—whether, indeed, such influences could survive distillation—is hotly debated.

Visitors to distilleries are sometimes invited to sample the water. It can taste intensely peaty. Yet the whisky may be barely peaty at all. This is the case at the famous Speyside distillery, Glen Grant. The explanation would seem to be that the peaty taste does not survive distillation. Speyside is also rich in heather. Is that why its whiskies are so floral? The circumstantial evidence is strong, but some distillers might argue that the flowery character actually results from reactions during maturation.

On the island of Islay, even the tap water can be tinged a peaty brown or ironstone red. Perhaps the water flowed over peat for a longer distance. Did it linger, and take up more peatiness? Or flow faster and dig up its peaty bed? The bed may also have contributed some ironstone, or some green, ferny, vegetal character. This time, the flavors do seem to carry over into the whisky. Perhaps the flavors were absorbed when the peaty water was used to steep the barley at the beginning of the malting process. Unlike the maltings on the mainland, those on Islay highlight the intensity of local peat. It is the use of peat fires in the drying of the grains that imparts the greatest degree of smokiness and "Islay character" to the malt. The peat in the kiln is the smoking gun. The Islay distiller has the soul of an outlaw.

PEAT

Not only is aroma the bigger part of taste—the drinks and foods that arouse the appetite and the imagination are often fragrant—but these same foods are in fact frequently grilled, barbecued, roasted, toasted, or smoked: the breakfast kippers, bacon, toast, and coffee; the steak sizzling on a

Tasting the *terroir*
The basis of terroir *is the earth. Here, it is sliced, and placed on a fire, so that its smoke pervades the malt. Some peat cutting on Islay is still done by hand.*

charcoal grill; the chestnuts roasting on an open fire. Of all the techniques historically used to kiln malt in different parts of Europe, the peat fires of Scotland surely produce the most evocative aromas. While some devotees of single malts have a catholic view, many take sides: will it be the peaty, briny whiskies of the islands and coasts; or the flowery, honeyed, sometimes sherried Speysiders?

The partisans for peat lust for its intensity (and love quoting ppm), but it also imparts a number of complex flavors and aromas. At least 80 aroma compounds have been found in peated malt.

While peatiness excites connoisseurs, it can alienate first-time tasters. When people say they "don't like" Scotch whisky, they often refer to a "funny taste," which turns out to mean peat. To take exception to such a fundamental element of the drink may seem odd, but distinctive, powerful flavors, especially if they are dry, can be challenging. Very hoppy beers are a perfect parallel. At a pinch, heavily oaked wines might also be drawn into the discussion.

In whisky, the dryness of peat provides a foil for the sweetness of barley malt, but that is a bonus, as is peat's rich content of anti-oxidants, the enemy of free radicals.

Peat was used in the first place because it is a convenient and plentiful fuel. Ninety percent of the world's peat bogs are in temperate-to-cold parts of the northern hemisphere. Two-thirds of Britain's bogland is in Scotland, which in land area is half the size of England. Scotland's northern Highlands has Europe's largest expanse of blanket bogs. These bogs, in the counties of Caithness and Sutherland, are said to set a standard in the worldwide study of the phenomenon.

The peat that seduces whisky lovers is on the distillery islands of Orkney and Islay. In both cases, the sea air and high winds add salty flavors to the peat. The coast of Islay is heavily fringed with seaweed, which adds an iodine, medicinal character to the atmosphere. This, too, penetrates the peat. The Orcadian peat is younger, more heathery, and incorporates a wide range of salt-tolerant maritime plants. In the western islands, especially Islay, the peat is rich in bog myrtle (*Myrica gale*), also known as sweet gale, which has a sweet, cypress-like aroma and bitter flavor. Bog myrtle was one of the flavorings used in beer before the hop plant was adopted, and clearly influences the flavors imparted by the peat.

When peat is being cut by hand, the spade digs out a cube with surfaces as shiny and dark as a bar of "black" chocolate. It sometimes looks as edible as Mississippi mud pie. A closer look at the muddy block sometimes reveals the fossil-like remains of mosses. The principal component is sphagnum, a spongy moss that intertwines with other plants to form a fibrous soil, which, under pressure, will eventually become coal. The peatbogs of Scotland began to grow between 7000 and 3000 years ago, and are up to 23 feet (7 meters) deep.

Ireland is also famously boggy, and no doubt its rural whiskey makers burned peat, but distilling quickly moved to an industrial scale, concentrated in the few big cities, and the lack of peat became a defining characteristic of the "smooth" Irish whiskies. The large, urban distillers used coke to fire smokeless maltings. Having been overtaken in volume long ago by the country next door, the Irish are now rediscovering the merit of variety. A peated single malt called Connemara was launched in 1995–96 by the Cooley distillery, and has gone on to win several judgings.

HEATHER

In the unofficial national anthem, the "Flower of Scotland" is Robert the Bruce; in heraldry, it is the thistle; in the world of drinks, it is surely heather. While the thistle is Scotland (prickly, defensive, and looking for a fight), heather is attractive and lucky. In Scotland, especially Orkney, it was traditionally the flavoring for an ale. When a whisky has a floral aroma, the flower is frequently heather. Often, it is not the flower itself but heather honey.

These characteristics are especially notable on Speyside and Aberdeenshire, where the hills are dense with heather. Glen Elgin and Balvenie are two whiskies with a notably heather-honey character. In

The color purple
Heather is a distinctive feature of the Scottish landscape. Its color does not affect the whisky, but the floral and honey aromas often seem to have jumped into the glass.

Aberdeenshire, Glendronach and Glen Garioch have an enjoyable touch of heather, balancing their dry maltiness.

Heather is a significant component of much peat in Scotland. At some distilleries, notably Highland Park, lore has it that sprigs of heather were thrown on to the peat fire in the maltings. Water flows over heather to several distilleries. Besoms, or brooms, made of heather twigs were once commonplace in Scotland, and were typically used to clean wooden washbacks (fermenting vessels). Whether their effect was to sanitize or inadvertently to inoculate with micro-organisms is a piquant question. Wild yeast activity is at its height in summer, when bees are pollinating, and heather is a favorite source of nectar.

The Greek for the word "brush" gives us the botanical name *Calluna vulgaris* for the purple ling heather, which carpets the hillsides from mid-August into September. The brighter, redder bell heather (*Erica cinerea*) and the pinker, cross-leafed variety (*Erica tetralix*) flower about a month earlier. The English name for this group of small evergreen shrubs derives from their liking of heaths, but they also grow in bogs and on mountainsides. All three occur in Scotland, where heather covers between 4 to 5 million acres (1.6 and 2 million hectares).

Some varieties are found throughout northern Europe, others are native to Scotland, which has the greatest abundance of the plants. Scottish settlers introduced heather to North America.

BARLEY

Everyone knows that wines and brandies are made from grapes, but what about beer or whisky? Many consumers are unsure. Beer is often thought, mistakenly, to be made from hops. And whisky?

In explaining, and therefore promoting, its natural qualities, the grape does rather better than the grain. Wine makers often indicate on their labels which varieties of grape they have used. They may do this even if the wine is not a varietal. They might even discuss their choice of grape varieties on a back label or hang tag, and in their public relations and advertising.

Whisky makers do not in general do this. Why not? Are they using poor-quality barley? No. Malting requires barley of good quality. The argument for reticence is threefold: barley's contribution to flavor in whisky is less than it would be in beer, and even less than that of the grapes in wine. Second, perhaps simply as a reflection of the above, the difference between varieties is less obvious when it comes to flavor. Third, perhaps explaining this, the act of distillation removes some characteristics, and others are masked by the flavors gained during maturation. All of this is true up to a point, but what the distiller puts into his vessels must be a factor in the liquid that issues from them.

Almost all whisky distillers buy their barley according to a set of technical criteria (corn size, nitrogen, moisture content, etc.), rather than by variety. Some varieties bred or selected in the period of innovation after World War II are still legends. The last of that line, Golden Promise, represented 95 percent of the harvest at its peak. Its short straw stands up to the wind; it ripens early (in August); and it produces nutty, rich flavors.

As the industry has grown, farmers have switched to varieties that give them more grain per acre, and therefore increase their profitability, while distillers have sought varieties that yield more fermentable sugars. These, however, do not necessarily produce delicious flavors, any more than do bigger, redder strawberries out of season. Nor do the varieties last much more than four or five seasons before being overtaken by something "better."

SEAWEED

The medicinal note in most Islay malts, especially Laphroaig, surely derives from seaweed, a source of iodine. The sea washes against the walls at all the distilleries, except Bruichladdich, and the coast is enwrapped with seaweed. How do the seaweedy, iron-like aromas get into the spirit? It seems likely that they are carried ashore by the winds and the rain, and permeate the peaty surface of the island. Then, when the rivers and burns flow over the peat to the distilleries, they pick up these flavors and impart them in the steep or the mash tun. If the boggy surface is, indeed, impregnated with the seaweedy rain, then a further opportunity will arise when the peat is cut and burned in the distillery's maltings.

The greatest scepticism concerns the belief that the casks in the warehouses "breathe in" the atmosphere. Distillers who use centralized warehouses, away from the distillery, especially favor this argument. Some age on site spirit which is destined to be bottled as single malt, but send to centralized warehouses spirit that is destined for blending.

Seaweed has been described as one of Scotland's most abundant natural resources. The harvesting of seaweed was once a significant industry in Scotland. There is some circumstantial evidence that the practice was introduced by monks on the islands of the west. This is the part of Scotland with the most seaweed. Skye has especially dense kelp forests, sometimes stretching 3 miles (5 kilometers) offshore and

Whisky and water
The village and distillery of Bowmore face the sea loch around which Islay wraps itself.
Some of the distillery's warehouses are below sea level. Even on a calm day, the atmosphere
is rich in the aromas of seaweed.

more than 65 feet (20 meters) deep. In the islands, kelp was
traditionally used as a fertilizer. It was also collected as a source of
iodine. More recently, it was used to provide alginates to clarify beer
and set jellies and desserts.

FLAVORS SHAPED AT THE DISTILLERY

In the balance of influences, much more importance has been
accorded in recent years to the way in which the distillery works.
Twenty-seven malt distilleries, (about a third of the industry's working
total) are owned by Diageo, the world's biggest drinks group; and
Diageo argues strongly that the most important influences on flavor
come from within the distillery itself.

The basic process of making malt whisky is the same throughout
Scotland, but there are endless small but significant areas of variation.
The degree of peating in the malt is one, similar to the choice of roasts
in coffee. Another example is the density (or original gravity) of the
malt-and-water mixture that goes into the mash tun (the "coffee
filter"). The time the mixture spends in the mash tun, the temperatures
to which it is raised, and the duration of each stage, all vary slightly
from one distillery to the next. Inside a traditional mash tun is a system

The infusion
Like coffee in a filter, the ground grains of malted barley are soaked in warm water, in a vessel with a sieve-like base. The stirring mechanism rotates and can be lowered so that its blades prevent the mixture from solidifying.

of revolving rakes to stir the mixture. In the more modern lauter system, developed in the German brewing industry, a system of knives is used. The German word "lauter" means pure or transparent, and refers to the solution of malt sugars that emerges from the vessel.

As in cooking, every variation affects everything that follows, so that the permutations are infinite. It can be very difficult to determine which aspect of procedure has what effect. Despite that, the industry in general has over the years adopted a rather casual attitude toward yeast's use in fermentation. The view taken was that yeast's influence on flavor would largely be lost in distillation, and that its job was simply to produce as much alcohol as possible.

For years, almost all of Scotland's malt distillers employed the same two yeast cultures. An ale yeast from one of the big brewers was used because it started quickly. Then there was a second pitching with a whisky yeast from Distillers' Company Limited (now long subsumed into a component of Diageo). This had less speed but more staying power. Mergers and changes in ownership resulted in different yeasts coming into the industry. Many distilleries now use only one culture; even Macallan, who insisted on three, have retreated to two.

The action of yeast in fermentation creates flavor compounds called "esters," which are variously fruity, nutty, and spicy. It is difficult to accept that none of these would survive distillation. Diageo believes that the amount of time spent in the fermenter is critical to the individuality of each distillate. The effect of a new yeast culture can be tasted in new make, but the final result will not be determined until the whisky is mature.

Fermentation vessels in Scottish malt distilleries are known as "washbacks." Some are closed vessels made of metal, usually stainless steel. These are easy to clean and relatively safe from contaminants. Despite this, some distilleries prefer wooden washbacks, usually made from larch or Oregon pine. These are open, with a movable lid. Although they are cleaned thoroughly, it is hard to believe that they accommodate no resident microflora. Perhaps these contribute to the house character of some of the more interesting whiskies. Meanwhile, whether the microclimate in and around the distillery has an influence is hotly debated.

Anyone who cooks will know that a recipe, however rigidly followed, will produce different results every time, depending upon the source of heat, the utensils, the cook, and so forth. The design of the stills is a factor increasingly emphasized by Diageo, but even this has an element of location. Some farmhouse distilleries clearly had stills designed to fit their limited space. Elsewhere, several distilleries in the same valley will have the same shape of still (in much the same way that train stations on the same line may look alike). Obviously, the local coppersmith had his own way of doing things. Distilleries are reluctant to change the shape or size of their stills when wear and tear demands replacement, or when an expansion is planned. The legend is that if a worn-out still has been dented at some time, the coppersmith will beat a similar blemish into its replacement, in order to ensure that the same whisky emerges.

Illegal distillers used just one small (and therefore portable), copper pot. Since then stills have grown, and are typically run in pairs (or occasionally threesomes), but the principles have not changed. It is clear that design has been largely empirical, with experiments and innovations introduced by individuals. It is often hard to imagine how a bit of extra piping here or there can make a difference. The ratio of surface areas to heat, liquid, vapor, and condensate have infinite effects that are not fully understood.

It is argued that in a tall, narrow still, much of the vapor will condense before it can escape. The condensate will fall back into the still and be redistilled. This is known as reflux. The result is a more thorough distillation and a more delicate spirit. Because there is far less

Water music?

Not a French horn, or any musical instrument, but the unromantically named worm tub. This is Edradour's. The coil is 80 ft (24.5 m) long. The diameter starts at 8 inches (20 cm) and finishes at 2 inches (5 cm).

reflux in a short, fat still, the spirit will be oilier, creamier, and richer. This is just the simplest example of how the still shape influences the character of the whisky.

Stills vary enormously in size and shapes range from "lantern" or "lamp" to "onion" or "pear." Some have a mini-column above the shoulders or, more often, a "boil ball." Others have pipes known as "purifiers" in order to create reflux. The pipe that carries the vapor to the condenser is sometimes at an upward angle, or it can be straight, or point downward. The first will create the most reflux and the last little or none.

The traditional method of condensing is in a worm tub. The vapors pass through a worm-like coil of copper piping in a tub of cold water. This tends to produce a more pungent, characterful spirit, with a heavier, maltier, cereal-grain character.

The more modern system has the opposite relationship between vapor and water. It involves a single large tube, inside which are packed smaller tubes. The small tubes are circulated with cold water, while the vapor passes through the large tube. This is called a shell-and-tube condenser. It is more efficient, and is said to produce lighter, grassier, fruitier spirits.

At a time when the industry was moving from worm tubs to shell-and-tube, Diageo made this change at its Dalwhinnie distillery. It was subsequently decided that the spirit had changed character to an unacceptable degree, and the distillery reverted to worm tubs.

One of the most important judgments in influencing flavor is deciding the speed at which the stills are run. A slower distillation leads to more contact between the liquid and the copper than a faster distillation, and this is usually desirable. Only part of the distillation is kept as useable spirit, though. Known at "the cut," this is the middle section of the distillation run. Judging the cut points is crucial.

In maturation, most distillery managers prefer a stone-built, earth-floored, cool, damp warehouse. Such an atmosphere is felt to encourage the casks to breathe. In this type of structure, known as a dunnage warehouse, the casks are normally stacked only three high, usually with planks between them as supports. The more modern type of warehouse has a concrete floor and fixed racking, and can contain several stories of maturing casks. The atmosphere is generally warmer and drier than in dunnage warehouses. As is often the case, the old, inefficient system, more vulnerable to the vagaries of nature, produces the more characterful result.

Still life

The creaminess of Macallan is attributed in part to its short, fat stills. In this picture, the stillman provides a sense of scale. The stills at Glenmorangie are twice as tall, and produce a spirit of legendary delicacy.

REGIONAL VARIATIONS

LIKE WINES—AND MANY OTHER DRINKS—the single malts of Scotland usually identify in their labeling not only their country of origin but also the region within it. To know where in Scotland a whisky was produced is to have a very general idea of its likely character. The differences arise from *terroir* and tradition; there are no regional regulations regarding production methods. In their aroma and palate, some whiskies speak of their region more clearly than others, as is the case with wines. Within Bordeaux, a particular Pomerol, for example, might have a richness more reminiscent of Burgundy; similar comparisons can be made in Scotland.

THE LOWLANDS

These are the most accessible whiskies, both in terms of palate and geography, but sadly they are few in number. From the border town of Carlisle, it is less than 100 miles (160 kilometers) to the southernmost Scottish distillery, Bladnoch, which has been back in production since December 2000.

Only two Lowlanders are in constant production. One of these is Auchentoshan, sometimes billed as "Glasgow's only working distillery." It is on the edge of the city, at Dalmuir, across the Dunbartonshire county line. In Lowland tradition, the whisky is light in both flavor and body, but surprisingly complex and herbal. Auchentoshan is now the sole practitioner of the Lowland tradition of triple distillation. The distillery does not have a visitor center, but professional tours are possible by arrangement. With its galleried mash house and uncluttered still-house, it is very visitor-friendly.

The other thriving Lowlander, at the opposite side of the country, is Glenkinchie, "The Edinburgh Malt." This pretty distillery is about 15 miles (25 kilometers) southeast of the city, in the direction of the border. Its spicy whisky has a popular following, and the distillery has a visitor center.

Maritime malt
Riveted, not welded, this pot still has a marine appearance befitting its region. Campbeltown's heyday was the era of coastal steamers. Fat stills make oily, muscular whiskies.

45

In the last couple of years, hope has faded for the reopening of the Lowland distilleries Littlemill and Rosebank, although various bottlings of both are still available. There is a possibility, too, that Rosebank's equipment may find future use in a planned new distillery at Falkirk. Rosebank, which triple distilled, was widely regarded as a classic, and its whisky is collectible. Half a dozen further whiskies are still to be found from Lowland distilleries, some of which closed as long ago as the 1970s.

There were never a great many Lowland malts, but to have only three active distilleries is perilously few. The delicacy of the Lowlanders makes its own contribution to the world of single malts. This style can be very attractive, especially to people who find the Highlanders and Islanders too robust.

The Lowlanders' problem has been that the Highlanders and Islanders have the romance. Many consumers like a gentle, sweetish malt such as is typical in the Lowlands, but they want the label to say it came from the Highlands. This is analogous with the wine industry, where consumers who like sweetish Chardonnays nevertheless insist that they are drinking a "dry white."

The notion of the Lowlands as a whisky region would be reinforced if it could annex two distilleries that are barely across the Highland line: Glengoyne and Loch Lomond. The first is very pretty, can be visited, and is barely outside Glasgow. Its malty whisky would be perfectly acceptable as a Lowlander. The second is a more industrial site, but a much more attractive distillery than it once was, and it makes a variety of whiskies. Pressed to "defect," both would probably cling to the Highland designation.

THE HIGHLANDS

The border between the Lowland and Highland distilleries is surprisingly southerly, following old county boundaries, stretching across the country between the rivers Clyde and Tay. Some commentators talk of a "southern Highlands," embracing the Tullibardine distillery and Deanston. Beyond these two, the spread is clearly eastern.

THE EASTERN HIGHLANDS includes, among others, the newly independent Edradour, the smallest distillery in Scotland. Another tiny, farm-style distillery, Glenturret, now finds itself greeting visitors as "The Famous Grouse Experience." The much larger but handsome Aberfeldy distillery has a similar role as "Dewar's World of Whisky."

The border
It is neither the Berlin Wall nor Hadrian's, but it is Border country. The outer wall of a warehouse is turned to brash advertisement at the otherwise discreet Bladnoch distillery. Several distilleries identify themselves with such bold wall paintings.

All of these, together with Blair Athol, are in Perthshire. Any of them could comfortably be visited in a day trip from Edinburgh (about 70 miles, or 112 kilometers, away), and all are on or near the main road north to Speyside. Perhaps for reasons of geology, several distilleries in this region have notably fresh, fruity whiskies. Farther north, in barley-growing Aberdeenshire, some heftier whiskies emerge from handsome distilleries such as Royal Lochnagar, Glen Garioch, and Glendronach.

SPEYSIDE is not precisely defined, but it embraces between a half and two-thirds of Scotland's distilleries, including the most widely recognized whisky names. A generous definition of Speyside is assumed in this book. Strictly speaking, the long-gone distilleries of Inverness were regarded as Highlanders, not Speysiders.

Again for the convenience of the visitor, this book divides the region into a series of river valleys. In some of these valleys, there do seem to be similarities between the whiskies of neighboring distilleries.

The Spey River itself is lined with distilleries on both banks, but a number of tributaries and adjoining rivers frame the region. Speyside's ascendancy rested not only on the Grampian mountain snow-melt and the malting barley of Banff and Moray, but also on the railroad era. Trains on a rustic branch alongside the Spey took workers and barley

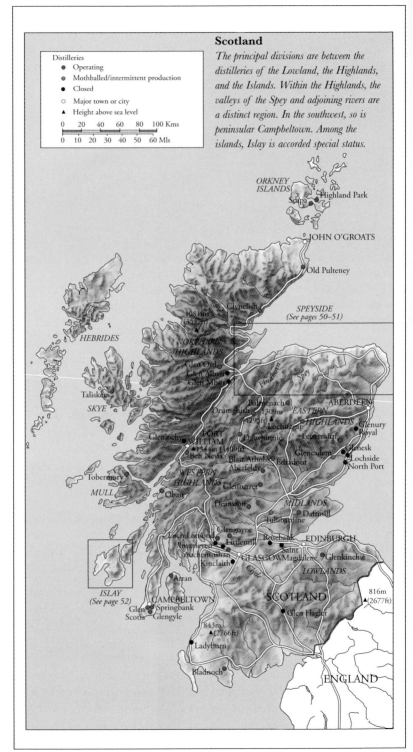

Scotland

The principal divisions are between the distilleries of the Lowland, the Highlands, and the Islands. Within the Highlands, the valleys of the Spey and adjoining rivers are a distinct region. In the southwest, so is peninsular Campbeltown. Among the islands, Islay is accorded special status.

Distilleries
- Operating
- Mothballed/intermittent production
- Closed
- Major town or city
- ▲ Height above sea level

| 0 | 20 | 40 | 60 | 80 | 100 Kms |
| 0 | 10 | 20 | 30 | 40 | 50 | 60 Mls |

ORKNEY ISLANDS
Scapa
Highland Park

JOHN O'GROATS

Old Pulteney

Clynelish

SPEYSIDE
(See pages 50–51)

HEBRIDES

1081m
(3537ft)

NORTHERN HIGHLANDS
Glen Ord
Glen Albyn
Glen Mhor

Talisker

SKYE

Balmenach
Drumguish 1309m
(4295ft)
Lochnagar
Dalwhinnie

ABERDEEN
EASTERN HIGHLANDS
Glenury Royal
Fettercairn

Glenlochy
FORT WILLIAM
1344m (4409ft)
Ben Nevis
Blair Athol
Aberfeldy
Edradour

Glencadam
Glenesk
Lochside
North Port

Tobermory

MULL

Oban

WESTERN HIGHLANDS
Glenturret

Deanston

MIDLANDS
Deanston
Daftmill
Tullibardine

Glengoyne
Loch Lomond
Inverleven
Littlemill
Rosebank
EDINBURGH
Auchentoshan
GLASGOW
Kinclaith
Saint Magdalene
Glenkinchie

Arran

ISLAY
(See page 52)

CAMPBELTOWN
Glen Scotia
Springbank
Glengyle

LOWLANDS

SCOTLAND

816m
(2677ft)

Glen Flagler

843m
(2766ft)

Ladyburn

Bladnoch

ENGLAND

or malt to the distilleries, and returned with whisky for the main line to Edinburgh, Glasgow, and London. Only vestiges of the Speyside railway survive today, though it is a popular walk. The active line from Aberdeen to Inverness (just over 100 miles or 160 kilometers) follows the main road. The rivers are crossed as follows:

DEVERON: This valley has Glendronach distillery and Macduff. There are five or six distilleries in the general area, but these are quite widely dispersed. Most produce firm, malty whiskies.

ISLA: This has nothing to do with island (it has a different spelling; there's no "y"). Dominican monks brewed here in the 1200s, and there is mention of heather ale in the records. The oldest distillery on Speyside is Strathisla (founded in 1786), showpiece of Chivas Brothers, in the town of Keith in the Isla Valley. There are four or five distilleries in this area, and some of its whiskies have a cedary dryness.

FIDDICH AND DULLAN: These rivers meet at Dufftown, one of the claimants to be the whisky capital of Scotland. There are still six working distilleries in the area, despite the loss of Pittyvaich in 2002. A couple more are currently silent. Some classically rounded, malty Speysiders are produced here, including the secret star, Mortlach.

LIVET: The most famous distillery is called after the river valley itself, and there are three others in the area, all producing light, soft, delicate whiskies. The Livet appellation was once widely copied, but has been increasingly protected. The hill town, Tomintoul, is a base for exploration.

SPEY: Macallan, Aberlour, and Glenfarclas, three of the heavier interpretations of Speyside malts, are all to be found on the most heavily whiskied stretch of the Spey. There are about 12 distilleries, each less than a mile from the next, immediately upstream of the village of Craigellachie, home to a famous hotel and whisky bar.

ROTHES BURN: Actually no more than a stream, this river is one of several that reach the Spey at Rothes, another whisky "capital." This one-street town has five distilleries, producing some very nutty whiskies. Speyburn, usually shot through the trees, is the most photographed distillery in Scotland, while Glen Grant has a spectacular "tropical" garden, a coppersmith's, and a "dark grains" plant, which turns residual malt into cattle feed.

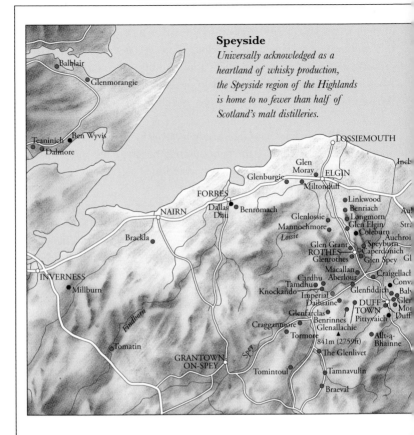

Speyside

*Universally acknowledged as a
heartland of whisky production,
the Speyside region of the Highlands
is home to no fewer than half of
Scotland's malt distilleries.*

LOSSIE: Was it the water that first attracted the Benedictines of Pluscarden to this region? They no longer brew there, but they still have a priory next door to the Miltonduff distillery. Two secret stars, Longmorn and Linkwood, are among the eight distilleries just south of Elgin. The world's most famous whisky shop, Gordon & MacPhail, is in Elgin itself. This sometimes ornate Victorian town is the undisputed commercial capital of Speyside and the county seat of Moray. The Lossie whiskies are sweetish and malty.

FINDHORN: Born-again Benromach is near the town Forres. Production restarted in 1998: the new make tasted creamy and flowery. The museum distillery of Dallas Dhu is nearby, and in the distance is Tomatin.

THE NORTHERN HIGHLANDS is a geographically clear-cut region, which runs from Inverness, straight up the last stretch of the east coast. The region's water commonly runs over sandstone, and there is a gentle maritime influence. There are four or five distilleries in short

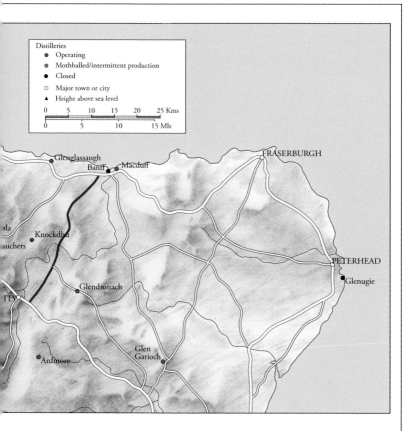

Distilleries
- ● Operating
- ● Mothballed/intermittent production
- ● Closed
- ○ Major town or city
- ▲ Height above sea level

| 0 | 5 | 10 | 15 | 20 | 25 Kms |
| 0 | | 5 | | 10 | 15 Mls |

Glenglassaugh
Banff   Macduff
FRASERBURGH

sla
Knockdhu
auchers

PETERHEAD
Glenugie

Glendronach

ILY

Glen
Garioch

Ardmore

order; including the energetic Glenmorangie and the rich Dalmore. Then there is a gap before the connoisseurs' favorite, Clynelish, and an even bigger gap before the famously salty Old Pulteney in Wick. As its distilleries have become more active, the northern Highlands has gained more recognition as a region. Its whiskies tend toward firm, crisp dryness and a light saltiness.

WESTERN HIGHLANDS The far northwest is the only sizeable stretch of the country with no legal whisky makers. It is just too rugged and rocky. Even the center cut has only two distilleries. On the foothills of Scotland's (and Britain's) highest mountain, Ben Nevis, the eponymous distillery can be regarded as being "coastal," according to its manager, Colin Ross. Why? Because it is on a sea loch. The Oban distillery certainly does face the sea, and has the flavors to prove it.

The other active mainland distilleries, Loch Lomond and Glengoyne, are so close to Glasgow that they might attract more attention reclassified as Lowlanders. In 2003, Glengoyne was acquired by Ian Macleod Ltd.

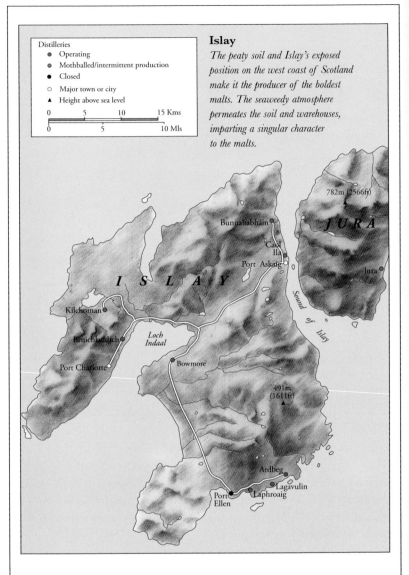

Islay

The peaty soil and Islay's exposed position on the west coast of Scotland make it the producer of the boldest malts. The seaweedy atmosphere permeates the soil and warehouses, imparting a singular character to the malts.

Distilleries
- Operating
- Mothballed/intermittent production
- Closed
- Major town or city
- ▲ Height above sea level

0   5   10   15 Kms
0   5   10 Mls

Bunnahabhain

Caol Ila

Port Askaig

JURA

782m (2566ft)

Jura

I S L A Y

Sound of Islay

Kilchoman

Bruichladdich

Loch Indaal

Port Charlotte

Bowmore

491m (1611ft)

Ardbeg

Lagavulin

Port Ellen

Laphroaig

THE ISLANDS

The greatest whisky island by far is Islay (above), with its eight distilleries—the newest being Kilchoman. The others have one apiece, except for Orkney, which has two distilleries.

ORKNEY For the moment, Highland Park is Scotland's northernmost distillery. Its whisky is one of the greats: peaty and smoky, and a superb all-rounder. Saltier whiskies from the Scapa distillery—slightly to the southwest of Highland Park—have a strong following.

SKYE Talisker whisky from Skye is a classic—volcanic, explosive, and peppery. The taste reflects the wild, looming *terroir*.

MULL Tobermory is a restrained islander, but the distillery also produces the peatier, smokier whisky called Ledaig.

JURA The decidedly piney Isle of Jura whisky has appeared in more expressions and has been better promoted since the owning group, Whyte and Mackay, seceded from its American parent, Jim Beam.

ISLAY There are currently eight distilleries bottling whisky on Islay now that Kilchoman is on line, and nine if you count the Bruichladdich bottlings under the Port Charlotte name. The Islay Festival in late May has established itself as an annual favorite.

ARRAN The first spirit from the Isle of Arran distillery ran in 1995. Its small stills produce a creamy spirit with only faint touches of island character: a touch of flowery pine in the finish.

CAMPBELTOWN

A temporary cessation in production occured at Springbank and its associated companies in 2008, but production began again in 2009. The first new distillery of the new millennium, Glengyle, opened in 2004 and it is hoped that there will be the release of an 8-year-old bottling in 2012 under the name Kilkerran.

The Springbank distillery itself produces three whiskies, using entirely its own malt—the Springbank maltings was restored a decade ago. This distillery has on occasion also assisted with the management of the other Campbeltown distillery, Glen Scotia, which is currently also in production.

Springbank, the independent bottlers Cadenhead, and the Eaglesome shop are all related businesses. The whisky veteran behind them all, Hedley Wright, has been determined to keep Campbeltown on the whisky map. Its remarkable history is evidenced by fragments of about 20 distilleries converted to other uses. There are said to have been 32 distilleries here in 1759. The town's location at the foot of the Kintyre peninsula provides not only a harbor, but also a location surrounded by the sea and often shrouded in mist.

WHAT IS THE PERFECT
AGE?

I T'S NOT UNCOMMON FOR A WHISKY MAKER to decide to change the age of the whisky sold as its core expression. As whisky enthusiasts have become more knowledgeable, it has become more widely understood that malt is an organic and evolving product, and advances in knowledge and technology have meant that while in the past many saw the age on the label as a statement of authenticity, in fact even relatively young whisky can have a strong and full flavor.

Glenfiddich, the world's biggest-selling malt, has changed its mind about age on more than one occasion, and other malts have moved to a different age. Some companies have left the age alone but have changed the liquid in the bottle markedly. Indeed, in the last two years, Glenmorangie, Dalmore, Ardbeg, and Deanston have all noticeably changed the whisky in the bottle, Auchentoshan has altered its standard expression from 10 years to 12, and Arran has bottled at consecutively older ages as the malt has become available.

There is another trend going on too, driven by shortages of malt. Increasingly distillers are focusing on taste and moving away from age statements. The intention is to persuade drinkers that even a young whisky can taste great—and that's all that really matters.

THE IMPOSSIBLE DECISION

Upgrading the age is not easy. Most distilleries have some reserves of maturing whisky that is older than they strictly need, but these stocks would not be sufficient to support such a major change. Had sales been falling sharply, a backlog of stock would have built up, but this was not the case. The decision to increase the age would have required sufficient stock to be laid down 12 years earlier, probably with a view to the change.

The person who makes such decisions has an impossible job. However good their judgment, knowledge, and understanding of the industry; however thorough the company's market research; and however many futurologists it consults, it is simply impossible to predict how much whisky will be required in five, ten or fifteen years.

Single but married
Glenfiddich Special Reserve is already 12 years old when it goes into this marrying tun for about four months. The object is to iron out natural differences and ensure a consistent product.

When the time comes, there is always too little or too much. Across the industry this is why distilleries open, close, are mothballed, and so frequently change ownership.

MAKING A VATTING

The components of a bottling may also embrace casks of various sizes and with different histories. Although the contents of the casks will be vatted according to a "recipe," adjustments will have to be made to account for the way in which the whisky has developed during maturation. No two casks, even with the same origin, are alike. Casks from the bottom of the warehouse will have matured at a different rate from those in the airier racks at the top. A warehouse nearer the sea may impart brinier characteristics. Some distilleries have only the classically damp, earth-floored, stone-built warehouses, with casks stacked three high, separated by planks of wood; others have fixed racking, with casks nine high; some have both. All of these factors may affect the distillers' choice of casks for a bottling.

Ages around six, seven, and eight years are commonly used in blends, but they could be used in a vatting for a single malt. If it carries an age statement, regulations demand that it be based on the youngest age, but as "6-year-old" might sound callow, the producer might prefer to manage without an age statement. When Glenfiddich was marketed as an 8-year-old, it probably included whiskies of nine and ten years or more. Now it is a 12-year-old and probably includes whiskies of up to 15 years old. Some of the lighter-bodied malts hit their stride at eight or ten years old, while 12 is so common as to be regarded by consumers in some markets as a standard for mature malt.

DEVELOPING A RANGE

If there were a "best" age for malt whisky, it would be universally adopted. In Italy, where the words "malt whisky" are potent, devotees are delighted with a 5-year-old. In Japan, where age is respected, a 30-year-old is appreciated. In recent years, distillers have offered not only a greater range of ages but also of strengths, types of cask, and finish. These have come to be known as different "expressions" of the same malt. For those consumers bored with consistency, there is the merit of greater individuality in some of the more unusual bottlings, particularly vintages, and especially those at cask strength.

To take Glenfiddich as an example, it also offers: a variation on the 12-year-old (involving casks from Islay); a 15-year-old (Solera Reserve); a 21-year-old (Millennium Reserve, with a variation employing

Vintage whiskies
While seeking consistency in its principal product, Glenfiddich offers diversity of character in its vintages. The barley harvest and climate differ slightly each year, but bigger differences develop in the cask.

Havana rum barrels); and several dated vintages (of which the 1961 was a single cask). A bottling from a single cask represents a very limited edition, with the merit of its own individuality. Such a bottling is made for malt lovers who wish to explore.

Glenfiddich's Malt Master, David Stewart, creates daring whiskies that dance on the tongue with balletic elegance. His 12-year-old is a deft transformation, but he might well have preferred to approach the task from a wider angle: retaining some younger malts from the 8-year-old, but increasing the proportion of older malts (or increasing their ages). Young malts can inject liveliness to a vatting, while the older ones add complexity. This might have produced an even more complex whisky. Why did he not follow that course? Because it would have precluded the use of the age statement "12 years old."

Blenders like to use a wide range of ages within a vatting, but are constrained by the marketing men, with their reliance on bold statements of maturity.

A whisky can be too woody at 21 years, or it can still be enjoyable at 50, but—like death and taxes—evaporation eventually takes its toll. Unlike a human being, a whisky that has over-stayed its time on earth is sure to meet the angels. Just as humans in ancient cultures revered trees, especially oaks, so *Quercus robur* and *Quercus alba* are the greatest influences on the maturation of *aqua vitae*.

THE PERFECT WOOD

D ID THE FLAVORS IN YOUR GLASS begin a dozen years ago, with the sowing of barley on the Black Isle? Or decades earlier, as a blizzard on the Grampians? If the malt was peated, you could be enjoying a few leaves of bog myrtle that have been waiting 7000 years for your rendezvous. Or did your favorite flavors emerge a century ago on a forest slope in Galicia, Spain? Or perhaps in the Ozark Mountains of Missouri?

The creation of alcoholic drinks in different parts of the world employs in various roles a whole alphabet of trees: for their fruits and berries; to make charcoal, to act as a filter; as a fuel in the kilning of malt; to provide vessels for fermentation or maturation, or simply to act as containers. Various drinks are stored in (or consumed from) cedar, juniper, and chestnut, but the wood most commonly used for all those purposes is oak. Its most attractive property is its pliability. It must bend to make a barrel, and the elegant curves of this traditional vessel strengthen it, just as an arch reinforces a building. Even in the most mechanized distillery, casks are rolled and occasionally dropped or bounced. They must be tough and not split or leak. They contain an increasingly precious product.

United States regulations insist that bourbon is matured in new oak, but the cask may subsequently cross the Atlantic and be filled three or four times with the spirit of Scotland. If each of those fillings is matured for only six or seven years, the cask will have seen two or three decades' service. If a cask is tapped at 25 years, then repeats the performance, it already has half a century under its belt. It must be tough, yet also able to breathe during the maturation of the whisky, and perhaps also have some flavors and aromas to donate.

OAK AND FLAVOR

Wooden casks were originally regarded simply as containers. Whisky was sold in the cask to inns and country houses, and customers noted that it mellowed in the cellar. Over the years, it has increasingly been recognized that the character of the wood plays a big part in the

Tough but pliable
Oak does not break under torture, but it bends to provide the elegant, strengthening curves of the cask. This cooperage is in Andalusia. Charring to enhance flavor is more typical in Kentucky.

development of the whisky's aromas and flavors, but how big? The perceived importance of wood has greatly increased across the industry in recent years, yet opinions differ more widely than ever.

The issue was not much discussed while former sherry casks were readily available for the maturation of whisky. These casks seem to have been accepted without much question, though they must have imparted a variety of characteristics. Some had been used in fermentation, others in maturation, others for transport. They had contained different styles of sherry—and sometimes other fortified wines.

As sherry fell out of fashion, exports to the United Kingdom diminished. Meanwhile, the dictator Franco died in 1975, Spain became a democracy, and its trade unions insisted that the bottling of wines be carried out by local labor in Spain.

Distilleries anxious to continue sherry aging now had to work directly with the bodegas in Jerez. Macallan has been the most consistently active proponent of this approach. So through several changes of control at Macallan, its top managers have each year swapped the granite and heather of Speyside for the orange trees and Moorish architecture of Jerez.

WHICH VARIETY OF OAK?

Setting aside those that grow as shrubs and bushes, there are more than half a dozen European species of oak tree. Two have traditionally been used in cooperage. The second choice is usually *Quercus petraea*, known as the sessile oak, for the way the acorns "sit" on the twigs. The first choice is *Quercus robur*, the pendunculate oak. The epithet refers to the way the acorns are suspended on stalks.

The *Q. robur* tolerates a wide range of growing conditions, and is typically found in England, France, and Iberia. In France, where region appellations are used, Limousin and Tronçais oaks are usually of the *Q. robur* variety.

The principal growing area in Spain is the northwest corner of the country, where the coast between the cities of Santander and Corunna faces the Bay of Biscay and the Atlantic. Behind the coast rise stony hills, the valleys between them dappled with oaks. These once fed shipyards making galleons; then Spanish oak was turned into barrels for wine; and now its final destination is Scotland.

The center of the timber industry is the city of Lugo, in the province of the same name, in the region of Galicia. A sawmill there cuts staves for Macallan. The staves are air-dried for 12 to 15 months by being left outdoors. The weather washes out some of the tannins, moderating the intensity of the wood, and the staves then become casks at a cooperage in Jerez. They are filled with newly pressed cloudy grape juice, for between two weeks and six months, and then used a second time, to mature sherry, before being sent to Scotland. The casks are shipped whole, thus maintaining the sherryish character of the wood. This would diminish if they were knocked down into staves.

Spanish wine makers, such as those of Jerez, increasingly prefer the sweeter, more vanilla-like character of American oak.

BUTTS, BARRELS, OR HOGSHEAD?

The casks used for the maturation of sherry are known as butts, and typically have a capacity of 500 liters (110 UK gallons or 132 US gallons). There is a beauty and an integrity to such vessels, but their size and weight make them difficult to handle.

The term "hogshead" refers to a traditional cask size of 250 liters (55 UK gallons or 66 US gallons). Sherry hogsheads can be found, but the designation is more commonly applied to a Scottish adaptation of an American barrel. In this instance,

Iron lady
Torture continues … this machine forces the hoops to hold the staves in position.

the barrel is broken down in the US and shipped as staves. It is then reassembled in Scotland with new heads (barrel ends) to increase the capacity of the cask. The new heads also freshen up the wood influence. The term "American oak" is sometimes used to indicate a bourbon barrel, which typically has a capacity of around 200 liters (44 UK gallons or 53 US gallons). Many single malts are vatted from a combination of sherry butts and bourbon barrels, usually with the latter in the majority.

Many producers of lighter-bodied, more delicate-tasting whiskies feel that they express their aromas and flavors more successfully when matured in bourbon barrels. A long-time proponent of this approach is the Glenmorangie distillery.

The man in charge of distillation and maturation for Glenmorangie, Bill Lumsden, has worked with the Blue Grass Cooperage in Louisville to develop a bourbon barrel that perfectly suits both sides of the Atlantic. More than 225 miles (360 kilometers) southwest and 100 miles (160 kilometers) south of St. Louis, Missouri, oak for the casks is grown around Altenburg, a town settled by immigrants from Saxony in Germany. The town sign still uses the word *"Stadt"* for "city."

This is an area of mixed deciduous woodland, with small, privately owned lots. The soils are very well drained. The part of the country has four definite seasons, but the winter cold has enough restraint not to damage the crop. The wood is clean, without knots, and with good pores. This is white oak, *Quercus alba.*

WHAT HAPPENS DURING AGING

Several processes take place during maturation. While the new distillate may have some harsh, "spirity" flavors, these can be lost by evaporation. With the expansion and contraction of the wood, caused by seasonal changes in temperature, spirit flavors may be exhaled and the natural aromas of the environment taken into the cask: piney, seaweedy, and salty "sea-air" characteristics can all be acquired in this way. Flavors are also imparted by the cask: sherry wood may add the nutty note of the wine; and bourbon barrels can impart caramel flavors, vanillins, and tannins.

Perhaps the most important influence on the flavor is that of a very slow, gentle oxidation of the whisky. While oxygen is regarded as an "enemy" by brewers and some wine makers, because it can cause "stale" flavors, its influence is also a part of the character of other drinks such as Madeira wines. The importance of oxidation in the

Steam heat

Scalded into submission ... after these sequences of tortures, the casks can settle down to a life of sipping sherry, then whisky.

maturation of whisky has been the subject of much work by Dr. Jim Swan, originally at the Pentlands Scotch Whisky Research Institute, and more recently by his own company. Dr. Swan argues that oxidation increases the complexity and intensity of pleasant flavors in whisky, especially fragrant, fruity, spicy, and minty notes.

As in the production of all alcoholic drinks, the flavors emerge from a complex series of actions and reactions. Traces of copper from the stills are the catalyst. They convert oxygen to hydrogen peroxide, which attacks the wood, releasing vanillin. This promotes oxidation, and additionally pulls together the various flavors present. These processes vary according to the region of origin of the wood, and its growth patterns. Vanillin is a component that occurs naturally in oak. As its name suggests, it imparts a vanilla-like flavor.

In Spain, trees from the most mountainous districts of Galicia are more resiny. In the US, growth is mainly in a belt across Ohio, Kentucky, Illinois, Missouri, and Arkansas. The western part of this contiguous region has the poorest soil and the most arid climate, and therefore the trees have to fight to survive. This optimizes spring growth, which has the most open texture and is the most active in the maturation process.

LIGHT, MEDIUM, OR ALLIGATOR?

Bourbon barrels are toasted or charred on the inside to enable the whiskey to permeate the wood. There are stories of this happy discovery having arisen from an accidental fire, but it seems more likely to have emerged from the technique of toasting the wood to make it pliable.

Charring gives the spirit access to positive properties and flavors in the wood, but also enables it better to expel undesirable flavors. American cooperages typically offer three degrees of char: light, medium, and alligator. The latter, the heaviest, leaves the wood looking like a log so heavily burned that it has formed a pattern of squares reminiscent of an alligator's skin.

A sherry butt or bourbon barrel will impart considerable aroma and flavor to its first fill of whisky. "First-fill sherry casks were used in the maturation of this whisky" is the type of claim that appears on the neck label of an especially voluptuous malt. Some distillers feel that the more restrained second fill provides a better balance. A third fill will impart little, but let the character of the spirit speak for itself. If there is a fourth fill, it is likely to go for blending after which, 30 or 40 years on, the inside of the cask might be recharred. The preferred word is "rejuvenated."

OWNERS, DISTILLERS, AND BOTTLERS

I N THE NEXT SECTION IS A REVIEW, in alphabetical order, of every
Scottish malt distillery that has ever witnessed its product in a
bottle. These are not "brands" (though their names may be registered);
they are actual distilleries: premises at which malt is turned into whisky.
Among today's distilleries, only the relatively new Kininvie has not
seen its product, a deliciously creamy whisky, bottled. Some of the
distilleries reviewed have long closed, but bottlings from their stocks
are still being made, or were within recent memory—and therefore
may still be on the odd shelf.

NAMES OF DISTILLERIES Some distilleries have been known over
the years by several different names. They are listed here by the most
recent name on the label of the principal bottlings, though reference
may be made in the text to earlier names. If you have bought, or are
considering buying, a malt that appears not to be in this book, check
the index. If it is not listed there, its name is not that of a distillery.
Importers, distributors, and supermarkets often buy malt whisky to
bottle under invented names (for example, Glen Bagpipe, Loch
Sporran). These products are not reviewed. The bottle will probably
contain whisky supplied by a reputable distiller who happens to have a
surplus, but the source could change at any time. The next bottle
under the same name might contain an entirely different whisky.

WHO OWNS THE DISTILLERIES? The biggest changes ever seen
in the ownership of distilleries have taken place in the first few years
of this millennium. Although the overall effect has been to concentrate
control of Scotland's distilleries yet further, it has also shaken loose a
handful into various degrees of independence.

Around one hundred distilleries are working or capable of being put
into operation. Ninety percent of them are owned by groups,
about half of which are international drinks companies. Some of the
world's biggest corporations own tiny, rustic distilleries.

THE INTERNATIONAL DRINKS COMPANIES

Diageo is the giant of the industry. It owns four maltings, 28 malt distilleries, including the new "super distillery" at Roseisle, and one grain distillery, since the closure of its Port Dundas plant. Some elements of this business date from the 1700s, but its emergence as a group can be traced to the 1880s, when a portfolio of distilleries was assembled to produce whiskies for blends. As the Distillers Company Limited (DCL), this group produced almost all the famous names in blended Scotch, and dominated the industry for 100 years. In the 1980s, DCL merged with Bell's to become United Distillers (UD).

The new company acknowledged the growing interest in malts by introducing bottlings from six distilleries, each highlighting a different region. These were dubbed The Classic Malts. The same whiskies have since been offered with wood finishes as The Distillers Edition. Although each malt in these two families has its own label design, the graphic genre is similar. This still left many UD distilleries without a bottled single malt to offer tourists in their region. A range with labels showing local flora and fauna was developed. This was purely for local sale, though it soon became more widely popular. UD then decided to bottle stocks they still held from distilleries that had closed or that had even been demolished. These were identified as The Rare Malts, and marketed at prices that reflected their scarcity value. As stocks diminished, this series then began to call upon rare vintages from distilleries still in operation. This was reflected in an extension of the series as Cask Strength Limited Editions. More recently, some whiskies that were appreciated by connoisseurs but not widely known have been released as Hidden Malts. Small, outstanding batches are bottled each year as Special Releases, though this rubric does not appear on the labels.

UD merged with Britain's other drinks giant, International Distillers and Vintners (IDV), in 1997 and coined the name Diageo, which is intended to speak of the daily pleasures of food and drink. The group owns Tanqueray gin, Smirnoff vodka, Cuervo tequila, Guinness stout, and many other drinks.

Chivas Brothers has 12 distilleries. This group began with two brothers from the Highlands and a wine and spirits shop established in Aberdeen in the mid-1800s. The business was acquired as a foothold in Scotland by Seagram, the Canadian whisky distillers. Taking advantage of the shutdown of US distilling during Prohibition, Seagram had become the world's biggest drinks company. It subsequently diversified into the entertainment industry, and withdrew from distilling. In one of the industry's biggest takeovers, its Scottish distilleries were acquired in 2001 by Pernod Ricard. This family-owned business, based on pastis, is now an international drinks company. Its subsidiaries include Irish Distillers Limited and Wild Turkey Kentucky Bourbon.

Beam Global became a major international whisky player after the break up of Allied Distillers in 2005, when Allied's distilleries were split between Beam and Pernod Ricard. Beam Global acquired the Teacher's blend and two heavyweight distilleries, Laphroaig on Islay and Ardmore in the Highlands. The company also took on some of the highly experienced and committed whisky team from Allied.

Three groups have five malt distilleries each:

The Edrington Group produces one of Britain's best selling blends, The Famous Grouse. Its malt distilleries include Macallan and Highland Park. The core of the group was known as Highland Distillers until a complex realignment in 1999/2000, involving several other old-established businesses in the Scottish whisky trade. It has links with Rémy-Cointreau, the French brandy and liqueur company.

Dewar's, the best-selling blend in the US, was owned by United Distillers until the merger that created Diageo. In approving the merger, the European Commission and the US Federal Trade Commission were both concerned about market domination. Diageo already owned Johnnie Walker and J&B. Dewar's principal distillery, Aberfeldy, and three others were sold to Bacardi, the rum producer.

Inver House has its origins in a long-gone American group, but was given its present shape by a management buy-out. During the 1990s, the company bought distilleries that were silent or surplus to the requirements of their owners. The Scottish management remains, but the company has since 2001 been owned by Pacific Spirits, a family-controlled drinks company in Thailand.

Two companies each have four malt distilleries:

Whyte and Mackay is an old established name that has been scrapped and reinstated over time, and the changes extend well beyond monikers, as the company has been through several ownerships. Most recently it was bought by Indian entrepreneur Vijay Mallya's United Spirits. Its malts include The Dalmore and Jura.

William Grant & Sons remains a family firm. The original William Grant was a distillery manager before he set up his own plant. He and his family built the Glenfiddich distillery in 1886, and Balvenie in 1892. Kininvie was added rather more recently, in 1990. William Grant also owns the Girvan grain distillery and, in 2008, opened a new malt distillery at the Ailsa Bay site. The company's growth has been a well-earned reward for its vision in pioneering the marketing of single malts.

Two companies each have a trio of malt distilleries:

Burn Stewart is owned by CL Financial, a major West Indian business that owns several alcoholic brands, including rums, wines, and now American whiskey under its Angostura Bitters division. Burn Stewart owned Deanston and Tobermory when it was bought by CL Financial in 2003 and added Bunnahabhain later that year.

Morrison Bowmore was a family business, built around the highly regarded maltings and distillery in the "capital" of Islay. The company also owns Auchentoshan, the last Lowlander to practise triple distillation. The third distillery in the group is Glen Garioch, in the Highlands. The Morrison family had a long cooperation with Suntory before the Japanese giant became the proud owner of this small but well-balanced business.

One company has two malt distilleries:

Glenmorangie was bought by Louis Vuitton Moët Hennessey in 2004 and, since then, the company has been radically shaken up. One of its three distilleries, Glen Moray, was sold in 2008, along with the company's headquarters. It has moved to new premises in Edinburgh and is focusing on its core malts, Glenmorangie and Ardbeg. The Glenmorangie was changed and repackaged in 2007.

Two more distilleries are in Japanese ownership:
Ben Nevis is owned by the Asahi subsidiary Nikka, old-established Japanese whisky distiller and competitor to Suntory.
Tomatin is owned by Takara Shuzo Co. Ltd., producers of the Japanese spirit shochu.

DEGREES OF INDEPENDENCE

In addition to the traditional producers listed above, the following companies, established as bottlers of blended and malt whiskies, each own two malt distilleries:

Loch Lomond owns the long-established malt distillery of the same name (with additionally a grain distillery on the site), and has now added Glen Scotia. (It also owned Littlemill, but this distillery is no longer operating and has been partially demolished).

Angus Dundee is a small company bottling under the name MacKillop's Choice. In reshuffles, it acquired the Tomintoul distillery from Jim Beam and Glencadam from Allied.

Other links between bottlers and distilleries:

Cadenhead has long shared ownership with Springbank.
Scott's Selection is owned by the Christie family, and opened the Speyside (Drumguish) distillery in 1990.
Gordon & MacPhail bought Benromach from UD and reopened it in 1998.
Murray McDavid has some common ownership with Bruichladdich, acquired from Jim Beam in 2000.
Signatory has the same principal as Edradour, acquired in 2003 from Pernod Ricard.
Ian Macleod acquired Glengoyne in 2003.

Distilleries not linked to other businesses:

Tullibardine was bought by a management consortium in 2003 and started distilling later that year. Since then it has launched a large range of bottlings made up of old stock and finished in various woods.
Arran was established in 1995 as an independent business.
Bladnoch was bought by a private individual from UD and restarted production in 2001.
Glenfarclas is the last family-owned single distillery. Licensed as a farm distillery in 1836, it was acquired two years later by John Grant, and is still in the family. (There is no connection with William Grant & Sons or the Glen Grant Distillery.)

THE CONFUSING WORLD
OF INDEPENDENT BOTTLERS

Newcomers to the world of single malts are often puzzled by the way in which whisky from the same distillery may appear under several different labels. Equally, whiskies from 20 or 30 different distilleries may all appear under labels which are almost identical. This is because most distilleries do not carry out their own bottling. The original farm distilleries pre-dated mechanized bottling. They sold their whisky by the cask to wealthy householders, hotels, or licensed grocers or wine and spirit merchants.

Two merchants, dating from the 1800s, kept malts alive after the industry turned its attention almost entirely to blends. (*See* Gordon & MacPhail *and* Cadenhead, *below*.) As the practice of blending grew, the trade of whisky broker emerged. Brokers buy casks of whisky, often speculatively, and supply them to blenders, bottlers, or merchants. A great deal of whisky is in the hands of brokers. With the growing interest in single malts, the availability of this whisky is exciting the interest of a growing number of independent bottlers. As most distilleries still supply the bulk of their output for blending, some do not wish to be concerned with the business of single malt, and are happy to leave it to the independent bottlers.

At the opposite extreme, some famous distilleries have very definite ideas about the way their whisky is presented as a single malt (age, strength, type of cask). Some have controlled stock, and even bought back casks, to prevent independent bottlings. Others have taken legal action. This can be difficult when the brand name is also a place.

The terms "distillery bottling" or "official bottling" are occasionally used in this book. These terms imply a bottling that has been made on behalf of the distillery's owners. Distilleries that are owned by groups will usually have a central bottling line, typically within easy reach of Glasgow and Edinburgh.

Statement of independence

This label is from a bottle released by Gordon & MacPhail. The whisky was produced at Benromach distillery and was bottled from two casks, numbered 112 and 114, which were refill sherry hogsheads.

Gordon & MacPhail is a family-owned shop in the Speyside heartland at Elgin, but its bottlings reach every corner of the world. Over the decades, it has acquired considerable stocks, which it has matured in its own warehouses. For this reason Gordon & MacPhail's bottlings of a particular malt have a consistency of style, often with a typical sherry-aged character, especially those in the Connoisseurs Choice Range.

Cadenhead has since the 1960s been owned by the proprietors of Springbank, in Campbeltown. The company is happy to buy small quantities of whiskies as they become available, so that bottling runs are short and the age or type of cask used may vary greatly. This makes for a great diversity of interesting bottlings. Cadenhead led the way in not chill filtering.

OTHER INDEPENDENTS

Adelphi Emphasizes cask strength. Tends toward full-flavored whiskies. Founded in the early 1990s by Jamie Walker, whose forebears owned the Adelphi Distillery (1825–1902) in Glasgow.

Berry Brothers Seek whiskies that are good examples of the distillery's character (*see* Glenrothes).

Blackadder The jocular name is appropriate. Bottlings range from the noble to the downright eccentric. Raw Cask is a sub-range. Whiskies bottled "on lees." Founded in 1995 by whisky writer Robin Tucek.

Coopers Choice Good regional diversity. Part of The Vintage Malt Whisky Company. Founded in 1992 by a former sales director of Morrison Bowmore.

Douglas Laing Likes to offer contrasting expressions from the same distillery. Typically bottles at 50 volume. Independent bottlings (as Old Malt Cask) since 1998, but family has been in the whisky trade since 1949.

Duncan Taylor Shop in Huntly, Aberdeenshire. Bottler since 2002. Large portfolio, based on inventory (some dating from the 1960s). Bequeathed by pioneering American importer, Abe Rosenberg.

Hart Brothers Emphasizes wood finishes and good oak character. Bottling since 1989. Wine background since 1960s.

Ian Macleod Rare malts at unusual ages or with distinctive finishes. Smart packaging. Chieftain's and Dun Bheagan ranges since 2000. Blender and broker since 1930s.

James MacArthur "Small is Beautiful." Low-profile business, started as a hobby in 1982. Selects in the basis of best age for each whisky.

Lombard Sensitive to age. Buys whiskies and continues to mature. Bottling recent, but brokers since late 1960s.

MacKillop's Choice Selections By Lorne MacKillop, Master of Wine. Bottler since 1998.

Murray McDavid Has sought in each bottling (since 1996) "the truest expression of the distillery." The Mission range is selected by Jim McEwan, of Bruichladdich.

Scott's Selection Emphasizes silent stills and rare malts. Started in mid-1990s by blender Rob Scott (now retired). Linked to the warehousing, blending, and bottling business established by George Christie (*see* Drumguish).

Signatory Father of the new wave of bottlers. Established in 1988 and one of the few to have its own bottling line. Signatory pioneered single cask bottlings. Founder Andrew Symington previously worked in hotels.

Wilson & Morgan Has used Marsala barrels. Based in Italy. Bottling since 1992. Importing since 1960s.

Whiskies reviewed include some bottlings for retailers in the UK. These include:
The Whisky Shop (Glasgow and branches), Royal Mile Whiskies (Edinburgh and London),
The Wee Dram (Bakewell, England), The Vintage House and The Whisky Exchange
(both London), and Oddbins (UK chain).

A–Z
OF SINGLE MALTS

WHATEVER THE ARGUMENTS about their relative prices, no one denies that a Château Latour is more complex than a mass-market table wine. The fine wines of the whisky world are the single malts. Some malts are made to higher standards than others, and some are inherently more distinctive than their neighbors. This cannot be obscured by the producers' blustery arguments about "personal taste." A tasting note cannot be definitive, but it can be a useful guide, and will tell you, for example, if the whisky is a light, dry malt, or if it is rich and sherryish, or peaty and smoky.

The tasting notes start with a comment on the house style—a quick, first, general indication of what to expect from each distillery's products, before looking at the variations that emerge in different ages and bottlings. I also suggest the best moment for each distillery's whiskies (such as before dinner, or with a book at bedtime). These suggestions are meant as an encouragement to try each in a congenial situation. They are not meant to be taken with excessive seriousness.

Tasting note example:

AUCHENTOSHAN 1973, 29-year-old, Sherry Butt No 793, 55.8 vol

COLOR Pinkish red. Almost rhubarb-like.
NOSE Jammy. Australian Shiraz. Red apples. Peaches.
BODY Textured. Fluffy.
PALATE An extraordinarily fruity whisky, with peach dominant. Peach-pit flavors, too. Underneath all that, it is hard to divine any Auchentoshan character. Severely marked down for those reasons.
FINISH Nutty dryness. With the cheese? After dinner?

SCORE **69**

COLOR The natural color of a malt matured in plain wood is a very pale yellow. Darker shades, ranging from amber to ruby to deep brown, can be imparted by sherry wood. Some distilleries use casks

A character-forming home
Skye forms a natural crucible, in which the flavors of a great whisky are fused. Living in the mountains and surrounded by sea, the whisky assumes a gusty salt-and-pepper house character.

that have been treated with concentrated sherry, and this can cause a caramel-like appearance and palate. Some add caramel to balance the color. I do not suggest that one color is in itself better than another, though a particular subtle hue can heighten the pleasure of a fine malt. We enjoy food and drink with our eyes as well as our nose and palate.

NOSE Anyone sampling any food or drink experiences much of the flavor through the sense of smell. Whisky is highly aromatic, and the aromas of malts include peat, flowers, honey, toasty maltiness, coastal brine, and seaweed, for example.

BODY Lightness, smoothness, or richness might refresh, soothe, or satisfy. Body and texture (sometimes known as "mouth feel") are distinct features of each malt.

PALATE In the enjoyment of any complex drink, each sip will offer new aspects of the taste. Even one sip will gradually unfold a number of taste characteristics in different parts of the mouth over a period of, say, a minute. This is notably true of single malts. Some present a very extensive development of palate. A taster working with an unfamiliar malt may go back to it several times over a period of days, in search of its full character. I have adopted this technique in my tastings for this book.

FINISH In all types of alcoholic drink, the "finish" is a further stage of the pleasure. In most single malts, it is more than a simple aftertaste, however important that may be. It is a crescendo, followed by a series of echoes. When I leave the bottle, I like to be whistling the tune. When the music of the malt fades, there is recollection in tranquillity.

SCORE The pleasures described above cannot be measured with precision, if at all. The scoring system is intended merely as a guide to the status of the malts. Each tasting note is given a score out of 100. This is inspired by the system of scoring wines devised by the American writer Robert Parker. In this book, a rating in the 50s indicates a malt that in my view lacks balance or character, and which—in fairness—was probably never meant to be bottled as a single. The 60s suggest an enjoyable but unexceptional malt. Anything in the 70s is worth tasting, especially above 75. The 80s are, in my view, distinctive and exceptional. The 90s are the greats.

A modest score should not dissuade anyone from trying a malt. Perhaps I was less than enthusiastic; you might love it.

ABERFELDY

PRODUCER John Dewar & Sons Ltd. (Bacardi)
REGION Highlands   DISTRICT Eastern Highlands
ADDRESS Aberfeldy, Perthshire, PH15 2EB
TEL 01887 822010   WEBSITE www.dewarswow.com
EMAIL worldofwhisky@dewars.com   VC

THE ORIGINAL JOHN DEWAR was born on a croft near Aberfeldy in 1806, and was introduced to the wine trade at the age of 22 by a distant cousin. The family moved into blending whisky, and, in 1896–98, established their own distillery at Aberfeldy. From the start, its job was to provide the heart of the malt whisky content of the Dewar's blends; it continued to do so in recent years under the ownership of United Distillers, and it persists with this role today, under the umbrella of Bacardi. Perhaps it is the Aberfeldy malt that imparts to Dewar's that fresh, lively crispness.

The hard water used at the distillery rises from whinstone flecked with iron and gold, and runs through pine, spruce, birch, and bracken on its way to the distillery. It is piped from the ruins of Pitilie, an earlier distillery, which closed for good in 1867. It took its name from the source of the water, the Pitilie Burn.

Aberfeldy still has its pagoda roof, though malting on site stopped in 1972. The owners at the time, DCL, were closing distillery maltings in favor of centralized sites for providing the malted barley. Some of the space liberated at the distilleries was then used to expand still-houses, at a time when production was being increased to meet demand. The upgraded still-house at Aberfeldy is in the classic design of the period. The stills themselves are tall, with a gentle contour. The distillery also has a small steam locomotive, no longer in operation.

When UD merged with IDV in 1998 and became Diageo, the new business had an embarrassment of distilleries. Then Aberfeldy, Aultmore, Craigellachie, and Royal Brackla were sold to become John Dewar & Sons, under the ownership of Bacardi.

HOUSE STYLE Oily, cleanly fruity, vigorous. Sociable, with dessert, or book-at-bedtime, depending upon ascending age.

ABERFELDY 12-year-old, 40 vol

COLOR Warm gold to bronze.

NOSE Lively. Orange zest. A hint of smokiness. Warm.

BODY Light on the tongue. Oily.

PALATE Emphatically clean fruitiness. Tangerines. Trifle sponges.

FINISH Like biting into a kumquat. Dust. Spicy. Gently warming.

SCORE 76

ABERFELDY 15-year-old, Flora and Fauna, 43 vol

COLOR Amber.

NOSE Oil, incense, heather, lightly piney, and peaty
(especially after water is added).

BODY Medium, very firm.

PALATE Very full flavors. Light peat, barley. Fresh, clean touches of
Seville orange. Rounded.

FINISH Sweetness moves to fruitiness, then to firm dryness.

SCORE 77

ABERFELDY 1980, 17-year-old, Bottled 1997, Cask Strength Limited Bottling, 62 vol

COLOR Pale gold.

NOSE Restrained, fragrant, pine, and heather. Dry.

BODY Medium, smooth, distinctly oily.

PALATE Creamy. Nutty. Hint of orange toffee. Still lively, but two or three
years in the cask has brought more tightly combined flavors.

FINISH Nutty, late pine. Leafy, peppery dryness.

SCORE 77

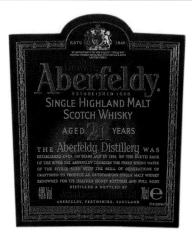

ABERFELDY 21-year-old, 40 vol

COLOR Warm gold to bronze. Very similar
to the Aberfeldy 12, but a touch darker.

NOSE Soft, sweet, warming. Notes of honey, vanilla, and oranges.

BODY Soft, yet robust. Slight oiliness.

PALATE A trace of peat, with notes of honey,
oak, and Seville oranges.

FINISH Dry. Lingers for a short moment, then drifts off in
a puff of smoke.

SCORE **77**

AN INDEPENDENT BOTTLING
ABERFELDY 1994 13-year-old, Duncan Taylor N.C.2, 46 vol

COLOR Yellowy green.

NOSE Melon- and grapefruit-flavored hard candies. Clean, sweet, and zesty.

BODY Gentle and medium-full.

PALATE Honey. Citrus fruits. Very clean. Fresh currants. Cooking apples.

FINISH Sharp fruits, some spice. Medium length.

SCORE **73**

ABERLOUR

PRODUCER Chivas Brothers (Pernod Ricard)
REGION Highlands DISTRICT Speyside (Strathspey)
ADDRESS Aberlour, Banffshire, AB3 9PJ
TEL 01340 881249 WEBSITE www.aberlour.co.uk VC

ANY FEARS THAT ABERLOUR'S parent company Pernod Ricard would pay less attention to its favorite malt since acquiring a host of neighboring brands eight years ago have long since been dispelled, and the French love affair with Aberlour has continued unabated.

Aberlour is at least a super-middleweight in body. With medals galore in recent years, it competes as a light-heavyweight, standing up well against bigger names, much as Georges Carpentier did. Aberlour rhymes with "power" in English, but most French-speakers make it sound more like "amour."

The regular range in Scotland and the rest of the United Kingdom comprises the 10-year-old, the a'bunadh, and the 15-year-old sherry wood finish, but there are larger selections in duty-free and in France. The overall range includes a great many minor variations.

Since 2002, visitors to the distillery have been able to hand-fill their own personally labeled bottle of Aberlour, from an identified single cask. A sherry butt and a bourbon barrel, each felt to provide a good example of its style, are set aside for this purpose. As each is exhausted, it is replaced by a similar cask. This personalized whisky is bottled at cask strength.

On the main road (A95) that follows the eastern bank of the Spey, an 1890s lodge signals the distillery, which is hidden a couple of hundred yards into the glen of the Lour River (little more than a stream). The Lour flows into the Spey. The site was known for a well associated with St. Drostan, from the epoch of St. Columba. The distilling water is soft. It rises from the granite of Ben Rinnes, by way of a spring in the glen of the Allachie, and is piped to the distillery.

HOUSE STYLE Soft texture, medium to full flavors,
nutty, spicy (nutmeg?), sherry-accented. With dessert,
or after dinner, depending upon maturity.

ABERLOUR 10-year-old, 43 vol

COLOR Amber.

NOSE Malty, spicy, mint toffee.

BODY Remarkably soft and smooth. Medium to full.

PALATE Distinctively clinging mouth feel, with long-lasting flavor development. Both sweetness and spicy, peppery dryness in its malt character. Nutmeg and berry fruit.

FINISH Lingering, smooth, aromatic, clean.

SCORE **83**

ABERLOUR a'bunadh ("The Origin"), No Age Statement, 59.6 vol

A single malt comprising Aberlours from less than 10 to more than 15 years, vatted together. All sherry-aging, with an emphasis on second-fill dry oloroso. No chill filtration.

COLOR Dark orange.

NOSE Sherry, mint, pralines. Luxurious, powerful.

BODY Full, creamy, textured, layered.

PALATE Rich, luxurious, and creamy, with a hint of mint and cherries behind.

FINISH Nougat, cherry brandy, ginger, faint smoke. Definitely after dinner.

SCORE **86**

ABERLOUR 12-year-old, Double Cask Matured, 43 vol

Vatting of first-fill sherry and unspecified refill casks.

COLOR Bronze.

NOSE Earthy, fruity. Pears. Apples. Tarte tatin.

BODY Medium, firm.

PALATE Melty pastry. Caramel sauce. Custard (in this instance,
let's call it crème anglaise). Leaves of garden mint.

FINISH More of the mint. Now it has become spearmint.
Ends rather abruptly and sharply.

SCORE **82**

ABERLOUR Cuvée Marie d'Ecosse, 15-year-old, 43 vol

A marriage of bourbon- and sherry-aged Aberlour, for the French market.

COLOR Amber.

NOSE Malty and toffeeish, developing flowering currant.

BODY Medium to full. Silky smooth.

PALATE Toffee, licorice, anise, crème brûlée.

FINISH Late spiciness and ginger. Long, soothing.

SCORE **83**

ABERLOUR 15-year-old, Sherry Wood Finish, 40 vol

A marriage of sherry and bourbon. Finished in sherry.

COLOR Fuller reddish amber.

NOSE Roses, candyfloss (cotton candy), slightly buttery.

BODY Very firm. Smooth.

PALATE Rounded, tightly combined flavors. Beautiful balance of
sherryish nuttiness, anise, and emphatic orange flower.

FINISH Cookies, licorice, toffee. Roots, spice, emphatic mint, late dryness.

SCORE **84**

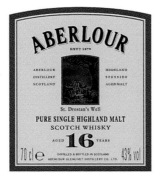

ABERLOUR 16-year-old, Double Cask Matured, 43 vol

Vatting of first-fill sherry and unspecified refill casks.

COLOR Bronze red.

NOSE Seville oranges, lemons. Turkish delight. Rose water.

BODY Gently rounded.

PALATE Smooth. Spun sugar. Caramel. Tightly combined flavors.
The extra years have made a big difference.

FINISH Cinnamon. Ground nutmeg. Nutty.

 SCORE **84**

ABERLOUR 18-year-old, Sherry Wood Matured, 43 vol

100% sherry-aged. Mainly for the North American market.

COLOR Bright orangey amber.

NOSE Sherryish but dry and slightly oaky.
Burned sugar. Spicy, rounded, teasing.

BODY Smooth. Nutty.

PALATE Well balanced. Spicy, flowery, nutty, fruity. Nutmeg.
Light, delicate flavors for this distillery and age.

FINISH Fresh sherry and oak.

SCORE **84**

ABERLOUR 100° Proof, No Age Statement
(Around 10 years), 57.1 vol

Mainly in duty-free outlets.

COLOR Bright orangey amber.

NOSE Fresh oak, giving way to light nuttiness and sherry.

BODY Firm. Crisp.

PALATE Dry oiliness. Delicious, soft fruitiness (apricots? cherries?).
Much more spiciness. Some butterscotch, toffee, and cough drops.
Both robust (tastes relatively young) and complex.

FINISH Big, firm, and dry. This version is more of a winter warmer.

SCORE **84**

ABERLOUR Warehouse No 1 Hand-filled
First-fill Bourbon Cask No 1684, 63.5 vol

A special treat reserved for distillery visitors.
Filled into cask July 17, 1994, bottled January 2009.

COLOR Bright gold.

NOSE Sweet, rock candy. Raw sugar with light vanilla.
Wonderfully rich, yet airy. Notes of lemons linger in the glass.

BODY Full, mouth-coating, rich.

PALATE Rich, floral, sweet. Violets, hard candy, hints of green apples.
Full-flavored, but also light and delicate, exhibiting lovely floral notes
mixed with ripe green apples. Like a female ninja—delicate, beautiful,
yet nimble and strong.

FINISH Long and sweet. Apples.

SCORE **91**

ABERLOUR Warehouse No. 1 Hand-filled
First-fill Sherry Cask No 9643, 62.6 vol

A special treat reserved for distillery visitors.
Filled into cask August 24, 1993, bottled January 2009.

COLOR Light Mahogany.

NOSE Hot varnish and coffee grounds. Leather and pencil erasers.

BODY Robust and creamy.

PALATE Well-balanced sherry; pronounced, but not overpowering.
Hints of cloves and cardamom, pecans with a dusting of nutmeg.
Striking a match from afar.

FINISH Lingering and spicy, with the nutty warmth of a tawny port.

SCORE **89**

ALLT-A-BHAINNE

PRODUCER Chivas Brothers (Pernod Ricard)
REGION Highlands DISTRICT Speyside (Fiddich)
ADDRESS Glenrinnes, Dufftown, Banffshire, AB55 4DB
TEL 01542 783200

A FLURRY OF CONSTRUCTION enlivened Speyside in the mid-1970s, with four or five new distilleries built. It was one of those periods when the industry tries to catch up with underestimated demand. This distillery and the present Braeval were built by Seagrams. Their light, airy architecture is a happy marriage of traditional allusions and modern ideas, but they are lacking in humanity. Both are designed to operate with minimal staff, and their spirit is matured in central warehousing elsewhere.

In Gaelic, Allt-á-Bhainne means "the milk stream," and the distillery lies to the west of the Fiddich River in the foothills of Ben Rinnes, near Dufftown. Its malt whisky is a component of the Chivas blends. There have been no official bottlings, so malt lovers curious to taste the whisky have had to rely on independents.

HOUSE STYLE Light, slightly vegetal, flowery-spicy. Aperitif.

ALLT-A-BHAINNE 11-year-old, James MacArthur, 56.9 vol

COLOR Rich gold.

NOSE Chocolate lime candy. Grape. some sulfur.

BODY Rich and full. Sherried fruits. Some sulfur, some smoke, and some oak.

FINISH Medium and sweet, but the sulfur is still there, masking a potentially very good malt.

SCORE **65**

ALLT-A-BHAINNE 17-year-old, Old Malt Cask, 50 vol

COLOR Pale straw.

NOSE Light. Toffee. Cereal. Pickled cabbage.

BODY Sweet and oily.

PALATE Sweet. Star anise. Sharp spice. Some astringency.

FINISH Short. Not very assertive.

SCORE **65**

ARDBEG

PRODUCER Glenmorangie plc
REGION Islay   DISTRICT South Shore
ADDRESS Port Ellen, Islay, Argyll, PA42 7EA
TEL 01496 302244   WEBSITE www.ardbeg.com
EMAIL oldkiln@ardbeg.com VC

ALREADY ONE OF THE WORLD'S GREAT DISTILLERIES in the days when single malts were a secret, and revived at a cost of millions (whether euros or dollars), Ardbeg shines ever more brightly. Its reopening was one of the first signs of the Islay revival, of which it has become both a principal element and a beneficiary. Its owners' ambitions for the distillery are being rewarded.

When Ardbeg reopened, one of the former kilns was turned into a shop, also offering tea, coffee, a dram, and a clootie (dumpling). The Old Kiln now serves meals and is used by local people as well as visitors to the distillery.

Ardbeg aficionados still cling to the hope that the second kiln may one day return to use. The maltings were unusual in that there were no fans, causing the peat smoke to permeate very heavily. This is evident in very old bottlings. The peaty origins of the water are also a big influence in the whisky's earthy, tar-like flavors. Some lovers of Ardbeg believe that an applewood, lemon-skin fruitiness derives from a recirculatory system in the spirit still.

The distillery traces its history to 1794. The maltings last worked in 1976–77, though supplies of their malted barley were no doubt eked out a little longer. Ardbeg closed in the early 1980s, but toward the end of that decade began to work again, albeit very sporadically, using malt from Port Ellen. Whisky produced at that time, but released by the new owners, is less tar-like than the old Ardbeg. Such heavily peated whisky as was inherited has been used in some vattings. Under the ownership by Glenmorangie, Ardbeg has released a significant number of innovative bottlings, and the iconic Islay distillery and its whisky seem in good hands.

HOUSE STYLE Earthy, very peaty, smoky, salty, robust. A bedtime malt.

ARDBEG 10-year-old, 46 vol

COLOR Pale gold.

NOSE Sweet, with soft peat, carbolic soap, and smoked fish.

BODY Medium, firm.

PALATE Burning peats and dried fruit, followed by malt
and a touch of licorice.

FINISH Long and smoky. Fine balance of cereal sweetness,
iodine, and dry peat.

SCORE **87**

ARDBEG 17-year-old, 40 vol

COLOR Full, shimmering, greeny gold.

NOSE Assertive, briney, seaweedy, tar-like. Hint of sulfur.

BODY Medium, oily. Very firm.

PALATE Peppery but also sweet. Cereal grains, oil, gorse. Tightly combined
flavors. More mature and rounded, but still robust. Very appetizing.

FINISH Oily. Lemon skins. Freshly ground white pepper.

SCORE **86**

ARDBEG "Lord of the Isles" 25-year-old, 46 vol

*"The supreme expression of Ardbeg," according to the label, but where is the smoke and
clamor of battle? This whisky is named after the island rulers who fought the Vikings.*

COLOR Full gold.

NOSE Sea air. Distant smoke.

BODY Silky.

PALATE The Ardbeg fruitiness, usually lemony and fragrant, has become more
assertive and complex with age. Here, there are flavors reminiscent of candied
orange peel and, especially, cherries. Lots of flavor development. Walnuts,
almonds. Marzipan. Bittersweet. The roundness of flavors masks the peat.

FINISH Long, haughty. Steely. Not as earthy as might have been hoped.

SCORE **89**

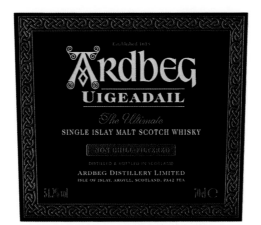

ARDBEG Uigeadail, 54.2 vol

COLOR Pale gold.

NOSE Intensely smoky. Dry, clean, tangy barbecue smoke.

BODY Light, firm.

PALATE Firm, very smooth, then explodes on the tongue.

FINISH Hot. Alcoholic. A shock to the system.

SCORE **92**

ARDBEG Still Young, 56.2 vol

Following Ardbeg's acquisition by Glenmorangie, the first of an ongoing series of releases of 1998 spirit appeared in 2003 as "Very Young." "Still Young" was marketed in 2006.

COLOR White wine.

NOSE. Fresh, with lemon zest and newly dug peat. A pinch of salt.

BODY Creamy.

PALATE Sweet peat, nuts, malt. Fresh pear notes with a peppery edge.

FINISH Warming and drying, with lingering almonds and pepper.

SCORE **84**

ARDBEG Almost There, 54.1 vol

The next release of 1998 Ardbeg spirit as part of the "Path to Peaty Maturity" series. Bottled 2007.

COLOR Pale straw.

NOSE Cereal-sweet, with vanilla and lemon, yet very phenolic and maritime.

BODY Medium, some oiliness.

PALATE Sweet, smoothly intense. Lemon, followed by spices and pepper. Complex.

FINISH Long and peaty, with milk chocolate and a peppery prickle.

SCORE **86**

ARDBEG Renaissance—We've Arrived! 55.9 vol

As the name implies, this is the final limited release of 1998 spirit,
bottled as a 10-year-old in 2008 at cask strength.

COLOR Straw.

NOSE Sweet peat, marzipan, bubblegum,
and floral notes. Later salt and spice.

BODY Medium to full; slightly oily.

PALATE Sweet and fruity. Chocolate ginger and spicy peat develop.

FINISH Lingering fruit, peat, persistent spice, and
a slight hint of Germolene.

SCORE **88**

ARDBEG Mor, 57.3 vol

Ten-year-old whisky, bottled in a limited edition of 1,000 x 450cl bottles.
"Mor" is Gaelic for big.

COLOR Straw, with copper highlights.

NOSE Unfettered Ardbeg. Phenolic, marine, tarry.

BODY Mouth-coating, oily.

PALATE Rich and bold, with peat, brine, and a citric edge.

FINISH Long and smoky, with ginger and dark chocolate.

SCORE **91**

ARDBEG Blasda, No Age Statement, 40 vol

Distilled from lightly peated malt.

COLOR Chardonnay.

NOSE Light and gently peaty, with a hint of lemon juice.

BODY Light, but not entirely insubstantial.

PALATE Sweet peat and canned peaches, moving to ripe eating apples.

FINISH Initially fresh, with developing and intensifying spicy peat.

SCORE **86**

ARDBEG Corryvreckan, No Age Statement, 57.1 vol

COLOR Gold.

NOSE Buttered kippers, freshly dug soil, citrus fruit, ginger and medicine cabinets.

BODY Full and viscous.

PALATE Quite dry, spicy and nutty, with savory and licorice notes, plus muted, background fruit, salt and peat.

FINISH Long, with peppery peat.

SCORE **88**

ARDBEG Airigh Nam Beist, 1990, 46 vol,

COLOR Ripening straw.

NOSE Soft, sweet, and medicinal, with nuttiness and subtle peat.

BODY Medium, oily.

PALATE Burning peat and seaweed. Oily and slightly peppery, cough lozenges, a hint of vanilla.

FINISH Lengthy, with strong coffee and licorice, but predominantly bonfire smoke.

SCORE **92**

ARDBEG 1976 Single Cask, No 2397, 52.4 vol

Matured in a sherry butt, 519 bottles.

COLOR Pale amber.

NOSE Seashore meets sherry.

BODY Medium and firm.

PALATE Rich, with golden raisins, raisins, toffee, and peat.

FINISH Medium in length, with dried fruit and slightly astringent oak.

SCORE **87**

ARDBEG Double Barrel 1974, Cask No 3160, 49 vol

Double Barrel features a luxury gun case presentation, which includes two bottles of 1974 Ardbeg. In total, eight single casks were used in the global allocation of 250 Ardbeg Double Barrels.

COLOR Amber.

NOSE Sweet and gentle, with malt, succulent fruits, and background smoke.

BODY Medium and insinuating.

PALATE Initially full, with over-ripe fruit, but soon showing signs of age.

FINISH Astringent, quite sooty, and woody.

SCORE **84**

ARDBEG Supernova, 58.9 vol

Supernova was launched in 2009 as "the peatiest Ardbeg ever." It boasts a peating level in excess of 100ppm, and comprises 70 percent spirit matured in first-fill bourbon barrels and 30 percent from former sherry casks.

COLOR Pale gold.

NOSE Blatant. Damp soil, peat smoke, tar, resin, and soft fruits.

BODY Muscular.

PALATE Lively. Complex mix of spices, including chili peppers, tobacco, peat, sea salt, and citrus fruit.

FINISH Long, with root ginger, black pepper, and dark chocolate.

SCORE **91**

AN INDEPENDENT BOTTLING
AR1, Elements of Islay, Speciality Drinks, 58.7 vol

A vattting of between 5 and 20 casks of varying ages, with no age statement.

COLOR Pale gold.

NOSE Full-on sweet peat, singed cloth, and iodine.

BODY Textured.

PALATE Sweet, smoky fruit, and big ginger notes merge and mesh nicely.

FINISH Long and peppery.

SCORE **90**

ARDMORE

PRODUCER Beam Global
REGION Highlands DISTRICT Speyside (Bogie)
ADDRESS Kennethmont, by Huntly, Aberdeenshire, AB54 4NH
TEL 01464 831213 VC

ARDMORE LIES ON THE EASTERN FRINGE of Speyside where Aberdeenshire barley country begins. Although not very well known, it is a sizeable distillery, makes a major contribution to Teacher's, and enjoys a healthy reputation as a single malt within some circles. When Allied broke up, it was taken over by Beam Global, who also now own Teacher's and Laphroaig. Ardmore's Traditional Cask is a new expression that uses malt partially matured in quarter-size casks. Enthusiasts hope that this will start to raise the distillery's profile.

HOUSE STYLE Malty, creamy, fruity. After dinner.

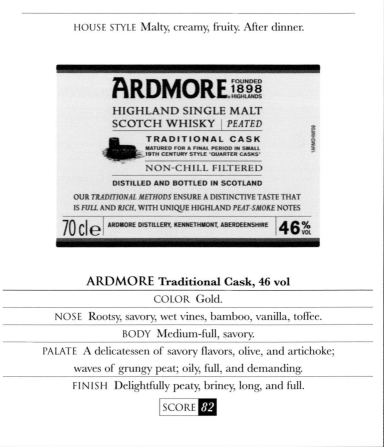

ARDMORE Traditional Cask, 46 vol

COLOR Gold.

NOSE Rootsy, savory, wet vines, bamboo, vanilla, toffee.

BODY Medium-full, savory.

PALATE A delicatessen of savory flavors, olive, and artichoke;
waves of grungy peat; oily, full, and demanding.

FINISH Delightfully peaty, briney, long, and full.

SCORE *82*

ARDMORE 12-year-old, Centenary Bottling, 40 vol

More elegant, but less robust, than the regular Gordon & MacPhail 12-year-old bottling.

COLOR Warm primrose.

NOSE Fresh, clean, sweet. Flowery-fruity. Cream. Sherry trifle.

BODY Light, but very smooth. Slippery smooth.

PALATE Delicate, fruity (raspberry?) flavors reminiscent of blancmange.

FINISH Flowery. Nutty dryness. Toasted almonds.

SCORE **73**

AN INDEPENDENT BOTTLING

ARDMORE 11-year-old, Provenance, 50 vol

COLOR Very pale yellowy green.

NOSE Earthy. Savory. Salami. Smoked meat.

BODY Oily and grungey.

PALATE Sardines at first. Nice balance between sweet vegetables, savory notes, and wispy spice. Big and complex.

FINISH Medium. Peat and spice.

SCORE **86**

ARRAN

PRODUCER Isle of Arran Distillers Ltd.
REGION Highlands   ISLAND Arran
ADDRESS Lochranza, Isle of Arran, Argyll, KA27 8HJ
TEL 01770 830264   WEBSITE www.arranwhisky.com
E-MAIL arran.distillers@arranwhisky.com   VC

SINCE IT OPENED IN 1995, and released its first whisky in 1998, the Isle of Arran distillery has inspired several similar projects elsewhere in Scotland. Its launch effectively marked the start of a prosperous and fertile spell in whisky's history.

The island, a favorite with hikers and bird-watchers, is easily accessible. From Glasgow it is a short drive south to the Ayrshire port of Ardrossan, whence a frequent ferry runs to Brodick, on the east of the island. A narrow road then winds its way round the north coast to the distillery, in the village of Lochranza. There is accommodation in Lochranza, and a ferry to Kintyre, for those who wish to visit the Campbeltown distilleries. A couple more ferries can be taken to extend the trip to Islay and Jura.

Arran has dramatic granite mountains, peaty land, and good water. The island was once known for its whisky, but spent a century and a half without a legal distillery. The inspiration for a new distillery came after a talk given at the Arran Society in 1992. Industry veteran Harold Currie, a retired managing director of Chivas, organized a scheme in which 2000 bonds were sold in exchange for whisky from the new distillery. As the Isle of Arran has many visitors, the distillery was seen as an additional attraction for tourists. It has a shop and a restaurant with an excellent kitchen.

HOUSE STYLE Creamy, leafy. Restorative or with dessert.
No obvious island character.

ISLE OF ARRAN 5-year-old, vol

COLOR Pale yellow.	
NOSE Straw, flower stem, clean, sherbet fruit.	
BODY Light, soft.	
PALATE Refreshing and clean; zingy; sweet lime, citrus.	
FINISH Medium, clean, and fruity, with a touch of cinnamon spice.	

SCORE **63**

ISLE OF ARRAN 10-year-old, 46 vol

COLOR Rich gold.

NOSE Light. Spearmint, vanilla, butterscotch.

BODY Creamy, oily, full.

PALATE Big rich melon, fresh barley, confectionery. Clean, sweet, chewy.

FINISH Vanilla, gentle spice. Rich.

SCORE **83**

ISLE OF ARRAN 12-year-old, 46 vol

COLOR Rich copper.

NOSE Barley sugar, ginger cubes, fresh mandarin, incense spices.

BODY Full, rich, sweet, creamy.

PALATE Tangerine. Orange liqueur, spice, some tannins.

FINISH Quite long, spicy, fruity and rich.

SCORE **79**

ISLE OF ARRAN Robert Burns 250th Anniversary Edition, 43 vol

COLOR Golden honey.

NOSE Floral, violets, perfume, sweet.

BODY Soft and rounded.

PALATE Sweet, vanilla, over-ripe melon. Clean and refreshing.

FINISH Medium, yellow fruits, drying at the end.

SCORE **73**

ISLE OF ARRAN Single Bourbon Cask, 1998, Bottled 2008

COLOR Rich orange.

NOSE Classic bourbon, with caramel and vanilla, stewed fruits, apricot.

BODY Full and mouth-coating.

PALATE Fine balance of yellow fruit and pineapple, clean barley,
sweet and sour, with sugar and spice. Some citrus notes.

FINISH Quite long, bitter lemon, sharp, spicy.

SCORE **77**

ISLE OF ARRAN 8-year-old St. Emilion finish, 50 vol

COLOR Red-brown.

NOSE Rosehip syrup, rosebuds. Sweet then earthy and rootsy; blueberry.

BODY Full, oily, rich, and chewy.

PALATE Plummy, green banana, grape.

FINISH Big and rich, uncloying, savory, and slightly sour fruit.

SCORE **78**

ISLE OF ARRAN 8-year-old Madeira Finish, 50 vol

COLOR Rich gold with a reddish hue.

NOSE Strawberry cream, guava, lime soda.

BODY Medium.

PALATE Clean, refreshing, with green fruit, strawberry, and vanilla ice cream

FINISH Medium but very refreshing and summery..

SCORE **86**

ISLE OF ARRAN Fontallaro Finish, 55 vol

COLOR Orangey brown.

NOSE Gentle and clean, but rich. Mandarin oranges, sweet citrus fruits.

BODY Sweet, oily, and full; mouth-coating.

PALATE Fresh, youthful fruit. Very clean and sweet. Nicely balanced
between grain and grape.

FINISH Sweet but not cloying, fruity, and fresh.

SCORE **83**

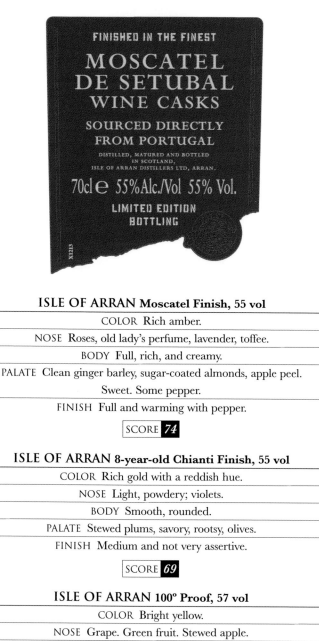

FINISHED IN THE FINEST

MOSCATEL DE SETUBAL
WINE CASKS

SOURCED DIRECTLY FROM PORTUGAL

DISTILLED, MATURED AND BOTTLED
IN SCOTLAND,
ISLE OF ARRAN DISTILLERS LTD, ARRAN.

70cl ℮ 55%Alc./Vol 55% Vol.

LIMITED EDITION
BOTTLING

ISLE OF ARRAN Moscatel Finish, 55 vol

COLOR Rich amber.

NOSE Roses, old lady's perfume, lavender, toffee.

BODY Full, rich, and creamy.

PALATE Clean ginger barley, sugar-coated almonds, apple peel. Sweet. Some pepper.

FINISH Full and warming with pepper.

SCORE **74**

ISLE OF ARRAN 8-year-old Chianti Finish, 55 vol

COLOR Rich gold with a reddish hue.

NOSE Light, powdery; violets.

BODY Smooth, rounded.

PALATE Stewed plums, savory, rootsy, olives.

FINISH Medium and not very assertive.

SCORE **69**

ISLE OF ARRAN 100° Proof, 57 vol

COLOR Bright yellow.

NOSE Grape. Green fruit. Stewed apple.

BODY Rich, full, and creamy.

PALATE Lime candies. Clean, sweet, strong barley.

FINISH Quite long, sweet, and clean.

SCORE **81**

ISLE OF ARRAN Single Sherry Cask, 59.4 vol
Cask 96/1754

COLOR	Rich dark brown.
NOSE	Full sherry, Christmas cake mix, red berries, kitchen pantry.
BODY	Rich, full, mouth-coating.
PALATE	Chewy raisin, rich red berries; some astringency from the wood.
FINISH	Long, rich, and fruity, drying at the end.

SCORE **86**

AN INDEPENDENT BOTTLING
ARRAN 1996, Bottled 2007, Berry's Own Selection, 46 vol

COLOR	Very pale greenish yellow.
NOSE	Cut grass. Summer meadow. Lemon sherbet bonbons.
BODY	Rich and full. Spicy.
PALATE	Clean barley, citrus juices. Then some peat and spice.
FINISH	Medium. Fresh and quite spicy.

SCORE **77**

AUCHENTOSHAN

PRODUCER Morrison Bowmore Distillers Ltd.
REGION Lowlands DISTRICT Western Lowlands
ADDRESS Dalmuir, Clydebank, Dunbartonshire, G81 4SJ
TEL 01389 878561 WEBSITE www.auchentoshan.com VC

THIS IS A CLASSIC LOWLAND DISTILLERY, not only in its location, but also in its adherence to triple distillation. Light-bodied whiskies result; light in flavor, too, but by no means bland. If you fancy single malts, but do not care for intensity, Auchentoshan offers the perfect answer: subtlety. Stan Getz rather than Sonny Rollins; Vivaldi, as opposed to Beethoven.

Auchentoshan ("corner of the field") is pronounced "och'n'tosh'n," as though it were an imprecation. The distillery is at the foot of the Kilpatrick Hills, just outside Glasgow. There are suggestions of a distillery on the site around 1800, but 1825 is the "official" foundation date. The distillery was rebuilt after World War II, re-equipped in 1974, and further overhauled ten years later, when it was acquired by Stanley P. Morrison. The acquisition provided a Lowland partner for their Islay and Highland distilleries, Bowmore and Glen Garioch. The company is now called Morrison Bowmore, and is controlled by Suntory. The Japanese cherish the distilleries, and the upkeep is superb. Much has been done to highlight the equipment at Auchentoshan and to show how the whisky is made.

HOUSE STYLE Light, lemon grassy, herbal, oily. Aperitif or restorative.

AUCHENTOSHAN Select, No Age Statement, 40 vol

COLOR Shimmery gold.

NOSE Appetizing, clean, warm, cereal grain.
Cookies fresh from the oven.

BODY Lightly oily.

PALATE Lemon grass notes. Toasty maltiness—
definite, but light. Cleanly sweet.

FINISH Light, crisp. Hint of lemon grass spiciness.

SCORE 79

AUCHENTOSHAN Classic, No Age Statement, 40 vol

Introduced in 2008, Classic is a replacement
for the previous Select bottling.

COLOR Pale gold.

NOSE Very sweet, with vanilla, coconut, peaches, and Madeira.

BODY Soft and quite light.

PALATE Granny Smith apples, malt, and creamy vanilla.

FINISH Fresh and floral, with ripe peaches.

SCORE **80**

AUCHENTOSHAN 10-year-old, 40 vol

COLOR Bright yellowy gold.

NOSE A warm embrace, with aromas of vanilla,
lemon grass, and saddles.

BODY Light but soft. Oily.

PALATE Lemon zest, marshmallow. Sweet but not cloying.

FINISH Longer. Lemongrass, faint ginger, vanilla,
perfumy. Soft.

SCORE **83**

AUCHENTOSHAN 12-year-old, 40 vol

A replacement for the now discontinued 10-year-old.
Contains a higher percentage of sherry wood matured spirit.

COLOR Honey-gold.

NOSE Floral and fruity, with mashed banana and nutty malt.

BODY Smooth, slightly oily.

PALATE Malt, caramel, oranges, a hint of sherry.

FINISH Medium in length and malty.

SCORE **85**

AUCHENTOSHAN 18-year-old, 43 vol

COLOR Deep gold.

NOSE Fresh fruits, honey, almonds, spices, and vanilla.

BODY Oily and quite full.

PALATE Initially fresh and floral, with developing maltiness,
fresh oak, and ginger.

FINISH Comparatively lengthy, with raisins, nutmeg,
and a final dry oak note.

 SCORE **86**

AUCHENTOSHAN Three Wood, 43 vol

*Released without an age statement, this whisky has at least ten years in bourbon wood,
a good year in oloroso and six months in the hefty Pedro Ximénez. In addition to offering
an unusual array of wood characteristics, it fills a gap in Auchentoshan's age range.*

COLOR Orange liqueur.

NOSE Soft. Orange zest, apricot, dates, marshmallow.

BODY Oily. Marshmallow-like.

PALATE Perfumy, lemon grass, cashews. A delicate interplay of flavors, but
the whisky struggles to assert itself among the woods.
Better with little or no water.

FINISH Long and creamy. Raisins, anise, fresh oak. Sappy dryness.

SCORE **85**

AUCHENTOSHAN 21-year-old, 43 vol

COLOR Full, deep gold.

NOSE Orange zest, date boxes, cedar, oil.

BODY Light to medium. Oily. Very smooth indeed.

PALATE Oily, citrusy, orange peel. Lightly spicy. Lots of flavor development. More oak character than previous entry. Fresh, with no obtrusive woodiness.

FINISH Cedar, vanilla, beautifully rounded, and aromatic.

SCORE **86**

VINTAGE-DATED AUCHENTOSHANS

The distillery has released a number of limited-edition vintage bottlings during the last few years, including, in late 2008, a 50-year-old expression, matured in an oloroso sherry butt, and a 31-year-old from 1965.

AUCHENTOSHAN 1965, 31-year-old, Cask No 2502, 49.3 vol

COLOR Old gold.

NOSE Some cotton-candy sweetness.

BODY Syrupy, then dusty. Cake icing. Cocoa powder.

PALATE Spun sugar. Quickly becoming drier. Nutty. Flavors reminiscent of peanut shells and coconut-fiber matting.

FINISH Dry, musty.

SCORE **72**

AN INDEPENDENT BOTTLING

AUCHENTOSHAN 19-year-old, Duthie's, 46 vol

COLOR Pale gold.

NOSE Soft, with caramel, mixed spices, and gentle honey.

BODY Rounded.

PALATE Fresh fruit, figs, and a developing creaminess.

FINISH Buttered fruit malt bread and lingering ginger.

SCORE **85**

AUCHROISK

PRODUCER Diageo
REGION Highlands   DISTRICT Speyside
ADDRESS Auchroisk Distillery Mulben, Banffshire, AB55 6XS
TEL 01542 885000   WEBSITE www.malts.com   VC

T OO YOUNG to make promises for eternity, but "Always Auchroisk" might be a wise text for the future. This distillery was established in 1974. Given that a distillery can survive two or three times as long as a human, Auchroisk is barely an adolescent. For several years, it was, in the hope of seducing foreigners, calling itself The Singleton. That term is sometimes used to indicate a single cask (in this case, a sherry butt). It was therefore thought to be an appropriate substitute for the original Gaelic name, which means "ford on the red stream."

The distillery, between Rothes and Dufftown, is on a ridge by the Mulben Burn, which flows into the Spey. Nearby is a spring called Dorie's Well, which determined the site of the distillery. The soft water and large stills make whisky of a delicacy that deserves a chance to show itself without sherry, and under its own name.

Phonetic guides can always be provided, except that no one agrees. Auch Roysk, says the manager; Ach Rask (or Rusk), insist the locals. There is schism over the "ch" being pronounced as a "th." Can the foreigners cope with this? Funny how the simply delicious Singleton never hooked as many sales worldwide as some unpronounceably complex whiskies from the west.

HOUSE STYLE Very soft. Berry fruits. Aperitif. Or with fruit salad.

AUCHROISK 10-year-old, 43 vol

COLOR Soft, burnished yellow.

NOSE Pronounced fruitiness. White grapes. Gooseberry. Berry fruits.

BODY Light, soft, seductive.

PALATE Lightly fruity, with a suggestion of figs.
Becoming nuttier and drier. Shortbread.

FINISH Faint sun-scorched grass and peat.

SCORE **78**

A 27-year-old independent bottling from Old Malt Cask, 43.8 vol, had a suggestion of bananas and creamy toffee. SCORE 77

AULTMORE

PRODUCER John Dewar & Sons Ltd.
REGION Highlands   DISTRICT Speyside (Isla)
ADDRESS Keith, Banffshire, AB55 6QY
TEL 01542 881800   VC

A FINE MALT IN THE OAKY STYLE that seems to characterize the whiskies made near the Isla River. This distillery, which is just north of Keith, was built in 1896, and reconstructed in 1971. In 1991, United Distillers, its owners at the time, introduced a bottling in their Flora and Fauna series. They issued a Rare Malts edition in 1996, and a cask strength limited bottling in 1997–98. These and other past releases were reviewed in the fourth edition of this book. In 1998, Aultmore was acquired by Bacardi.

HOUSE STYLE Fresh, dry, herbal, spicy, oaky. Reminiscent of a fino sherry, albeit a very big one. Before dinner.

AULTMORE 12-year-old, Old Malt Cask, 50 vol

COLOR Rich gold.

NOSE Light. Floral. Vanilla. Rose petal.

BODY Medium and pleasant.

PALATE Nicely balanced. Quite minty. Mixed fruits. Nice balance of sweetness and spice.

FINISH Quite short but very sweet and pleasant.

SCORE 79

AULTMORE 1995, Connoisseurs Choice, 43 vol

COLOR Lemon yellow.

NOSE Over-ripe fruit bowl. A mix of juicy fruits, including lime and melon.

BODY Distinctively firm, smooth, and oily.

PALATE Soft. Melon. Sugared barley. Vanilla. Very pleasant and palatable.

FINISH Medium, rounded, and balanced.

SCORE 86

BALBLAIR

PRODUCER Inver House Distillers Ltd.
REGION Highlands DISTRICT Northern Highlands
ADDRESS Edderton, Tain, Ross-shire, IV19 1LB
EMAIL enquiries@inverhouse.com WEBSITE www.inverhouse.com

INVER HOUSE HAS WORKED SLOWLY and surely on its distilleries since it purchased them in 2001, making gradual but distinctive improvements to both the properties and malts, expanding the portfolios, and picking up awards along the way. Then, in 2008, the company took the dramatic step of not only repackaging its Balblair range, but also changing the whisky, branding the malt by distillation year rather than age and boldly repositioning the distillery's bottles in a more premium category. None of the company's distilleries is a household name, but they are all respected and are building a growing reputation under their newish owners.

The typically spicy and fresh dryness of the Northern Highlands is now complemented by a richer fruit sweetness in the new Balblairs and the relatively older expressions are a real and welcome surprise. They are made using water that has flowed from the piney hillsides of Ben Dearg and over dry, crumbly peat towards the river Carron and the Dornoch firth. A burn (stream) near the distillery feeds Balblair, which is amid fields at Edderton, close to the firth and the sea. There is said to have been brewing and distilling in the vicinity in the mid-1700s. Balblair is among Scotland's oldest distilleries. It began in 1790, and the present building dates from the 1870s.

HOUSE STYLE Light, firm, dry. Aperitif when young.
Can be woody when older.

BALBLAIR "Elements", No Age Statement, 40 vol

COLOR Full gold.

NOSE Sea breezes. Slight salt. Barley-malt sweetness.

BODY Lean but smooth. Textured.

PALATE Teasing, appetizing balance of slight salt and shortbread-like fresh malt. Faint hint of raspberries.

FINISH Plum-skin dryness.

SCORE 76

BALBLAIR 10-year-old, 40 vol

COLOR Shimmery, pale gold.

NOSE Fresh. Salty. Vanilla. A hint of chocolate.

BODY Light on the tongue.

PALATE Malty dryness. Shortbread sprinkled with sugar.
Custard. Berry pudding.

FINISH Concentrated fruity dryness. Berry pudding. Comforting.

COMMENT Approachable and well structured, with delicious flavors.

SCORE 77

BALBLAIR 16-year-old, 40 vol

COLOR Pale amber.

NOSE Nutty. Light, fresh spiciness. Fragrant.

BODY Firm, smooth, textured.

PALATE Smooth and surprisingly satisfying. Again, the saltiness and
shortbread. This time, it is chocolate shortbread. A light whisky,
but packed with flavors. Very lively.

FINISH Toffee apples. Cedary dryness.

SCORE 78

BALBLAIR 1997, 43 vol

COLOR Rich gold.

NOSE Fresh, lime, kumquat, orange peel.

BODY Full, fresh, and mouth-coating.

PALATE Rich ginger barley, lime citrus. Then later sweet pepper
and lime cordial.

FINISH Medium and sweet.

SCORE 76

BALBLAIR 1990, 43 vol

COLOR Rich gold.

NOSE Pineapple, green fruits, vanilla. Sweet.

BODY Sweet and thin syrup.

PALATE Canned pears, lots of clean fruit, sugary spices. Very pleasant.

FINISH A mix of fruit and sweet spice, with the merest hint of oak.

SCORE **72**

BALBLAIR 1989, 43 vol

COLOR Rich gold.

NOSE Sherbet fruits, vanilla. Zesty. Strawberry Starburst.

BODY Medium, sweet, balanced.

PALATE Sweet, citrus Starburst, clean barley, lime, guava, exotic fruits.

FINISH Medium-sweet, like an alcohol-soaked bowl of exotic fruits.

SCORE **83**

BALBLAIR 1975, 46 vol

COLOR Rich mahogany.

NOSE Bourbony, vanilla, red fruits, orange marmalade. Oaky.

BODY Full, mouth-coating.

PALATE Soft but complex mix of barley, sweetness, dark chocolate,
cherry, orange liqueur, and oak.

FINISH Cherry liqueur and dark chocolate linger. Wonderful.

SCORE **90**

AN INDEPENDENT BOTTLING
BALBLAIR 1990, Cask 1143, A.D. Rattray, 62.4 vol

COLOR Deep gold.

NOSE Grapeskin. Oil paint. Gooseberry.

BODY Medium and sweet.

PALATE Sweet. Some soft fruits, including orange and tangerine.
Some chewy barley.

FINISH Short, sweet, not much depth.

SCORE **70**

BALMENACH

PRODUCER Inver House Distillers Ltd.
REGION Highlands   DISTRICT Speyside
ADDRESS Cromdale, Grantown-on-Spey, Morayshire, PH26 3PF
EMAIL enquiries@inverhouse.com   WEBSITE www.inverhouse.com

O F THE FOUR DISTILLERIES that Inver House acquired in the 1990s, Balmenach is the one that has received the least attention, despite early mutterings that it was to be the group's flagship. Traditionally its distillate has the most powerful aromas and flavors but it has become something of a remote distillery. In the upper reaches of Speyside, beyond the Livet and Avon, the bowl known as Cromdale ("crooked plain") was once alive with illicit distillers. When Balmenach emerged there as a legal distillery in 1824, it was in the heart of whisky country.

The family that founded Balmenach, in 1824, also produced two appropriately distinguished authors: Sir Compton Mackenzie (*Whisky Galore*) and Sir Robert Bruce Lockhart (*Scotch: The Whisky of Scotland in Fact and Story*, and other books on soldiering, espionage, and travel). Balmenach later had its own spur on the Strathspey railroad. The distillery contributed malt whisky to many blends, especially Crabbie's and Johnnie Walker.

In 1991 a bottled single malt was issued at 43 vol in the flora and fauna series. A review appeared in subsequent editions of this book, praising the whisky for its depth of heather-honey flavors, herbal dryness, and sherry (SCORE 77). Two years later, United Distillers announced that Balmenach was to be mothballed. Four years on, it passed to Inver House. In the interim, very flowery expressions of Balmenach were bottled under the name Deerstalker, by Aberfoyle & Knight, of Glasgow (SCORE 79).

HOUSE STYLE Big, herbal, savory. Hints of peat. Surprisingly food-friendly.

BALMENACH 27-year-old,
Bottled 2001, Highland Selection, 46 vol

NOSE Sweet tropical fruits. Bananas. Plantains being cooked on a barbecue.

PALATE Becoming drier. Vegetal. Yeasty. Perhaps the meal is in Thailand or China?

FINISH A touch of smokiness. Roasted bell peppers. Some chili pepper-like heat.

SCORE **79**

BALMENACH 1972, 28-year-old,
Highland Selection, 46 vol

NOSE Sweet at first. Honeydew melons. Then leafy: a suggestion of sorrel. A hint of grass and peat smoke.

PALATE Lightly honeyish, becoming creamy. Quite rich. Leathery. Some peat.

FINISH Dry. Big. Gingery. Blackstrap molasses. Smoky, sulfury, heady.

COMMENT A robust malt, but with many subtleties of character.

SCORE **80**

TWO INDEPENDENT BOTTLINGS
BALMENACH 8-year-old, Provenance, 46 vol

COLOR Very pale yellow.

NOSE Grapey barley. Grassy. Damp straw. Trace of citrus fruit—lime?

BODY Medium and sweet.

PALATE Anise. Sweet but nicely counter-balanced by some earthy peat. Rich barley. Marzipan.

FINISH Medium, sweet, pleasant.

SCORE **75**

BALMENACH 18-year-old, Old Malt Cask, 50 vol

COLOR Light yellow.

NOSE Citrus. Grapefruit. Resiny.

BODY Soft, sweet, and creamy.

PALATE Mix of peat, clean barley, and sweet fruits, with late spice and some oaky tannins.

FINISH Sweet and spicy.

SCORE **77**

THE BALVENIE

PRODUCER William Grant & Sons Ltd.
REGION Highlands   DISTRICT Speyside (Dufftown)
ADDRESS Dufftown, Banffshire, AB55 4BB
TEL 01340 820373   WEBSITE www.thebalvenie.com

As SEDUCTIVELY HONEYED AS A SPEYSIDER can be; ever more aristocratic, in recent years introducing vintages as though they were eligible offspring, The Balvenie is increasingly recognized far from her domain. Her tendency toward voluptuousness, and her ready charm, win friends easily. A dalliance by the sea resulted in the birth, in 2001, of The Balvenie Islay Cask. Fellow Speysiders resented the notion of a whisky from their elevated territory even contemplating the addition of "Islay" to its name. Meanwhile, Islanders complained that The Balvenie was merely courting popularity. There have been no more Islay Casks. It was a holiday romance.

She may be a notably rich spirit, but Bad Penny offers the easiest mnemonic for Balvenie's vowel sounds. The Balvenie distillery was built in 1892 by the Grant family, who had already established Glenfiddich in 1886. It is highly unusual for a distillery to remain in the same ownership throughout its history, but both Glenfiddich and Balvenie have done so, on their original sites, which adjoin one another. One became the world's biggest selling malt and the other the epitome of luxury, but both were established, thriftily, with second-hand stills. Balvenie's are more bulbous, and that feature no doubt contributes to the distinct character of the whisky. The distillery also has its own small floor maltings, using barley from the family farm.

In 1990, Grant's added to the site a third distillery, Kininvie. This also produces a creamy spirit, but Kininvie has not thus far been bottled as a single malt. Adjoining the site is the silent Convalmore distillery, acquired by Grant's in 1992 to augment warehousing capacity.

Grant's site is at Dufftown, where the rivers Fiddich and Dullan meet on their way to the Spey. The Balvenie distillery is near the castle of the same name, which dates at least from the 1200s. The castle was at one stage known as Mortlach and was at another stage occupied by the Duff family, and is now owned by the nation of Scotland.

HOUSE STYLE The most honeyish of malts, with a distinctively orangey note.
Luxurious. After dinner. Ages well.

THE BALVENIE Founder's Reserve, 10-year-old, 40 vol

Matured in 90% American oak and 10% sherry.

COLOR Bright gold.

NOSE Orange-honey perfume. Musky. Faint hint of peat.

BODY Medium.

PALATE Honeyed sweetness, drying to lightly spicy notes. Very lively.
Just a touch of sherry.

FINISH A tingly surge of flavors, with lingering, syrupy honey.

SCORE **85**

THE BALVENIE Signature, 12-year-old, 40 vol

COLOR Deep golden orange.

NOSE Pencil shavings, dry, woody, dusty, sweet satsuma,
and orange. Complex.

BODY Soft, rounded, and medium-full.

PALATE Sharp, clean barley, but without enough body. Fruitcake.
An array of orange fruits, including tangerine and mandarin oranges.

FINISH Pleasant, medium-long, fruity.

SCORE **70**

THE BALVENIE Double Wood, 12-year-old, 40 vol
First- and second-fill bourbon casks, then six to twelve months in sweet oloroso casks.

COLOR Amber.

NOSE Sherry and orange skins.

BODY Medium, rich.

PALATE Beautifully combined mellow flavors: nutty, sweet, sherried.
A very orangey fruitiness. Heather. Cinnamon spiciness.

FINISH Long, tingling. Very warming.

SCORE **87**

THE BALVENIE Roasted Malt, 14-year-old, 47.1 vol

COLOR Deep golden orange.

NOSE Praline, soft barley, hay. Buttery. Pencil shavings.

BODY Sweet, soft, and quite rich.

PALATE Burned toffee, pralines. Sweet. Later sweet spice
and toasted tannin notes.

FINISH Quite long. Toast, malted milk, some orange. Very pleasant.

SCORE **84**

THE BALVENIE Rum Finish, 17-year-old, 43 vol

COLOR Deep gold.

NOSE The rum influence is strong. Molasses, and a dark chocolate
note that gives a delightful rum-raisin combination.
Rich fruitcake, summer meadow.

BODY Rich and full, sweet and delightful.

PALATE Apple seed, almond, then lime and mango. Citrus fruits,
sharp spices, and oak later on. A hint of apples.

FINISH Quite long, sharp, and spicy.

SCORE **80**

THE BALVENIE Single Barrel, 15-year-old, 50.4 vol
All first-fill bourbon casks.

COLOR Pale gold.

NOSE Assertive. Dry, fresh oak. Heather. Rooty. Coconut. Lemon pith.

BODY Firm.

PALATE Lively. Cedar. Orange skins, pineapple-like sweetness
and acidity.

FINISH Very dry. Peppery alcohol.

SCORE **85**

THE BALVENIE Single Barrel, 15-year-old, 47.8 vol

COLOR Lemony gold.

NOSE Fresh and clean. Starburst, tutti frutti ice cream. Perfumed.

BODY Full, rich, and fruity.

PALATE Massive burst of lemon and lime, clean and sweet barley, and vanilla. Then some late cake icing and spice. Very summery, very refreshing, very moreish.

FINISH Sublime. Long, sweet, and fruity, with a late burst of spice.

SCORE **90**

THE BALVENIE Islay Cask, 43 vol

Seven years in bourbon barrels, then finished for six months at Balvenie in casks that had held Islay whisky for six months.

COLOR Bronze with a pinkish tinge.

NOSE Restrained, but distinct. Seaweed and salt.

BODY A touch of syrupiness in the middle.

PALATE Honeyed, then some peaty smokiness. The smokiness is enwrapping, rather than attacking, as it might be in an Islay malt.

FINISH Fragrantly smoky. Orangey flavors emerge. Lively, emphatic finish. A bold idea.

SCORE **89**

THE BALVENIE Port Wood, 21-year-old, 40 vol

Primarily matured in bourbon casks, then a short period in first-fill port pipes.

COLOR Reddish amber.

NOSE Perfumy, fruity. Passion fruit. Raisiny. Nutty dryness. Marzipan.

BODY Rich.

PALATE Very complex. Toffee, creamy, winey, anise.

FINISH Long, cedary, dry.

SCORE **88**

THE BALVENIE Single Barrel, 25-year-old, 46.9 vol

COLOR Pale, bright gold.

NOSE Honeyed.

BODY Lightly syrupy.

PALATE Surprisingly peaty, though the characteristic honey is there.

FINISH Firm. Peaty.

SCORE **86**

SOME VINTAGE BOTTLINGS OF THE BALVENIE
THE BALVENIE Vintage Cask, 1972, 49.4 vol

COLOR Rich, warm, gold to amber.

NOSE Buttery richness. Butterscotch pudding. Bread and butter pudding. Honey.

BODY Rich, soft, delicious. Astonishingly syrupy smooth.

PALATE Still evoking thoughts of desserts, but the honeyed pastries of the Balkans. Then a suggestion of chocolate powder hints at tiramisu.

FINISH Bitter chocolate. Chocolate oranges.
The ultimate dessert whisky. Beautifully composed.

SCORE **92**

THE BALVENIE 1968, Vintage Cask, 50.8 vol

COLOR Full gold to bronze.

NOSE Clear liquid honey. Heathery.
More perfumy and orangey when water is added.

BODY Fudgey, soft.

PALATE Honeyed. Very pronounced orange zest. Lots of flavor development.
With water. Hazelnut or almond. Some smoke. Slight menthol. Mint.

FINISH Lemony. Dry. Warming. Very long.

SCORE **90**

THE BALVENIE Vintage Cask 1967, 49.7 vol

COLOR Full gold.

NOSE Very aromatic. Butterscotch, honey. Acacia. Faint peat.

BODY Light syrupy. Slightly drying. Nutty. Chewy.

PALATE Buttery maltiness. Honey. Orange. Linctus-like.
Hint of vanilla. Juicy oak.

FINISH Orange skins. Lemon grass. Lightly peaty balancing dryness.

SCORE **88**

THE BALVENIE Vintage Cask 1976, 52.8 vol, Cask 6570

COLOR Rich honey.

NOSE Hazelnut, wood, syrup, sweet spice, gloopy honey, fruity cake mix.

BODY Full and mouth coating, quite oily.

PALATE Prune juice, soft and rounded grape and melon fruits battling against drying tannins and just about winning, some spice.

FINISH Astringency from the wood first, and finally the fruit mix wins out.

SCORE **89**

THE BALVENIE Vintage Cask 1976, 53.8 vol, Cask 6568

COLOR Bronze.

NOSE Sharp, hazelnut, root vegetable, musk, damp leaves.

BODY Full, creamy, mouth-filling and oily.

PALATE Sweet fruit at first but then bitterness, nuttiness and tannins. Sweet chili peppers and oakiness is replaced by grape and citrus fruits.

FINISH Long, warming and balanced, sweeter than the body might have suggested, with the bitter tannins held in check.

SCORE **88**

THE BALVENIE Vintage Cask 1975, Cask 15354, 47.3 vol

Exclusive to Taiwan

COLOR Lemon yellow.

NOSE Light, lemon and orange zest, vanilla, honey, sweet.

BODY Medium-full, sweet and juicy.

PALATE Anise, spearmint, sweet pepper, tannins, some pear.

FINISH Nice balance of sweet fruit, spices and oakiness. Long.

SCORE **85**

THE BALVENIE 1964, 41.3 vol

Exclusive to Hong Kong

COLOR Pale lemon.

NOSE Pineapple, sherbet, zesty, grapefruit.

BODY Shy, quite thin, unassertive.

PALATE Delicate. Citrus fruits, grapefruit. Refreshing lime cordial. Summery.

FINISH Medium, sweet lemon, cake icing.

SCORE **87**

BANFF

PRODUCER DCL
REGION Highlands   DISTRICT Speyside (Deveron)
SITE OF FORMER DISTILLERY Inverboyndie, on B9139, 1 mile west of Banff

D ATING FROM AT LEAST 1824, Banff closed in 1983, leaving a substantial amount of stock for independent bottlings. Its buildings have gradually been dismantled, though remnants loom through the sea mist. The distillery stood near the adjoining towns of Banff and MacDuff, which face each other across the Deveron, where the river flows into the Moray Firth. Before being subsumed into Aberdeenshire, the county of Banffshire once formed the eastern flank of Speyside and embraced half the region's distilleries. It has fewer today, but this coastal strip is still very much barley country.

HOUSE STYLE Fragrant. Lemon grass. Sweet. Restorative or after dinner.

BANFF 1975, Celtic Heartlands, 48.1 vol

COLOR Pale gold with a greenish tinge.

NOSE Gentle. Pineapple. Exotic fruits. A touch of oak.

BODY Full. Creamy. Sweet.

PALATE Honey. Fruit syrup. Apricots. Late dryness.

FINISH Sugary sweetness remains but is joined by sweet spice. Quite long.

SCORE **83**

BANFF 1976, Connoisseurs Choice, 40 vol

COLOR Pale gold.

NOSE Fresh cut barley soaked in lemon juice. Old lady's perfume. Violets.

BODY Quite creamy. Soft and full.

PALATE Juicy barley. Soft fruits. Blemish-free. Lemon and lime bonbons.

FINISH Relatively short. Sweet lemon sweets.

SCORE **86**

BANFF 37-year-old, Old & Rare, 53 vol

COLOR Pale gold.

NOSE Big. Crispy vegetables. Grapefruit.

BODY Medium and zesty.

PALATE Burned wood. Very sweet. A battle between citrus fruits and wood.

FINISH Medium. Drying. Spicy.

SCORE **70**

BEN NEVIS

PRODUCER Ben Nevis Distillery Ltd. (Nikka)
REGION Highlands DISTRICT West Highlands
ADDRESS Lochy Bridge, Fort William, PH33 6TJ
TEL 01397 702476 WEBSITE www.bennevisdistillery.com VC

SOME CARE NEEDS TO BE TAKEN when looking for Ben Nevis malt, as it is one of the few whiskies to be bottled both as a single malt and as a blend bearing the same name. The distillery was established in 1825 and is now owned by Nikka of Japan. It is situated in Fort William, at the foot of Scotland's highest mountain, Ben Nevis (4409 ft / 1344 m). It is a very visible spot, on a road with heavy tourist traffic, but Ben Nevis is relatively distant from any other distilleries. Its regional appropriation to the western Highlands is supported by its being close to a sea loch. "We are a coastal distillery" insists manager Colin Ross, standing in front of the mighty mountain.

HOUSE STYLE Fragrant. Robust. Waxy fruitiness. Tropical fruit. Oily. A touch of smoke. Restorative or book-at-bedtime.

BEN NEVIS 10-year-old
Found at both 40 vol and 43 vol, depending on the market.

COLOR Warm bronze to amber.

NOSE Perfumy, spicy, soft. Waxed fruit. Kumquats. Hard dark chocolate.

BODY Emphatically big, firm, and smooth.

PALATE Orange-cream pralines in dark chocolate. Belgian toffee wafers.

FINISH Orange zest. Pithy dryness. A touch of cigar smoke.

SCORE **77**

TWO INDEPENDENT BOTTLINGS
BEN NEVIS 10-year-old, Provenance, 46 vol

COLOR Pale yellow. NOSE Soft toffee. Frosted coconut. BODY Thin. PALATE Quite zesty. Some peaty earthiness. FINISH Medium. Fruity. A touch of pepper. SCORE 70

BEN NEVIS 10-year-old, James MacArthur & Co., 57.9 vol

COLOR Amber. NOSE Hint of anise, then melon. Vanilla. BODY Medium. PALATE Soft yellow fruit. Fruitcake. Pepper. FINISH Medium-long, with fruit and spice. SCORE 80

BENRIACH

PRODUCER Benriach Distillery Company
REGION Highlands   DISTRICT Speyside (Lossie)
ADDRESS Longmorn, Elgin, Morayshire, IV30 3SJ
TEL 01343 862888   WEBSITE www.benriachdistillery.co.uk

O F ALL SCOTLAND'S DISTILLERIES, only Bruichladdich can match
Benriach for the scale of transformation which has taken place
since the last edition of this book. Having been mothballed by Pernod
Ricard, it was bought in 2004 by a South African consortium headed
by former Burn Stewart whisky maker and director Billy Walker. It is
close to Longmorn distillery, and for some years it was known as
Longmorn No 2. But its output was not altogether typical of the
region, and its previous owners had experimented with peated
distillations to make up for the fact that the company had no Islay
distillery. In the last few years, Walker and his team have launched an
array of different malts, including rich, heavily peated whiskies,
capable of giving the islands a run for their money. As a result,
Benriach has grown into one of the most fascinating distilleries in
Scotland. In 2009 it even started using the floor maltings again.

HOUSE STYLE Cookie-like, with touches of butterscotch. Restorative.
A mid-afternoon malt?

BENRIACH Heart of Speyside, 40 vol

COLOR Rich yellow honey.

NOSE Sweet and creamy, vanilla, pineapple cubes, syrup, lychee.

BODY Gentle, sweet, medium-full.

PALATE Clean barley, pineapple. Pure and clean. Grapefruit and other citrus fruits. Some late, sweet spice.

FINISH Medium, sweet, and with some spice.

SCORE **64**

BENRIACH Curiositas, 46 vol

The original release, which was bottled at 46 vol.

COLOR Deep yellowy gold.

NOSE Complex. Lots of charcoal smoke, soot, lemon, and other citrus fruits, cocoa powder.

BODY Soft, sweet, honeyed and rounded.

PALATE A beautiful oral explosion. Sugar and spice, big peat and smoke, but lots of fruit too, with melon and peach in the mix. Overall, lots of big and weighty flavors.

FINISH A curious mix of very sweet fruit and barley, and an acerbic wet fire ash. Long and lingering.

SCORE **91**

BENRIACH Curiositas, 40 vol

The 2009 release, with a weaker bottling strength.

COLOR Straw yellow.

NOSE Sooty peat and smoke. Bitter, citrusy.

BODY Rounded, soft, gentle. Very pleasant.

PALATE Sooty smoke, lots of canned exotic fruits, peat, and barley cocoa. A gorgeous mix but lacking full bite.

FINISH Sweet peat, smoke, cocoa, ash.

SCORE **80**

BENRIACH 12-year-old, 43 vol

COLOR Gold.

NOSE A rich blend of fruits, vanilla, and honey. Classic Speyside.

BODY Medium, rich, and sweet.

PALATE Honey, ripe fruits, vanilla, and barley. Balanced, rounded, pleasant.

FINISH Medium, summer fruits.

SCORE **70**

BENRIACH Heredotus Fumosus, 12-year-old, 46 vol

COLOR Straw yellow.

NOSE Rich peat, but lots of fruit, including soft melon. Soot.

BODY Very full, oily, and mouth-coating.

PALATE A bold and delightful mix of sooty smoke and sweet fruit.
Chunky masses of blackcurrant, smoky Turkish Delight.

FINISH Immense. Long, rich, sooty, smoky, and full. Unforgettable.

SCORE **91**

BENRIACH Importanticus Fumosus, 12-year-old, 46 vol

COLOR Copper with a reddish hue.

NOSE A somewhat confused mix of rich wine and fruits,
coastal brine, rich peat, and some floral and vanilla notes.

BODY Full and mouth-coating. Big in every sense.

PALATE Sweet, with lemon and grapefruit, full port notes,
and a heavy dose of smoke and peat.

FINISH Long, rich, and lingering.

SCORE **88**

BENRIACH Aromaticus Fumosus, 12-year-old, 46 vol

COLOR Rich yellow.

NOSE Delightful mix of smoke and sweet fruits.

BODY Full and dominant. Creamy.

PALATE Peat fire, smoking embers, some yellow fruits.
Very sweet, pink bonbons, dark roast coffee, cinnamon.

FINISH Long, sweet, and smoky.

SCORE **89**

BENRIACH Maderensis Fumosus, 13-year-old, 46 vol

COLOR Lemon yellow.

NOSE Sooty smoke, oily, and powerful. Like a steam engine,
but with soft pear and melon.

BODY Rich, sweet, and full, but still soft and smooth.

PALATE Delicious and outstanding balance between
heavy industry sooty smoke and canned exotic fruits,
as well as soft pears and melon.

FINISH Classic sooty Benriach battling with sweetness
in a long and impressive finish.

SCORE **89**

BENRIACH Pedro Ximénez Finish, 15-year-old, 46 vol

COLOR Suntan brown.

NOSE Toffee, mince pie, some apple. Quite restrained.

BODY Full and mouth-coating, but still soft, sweet, rich and very welcoming.

PALATE Ripe grapes, soft berries, apple seeds, almonds, and gentle tannins and spices. Sophisticated.

FINISH Full, long, very soft, sweet, and delicious.

SCORE **83**

BENRIACH Dark Rum Finish, 15-year-old, 46 vol

COLOR Pale yellow straw.

NOSE Milk chocolate, honey, caramel, Crunchie bar, apple, spice.

BODY Oily and creamy. Mouth-coating, rich, and full.

PALATE Very sweet. Rum-raisin to the fore. Exotic fruits, milk chocolate, vanilla. Full, but quite one-dimensional.

FINISH Sweet and full, with a touch of spice and oak at the end and a hint of peat very late on.

SCORE **78**

BENRIACH Tawny Port Finish, 15-year-old, 46 vol

COLOR Rich copper with a reddish hue.

NOSE Rich wine, then rosehip, chestnut, chicory coffee, sweets. Odd.

BODY Smooth, gentle, rounded, and sweet.

PALATE Nice balance. Sweet and grapey, with icing sugar, clean barley, and full soft fruit.

FINISH Long, sweet, and spicy; slightly spicy cake icing. Clean and ordered.

SCORE **82**

BENRIACH Madeira Finish, 15-year-old, 46 vol

COLOR Auburn, copper bronze.

NOSE Lively mix of melon, pear, and vanilla. Sweet and welcoming.

BODY Full, creamy, sweet.

PALATE Clean and fresh. Sweet lime cordial, milk chocolate, and then some astringency. Tannin and spice towards the end.

FINISH Very sweet, spicy, and long.

SCORE **89**

BENRIACH Sauternes Finish, 16-year-old, 46 vol

COLOR Rich orange syrup.

NOSE Chinese food, sweet stewed bamboo shoots, musty sweetness, savory root, doughballs.

BODY Quite full and oily, coats the mouth, but has a distinctive zip.

PALATE Much better than the nose. Soft, sweet grape, berries, plum, lots of vanilla, and a slash of spice.

FINISH Excellent mix of plummy fruit, sweet pepper, and tannins. Long and tingling.

SCORE **86**

BENRIACH 16-year-old, 40 vol

COLOR Amber.

NOSE Honey, vanilla, lots of sweet fruit.

BODY Sweet, creamy, and full.

PALATE A bowl of sweet fruits. Stewed apples with vanilla ice cream—and honey in the mix. Some late tannin and spice to add balance.

FINISH Sweet, clean, fruity, and with some gentle spice.

SCORE **80**

BENRIACH 20-year-old, 43 vol

COLOR Rich bronze.

NOSE Subtle and restrained, with grape, pear, and apple. Marzipan. Sweet.

BODY Rich and rounded, soft and clean.

PALATE Subtle, sophisticated, and balanced, with honey, vanilla, oak, and clean melon and pear.

FINISH Medium-long, restrained, and with a delightful burst of oak and spice late on.

SCORE **84**

BENRIACH Authenticus, 21-year-old, 46 vol

COLOR Rich bronze.

NOSE Smoked crab and sweet-cured fried bacon. Smoky, but layered with apples and peach.

BODY Oily, sweet, full, and mouth-coating.

PALATE Stunning mix of sweet canned exotic fruits, blackcurrant, and chocolate, with full peat and smoke, some astringency from the oak, and a delightful spicy bite.

FINISH Very long and oily, with the charcoally smoke sticking to the mouth with the gloopy fruitiness. Some oaky tannins.

SCORE **92**

BENRIACH 30-year-old, 50 vol

COLOR Deep orangey gold.

NOSE Dusty wood, polish, honey, sweet citrus, oak-panelled office.

BODY Extremely soft and gentle, but still pleasantly assertive.

PALATE At first sweet orange and tangerine; citrus fruit.
Then pepper and a hefty dose of oak and tannins.

FINISH Quite sharp and bitter. Marmalade. Oakiness battles the
fruit with the fruit winning out in the end.

SCORE **89**

INDEPENDENT BOTTLINGS
BENRIACH 18-year-old, Single Malts of Scotland, 55.7 vol

COLOR Pale lemon.

NOSE Tutti frutti ice cream. Pineapple. Vanilla.

BODY Sweet. Creamy. Mouth-coating.

PALATE Tinned fruits. Some green fruits with a touch of peat.
Restrained tannins.

FINISH Medium, with tannin astringency reining in the sweetness.
Sugared spice at the end.

SCORE **85**

BENRIACH 23-year-old, Single Malts of Scotland, 54.2 vol

COLOR Gold with a greenish hue.

NOSE Fruity and light, with gentle wafts of peat.

BODY Creamy, sweet, and full.

PALATE Rich, sweet toffee fudge, with a gentle peat base underneath.

FINISH Long, sweet, toffeeish, and with a trace of peat and tannin.

SCORE **88**

BENRINNES

PRODUCER Diageo
REGION Highlands   DISTRICT Speyside
ADDRESS Aberlour, Banffshire, AB38 9WN
TEL Contact via Dailuaine 01340 872500

As a mountain, Ben Rinnes spreads itself to two words and is hard to miss; as a distillery and a whisky, Benrinnes compounds itself so neatly that it is too easily overlooked. It is no novice. Benrinnes may have been founded as early as the 1820s, and was largely rebuilt in the 1950s. The distillery had a long association with the Crawford blends. Its malt whisky did not have official bottling until 1991, in a Flora and Fauna edition. Benrinnes' system of partial triple distillation places it among the handful of quirky, individualistic distilleries in the Diageo group.

HOUSE STYLE Big, creamy, smoky, flavorsome. Restorative or after dinner.

BENRINNES 15-year-old, Flora and Fauna, 43 vol

COLOR Autumnal reddish brown.

NOSE Heavy, almost creamy. A whiff of sherry, then a firm, smoky, burned-toffee character.

BODY Medium to full. Firm.

PALATE Dry, assertive, rounded. Flavors are gradually unlocked. Hints of licorice, anise, vanilla, bitter chocolate, smoke.

FINISH Satisfying, soothing. Faintly sweet and smoky.

SCORE 79

SOME INDEPENDENT BOTTLINGS
BENRINNES 10-year-old, Provenance, 46 vol

COLOR Pale gold.

NOSE Peardrop. Slight touch of anise. Perfume.

BODY Soft and gentle.

PALATE Anise/spearmint is there at first, then
a sliver of unripe plum, lemon and citrus fruits, and then some
pepper and sharpness.

FINISH Short and quite sharp.

SCORE **68**

BENRINNES 1991, Bottled 2007,
Berry's Own Selection, 46 vol

COLOR Pale yellow.

NOSE Stir-fried Chinese vegetables. With time, freshly cut bamboo.
Vines. Sweet, soft, citrus hard candies.

BODY Light and unassertive.

PALATE Some sweet lime, but mainly a pleasant but unexceptional
clean barley core. Some earthiness.

FINISH Medium, clean, and with some pepper.

SCORE **73**

BENRINNES 1993, Scotch Malt Whisky Society,
No 36.42, Cask 1077

COLOR Orange.

NOSE Wet cane. Damp straw. Vegetable stew.

BODY Rich and creamy.

PALATE Sweet. Traces of mint. Some peat. Chunky barley. Celery.
Quite clean and fresh, but with savory notes.

FINISH Savory and spicy.

SCORE **78**

BENRINNES 17-year-old,
Single Malts of Scotland, 55.8 vol

COLOR Deep banana yellow.

NOSE Fresh and clean. Cut straw. Green fruit. Oaky.

BODY Full and assertive.

PALATE Almond. Vanilla. Barley. Traces of citrus fruit. Clean.

FINISH Medium, with some late sweet pepper spice.

SCORE **78**

BENROMACH

PRODUCER Gordon & MacPhail
REGION Highlands DISTRICT District Speyside (Findhorn)
ADDRESS Invererne Road, Forres, Moray, IV36 3EB
TEL 01309 675968 WEBSITE www.gordonandmacphail.com
EMAIL info@gordonandmacphail.com VC

PRINCE CHARLES IS NO DOUBT among the malt lovers keen to taste this 100-year-old distillery's born-again whisky. Benromach appeared to have died while in the care of United Distillers in the mid-1980s. The distillery, the most immediately visible to travellers approaching Speyside from Inverness, was closed. Sadder still, its valuable copper stills were removed. United did subsequently issue one Rare Malts edition, at 20 years old. Apart from that isolated instance, Benromach was for many years available only in independent bottlings.

A flowery 12-year-old and a more fruity 15-year-old, both popular ages, and each scoring 77, dried up after the fourth edition of this book appeared. However much inventory a distillery has, its stocks are finite. Devotees mourn, and independent bottlers lose a source. On this occasion, Gordon & MacPhail decided to try and buy the distillery. Having succeeded, they re-equipped it with smaller stills. The idea was to adapt it to present demand, but also to produce a richer spirit. With its new still-house, Benromach was reopened in 1998—by Prince Charles. There have subsequently been a significant number of varied and enterprising bottlings of Benromach, breathing new life into this happily revived distillery and its single malt. After "Bottled by Gordon & MacPhail" and then "by the Proprietors", the legend now says "Distilled and bottled by Gordon & MacPhail."

HOUSE STYLE Assertive, flowery, sometimes creamy. With dessert or after dinner.

BENROMACH Traditional, 40 vol

COLOR Straw.	
NOSE Fresh, with citrus fruits, cereal, and peat smoke.	
BODY Medium, rounded.	
PALATE Sweet and gently spiced, with smoky malt.	
FINISH Medium in length, spicy, with smoke and cocoa.	

SCORE 76

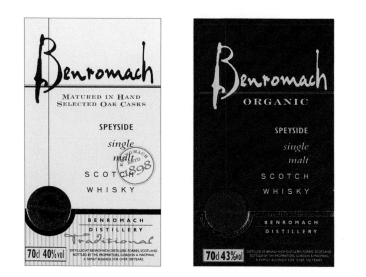

BENROMACH Organic, 43 vol

COLOR	Golden brown.
NOSE	Sweet oak, banana, and vanilla.
BODY	Smooth.
PALATE	Velvety mix of malt, soft toffee, oak, and cloves.
FINISH	Drying steadily through sweet oak and fresh fruit.

SCORE **77**

BENROMACH Peat Smoke, 46 vol

COLOR	Pale straw.
NOSE	Sweet peat and cigarette smoke over fresh, fruity notes.
BODY	Medium.
PALATE	Smoky, fruity malt and spice. Lovely balance.
FINISH	Long and kippery.

SCORE **79**

BENROMACH Origins, 50 vol

Distilled from Golden Promise barley.

COLOR	Deep gold.
NOSE	Initially sourdough bread, with developing malt and smoky sherry notes.
BODY	Full and creamy.
PALATE	Spicy, then very malty, with sherry and peat smoke.
FINISH	Long and fruity, with spicy smoke and sherry. Lingering molasses.

SCORE **76**

BENROMACH Latitude 57°, 57 vol

COLOR Bright chestnut.

NOSE Expansive, spicy. Christmas cake.

BODY Medium to full.

PALATE Quite dry, with raisins, walnuts, and developing figs.

FINISH Steadily drying. Nutty, with developing oak.

SCORE **75**

BENROMACH 10-year-old, 40 vol

Introduced in 2009.

COLOR Gold.

NOSE Initially quite smoky, with wet grass, butter,
ginger, and brittle toffee.

BODY Firm.

PALATE Spicy and nutty, with developing citrus fruits.

FINISH Warming, with lingering barbecue notes.

SCORE **79**

BENROMACH 21-year-old, 43 vol

COLOR Bright gold.

NOSE Herbal and delicate, with ripe, soft fruits. Developing linseed oil.

BODY Full.

PALATE Rich, with sherry, spices, and caramel.

FINISH Long and sherried.

SCORE **78**

BENROMACH Cask Strength 1981, 54.2 vol

COLOR Gleaming amber.

NOSE Brittle toffee, pineapple, and delicate sherry notes.

BODY Rich.

PALATE Very sweet and mouth-coating. Sherry and smoky spice.

FINISH Slowly drying, with fresh fruit and, finally, cocoa.

SCORE **78**

BENROMACH Vintage 1968, 43 vol

COLOR Deep amber.

NOSE Rich and floral, with orchard fruits, background licorice, and smoke.

BODY Full-bodied, luscious.

PALATE A moist fruitcake, with lots of sherry. Dries through smoke.

FINISH Long and smoky, with ever-present sherry and licorice sticks.

SCORE **80**

BLADNOCH

PRODUCER Raymond Armstrong
REGION Lowlands DISTRICT Borders
ADDRESS Bladnoch, Wigtownshire, DG8 9AB
TEL 01988 402605 WEBSITE www.bladnoch.co.uk VC

NINE YEARS AFTER THE RECOMMENCEMENT of whisky production at Bladnoch, the distillery is coming of age, producing its own malts to put alongside older stock bought in by proprietor Raymond Armstrong. In the process, it is also restoring pride in a remote region of the Lowlands, in the deep southwestern corner of Scotland. All the signs are encouraging, and there has been a nice mix of malts, some peated, some not, but all distinctive and impressive.

Bladnoch is the southernmost working distillery in Scotland. It takes its water from the river Bladnoch, which flows into the Solway Firth, which forms the border with England.

The pretty little distillery, established between 1817 and 1825, was originally attached to a farm, and used local barley. For a time, it triple distilled. It was mothballed in 1993 by its then owner, United Distillers.

The distillery gave rise to the hamlet of Bladnoch. Nearby is Wigtown, noted for its bookshops. A little farther away is Dumfries, where Robbie Burns's house can be visited.

Raymond Armstrong, from Northern Ireland, bought the distillery buildings with a view to converting them into a vacation home, but came to feel they should be returned to their original purpose. He spent two years restoring the distillery to working order. Armstrong, a surveyor and builder, had no connections with the whisky industry, but had family links with Wigtownshire. The area is geographically very close to Northern Ireland.

HOUSE STYLE Grassy, lemony, soft, sometimes with a suggestion of bananas. A classic Lowlander. Perhaps a dessert malt.

BLADNOCH 7-year-old, Lightly Peated, 58.5 vol

COLOR Rich pale gold.

NOSE Very shy and requires water to open it. Sweet peat, blackcurrant, cocoa powder.

BODY Full, rich, oily.

PALATE Soft. Gentle peat, smoke, and spice. Apple and other soft fruits. Drying. Honey.

FINISH Peat. Pine needles. Savory, earthy flavors.

SCORE **75**

BLADNOCH 15-year-old, 40 vol

COLOR Pale lemony yellow with a greenish hue.

NOSE Delicate, wispy, fresh pear. Almost Irish.

BODY Light. Quite thin. Refreshing.

PALATE Green fruit, especially apple and pear. The slightest trace of oak. Clean, crisp, apple pip.

FINISH Medium. Very refreshing, with fruit and the merest hint of spice.

SCORE **82**

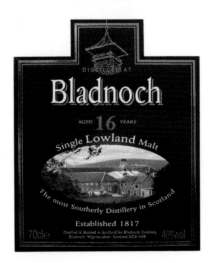

BLADNOCH 16-year-old, 46 vol

COLOR Pale lemon.

NOSE Delicate smoke, green fruit—pear? Autumn garden.

BODY Soft, rounded, and sweet.

PALATE Pear and vanilla ice cream, in a gentle peaty and earthy wrap.

FINISH Spice and smoke. Canned pears in ash.

SCORE **85**

BLADNOCH 16-year-old, Sherry Matured, 55 vol

COLOR Fluorescent orange.

NOSE Toffee, earthy. Mince pies. Soggy fruitcake.

BODY Full, sweet, sherried, creamy.

PALATE Lots of rich sherry and full berries. Sweet toffee, chicory coffee.

FINISH Sweet, long, full, and fruity.

SCORE **75**

BLADNOCH 18-year-old, 55 vol

COLOR Pale greeny yellow.

NOSE Apple, grape, barley sugar, gooseberry.

BODY Soft, full, sweet, and creamy.

PALATE Sweet and clean. Very pure. Green fruits and sweet pepper.

FINISH Very full and fruity, with a gentle but definite oak and spice finale.

SCORE **85**

AN INDEPENDENT BOTTLING
BLADNOCH 16-year-old, Old Malt Cask, 50 vol

COLOR Light yellow with a greenish hue.

NOSE Cucumber. Vegetal. Grassy meadow. Hay.

BODY Medium-full.

PALATE Subtle, but clean and refreshing. Cucumber salad.
Gentle spices and oak late on.

FINISH Medium, with some tannin and spice.

SCORE **67**

BLAIR ATHOL

PRODUCER Diageo
REGION Highlands   DISTRICT Eastern Highlands
ADDRESS Pitlochry, Perthshire, PH16 5LY
TEL 01796 482003
WEBSITE www.discovering-distilleries.com/www.malts.com   VC

B LAIR IS A SCOTTISH NAME, referring to a tract of flat land, a clearance, a battlefield, or someone who originates from such a place. Blair Castle is the home of the Duke of Atholl. The village of Blair Atholl ends with a double "l", while the distillery prefers to keep it single. The distillery is nearby at the inland resort of Pitlochry. It is well-designed, beautifully maintained, and can trace its origins to 1798.

Its malt whisky is extensively used in the Bell's blends. The whisky matures quickly, and behaves like a gentleman. It is a sturdy, well-proportioned whisky rather than a big bruiser, but it can take a lot of sherry without becoming showy or belligerent.

HOUSE STYLE Redolent of shortbread and ginger cake.
Spicy, nutty. A mid-afternoon malt?

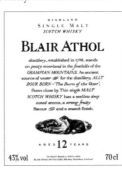

BLAIR ATHOL 12-year-old, 43 vol
Released in 2000 in the Single Distillery Malt series, a further development of the Flora and Fauna selections.

COLOR Attractive dark orange. Satin sheen.

NOSE Rich, moist, cake-like. Lemon grass. Assam tea (a hint of peat?).

BODY Silky smooth.

PALATE Spiced cake. Candied lemon peel. Lots of flavor development.

FINISH Lightly smoky. Rooty. Syrupy. Impeccable sweet and dry balance.

SCORE 78

BLAIR ATHOL 12-year-old, Commemorative Limited Edition, 43 vol

A much more sherryish version.

COLOR Distinctively deep. Orange liqueur.

NOSE Very complex. Fragrant, candied orange peels, dried fruit, cinnamon.

BODY Medium, silky.

PALATE Walnuts. Sweetish. Cakey. Faint treacle or molasses.

FINISH Very smooth, round, soothing, lightly smoky.

Very sophisticated for its age. Blair Athol matures quickly,
gaining perfuminess, sweetness, richness, spiciness, complexity,
and length. The sherry helps to emulsify the elements.

SCORE **77**

BLAIR ATHOL 18-year-old, Bicentenary Limited Edition, 56.7 vol

COLOR Full peachy amber (but less dark than the 12-year-old).

NOSE Very delicate. Finessed. Orange and cinnamon.

BODY Bigger and firm.

PALATE Dates. Raisins. Dried figs. Moist cake. Butter.

FINISH Toasty. The slightly burned crust on a cake.

SCORE **78**

BLAIR ATHOL 1981, Bottled 1997, Cask Strength Limited Bottling, 55.5 vol

Now becoming hard to find.

COLOR Deep, bright orange red.

NOSE Oakier and smokier, but appetizingly so.

BODY Medium, firm, smooth.

PALATE Delicious, clean toffee. Firm, slightly chewy. Blackstrap molasses
treacle. Lively. Hints of banana, orange, lemon. Faint fragrant smokiness.

FINISH Ginger. Toasty oak.

SCORE **78**

AN INDEPENDENT BOTTLING
BLAIR ATHOL 30-year-old, Distilled 1997, Bottled 2008, Cask No 05543, Duncan Taylor, 54.3 vol

COLOR Amber.

NOSE Pretty, floral aromas and fresh citrus fruits.
Gentle caramel and smoke.

BODY Full and rounded.

PALATE Rich, brittle toffee and spicy oak. Becoming fudgy.

FINISH Medium in length. Spicy, dried fruits.

SCORE **78**

BOWMORE

PRODUCER Morrison Bowmore Distillers Ltd.
REGION Islay   DISTRICT Lochindaal
ADDRESS Bowmore, Islay, Argyll, PA34 7JS
TEL 01496 810441   WEBSITE www.bowmore.com   VC

E VOCATIVE NAMES like Dawn, Darkest, Voyage, and Legend accentuate the dream-like nature of the place. The village of Bowmore is the "capital" of Islay, but barely more than a hamlet, where the Laggan River flows into Lochindaal. On the edge of the boggy moor, the round church looks down the hill to the harbor.

The distillery, founded in 1779, is kept in beautiful condition—but is not to be confused with the local school, which has decorative pagodas. In both geography and palate, the whiskies of Bowmore are between the intense malts of the south shore and the gentlest extremes of the north. Their character is not a compromise but an enigma, and tasters have found it difficult to unfold its complexity. The water used rises from iron-tinged rock, and picks up some peat from the earth as it flows by way of the Laggan, through moss, ferns, and rushes, to the distillery. While the peat higher on the island is rooty, that at Bowmore is sandier.

The company has its own maltings, where the peat is crumbled before it is fired to give more smoke than heat. The malt is peated for a shorter time than that used for the more intense Islay whiskies. Up to 30 percent of the whisky is aged in sherry. The distillery is more exposed to the westerly winds than others, so there may be more ozone in the complex of aromas and flavors.

HOUSE STYLE Smoky, with leafy notes (ferns?) and sea air.
Younger ages before dinner, older after.

EXPRESSIONS WITH NO AGE STATEMENT
BOWMORE Legend, 40 vol

A light, young version, identified in some markets as an eight-year-old.

COLOR Full gold.

NOSE Firm, peaty, smoky, very appetizing.

BODY Slightly sharp.

PALATE Very singular flavors, deftly balanced: leafy, ferny, peaty;
a touch of iron. Underlying earthy sweetness.
A fresh, young whisky, but no obvious spiritiness.

FINISH Sweet, then salty.

SCORE **80**

BOWMORE Surf, 43 vol

Now exclusive to travel retail outlets.

COLOR Bright gold.

NOSE Fresh peat smoke.

BODY Light but smooth.

PALATE Light, dry, some nutty malt. A light, smooth,
entry-level Bowmore. Seems very tame at first,
with a cookie-like maltiness, but the characteristic
ferny lavender, fragrant smoke, and sea air gradually emerge.
One of the sweeter Bowmores.

FINISH Sweet smokiness. With water, late saltiness; honey-roast peanuts.

SCORE **78**

BOWMORE Dawn, Ruby Port Cask Finished, 51.5 vol

COLOR Very interesting pinkish amber.

NOSE Sooty smoke.

BODY Soft, textured, lightly toffeeish.

PALATE Smoky and fruity. Lively.

FINISH Leafy, peaty. Slightly chewy.

SCORE **83**

BOWMORE Voyage, Port Casked, 56 vol

COLOR Bright orange.

NOSE Less obviously smoky. More perfumy. Drier.

BODY Less toffeeish than most port finishes.

PALATE Smooth. Light on the tongue. Develops some fruitiness.

FINISH More lively. Seems crisp at first, but lingers
very warmly, with late saltiness.

SCORE **84**

BOWMORE Cask Strength, 56 vol

Vatting of whiskies in mid-teens.

COLOR Sunny, yellowy gold.

NOSE Sea air. Cereal-grain oiliness. Nutty. Malty sweetness. Syrupy. Scenty.

BODY Medium, substantial, smooth.

PALATE Earthy dryness. Some tasters have found "wet wool." Others find it carbolic. Lively. Flavors not very well integrated.

FINISH Orange peel. Leafy. Ferns. Peaty.

SCORE **81**

BOWMORE 12-year-old, 40 vol

COLOR Mid-amber.

NOSE Lemon, honey, and gentle brine.

BODY Medium.

PALATE Smoky and citric, with developing cocoa notes.

FINISH Lengthy, with hard candies, milk chocolate, and sweet peat.

SCORE **82**

BOWMORE Enigma, 12-year-old, 40 vol

Exclusive to travel retail outlets.

COLOR Full bronze.

NOSE Reticent peat, sherry, honey, and malt.

BODY Some oiliness.

PALATE Sweet fruit and sherry, with developing smoke and notes of lemon.

FINISH Long and harmonious. Sweet peat and brine.

SCORE **83**

BOWMORE Mariner 15-year-old, 43 vol

Exclusive to travel retail outlets.

COLOR Copper.

NOSE Cocoa and toffee, with background peat smoke.

BODY Smooth.

PALATE Stewed apples and rhubarb, with dark chocolate and oak.

FINISH Lengthy, with ginger, bitter chocolate,
and a sprinkling of brine.

SCORE **81**

BOWMORE Darkest 15-year-old, 43 vol

Matured for a final three-year period in oloroso sherry casks.

COLOR Deep bronze.

NOSE Dark chocolate and smoky, sherried vanilla.

BODY Viscous.

PALATE Rich, dark notes: old sherry, bitter chocolate, molasses, smoke.

FINISH Toffee and dried fruit. Robust.

SCORE **84**

BOWMORE 17-year-old, 43 vol

Exclusive to travel retail outlets.

COLOR Warm gold.

NOSE Toffee, ripe fruit, delicate peat.

BODY Medium- to full-bodied.

PALATE Fresh fruits, creamy malt, and smoke.

FINISH Long and warming, with lingering spicy smoke.

SCORE **87**

BOWMORE 18-year-old, 43 vol

COLOR Mahogany.

NOSE Gingery fruit, malt, and subtle peat, plus muted sherry.

BODY Rounded.

PALATE Initially floral, with sherry and stewed fruit. Complex.

FINISH Long and nutty, with lingering peatiness.

SCORE **87**

BOWMORE 25-year-old, 43 vol

COLOR Deep mahogany.

NOSE Rich, with sweet sherry and just a hint of smoke.

BODY Full.

PALATE Perfumed fruits, toffee, and sherry. A suggestion of peat and oak tannins.

FINISH Long, with dark chocolate, nuts, and gentle, smoky oak.

SCORE **88**

SOME INDEPENDENT BOTTLINGS
BOWMORE 13-year-old, Distilled 1995, Bottled 2008, Cask No 419, The Single Malts of Scotland, 56.4 vol

COLOR Rich amber.

NOSE Medium sherry, worn leather, and pipe tobacco. Slightly meaty.

BODY Full.

PALATE Rich, smooth, sweet peat, and pepper.

FINISH Citrus fruit and gunpowder. Very long.

SCORE **86**

BOWMORE, 1989, Dewar Rattray, Cask No 7914, 51.9 vol

COLOR Mid-gold.

NOSE Fresh, with brine, resin, malt. Some citrus fruit.

BODY Rounded.

PALATE Sweet and full, developing spice
and smoky, maritime notes.

FINISH Long and spicy, with an edge of sea salt.

SCORE **82**

BOWMORE 1987, Berry's Own Selection, 48.8 vol

COLOR Pale gold.

NOSE Apple blossom, citrus fruits, smoked fish, tobacco.

BODY Medium. Some oil.

PALATE Pleasing interplay of heather, peat smoke, and ripe apples.

FINISH Brittle toffee. Dry. Pepper

SCORE **86**

BOWMORE 26-year-old, Distilled 1982, Bottled 2008, Cask No 85031, Duncan Taylor, Rare Auld range, 52.1 vol

COLOR Bright gold.

NOSE Bright, creamy, lemon fruit sorbet.

BODY Rich.

PALATE Kiwi fruits, sherry, smoldering heather.
Nicely balanced.

FINISH Long and gentle, with a citric note.

SCORE **84**

BOWMORE 40-year-old, Distilled 1966, Bottled 2006, Duncan Taylor, 43.2 vol

COLOR Amber.

NOSE Intensely orangey. Could be a liqueur!

BODY Syrupy.

PALATE Initial carry-over of orange from the nose—now blood
orange—but soon assertive, slightly rubbery oak
takes over. Peppery peat also.

FINISH Somewhat bitter old oak, with the orange manfully
fighting back. Fascinating!

SCORE **85**

BRAEVAL

PRODUCER Chivas Brothers (Pernod Ricard)
REGION Highlands   DISTRICT Speyside (Livet)
ADDRESS Chapeltown, Ballindalloch, Banffshire, AB37 9JS
TEL 01542 783200

THE REOPENING OF BRAEVAL in 2008 was further good news for Scotland's whisky industry, though you suspect that they weren't celebrating at Dalwhinnie. Its claim to be Scotland's highest working distillery was firmly knocked on the head.

Originally the distillery was called Braes of Glenlivet, and this was the distillery's name when the whiskies reviewed here were distilled. This name had the merit of linking this distillery with its famous neighbor and parent—but made it difficult for the owners to dissuade other companies from treating Glenlivet as a region or style. The current name, Braeval, is an even older form. Brae is Scottish Gaelic for a "hillside" or "steep bank." Against a mountain ridge, this distillery is perched over a stream that feeds the Livet River. Despite its romantic name, and handsomely monastic appearance, it is a modern distillery, built between 1973 and 1978. It can be operated by one person, or even from its parent distillery, Glenlivet. Braeval's whisky has been a component of Chivas Regal, among other blends.

HOUSE STYLE Light, sweet, honeyish, with a zesty finish. Aperitif.

BRAES OF GLENLIVET 1975,
Connoisseurs Choice, 40 vol

COLOR Very pale greeny gold.

NOSE Fragrant. Vanilla.

BODY Dancing on the tongue.

PALATE Flowery. Herbal. Very appetizing.

FINISH Lightly dry. Zesty.

SCORE **77**

BRAEVAL 10-year-old, Old Malt Cask, 50 vol

COLOR Lemon

NOSE Floral. Buttercup. Lemon. Soft toffee.

BODY Medium. Creamy. Sweet.

PALATE Furniture polish. Honey. Clean and sweet.
Some spice.

FINISH Medium, sweet and zingy.

SCORE **75**

BRAEVAL 10-year-old, Provenance, 46 vol

COLOR Pale gold.

NOSE Aniseed. Pernod. Cucumber and lettuce.

BODY Full and creamy. Mouth-coating.

PALATE More anise. Vanilla. Sweet.

FINISH Quite short. Pleasant. Late peppery spice.

SCORE **74**

BRAEVAL 12-year-old, Old Malt Cask, 50 vol

COLOR Rich prune brown.

NOSE Plums. Traces of smoke and sulfur (but not in a bad way).
Blackcurrant.

BODY Creamy and full.

PALATE Sherried fruits at first. Some peat. Strange mix of aged red fruits
and zestier and younger-tasting citrus fruits.

FINISH Long, sherried, and peaty.

SCORE **81**

BRUICHLADDICH

PRODUCER The Bruichladdich Distillery Co. Ltd.
REGION Islay   DISTRICT Loch Indaal
ADDRESS Bruichladdich, Islay, Argyll, PA49 7UN
TEL 01496 850221   WEBSITE www.bruichladdich.com
EMAIL laddie@bruichladdich.com   VC

ISLANDERS CARRIED CHILDREN on their shoulders to witness the historic moment. They lined the Islay shore to watch the reopening in 2001 of Bruichladdich. The single morning plane, bringing more guests, was running late. The people on the shore scanned the skies. They had waited ten years; what was another hour? Lovers of Bruichladdich had come from London, Seattle, and Tokyo. There were tears of joy, a ceilidh, and fireworks at midnight.

The new owners, headed by Mark Reynier, inherited plenty of maturing stock and a large mix of sherry and bourbon casks at various stages of maturation and in first, second, and third fill casks. As a result, veteran Islay whisky maker Jim McEwan has spent the years since creating a broad range of different whisky styles. Some have been light and delicate, others more robust, and, although the distillery is not known for producing a typical Islay-style whisky, there have been plenty of experiments with peat, too. One of the distillery's whiskies is actually quadruple distilled.

The whisky has long combined light, firm maltiness with suggestions of passion fruit, seaweed, and salt. McEwan has coaxed out more fruitiness and some sweetness, and has given everything more life and definition. The latter qualities are heightened by the use of the distillery's own water in reduction and by the lack of chill filtration. These changes in procedure were made possible by the installation in 2003 of a bottling line. Bruichladdich thus becomes the third distillery to have its own bottling line on site. (The others are Springbank and Glenfiddich/Balvenie.)

When Bruichladdich reopened, McEwan immediately reset the stills to produce a spirit to his requirements. This will remain light to medium in its peating. Two new spirits were added, with a heavier peating.

Bruichladdich (pronounced "brook laddie") is on the north shore of Lochindaal. The new owners have promoted the nickname "The Laddie," and introduced labels in a pale seaside blue to match the paintwork at the distillery. The distillery's water rises from iron-tinged stone, and flows lightly over peat. Unlike the other Islay distilleries, Bruichladdich is separated from the sea loch, albeit only by a quiet, coastal road.

The distillery was founded in 1881, rebuilt in 1886 and, despite an extension in 1975, remains little changed. All maturing spirit in its ownership is warehoused on the island, either at Bruichladdich or in the vestiges of the Lochindaal distillery, at Port Charlotte, the nearest village. Some independent bottlers of Bruichladdich have labeled the whisky Lochindaal.

Bruichladdich has started to bottle some of its more heavily peated whisky under the name Port Charlotte and its most heavily peated whisky—informally known as The Beast and a remarkable whisky even by this island's high standards—is called Octomore, after another former distillery at Port Charlotte. Parts of that distillery survive as Octomore Farm, home of Port Charlotte's lighthouse keeper, fire fighter, and lifeboatman. He was also one of the pipers on the opening day at Bruichladdich. In late 2008 the distillery passed another milestone when it bottled a malt made entirely from spirit distilled after the 2001 reopening.

HOUSE STYLE Light to medium, very firm, hint of passion fruit, salty, spicy (mace?). Very drinkable. Aperitif.

AGE STATEMENT AND VINTAGE DATED BOTTLINGS
BRUICHLADDICH 10-year-old, 46 vol

COLOR Bright greeny gold.

NOSE Fresh. Clean. Very soft "sea air." Wild flowers among the dunes. A picnic at the beach.

BODY Satin.

PALATE Summer fruits. Passionfruit. Zesty, almost effervescent. Bruichladdich at its fruitiest.

FINISH The flavors meld, with a late frisson of sharpness.

SCORE **82**

BRUICHLADDICH Oloroso Finish,
10-year-old, Distilled 1998, 46 vol

COLOR Rich golden brown.

NOSE Soft, toffee apple, pineapple, sweet red berries.

BODY Full, creamy, rich, and sweet.

PALATE Peach, soft melon, canned sweet fruits. Full.

FINISH Quite long. A delicious mix of sweetness, fruitiness, and sherbety spice.

SCORE **87**

BRUICHLADDICH Manzanilla Finish,
10-year-old, Distilled 1998, 46 vol

COLOR Nutty brown.

NOSE Sweet and flighty, light tangerine, cocoa.

BODY Soft and rounded, medium-rich, balanced.

PALATE Better than the nose. Quite zingy, rich fruit, nut, chocolate bar, honeycomb.

FINISH Relatively short but soft, gentle and pleasant.

SCORE **73**

BRUICHLADDICH 12-year-old, 46 vol

COLOR Liquid honey.

NOSE Very clean and fresh. Citrus, pear, vanilla, sweet fruits.

BODY Delightfully soft, sweet, and mouth-filling.

PALATE Very clean and refreshing. A bowl of sweet exotic fruits. Vanilla.

FINISH Mainly soft and honeyed, but with a delicate touch of pepper. Blemish-free.

SCORE **80**

BRUICHLADDICH 15-year-old, Birkdale, 46 vol

COLOR Ripe yellow hay.

NOSE Earthy, rootsy, wet straw, and a touch of peat.

BODY Oily. Quite full. Tingling.

PALATE Intriguing mix of clean barley, grape, and green fruit, with Highland-style earthiness and some tannin and spice later on.

FINISH Medium, spicy, and with some woodiness and astringency late on.

SCORE **68**

BRUICHLADDICH 16-year-old, Bourbon/Latour, 46 vol

COLOR Soft golden yellow.

NOSE Vanilla ice cream, soft melon, pineapple, sweet yellow fruits.

BODY Sweet, creamy, balanced.

PALATE Vanilla, squidgy soft yellow fruit, then later a touch of astringency from the oak, a dose of spice, and tannin. All very balanced.

FINISH Quite long and a trade-off between fresh fruit, spice, and a touch of oak and peat.

SCORE **80**

BRUICHLADDICH 16-year-old, Bourbon/Margaux, 46 vol

COLOR Orange with a pinkish hue.

NOSE Winey, awkward rootsy note. Musty. Fruit arriving late.

BODY Not very assertive. Rounded, and gentle. Light.

PALATE Pleasant but not very commanding. Grape, rosewater, dry tannins.

FINISH Dry and medium, with some spice.

SCORE **68**

BRUICHLADDICH 16-year-old, Bourbon/Lafleur, 46 vol

COLOR Rich reddish orange.

NOSE Soft toffee, apricot jam, strawberry preserve.

BODY Medium-full, prickly, and fruity.

PALATE Cherry and blackcurrant sherbet, some sweet citrus.

FINISH Medium-full. Fruit, with the spice arriving late.

SCORE **77**

BRUICHLADDICH 16-year-old, Bourbon, 46 vol

COLOR Deep yellow.

NOSE Lots of vanilla and honey. Rich and sweet.

BODY Quite full. Sweet and rounded.

PALATE Clean, ginger barley, sweet vanilla, soft fruit,

then late spice and tannin.

FINISH Quite long and sweet, with sweet pepper spice.

SCORE **84**

BRUICHLADDICH 16-year-old, Bourbon/D'youem, 46 vol

COLOR Rich deep orange.

NOSE Fragrant. Melon, soft toffee, vanilla. Dustiness.

BODY Quite oily and creamy.

PALATE Yellow fruits, sweet pear, and apricot juice.

Some oakiness and tannins.

FINISH Short, leaving a tingling spiciness.

SCORE **66**

BRUICHLADDICH 16-year-old, Bourbon/Lafitte, 46 vol

COLOR Sunset orange with a pinkish hue.

NOSE Beautiful sweet mix of toffee apple, butterscotch, and vanilla.

BODY Creamy, rich, and full.

PALATE Big blast of orange marmalade, dark chocolate-coated cherry,

and then cheek-sucking astringency to rein in the sweetness.

FINISH Bitter dark chocolate, cherry, chili spice, and oak.

SCORE **82**

BRUICHLADDICH 18-year-old, 46 vol

COLOR Pale gold with a hint of green.

NOSE Rootsy. Stewed chestnuts, bamboo, damp vegetation.

BODY Medium-full. Winey.

PALATE Grape, clean barley, then pepper and tannins.
Pleasant but no great depth.

FINISH Medium, with some fruits, a saltiness, and some savory notes.

SCORE **77**

BRUICHLADDICH 20-year-old, 46 vol

COLOR Orange marmalade.

NOSE Subtle, with peach, apricot, canned pear, a slight mustiness,
and a touch of tannin.

BODY Medium-full, rounded, balanced, and pleasant.

PALATE Clean, with apples, exotic fruits, sweets, and some bewitching
peppermint. Some peat and drying tannins. Very sophisticated; subtle.

FINISH Soft fruit. Delicate and medium-long, with sweet pepper and spice.

SCORE **82**

BRUICHLADDICH 21-year-old, 46 vol

COLOR Deep autumnal brown with a greenish hue.

NOSE Rich, dried fruits; orange jelly.

BODY Soft, rich, rounded, and full.

PALATE Bold mix of peach and apricot, then a big splash of tannin
and pepper, reflecting its age.

FINISH Quite long, astringent, and spicy.

SCORE **80**

BRUICHLADDICH 35-year-old, Legacy series, 40.7 vol

COLOR Rich orange gold.

NOSE Nougat, vanilla, hard candies, bourbon notes.

BODY Medium and soft.

PALATE Lemon and lime sherbet sweets. Flighty fruit spices. Battle between drying tannins and a youthful sweetness.

FINISH Shy, almost stately, but long and sherbety, with pepper at the end.

SCORE **79**

BRUICHLADDICH 40-year-old, 40 vol

COLOR Golden yellow.

NOSE Sweet pineapple candy, sherbet, vanilla, soft chews.

BODY Medium, sweet, and pleasant.

PALATE A big dose of sweet vanilla, pineapple, pear, melon, tropical fruits.

FINISH Lots of fruit and sugar, but some drying tannins and spiciness too.

SCORE **90**

NON-AGE STATEMENT BOTTLINGS
BRUICHLADDICH Waves, 46 vol

COLOR Pale yellowy bronze.

NOSE Rich, full, seaweed, and seaside peat. Smoked fish.

BODY Oily. Medium. Peaty.

PALATE A beautiful balancing act between grain, smokiness, and sweet, rich stewed fruits. Sweet wins over the phenols.

FINISH A sweet and peaty two-step. Blemish-free. Quite long. Delicious.

SCORE **86**

BRUICHLADDICH "WAVES": *A lightly peated Islay single malt. Matured on the rugged shores of the Atlantic Ocean, this Bruichladdich has been lashed by winter gales for years, the maturing barrels breathing the Hebridean marine air providing wave after wave of bracing flavours as the spirit opens up in your glass.*

700ML 46% ALC./VOL
ISLAY SINGLE MALT SCOTCH WHISKY

BRUICHLADDICH "PEAT": *One of the peatiest Islay single malt whiskies around. Distilled on Bruichladdich's uniquely tall, narrow-necked stills, so refreshingly free from "medicinal" overtones - just evocative and beguiling peat aromas. A three dimensional flavour obtained from three strengths of peated barley.*

700ML 46% ALC./VOL
ISLAY SINGLE MALT SCOTCH WHISKY

BRUICHLADDICH Peat, 46 vol

COLOR Rich orange.

NOSE Rich. The seashore, a barbecue, peat, burned fish.

BODY Oily, but pleasantly soft and rounded.

PALATE Sweet pear and apricot juice in gentle, wispy smoke. A rugged peat carpet. Beautifully balanced.

FINISH Soft, sweet, smoky. Lovely.

SCORE **83**

BRUICHLADDICH 3D, Third Dimension, 46 vol

COLOR Pale sand yellow.

NOSE Distinctive aromas of the seaside, with some seaweed, salt air, barbecue smoke, and peat.

BODY Medium-full, pleasant, and quite oily.

PALATE Green fruits, perhaps kiwi fruit or gooseberry, a delightful wallop of peat, and then a sweet fruit finale.

FINISH Quite long. Spicy. Tingling.

SCORE **83**

BRUICHLADDICH Laddie, 2001, 46 vol

COLOR Brass.

NOSE Chinese food: stewed beanshoots, onions, soy; musty.

BODY Firm and structured. Medium-full.

PALATE Spirity, spicy, almost floral, with a touch of peat and a savory balance. Green salad with a sharp dressing. Very different to anything else from this distillery.

FINISH Pleasant enough, but short, and with a final peat flourish.

SCORE **71**

BRUICHLADDICH Infinity, 52.5 vol

COLOR Golden honey.

NOSE Seaside on Islay. Winter beach. Damp, seaweedy, salty.

BODY Soft, medium-full, sweet, and rounded.

PALATE Like chewing exotic canned fruit while smoking. A beautiful
interplay between smoky peat and a delicious sweetness.

FINISH A lengthy tangle of smoke and sweetness.
Utterly compelling.

SCORE 89

BRUICHLADDICH Yellow Submarine, 46 vol

COLOR Orangey gold.

NOSE Honeyed, soft melon, stewed plum. Sweet.

BODY Soft, rounded, and medium-full.

PALATE Unripe banana, clean malt, melon, and then peppery spice.

FINISH Medium, with fruit and a spicy and
savory conclusion.

SCORE 70

BRUICHLADDICH Redder Still, 50.4 vol

COLOR Marmalade orange with reddish hue.

NOSE Alcoholic dandelion and burdock. Part florist, part hairdresser's.
Blackcurrant cordial.

BODY Rich full and mouth-coating.

PALATE Intense, rich, blemish-free. Tropical fruits,
sweet citrus, blackcurrant.

FINISH Long, clean, and very moreish.

SCORE 87

BRUICHLADDICH Blacker Still, 50.7 vol

COLOR Deep prune brown.

NOSE Monstrous and growling. Prune juice, dried currents,
pantry spices, damp vegetables.

BODY Very full, aggressive, and mouth-coating.

PALATE Full and rich sherry, big sweet dollops of over-ripe fruit,
and a big dose of tannins, suggesting age, Japanese-like.
Everything at full volume.

FINISH Sweet, dried fruits, oak, and spices, but all balanced
and utterly irresisitble.

SCORE 92

PORT CHARLOTTE AND OCTOMORE BOTTLINGS
BRUICHLADDICH Port Charlotte PC 6, 61 vol

COLOR Rich orange.

NOSE Deep tar, seaweed, coastal, rich.

BODY Very full but soft. Delightfully oily.

PALATE Soft fruit, peat, seaweed, barbecue smoke. Rounded and chewy.

FINISH Long but gentle, a balance of smoke and fruit.

SCORE **89**

BRUICHLADDICH Port Charlotte PC 7, 60.5 vol

COLOR Orangey yellow.

NOSE Musty damp wood, then light and sweet peat. Subtle and restrained.

BODY Full, sharp, oily, and intense.

PALATE Charcoal, rich tarry peat, then sweet fruits. Strawberry.

FINISH Long and very impressive. A delicious mix of sweetness and smoke.

SCORE **90**

BRUICHLADDICH Octomore, 63.5 vol

COLOR Pale yellow.

NOSE Classic Islay in neon lights: barbecued fish, seaweed, beach, smoke.

BODY Oily, full, and mouth-coating.

PALATE Needs water, but is even more stunning for it. Very sweet, very peaty.
Charcoal. Lemon drizzled on barbecued trout.

FINISH Long and lingering. Faultless and perfectly balanced between
the fruit, smoke, and peppery spices.

SCORE **93**

BUNNAHABHAIN

PRODUCER Burn Stewart Distillers plc
REGION Islay   DISTRICT North Shore
ADDRESS Port Askaig, Islay, Argyll, PA46 7RP
TEL 01496 840646   WEBSITE www.blackbottle.com
EMAIL enquiries@burnstewartdistillers.com   VC

A NEW LIFE for the elusive Bunnahabhain set the seal on the Islay revival in the new millennium. Elusive? Bunnahabhain has the most hidden location of the Islay distilleries, the most superficially difficult name (pronounced "boona'hhavn"), and the most delicate whisky. Even its new owners, since 2003, are the smallest group in the industry. Bunnahabhain joins the Tobermory and Deanston distilleries in the Burn Stewart group, well known in the Far East for its Scottish Leader blends. With the acquisition of Bunnahabhain, Burn Stewart also gain the cult blend Black Bottle, which contains malts from all the Islay distilleries. At the time of the takeover, Burn Stewart had recently joined the worldwide group that includes the "super-premium" vodka Belvedere and has as its unlikely flagship Angostura Bitters.

The Bunnahabhain distillery had been well maintained by its previous owners, Edrington, but both production and marketing of its products had been sporadic. Stocks were sinking—not a happy state of affairs for the whisky whose packaging bears the words of the Islay anthem, "Westering Home." Despite its delicacy, Bunnahabhain does have a touch of Islay maritime character.

The distillery, expanded in 1963, was built in 1881. It is set around a courtyard in a remote cove. A kerb has been built to stops visitors' cars from rolling into the sea. A ships' bell, salvaged from a nearby wreck, hangs from the wall. It was at one time used to summon the manager from his home if he were urgently needed. The distillery's water rises through limestone, and because it is piped to the distillery, it does not pick up peat on the way. The stills are large, in the style that the industry refers to as onion-shaped.

HOUSE STYLE Fresh, sweetish, nutty, herbal, salty. Aperitif.

BUNNAHABHAIN 12-year-old, 43 vol

COLOR Gold.

NOSE Remarkably fresh. Sweet. Sea-air aroma.

BODY Light to medium; firm.

PALATE Gentle, clean, with a nutty-malty sweetness.

FINISH Very full flavor development. Refreshing.

SCORE **77**

BUNNAHABHAIN 14-year-old, 52.6 vol

Bottling for Feis Ile, 2006. Finished in Pedro Ximénez casks.

COLOR Mid-amber.

NOSE Powerful and sweet, with apricots, spicy bananas, and Brazil nuts.

BODY Creamy.

PALATE Sweet and spicy; port-like.

FINISH Long and drying. Ginger and tannins.

SCORE **79**

BUNNAHABHAIN 18-year-old, 43 vol

COLOR Pale amber, with golden highlights.

NOSE Sherry, spicy, ripe apples, marshmallow.

BODY Medium to full.

PALATE Nutty, quite dry, sprinkling of pepper.

FINISH Caramelized fruits, sherry, and dry oak.

BUNNAHABHAIN 21-year-old, 1986 vintage, 46.7 vol

Bottling for Feis Ile, 2008.

COLOR Chestnut brown.

NOSE Moist fruitcake and sherry, balanced by brine.

BODY Rounded.

PALATE Nutty sherry, malt, and delicate oak.

FINISH Lengthy, spicy, and drying, with another splash of brine.

BUNNAHABHAIN 25-year-old, 43 vol

COLOR Mid-amber, with golden highlights.

NOSE Floral, with a hint of background salt.

BODY Medium to full.

PALATE A little salt, balanced by sherry, baked apple crumble, and cream.

FINISH Medium to long. Lingering sherry drying to cocoa.

SCORE 84

BUNNAHABHAIN 34-year-old, 1968, 43.5 vol

COLOR Light gold.

NOSE Enticingly floral, fruity, and sherried.

BODY Medium.

PALATE Less full than expected. Tannins, with developing
bubble gum.

FINISH Fruits and tannins fight it out.

SCORE **78**

BUNNAHABHAIN 40-year-old, 1963, 42.9 vol

COLOR Pale gold.

NOSE Sweet sherry, fresh fruits, nutmeg.

BODY Medium to full.

PALATE Complex and supple. Orange, pepper, and spice.

FINISH Long, with some brine.

SCORE **83**

BUNNAHABHAIN Auld Acquaintance Hogmanay Edition, 1968, Bottle 1 of 2000, 43.8 vol

Also subsequently bottled as Bunnahabhain 32-year-old.

COLOR Orange satin, with pinkish tinge.

NOSE A rich, moist Dundee cake. Toasted nuts. Salty. Sea breezes.

BODY Creamy.

PALATE Malted milk. Chocolate. Nonetheless avoids
being cloying. Deftly balanced.

FINISH Dark cocoa powder.

COMMENT A brilliantly sunny winter's day; a long walk by the sea in the
late afternoon; oatcakes and cheese; Dundee cake; a dram at dusk. Still
recognizably Bunnahabhain, but so different. More such essays, please.

SCORE **86**

BUNNAHABHAIN Darach Ur, 46.3 vol
Exclusive to global travel retail outlets.

COLOR Bright amber.

NOSE Fresh oak, spice, and pine nuts.

BODY Firm.

PALATE Citrus fruit, spicy vanilla, cloves, and cinnamon.

FINISH Medium. Gingery and drying.

SCORE 82

SOME INDEPENDENT BOTTLINGS
BUNNAHABHAIN 28-year-old, Distilled 1979, Bottled 2008
Cask No 18831, The Single Malts of Scotland, 46 vol

COLOR Pale gold.

NOSE Gently perfumed, fresh for its age,
with ripe barley and soft toffee.

BODY Rounded.

PALATE Mixed spices, apple pie, and almonds.

FINISH More perfume, Parma Violets, buttery oak.

SCORE 82

BUNNAHABHAIN 31-year-old, Distilled 1976, Bottled 2008
Cask No 6223, Dewar Rattray, 49.1 vol

COLOR Mid-amber.

NOSE Spicy malt, brine, and a fresh, lemon edge.

BODY Smooth.

PALATE Dry, nutty, sherry, spice; progressively peppery.

FINISH Long, peppery oak.

SCORE 79

BUNNAHABHAIN 38-year-old,
Distilled 1970, Bottled 2008
Cask No 4075, Duncan Taylor, 40.2 vol

COLOR Gold.

NOSE Soft and fragrant, backed by brittle toffee
and mild maritime aromas.

BODY Quite firm.

PALATE Spice and brine, citrus fruits, cocoa powder,
then fruit-and-nut milk chocolate.

FINISH Lengthy, with benign oak and milky cocoa.

SCORE 82

CAOL ILA

PRODUCER Diageo
REGION Islay   DISTRICT North shore
ADDRESS Port Askaig, Islay, Argyll, PA46 7RL
TEL 01496 302760   Distillery has shop
WEBSITE www.discovering-distilleries.com/www.malts.com

AT THE ISLAY FESTIVAL OF 2002, three stylishly boxed expressions of Caol Ila were released by owners Diageo, as part of a new range with the rubric "Hidden Malts." It was further announced that Hidden Malts would also emanate from another three Diageo distilleries: Clynelish, Glen Elgin, and Glen Ord. The launch of Caol Ila in an official bottling—in such a public way, too, and, implicitly at least, as the flagship in the new range—finally confirmed that it was far from hidden. Its malts had become more readily available, and appreciated, in recent years.

The name, pronounced "cull-eela," means "Sound of Islay." The Gaelic word "caol" is more familiar as "kyle." The distillery is in a cove near Port Askaig. The large windows of the still-house overlook the Sound of Islay, across which the ferry chugs to the nearby island of Jura. The best view of the distillery is from the ferry.

Its 1970s façade is beginning to be accepted as a classic of the period. Inside, the distillery is both functional and attractive: a copper hood on the lauter tun; brass trim; wash stills like flat onions, spirit stills more pear-shaped; Oregon pine washbacks. Some of the structure dates from 1879, and the distillery was founded in 1846.

Behind the distillery, a hillside covered in fuchsias, foxgloves, and wild roses rises toward the peaty loch where the water gathers. It is quite salty and minerally, having risen from limestone. As a modern, well-engineered distillery, making whisky for several blends, Caol Ila has over the years used different levels of peating. This is apparent in the independent bottlings.

HOUSE STYLE Oily, olive-like. Junipery, fruity, estery.
A wonderful aperitif.

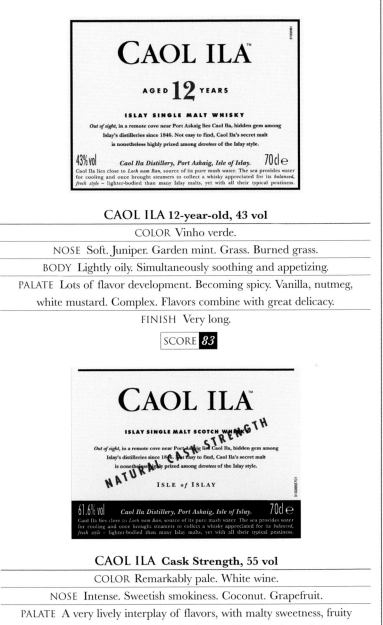

CAOL ILA 12-year-old, 43 vol

COLOR Vinho verde.

NOSE Soft. Juniper. Garden mint. Grass. Burned grass.

BODY Lightly oily. Simultaneously soothing and appetizing.

PALATE Lots of flavor development. Becoming spicy. Vanilla, nutmeg, white mustard. Complex. Flavors combine with great delicacy.

FINISH Very long.

SCORE 83

CAOL ILA Cask Strength, 55 vol

COLOR Remarkably pale. White wine.

NOSE Intense. Sweetish smokiness. Coconut. Grapefruit.

PALATE A very lively interplay of flavors, with malty sweetness, fruity esteriness, and peppery dryness. Perfumy, with suggestions of thyme.

FINISH The flavors come together in a rousing finale, with the alcohol providing a backbeat.

SCORE 85

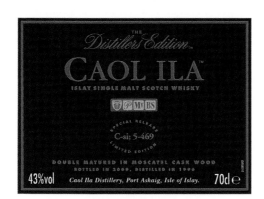

CAOL ILA 1995, Distillers Edition,
Double Matured, Bottled 2007, 43 vol

Finished in Moscatel casks.

COLOR Bright gold.

NOSE Sweet peat smoke, cloves, succulent fresh fruits.

BODY Smooth.

PALATE Initially very suave, then brine, fruit, and gingery peat.

FINISH Warming. Smoky spice.

SCORE **83**

CAOL ILA 18-year-old, 43 vol

COLOR Fino sherry on a sunny day.

NOSE Fragrant. Menthol. Markedly vegetal. Nutty vanilla pod.

BODY Firmer. Much bigger.

PALATE More assertively expressive. Sweeter. Leafy sweetness.
Spring greens. Crushed almonds. Rooty, cedary.

FINISH Powerful reverberations of a remarkable whisky.

SCORE **86**

CAOL ILA 25-year-old, Cask Strength,
Distilled 1979, 58.4 vol

COLOR Mid-gold.

NOSE Sweet, spicy, and peaty, with warm soil.

BODY Medium and oily.

PALATE Sweetness is balanced by lemon, pepper, and olives.

FINISH Lengthy and drying, with bonfire embers,
gauze bandages, and shellfish.

SCORE 84

CAOL ILA 8-year-old, 64.2 vol
Special Releases 2008

COLOR Pale gold.

NOSE Spicy caramel and stewed apples with cream.

BODY Light and slightly oily.

PALATE Herbal and smoky, with balancing fresh fruit notes.

FINISH Short to medium, dry, and herbal.

SCORE 82

SOME EARLIER OFFICIAL BOTTLINGS THAT ARE
NOW HARD TO FIND
CAOL ILA 1981, Bottled 1997,
Cask Strength Limited Bottling, 63.8 vol

COLOR Bright limey yellow.

NOSE Fragrant peat smoke, juniper, seaweed. Very appetizing.

BODY Firm, oily.

PALATE Assertively oily, junipery. Late surge of
peaty dryness. Very dry.

FINISH Wonderfully long and warming.

SCORE 82

CAOL ILA 20-year-old, Bottled 1996, 57.86 vol
150th Anniversary Edition

COLOR Orange.

NOSE Sweet seaweed. Juniper. Pine nuts.

BODY Medium, smooth, rounded.

PALATE Enormously complex and distinctive. Nutty, appetizingly seaweedy,
peppery, salty. Tightly combined flavors. Beautifully balanced.

FINISH Sherry, toasty oak, seaweed, lemon peel, pepper.

SCORE 85

SOME INDEPENDENT BOTTLINGS
CAOL ILA 18-year-old,
Scotch Malt Whisky Society, 53.126, 56.7 vol

COLOR Pale amber, with gold highlights.

NOSE Brine, peat smoke, mildly fishy. Adhesive bandages.
Balancing sweetness.

BODY Smooth.

PALATE Smoky, sweet and rich, with coconut, developing maritime notes,
sea salt, and spice.

FINISH Long and warming.

SCORE **84**

CAOL ILA 27-year-old, Distilled 1981, Bottled 2008
Cask 2932, Duncan Taylor, Rare Auld Range, 53.8 vol

COLOR Mid-gold.

NOSE Damp tweed, peat, and slight iodine.

BODY Robust.

PALATE Lemon and lime. Quite big peat notes. Pepper and ginger.

FINISH Medium to long. More peat, slightly oily, and perfumed.

SCORE **83**

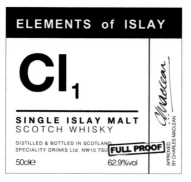

CI1 Elements of Islay, Speciality Drinks Co, 60.8 vol

COLOR Pale yellow.

NOSE Sweet zingy lemon. Wispy smoke. Melon. Pineapple chunks.

BODY Oily, full, rich, smoky.

PALATE Yellow fruits. Lemon bonbons in fire ashes. Smoky. Rounded.
Over-ripe melon.

FINISH Long, oily, smoky, with citrus and late spice. Peat and spice linger.

SCORE **84**

CAPERDONICH

PRODUCER Chivas Brothers
REGION Highlands DISTRICT Speyside (Rothes)
ADDRESS Rothes, Morayshire, AB38 7BN

CAPERDONICH WAS MOTHBALLED IN 2002, and there are no current plans to reopen it. It is the lesser known partner to Glen Grant—the two distilleries stand across the street from one another in the whisky town of Rothes and share the same ownership. Caperdonich, founded in 1898, was rebuilt in 1965 and extended in 1967. Its name is said to indicate a "secret source." From the start, it has been a back-up to Glen Grant. When young, the malts of both distilleries are light and fragrant in their bouquet, medium-bodied, and nutty-tasting.

Of the two, Caperdonich is perhaps a dash fruitier and slightly more smoky. It, too, is a component of the Chivas Regal blend. The Chivas group kept a tight control of its malts during the last years of its ownership by Seagram, of Canada. This policy was maintained following the takeover by Pernod Ricard, of France. There are no official bottlings of Caperdonich, and the independent bottlings tend to be from very old stock.

HOUSE STYLE Dried fruits, grainy, toasty. Breakfast? After dinner?

CAPERDONICH Aged 40 years, Old Malt Cask, 42.9 vol

COLOR Rich gold.

NOSE Rich and full. Orange and mandarin orange. Soft jelly. honeycomb.

BODY Medium, sweet, and full.

PALATE Berries. Blood orange marmalade. A battle for the fruit against wood and pepper.

FINISH Quite long and very spicy. Big oak notes.

SCORE 79

CAPERDONICH 11-year-old, Provenance, 46 vol

COLOR Pale yellow.

NOSE banana-and-toffee pie. Banana milkshake. Milk chocolate.

BODY Thin and unassertive.

PALATE Sweet. Minty. Ginger barley. Touch of citrus.

FINISH Short and sweet.

SCORE 65

CARDHU/CARDOW

PRODUCER Diageo
REGION Highlands DISTRICT Speyside
ADDRESS Aberlour, Banffshire, AB38 7RY
TEL 01340 872555 WEBSITE www.discovering-distilleries.com VC

A FEW YEARS AGO Cardhu became famous for all the wrong reasons when Diageo added two other malts from its portfolio to Cardhu Single Malt and renamed it Cardhu Pure in a bid to stretch supplies further to slake the thirst of drinkers in Spain, where it enjoys enormous popularity. The move caused outrage and Diageo backed down, but the furore led to a change in rules by the Scotch Whisky Association.

Cardow has several claims to renown. It provided the industry with a dynastic family, the Cummings, and contributed twice to the tradition of strong women running distilleries. Helen Cummings distilled illegally on the family farm. Her daughter-in-law, Elizabeth, developed the legal distillery, which produced malt whisky as a substantial component of the Johnnie Walker blends.

The distillery was founded as Cardow (Gaelic for "black rock," after a nearby point on the river Spey). An alternative spelling, "Cardhu," better reflecting the pronunciation, was adopted when the distillery began to promote a bottled single malt. This mild, easily drinkable whisky was launched to compete with the popular malts in the early days of consumer interest.

It was a modest success in the United Kingdom, but enjoyed far greater sales in new markets for malts, such as France and Spain. In the latter country, the distinction between malts and blends seems to engage the consumer less than the age statement. Cardhu found itself head to head with the blend Chivas Regal, both being 12 years old. The Spaniards' taste for Scotch whisky is so great that the success of Cardhu in that market rendered it the world's fastest growing malt, outstripping the capacity of the distillery.

HOUSE STYLE In the original form: light, smooth, delicate;
an easy-drinking malt. Greater ages are richer, more toffeeish,
and often work well with desserts.

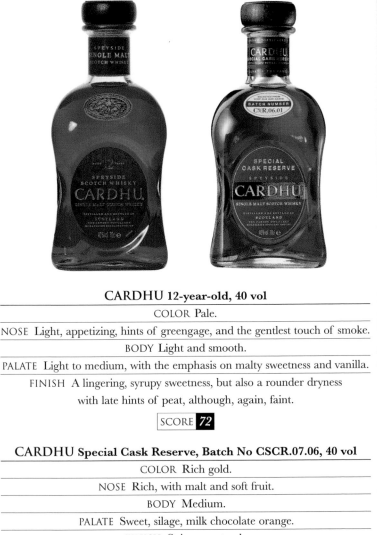

CARDHU 12-year-old, 40 vol

COLOR Pale.

NOSE Light, appetizing, hints of greengage, and the gentlest touch of smoke.

BODY Light and smooth.

PALATE Light to medium, with the emphasis on malty sweetness and vanilla.

FINISH A lingering, syrupy sweetness, but also a rounder dryness with late hints of peat, although, again, faint.

SCORE 72

CARDHU Special Cask Reserve, Batch No CSCR.07.06, 40 vol

COLOR Rich gold.

NOSE Rich, with malt and soft fruit.

BODY Medium.

PALATE Sweet, silage, milk chocolate orange.

FINISH Spicy, sweet oak.

SCORE 78

CARDHU Managers' Choice, Distilled 1997, Bottled 2009, 58.3 vol

COLOR Pale yellow.

NOSE Lemon and lime. Clean barley. Crisp and fresh.

BODY Medium-full, oily, mouth-coating.

PALATE Mint. Kiwi. Melon. A late surge of pepper.

FINISH Long and spicy.

SCORE 78

CLYNELISH

PRODUCER **Diageo**
REGION **Highlands**   DISTRICT **Northern Highlands**
ADDRESS **Brora, Sutherland, KW9 6LR**
TEL **01408 623003**
WEBSITE **www.discovering-distilleries.com/www.malts.com**   VC

CULT STATUS SEEMS TO have been conferred in recent years on the Clynelish distillery and its adjoining predecessor, Brora, which command the middle stretch of the northern Highlands.

The appeal of their malts lies partly in their coastal aromas and flavors. Sceptics may question the brineyness of coastal malts, but some bottlings of Brora and Clynelish make that characteristic hard to deny. They are the most maritime of the East Coast malts, and on the Western mainland are challenged only by Springbank.

For a time, the big flavors of Clynelish and Brora were heightened by the use of well-peated malts. Clynelish cultists are always keen to identify distillates from this period. A similar preoccupation is to distinguish malts made at the Brora distillery from those that were distilled at Clynelish.

The two distilleries stand next door to each other on a landscaped hillside near the fishing and golfing resort of Brora. They overlook the coastal road as it heads toward the northernmost tip of the Scottish mainland.

The older of the two distilleries was built in 1819 by the Duke of Sutherland to use grain grown by his tenants. This distillery was originally known as Clynelish: the first syllable rhymes with "wine," the second with "leash." The name means "slope of the garden." After a century and half, a new Clynelish was built in 1967–68, but demand was sufficient for the two distilleries to operate in tandem for a time. They were initially known as Clynelish 1 and 2. Eventually, the older distillery was renamed Brora. It worked sporadically until 1983.

Brora is a traditional 19th-century distillery, in local stone (now overgrown), with a pagoda. Clynelish's stills greet the world through the floor-to-ceiling windows, in the classic design of the period, with a fountain to soften the façade.

Inside, the still-house has its own peculiarities, in which the deposits in the low wines and feints receivers play a part. The result is an oily, beeswax background flavor—another distinctive feature.

For years, this robustly distinctive malt was available only as a 12-year-old, bearing a charmingly amateurish label, from Ainslie and Heilbron, a DCL subsidiary, whose blends were given brand names of equal charm. The Real McTavish was a good example. Since the United Distillers and Diageo eras, Brora and Clynelish have been positively anthologous. Editions have been issues by Flora and Fauna, The Rare Malts, Cask Strength Limited Editions, Hidden Malts, as well as Special Releases.

HOUSE STYLE Seaweedy, spicy. Mustard-and-oil.
With a roast-beef sandwich.

CLYNELISH, 14-year-old, Hidden Malts, 46 vol

Replaces the more seaweedy Flora and Fauna edition.

COLOR Bright pale orange.

NOSE Fragrant. A stroll in the sand dunes.

BODY Firm, oily and seductively smoky.

PALATE Firm hit of cleansing flavors. Coriander. Orange. Dry. Spicy.
Distinctively mustardy.

FINISH The spiciness becomes yet more perfumy and exotic.
Both satisfying (without being satiating).

SCORE 81

CLYNELISH 1991, 15-year-old, Distillers Edition, 46 vol

COLOR Orangey gold.

NOSE Nutty. Rich. Oranges. Madeira cake.

BODY Full. Intense. Creamy. Rich.

PALATE Big wave of brine and peat. Intense, almost oily.
Then fragrant fruit. Part industrial, part flower garden.
Dominant and dramatic.

FINISH Rich, intense, liqueur-like, but briney.

SCORE **81**

BOTTLINGS OF BRORA MALTS
BRORA 30-year-old, 52.4 vol

COLOR Deep golden brown.

NOSE Halfway between a florists and the fruit store.
Delightfully fruity, but with hints of spice
and peat. Smoky.

BODY Rich. Full. Very assertive.

PALATE Captivating. A perfectly balanced blend
of pepper, peat, big orangey fruits,
and brine. Plenty of oak.

FINISH Perfectly balanced, peaty, fruity, and peppery.

SCORE **94**

BRORA 25-year-old, Special Release 2008, 56.3 vol

COLOR Clear honey.

NOSE Perfumed. Lemon cleaner. Wax polish. Cookies.

BODY Rich, full, and creamy.

PALATE Mint. Anise. Green fruit. Oak, spice,
and wafts of smoke.

FINISH Long, intense, and peppery.

SCORE **88**

BRORA 30-year-old, Special Release 2006, 55.7 vol

COLOR Orange.

NOSE Pencil shavings. Sweet yellow fruit. Tarry peat.

BODY Rich, creamy, and full.

PALATE Liquorice. Lots of peat. Zesty. Dusty spice.

FINISH Long, full, peaty, and peppery.

SCORE **90**

BRORA 30-year-old, Special Release 2005, 56.3 vol

COLOR Rich orange.

NOSE Islay-like. Seaweed, coal tar, and peat.

BODY Medium.

PALATE Aniseed, then red licorice. Apple and unripe pear.
Finally peat and tar, but evolving and rounded.

FINISH In two parts: fruit, which disappears quickly;
then smoke, tars, and spices.

SCORE **85**

INDEPENDENT BOTTLINGS OF CLYNELISH
AND BRORA MALTS

CLYNELISH 11-year-old, Provenance, 46 vol

COLOR Pale straw.

NOSE Melon. Grapefruit. Pineapple. Tingling.

BODY Medium-full and oily.

PALATE Sharp barley. Earthy peat. Quite sweet. Pepper.

FINISH Savory. Spicy. Quite long.

SCORE **64**

CLYNELISH 1993, Bottled in 2008,
Berry's Own Selection, 46 vol

COLOR Lemon yellow.

NOSE Cooking apples. Horse-chestnut shells. Vanilla.
Clean and rapier-like.

BODY Medium-full. Savory.

PALATE Sharp green and orange fruits. Almond. Apple seed.
Clean and refreshing. A touch of mint.

FINISH Long and clean, with a touch of pepper, mint, and oak.

SCORE **82**

CLYNELISH 16-year-old, Duncan Taylor, N.C.2, 46 vol

COLOR Lemon yellow.

NOSE Toffee. Fresh flowers. Grassy perfume.

BODY Creamy and full.

PALATE Orange barley sugar. Vanilla. Almost chewy.

FINISH Quite long. Fruity. A touch of pepper late on.

SCORE **82**

CLYNELISH 17-year-old, Chieftains, 46 vol

COLOR Bronze.

NOSE Butterscotch and vanilla at first. Then kiwi fruit and kumquat.

BODY Medium. Sweet. Creamy.

PALATE Refreshing. Canned fruit syrup. Wedding cake.
Banana peel.

FINISH Medium, with fruit and long sugary spice.

SCORE **88**

CLYNELISH 34-year-old,
Single Malts of Scotland, 50.5 vol

COLOR Orange gold.

NOSE Great mix of honey, citrus fruits, and oak.

BODY Soft. Creamy, fresh, and intense.

PALATE Soft. Honeyed, with sharp lemon and over-ripe peach to start,
then oak, but not too dramatically.

FINISH Medium, honeyed, and oaky. Spices linger. Some tannins.

SCORE **86**

BRORA 1982, Connoisseurs Choice, 43 vol

COLOR Pale yellow.

NOSE Lemon-flavored flu powder and intense smoke.

BODY Rich. Intense. Oily.

PALATE Intense barley with some sweetness. Citrus. Peat.

FINISH Long. Sweet. Lemon and peat.

SCORE **83**

BRORA 27-year-old, Cask 1427,
Duncan Taylor, 53.8 vol

COLOR Lemon yellow.

NOSE Lemon zest. Clean. Traces of peat, but also rich and honeyed.

BODY Sweet. Oily. Full.

PALATE Crunchie bar. Honeycomb. Soft and sugary. Intense barley.

FINISH Very pleasant. Rich honeyed barley. Very clean.
A trace of late tannin. Very fruity.

SCORE **89**

COLEBURN

PRODUCER Diageo
REGION Highlands   DISTRICT Speyside (Lossie)
ADDRESS Longmorn by Elgin, Moray, IV38 8GN

THE USHER'S WHISKIES, pioneer blends, once relied heavily upon malt from this distillery. Coleburn was built in the booming 1890s. It closed in the grim 1980s, the year before its owners DCL were subsumed into United Distillers, which in turn became part of Diageo. The Coleburn distillery has not been licensed since 1992, and is unlikely to work again. There have been sporadic proposals to redevelop the site for other uses. Its whisky, always intended for blending, was never destined for solo stardom. A valedictory Rare Malts vintage was as enjoyable as any Coleburn to have been bottled in recent decades.

HOUSE STYLE Dry, fruity. Aperitif.

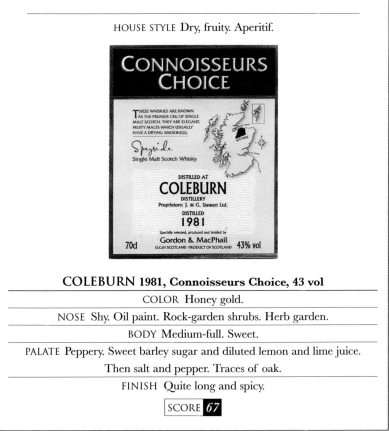

COLEBURN 1981, Connoisseurs Choice, 43 vol

COLOR	Honey gold.
NOSE	Shy. Oil paint. Rock-garden shrubs. Herb garden.
BODY	Medium-full. Sweet.
PALATE	Peppery. Sweet barley sugar and diluted lemon and lime juice. Then salt and pepper. Traces of oak.
FINISH	Quite long and spicy.

SCORE 67

CONVALMORE

PRODUCER William Grant & Sons Ltd.
REGION Highlands DISTRICT Speyside (Dufftown)
ADDRESS Dufftown, Banffshire, AB55 4BD

THE PAGODAS OF DUFFTOWN make an impressive congregation of landmarks, and Convalmore's is one of the most strikingly visible. Sadly, the distillery no longer operates.

For much of its life, Convalmore contributed malt whisky to the Buchanan/Black & White blends. The distillery was built in the 1870s; seriously damaged by fire, and rebuilt in 1910; modernized in 1964–65, but mothballed a couple of decades later by its owners at the time, DCL. Their successors, Diageo, still have the right to issue bottlings of Convalmore whisky from stock, but most appearances currently are independent bottlings. In 1992, the premises were acquired by William Grant & Sons, owners of nearby Glenfiddich and Balvenie, but their use is purely for warehousing.

HOUSE STYLE Malty, syrupy, fruity, biggish. After dinner.

CONVALMORE 1984, Connoisseurs Choice, 43 vol

COLOR Pale orange.

NOSE Plastic bandage. Some toffee. Traces of potpourri and citrus.

BODY Sweet and creamy.

PALATE Sweet fruit, then spearmint. Unripe green fruit. Apple. A touch of spice. Hefty barley backbone.

FINISH Medium. Savory. Balanced.

SCORE 75

CONVALMORE 32-year-old, Old Malt Cask, 48 vol

COLOR Orangey brass.

NOSE Lemon and lime. Orange sherbet.

BODY Medium and sweet.

PALATE Blood orange. Bitter lemon. Vanilla, then late spice. Surprisingly fresh and zesty for its age.

FINISH Quite long and citrusy, with pepper at the end.

SCORE 83

CRAGGANMORE

PRODUCER Diageo
REGION Highlands   DISTRICT Speyside
ADDRESS Ballindalloch, Banffshire, AB37 9AB   TEL 01479 8747000
WEBSITE www.discovering-distilleries.com/www.malts.com

SPECIAL RELEASES IN RECENT YEARS have demonstrated just what a complex and special malt this is. Despite being one of the original six Classic Malt selections, this Speyside great still isn't as well known as it could be. The distillery, founded in 1869–70, is very pretty, hidden in a hollow high on the Spey. Its water, from nearby springs, is relatively hard, and its spirit stills have an unusual, flat-topped shape. These two elements may be factors in the complexity of the malt. The usual version from refill sherry casks, some more sherried independent bottlings, and the port finish, are each, in their own ways, almost equal delights. Cragganmore is a component of the Old Parr blends.

HOUSE STYLE Austere, stonily dry, aromatic. After dinner.

CRAGGANMORE 12-year-old, 40 vol

COLOR Golden.

NOSE The most complex of any malt. Astonishingly fragrant and delicate, with sweetish notes of cut grass and herbs (thyme perhaps?).

BODY Light to medium, but very firm and smooth.

PALATE Delicate, clean, restrained; a huge range of herbal, flowery notes.

FINISH Long.

SCORE **90**

CRAGGANMORE 1984, Double Matured, 40 vol
Finished in ruby port.

COLOR Pale amber.

NOSE Heather honey. Scented. Beeswax. Hessian.

BODY Firm and smooth. Fuller than the 12-year-old.

PALATE Flowery. Orange blossom. Sweet oranges. Cherries. Port.

FINISH Flowery, balancing dryness. Warming. Soothing.

COMMENT Connoisseurs might miss the austerity of the original—or enjoy the added layer of fruity, winey sweetness.

SCORE **90**

CRAGGANMORE Distillers Edition, 40 vol

COLOR Deep golden brown.

NOSE Coffee. Rich vanilla. Prunes. Stewed fruits. Cooked raisins.

BODY Rich and rounded. Soft and delicate.

PALATE Soft and sweet. Peach. Soft fruit.
A hint of smoke. Berries. Evolving.

FINISH Medium but very pleasant, rounded,
and balanced. Complex and beguiling.

SCORE **90**

SOME INDEPENDENT BOTTLINGS
CRAGGANMORE 1993
Cask 1910, Duncan Taylor, 59.8 vol

COLOR Pale yellowy green.

NOSE Fruity. Vegetal. Some citrus. Watermelon.

BODY Sweet and creamy.

PALATE Sweet and full. Green fruit. Melon. Anise.

FINISH Quite long, with anise and pepper.

SCORE **72**

CRAGGANMORE 15-year-old, Duthies, 46 vol

COLOR Straw.

NOSE Shy and subtle. Fresh grape. Clean juicy fruits. Sweet.

BODY Soft, creamy, and full.

PALATE Lime Starburst. Creamy and sweet. Fresh.
Exotic canned fruits.

FINISH Medium-long. Lemon and lime cordial. Rounded.

SCORE **86**

CRAIGELLACHIE

PRODUCER John Dewar & Sons Ltd. (Bacardi)
REGION Highlands   DISTRICT Speyside
ADDRESS Craigellachie, Banffshire, AB38 9ST
TEL 01340 872971

THE VILLAGE OF CRAIGELLACHIE—between Dufftown, Aberlour, and Rothes—is at the very heart of the Speyside distillery country. It also has the Speyside Cooperage. Here, the Fiddich meets the Spey, and the latter is crossed by a bridge, designed by the great Scottish engineer Thomas Telford. Craigellachie, founded in 1891 and remodelled in 1965, is pronounced "Craig-ella-ki"—the "I" is short.

The whisky of Craigellachie had a very low profile under the ownership of Diageo; perhaps it will rediscover itself under Dewar's, which released a 14-year-old for a period.

HOUSE STYLE Sweet, malty-nutty, fruity. After dinner.

CRAIGELLACHIE 14-year-old, Flora and Fauna, 43 vol

COLOR Old gold.
NOSE Fragrant. Lightly smoky. Plenty of sweet, crushed-barley maltiness.
BODY Medium.
PALATE Starts sweet, slightly syrupy, and malty, then becomes nutty, developing a very fruity, Seville-orange character.
FINISH Orangey. Lightly smoky. Aromatic and warming.

SCORE 75

DAILUAINE

PRODUCER Diageo
REGION Highlands   DISTRICT Speyside
ADDRESS Carron, Aberlour, Banffshire, AB38 7RE
TEL 01340 872500

Between the mountain ben rinnes and the Spey River, at the hamlet of Carron, not far from Aberlour, the Dailuaine ("Dal-oo-ayn") distillery is hidden in a hollow. The name means "green vale," and that accurately describes the setting. It was founded in 1852, and has been rebuilt several times since.

It is one of several distilleries along the Spey valley that once had its own railroad flag stop for workers and visitors—and as a means of shipping in barley or malt and despatching the whisky. A small part of the Speyside line still runs trains for hobbyists and visitors, at the Aviemore ski resort, and Dailuaine's own shunting locomotive has appeared there under steam, but is now preserved at Aberfeldy, a distillery formerly in the same group. Most of the route from the mountains to the sea is now preserved for walkers, as the Speyside Way. Dailuaine's whisky has long been a component of the Johnnie Walker blends. It was made available as a single malt in the Flora and Fauna series in 1991, and later in a Cask Strength Limited Edition.

HOUSE STYLE Firmly malty, fruity, fragrant.
After dinner.

SPEYSIDE
SINGLE MALT SCOTCH WHISKY

DAILUAINE

is the GAELIC for "the green vale". The *distillery*, established
in 1852, lies in a hollow by the *CARRON BURN* in *BANFFSHIRE*. This
single Malt Scotch Whisky has a *full bodied fruity* nose and a *smoky* finish.
For more than a *hundred years* all *distillery supplies* were despatched by
rail. The *steam locomotive* "DAILUAINE NO.1" was in use
from 1939 ~ 1967 and is *preserved* on the *STRATHSPEY RAILWAY*.

AGED 16 YEARS

43% vol   Distilled & Bottled in SCOTLAND. DAILUAINE DISTILLERY, Carron, Aberlour, Banffshire, Scotland.   70 cl

DAILUAINE 16-year-old, Flora and Fauna, 43 vol

COLOR Emphatically reddish amber.

NOSE Sherryish but dry. Perfumy.

BODY Medium to full; smooth.

PALATE Sherryish, with barley-sugar maltiness, but balanced by
a dry cedar or oak background.

FINISH Sherryish, smooth, very warming. Long.

SCORE **76**

SOME INDEPENDENT BOTTLINGS
DAILUAINE 9-year-old, Provenance, 46 vol

COLOR Rich gold.

NOSE Soft caramel. Banana toffee.

BODY Full, creamy, and pleasant.

PALATE Sweet banana toffee at first. Then chunky
and chewy malt. Finally cake icing.

FINISH Long. Like licking the cake icing bowl.

SCORE **77**

DAILUAINE 13-year-old, 1993
Connoisseurs Choice, 43 vol

COLOR Pale gold.

NOSE Restrained. Subtle. Flowery. Perfumy.

BODY Medium-full, sweet, and quite oily.

PALATE Sweet and clean barley. Green fruit.
Gooseberry. Some spice.

FINISH Quite short and spicy.

SCORE **73**

DAILUAINE 14-year-old, Duncan Taylor, N.C.2, 46 vol

COLOR Straw yellow.

NOSE Spring meadow. Floral. Lemon.

BODY Melon. Rich and sweet.

PALATE Lemon sherbet. Grapefruit squash. Refreshing.

FINISH Short and spicy.

SCORE **70**

DALLAS DHU

PRODUCER DCL
REGION Highlands   DISTRICT Speyside (Findhorn)
ADDRESS Forres, Morayshire, IV36 2RR
TEL 01309 676548   VC

THE NAME MEANS "black water valley." This Dallas accommodates a hamlet rather smaller than its indirect descendant in Texas (named after US Vice-president George Mifflin Dallas, who seems to have been of Scottish origin). The Dallas Dhu distillery was established in 1899. Despite a fire in 1939, it does not appear to have changed greatly. Latterly, its whisky appeared in the Benmore blends and vattings, and as Dallas Mhor single malt.

The distillery closed in 1983 and reopened to the public in 1988, under the aegis of Scotland's Historic Buildings and Monument Directorate. There are no plans to restart production, but the later batches continue to appear in independent bottlings.

HOUSE STYLE Silky, honeyish, sometimes chocolatey. After dinner.

DALLAS DHU 26-year-old, 1981, Duncan Taylor, 55.8 vol

COLOR	Pale yellow.
NOSE	Zesty lemon and lime sherbet. Lime soda. Perfumed bath salts.
BODY	Medium-full and pleasant.
PALATE	Honey. Vanilla. Barley. Citrus fruits. Clean and refreshing. Tastes sprightly for its years. Some late pepper.
FINISH	A delightful mix of fruit, barley, and spice. Lengthy.

SCORE **86**

THE DALMORE

PRODUCER Whyte and Mackay Ltd.
REGION Highlands   DISTRICT Northern Highlands
ADDRESS Alness, Morayshire, IV17 0UT
TEL 01349 882362   WEBSITE www.dalmoredistillery.co.uk

A RECORD PRICE FOR A BOTTLE OF WHISKY was established in 2002, when a Dalmore 62-year-old single malt was sold at auction to an anonymous bidder for just over $38,000/£25,000. Records are made to be broken, but this was a timely boost to the distillery, not long returned to Scottish ownership. The record-breaking sale took place at McTear's, the Glasgow auction house. The whisky was vatted from vintages of 1868, 1878, 1926, and 1939. Over the years, it had been racked several times, latterly in an oloroso sherry butt from Gonzalez Byass.

The man who makes the vattings and blendings for Whyte and Mackay, Richard Patterson, is one of the industry's extroverts. He may well have celebrated with a cigar. One of his creations is

Dalmore Gran Reserva, a rich whisky that is the ideal accompaniament to a fine Havana. It is easy to imagine the finest cigars being smoked in the oak-paneled offices at Dalmore. The panels previously graced a shooting lodge.

Dalmore, said to have been founded in 1839, was once owned by a distinguished local family, the Mackenzies, friends of James Whyte and Charles Mackay, who created a famous name in blended Scotch. Latterly, the proprietor was Jim Beam, of Kentucky. The management buy-out of Jim Beam's Scottish distilleries led to the restoration of the Whyte and Mackay name, and in 2007 the company was acquired by the Indian-based UB Group.

Dalmore has an unusual still-house. The wash stills have a conical upper chamber and the spirit stills are cooled with a water jacket— another distinctive feature. There are two pairs of stills, identical in shape but different sizes. The warehouses are by the waters of the Cromarty Firth. About 85 percent of the whisky is matured in bourbon casks, mainly first-fill, the rest in sweet oloroso and amontillado, but it is all married in sherry butts.

HOUSE STYLE Rich, flavorful, orange marmalade. After dinner.

THE DALMORE 12-year-old, 40 vol

COLOR Antique gold.

NOSE Vanilla fudge, thick-cut orange marmalade, sherry, and a whiff of leather.

BODY Velvety smooth.

PALATE Sherry and spice, plus delicate citrus notes.

FINISH Medium, with ginger, Seville oranges, and a hint of vanilla.

SCORE 81

THE DALMORE 15-year-old, 40 vol

COLOR Fresh copper.

NOSE Generous. Sweet. Toffee, medium sherry, and ripe oranges.

BODY Medium, firm. Lush malt and a drier, gingery nuttiness.

PALATE Sherry and Christmas spices.

FINISH Quite long and nutty, with final note of vanilla.

SCORE 83

THE DALMORE Gran Reserva, 40 vol

Formerly known as Cigar Malt. A marriage of Dalmore whiskies between
10 and 20 years old, mainly in the mid-teens.

COLOR Dark orange.

NOSE A soft smokiness. Suggestions of black chocolate and orange creams.

BODY Firm.

PALATE Rich, rounded. A hint of rum butter, then dryish and firm.
Hard caramel toffee. Hint of burned sugar. Faint smoke. Never cloying.
With the cigar, a complement rather than a contrast.

FINISH Light, smoky, wood bark, ground almonds, dryness.
Scores points for originality and for balance.

SCORE **81**

THE DALMORE 1263 King Alexander III, 40 vol

Matured in vintage oloroso and Madeira butts,
vintage bourbon barrels, and Cabernet Sauvignon barriques.

COLOR Warm amber.

NOSE Almonds, hedgerow berries, plums, brittle toffee,
and a faint whiff of treacle.

BODY Firm.

PALATE Complex, with sherry and fresh berries,
plums, vanilla, and toffee.

FINISH Blackcurrants and a tang of molasses. Lingering.

SCORE **83**

THE DALMORE 1973
Chateau Haut Marbuzet Cabernet Sauvignon, 40 vol

COLOR Ruby, with amber highlights.

NOSE Grape pulp, prunes, and fudge. Then soft fruit and honey.

BODY Medium, rounded.

PALATE Quite citric, with blackberries, licorice, and fruity red wine.

FINISH Long and spicy. Plums and persistent berries.

SCORE **83**

THE DALMORE 1974, 42 vol

COLOR Deep amber gold.

NOSE Chocolate orange, bananas, sweet sherry, and background coffee.

BODY Big and smooth.

PALATE Complex, with oranges, dark chocolate, walnuts, and old sherry.

FINISH Lengthy and fruity. Gently drying.

SCORE **85**

THE DALMORE 40-year-old, 40 vol

COLOR Rich amber.

NOSE Classic Dalmore: orange, plum pudding notes, background oak.

BODY Big and rounded.

PALATE Brittle toffee and bitter chocolate combine
with spicy orange and almonds.

FINISH Long and quite sweet. A touch of licorice.

SCORE **84**

THE DALMORE 50-year-old, 52.6 vol

Occasional bottlings. Some have contained proportions of far older whiskies, dating to 1868. The enjoyment is in the pleasure of tasting history. A whisky of this age has more memory than muscle. Available at the Sheraton Hotel, Edinburgh.

COLOR Chestnut.

NOSE Astonishingly, the fruit is still discernible. Perfumy, polished oak. Quickly moving to surprisingly fresh smokiness and oakiness.

BODY Has lost some fullness with age, but still some substance.

PALATE Orange, lemon pith, flowering currant, sap, oak, smoke.

FINISH Caramelized charred oak.

SCORE 85

THE DALMORE 62-year-old, 40.5 vol

COLOR Dark oak.

NOSE Hickory smoke. Mesquite. Or perhaps applewood. Very appetizing.

BODY Beeswax oiliness.

PALATE Orange. Mint. Menthol. Pipe tobacco. The big Dalmore flavors have settled down in harmonious maturity.

FINISH Mild. Surprising lack of woody astringency. There is even some sweetness.

SCORE 86

AN INDEPENDENT BOTTLING
DALMORE 18-year-old, Distilled 1990, Bottled 2009
Cask No 7329, Duncan Taylor, 56.7 vol

COLOR Gold, with copper highlights.

NOSE Mildly herbal, quite dry, and nutty.

BODY Rich.

PALATE Full and intensely sweet. Fruit bonbons and sugar-coated almonds, with a spicy kick.

FINISH Long; ultimately fruit candies.

SCORE 80

DALWHINNIE

PRODUCER Diageo
REGION Highlands DISTRICT Speyside
ADDRESS Dalwhinnie, Inverness-shire, PH19 1AB
TEL 01540 672219 VC
WEBSITE www.discovering-distilleries.com/www.malts.com

O NE OF THE HIGHEST DISTILLERIES in Scotland, at 1073 feet (326 meters), Dalwhinnie has the Monadhlaith Mountains to one side, and the Forest of Atholl, the Cairngorms, and the Grampians to the other. Its name is Gaelic for "meeting place." The village of the same name stands at the junction of old cattle-droving routes from the west and north down to the central Lowlands. Much whisky smuggling went on along this route. The distillery was called Strathspey when it opened in 1897.

HOUSE STYLE Lightly peaty. Cut grass and heather honey. Clear flavors against a very clean background. Aperitif.

DALWHINNIE 15-year-old, 43 vol

COLOR	Bright gold.
NOSE	Very aromatic, dry, faintly phenolic, lightly peaty.
BODY	Firm; slightly oily.
PALATE	Remarkably smooth; long-lasting flavor development. Aromatic, heather-honey notes give way to cut grass and malty sweetness, which intensifies to a sudden burst of peat.
FINISH	A long crescendo.

SCORE 76

DALWHINNIE 15-year-old,
Friends of the Classic Malts Bottling, 56.9 vol

COLOR Light gold.

NOSE Hard to get much on the nose: sulfur, guava,
coconut cream. Alcohol.

BODY Light and delicate.

PALATE Delicate, but with better weight than the nose suggests.
Tropical fruit. More about feel than aroma.

FINISH Crisp. Oaky.

SCORE **70**

DALWHINNIE 1980, Double Matured, 43 vol
Oloroso finish.

COLOR Sunny gold to bronze.

NOSE Oloroso sherry, licorice. Rooty, grassy.

BODY Firm, rounded.

PALATE Very sweet, toffeeish start. Honey. Lemons. Long flavor development
to peatiness, cut grass, vanilla, and fresh oak. Beautiful interplay and balance.
The sherry sweetness seems, by contrast, to accentuate the usually light
peatiness of Dalwhinnie.

FINISH Very long. Cut grass, peat, smoke, oak.

SCORE **79**

DALWHINNIE Distillers Edition, 1990, 43 vol

COLOR Copper orange.

NOSE Honey. Lots of sweet citrus. Some tangerine and mandarin.
Quite full and rich.

BODY Sweet. Soft. Treacly.

PALATE Honey. Juicy barley. Milk chocolate.
Late spice and pepper. Peat.

FINISH Quite long. Mix of honey, spice and peat.
Balanced and pleasant.

SCORE **86**

DEANSTON

PRODUCER Burn Stewart Distillers plc
REGION Highlands   DISTRICT Eastern Highlands
ADDRESS Deanston, near Doune, Perthshire, FK16 6AG
TEL 01786 841422   WEBSITE www.burnstewartdistillers.com
enquiries@burnstewartdistillers.com

THE TOWN OF DOUNE was known in the 17th century for the manufacture of pistols, some of which may have seen service on the Spanish Main. Now the old empire strikes back. The Trinidadian drinks company, Angostura, has acquired Burn Stewart, owners of the town's Deanston distillery. That enterprise itself has an interesting history. It is housed in a cotton mill, designed in 1785 by Richard Arkwright and extended in 1836. The mill was driven by the waters of the Teith River The supply of good water apparently contributed to the decision to turn the building into a distillery at a time when the whisky industry was doing very well.

It opened as the Deanston distillery in 1965–66, with the vaulted weaving shed serving as a warehouse. The distillery prospered during the 1970s, but closed during the difficult mid-1980s. At the time it was owned by Invergordon. With the growth of interest in single malts in the late 1980s and early 1990s, Deanston was bought by the blenders, Burn Stewart, and more versions of this pleasant whisky became available.

HOUSE STYLE Light, slightly oily, nutty, accented toward a notably clean, malty sweetness. Restorative.

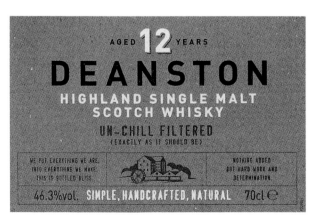

DEANSTON 12-year-old, 46.3 vol

COLOR Antique gold.

NOSE Fresh and fruity, with malt and honey.

BODY Medium

PALATE Cloves, ginger, honey, and malt.

FINISH Long, quite dry, and pleasantly herbal.

 SCORE **75**

DEANSTON 12-year-old, 40 vol

Exclusive to Marks & Spencer

COLOR Light gold.

NOSE New-mown hay, barley, toffee, honey, and fresh oak.

BODY Smooth.

PALATE Sweet, with vanilla, honey, and spices.

FINISH Medium in length and spicy, with attractive oak and cloves.

 SCORE **73**

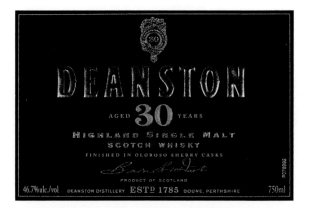

DEANSTON 30-year-old, 46.7 vol

Finished in an oloroso sherry cask.

COLOR Mid-gold.

NOSE Caramel, almonds, and chocolate orange.

BODY Firm.

PALATE Big and fruity, with developing green oak.

FINISH Medium to long. Nutty.

SCORE **75**

DUFFTOWN

PRODUCER Diageo
REGION Highlands   DISTRICT Speyside (Dufftown)
ADDRESS Dufftown, Keith, Banffshire, AB55 4BR
TEL 01340 822100   WEBSITE www.malts.com

THE EARL OF FIFE, James Duff, laid out this handsome, hilly little town of stone buildings in 1817. The town's name is pronounced "duff-ton." Dufftown lies at the confluence of the Fiddich and Dullan rivers on their way to the Spey. There are six active malt distilleries in the town; a further two survive as buildings but are highly unlikely ever to operate again. A ninth, Pittyvaich, has recently been bulldozed.

Only one of the distilleries appropriates Dufftown as its name. This distillery and Pittyvaich, its erstwhile next-door neighbor, were both owned by Bell's until that company was acquired by United Distillers, now Diageo. Dufftown's stone-built premises were a grain mill until 1896, but they have since sprouted a pagoda, and were twice expanded in the 1970s. They now comprise one of Diageo's larger distilleries, but most of its output goes into Bell's, the biggest selling blend in the UK.

HOUSE STYLE Aromatic, dry, malty. Aperitif.

SINGLETON OF DUFFTOWN, 40 vol

COLOR Deep gold.	
NOSE Vegetal. Rootsy. Toffee. Slight.	
BODY Unassertive. Inoffensive.	
PALATE Off-key and unimpressive. Sweet, with some barley and fruit, but wispy. Weak spice. Bland.	
FINISH Medium and spicy.	

SCORE **64**

AN INDEPENDENT BOTTLING
DUFFTOWN 1976, AD Rattray, 55.4 vol

COLOR Lemony yellow.
NOSE Flower cuttings. Freshly cut grass. Lemon Turkish delight.
BODY Sweet and creamy.
PALATE Sweet. Lime. A touch of anise. Celery. Barley.
FINISH Medium. Rootsy, with some oak and spice.

SCORE **75**

EDRADOUR

PRODUCER Signatory Vintage Scotch Whisky Co. Ltd.
REGION Highlands   DISTRICT Eastern Highlands
ADDRESS Pitlochry, Perthshire, PH16 5JP   TEL 01796 472095
WEBSITE www.edradour.co.uk   EMAIL info@edradour.fsbusiness.co.uk   VC

THE COUNTRY'S SMALLEST DISTILLERY was returned to Scottish— and independent—ownership in 2002. Edradour is a working commercial distillery on a farmhouse scale, using very old, open equipment, the function of which is easy to understand—a bonus for the visitor. It is near the inland resort of Pitlochry, and within easy reach of Edinburgh and Glasgow. The change in the ownership of Edradour was greeted with widespread goodwill.

With the much bigger Speyside distillery, Aberlour, it had for some years been a Scottish outpost of Pernod Ricard. With the acquisition of Chivas Brothers' ten distilleries, the French found their hands full. They had looked after Edradour well, but such a small distillery might benefit from ownership by an individual. It was sold to Andrew Symington, the enterprising founder of the independent bottler Signatory. A wide range of diverse Edradour bottlings have subsequently appeared, including single cask, cask strength variants, and numerous "finished" expressions, while heavily peated Edradour spirit has been distilled under the name Ballechin.

Edradour likes to trace its history back to the beginning of legal whisky production in the Highlands in 1825, although the present distillery is believed to have been founded in 1837. The distillery, at the hamlet of Balnauld, above Pitlochry, is secreted by the hills.

HOUSE STYLE Spicy. Minty. Creamy. After dinner.

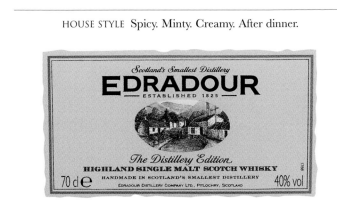

EDRADOUR 10-year-old, 40 vol

COLOR Antique gold.

NOSE Floral, with vanilla, caramel, and faintly earthy notes.

BODY Smooth.

PALATE Rich, sweet, spicy, and fruity.

FINISH Lengthy and sweet.

SCORE **81**

EDRADOUR 10-year-old, 1998, Un-chillfiltered, 46 vol

COLOR Gold with amber highlights.

NOSE Sweet orange marmalade, fresh cut flowers, caramel, mild licorice.

BODY Smooth and rounded.

PALATE Butterscotch, spice, mild pepper.

FINISH Medium to long; spicy.

SCORE **83**

EDRADOUR 12-year-old, 1995, Cask No 460, 57.2 vol

COLOR Mid-amber.

NOSE Nougat, ripe oranges, and golden raisins.

BODY Slightly oily and full.

PALATE Spicy malt, dried fruits, and a hint of warm leather.

FINISH Long and mildly gingery.

SCORE **84**

EDRADOUR 2003, Port Cask Matured, Cask No 378, 46 vol

Released August 2008

COLOR Bronze with pink highlights.

NOSE Clean and fragrant, with cherries and summer berries.

BODY Medium.

PALATE Fruity, with pineapples and red wine.

FINISH Lengthy, with slightly smoky raspberry jam.

SCORE **83**

EDRADOUR 10-year-old, 1997, Straight from the Cask, D'Yquem Finish, 57.7 vol

COLOR Pale gold.

NOSE Medium-sweet, with apricots and nougat.

BODY Rounded.

PALATE Sweet, with chocolate orange, almonds, and instant coffee.

FINISH Long, spicy, and nutty.

SCORE **83**

EDRADOUR 10-year-old, 1998, Straight from the Cask, Sherry Finish, Cask No 325, 58.1 vol

COLOR Bright amber.

NOSE Slightly menthol; medium sherry.

BODY Rich.

PALATE Full and rounded. Big, leathery, fruity sherry flavors.

FINISH Medium to long. Golden raisins, leather, and spice.

SCORE **84**

EDRADOUR 10-year-old, 1998, Straight from the Cask, Sassicaia Finish, 58.1 vol

COLOR Rosé.

NOSE Rich, scented, and creamy.

BODY Medium.

PALATE Mellow, with summer berries, custard, and milk chocolate notes.

FINISH The chocolate darkens slightly and spices develop.

SCORE **83**

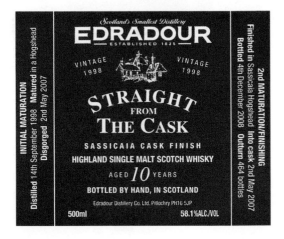

EDRADOUR 11-year-old, 1997, Straight from the Cask, Moscatel Finish, 58.3 vol

COLOR Amber with golden highlights.

NOSE Aerosol furniture polish, candied lemon, and pepper.

BODY Soft and rounded.

PALATE Quite dry. Fruit notes. Slightly herbal.

FINISH Medium, drying.

SCORE **81**

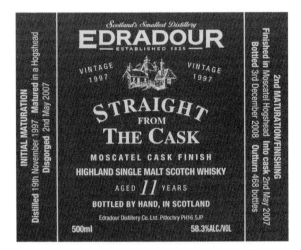

EDRADOUR 12-year-old, 1996, Straight from the Cask, Madeira Finish, 56.7 vol

COLOR Pale gold.

NOSE Raisins, wax, and citrus fruits.

BODY Lush.

PALATE Soft toffee and cinnamon.

FINISH Lengthy, with intensifying ginger and pepper notes.

SCORE **82**

EDRADOUR 12-year-old, 1995, Straight from the Cask, Chardonnay Finish, 56.9 vol

COLOR Amber.

NOSE Dense and aromatic. Prunes, new leather, and mild smoke.

BODY Medium to full.

PALATE Very focused fruitiness; developing spiciness.

FINISH Long, with slightly rubbery spice.

SCORE **81**

EDRADOUR 12-year-old, 1996, Straight from the Cask, Port Wood Finish, 57 vol

COLOR Pale gold with copper highlights.

NOSE Very fruity, with sweet, musky wine.

BODY Syrupy.

PALATE Rich and gingery, with developing confectionery notes.

FINISH Long and peppery.

SCORE 82

EDRADOUR 25-year-old, 1983, Port Wood Finish, 52.5 vol

COLOR Bright copper.

NOSE Soft and mature. Cherries, golden raisins, and a whiff of smoke.

BODY Quite full.

PALATE Fruity and intense, with emerging mild licorice.

FINISH Raisins and slightly bitter oak.

SCORE 82

EDRADOUR Ballechin, Discovery Series, Burgundy, 46 vol (2006)

COLOR Antique gold.

NOSE Soft peat and strawberries. Developing nut and coal notes.

BODY Rounded.

PALATE Very spicy peat smoke. Quite dry, with emerging blackcurrants and coffee.

FINISH Medium in length, with malt and lingering peat.

SCORE 81

EDRADOUR Ballechin, Discovery Series, Madeira, 46 vol (2007)

COLOR Pale gold.

NOSE Dairy barns, dried flowers, charcoal, and background peat.

BODY Soft.

PALATE Slightly herbal, with almonds, discreet peat, and oatmeal.

FINISH Medium to long, sweetish peat, closing with paprika.

SCORE 82

EDRADOUR Ballechin, Discovery Series, Port, 46 vol (2008)

COLOR Light gold.

NOSE Mild iodine, nutty, spicy peat, summer fruits.

BODY Medium and silky.

PALATE Apricots and ginger, with a splash of cream.

FINISH Spicy, with developing peat.

SCORE 84

FETTERCAIRN

PRODUCER Whyte and Mackay Ltd.
REGION Highlands   DISTRICT Eastern Highlands
ADDRESS Distillery Road, Fettercairn, near Laurencekirk,
Kincardineshire, AB30 1YE   TEL 01561 340244   VC

THE ESTATE OF THE GLADSTONE FAMILY, who provided Queen Victoria with a famous Prime Minister, accommodates Fettercairn. This pretty, cream-painted distillery is amid farmers' fields on the edge of the village of attractive Georgian cottages from which it takes its name. The distillery was founded in 1824, and that date is now incorporated in the names of the whiskies. A malt called Fettercairn 1824, at 12 years old, was introduced to replace the previous 10-year-old bottling in 2001. It is pleasing to see that there have subsequently been a number of limited edition "house" bottlings of this often neglected single malt.

HOUSE STYLE Lightly earthy, nutty.
Easy drinking or aperitif.

FETTERCAIRN 1824, 12-year-old, 40 vol

COLOR Pale amber, with golden highlights.

NOSE Fresh and light. Caramel and faint peat.

BODY Medium.

PALATE Medium-dry and nutty. Perfumed toffee.

FINISH Medium length. Spice and subtle peat. Slightly metallic.

SCORE **77**

FETTERCAIRN American White Oak Cask, 15-year-old, 62.6 vol

COLOR Bright gold.

NOSE Attractive floral notes, vanilla, and honey.

BODY Medium, silky.

PALATE Well-balanced. Toffee, hazelnuts, and marzipan.

FINISH Medium in length, persistently honeyed, and spicy.

SCORE **78**

FETTERCAIRN Spanish Oak Cask, 15-year-old, 64 vol

COLOR Dark oak.

NOSE Malt, caramel, spice, and Demerara sugar.

BODY Full.

PALATE Bold sherry, hints of honey, and licorice. Developing
spices and pepper.

FINISH Medium to long. Drying, with bitter chocolate notes.

SCORE **79**

FETTERCAIRN 23-year-old, Cask Strength, 52 vol

COLOR Mahogany.

NOSE Rich, with dark sherry, stewed fruits, spices, and molasses.

BODY Full.

PALATE Sweet and fruity. Nuts and smoky toffee.

FINISH Dries quite quickly, with walnuts, a lick of licorice, and oak.

SCORE **78**

AN INDEPENDENT BOTTLING
FETTERCAIRN 1992, Gordon & MacPhail, 46 vol

COLOR Pale gold, with copper highlights.

NOSE Initially vegetal. Nuts and faint sherry.

BODY Soft.

PALATE Malt, hazelnuts, cedar, and spice.

FINISH Drying, with gentle oak and spice notes.

SCORE **74**

GLEN ALBYN

PRODUCER DCL
REGION Highlands   DISTRICT Speyside (Inverness)
SITE OF FORMER DISTILLERY Telford Street, Inverness,
Inverness-shire, IV3 5LD

A COMPUTER SUPERSTORE AND a home-improvement store now stand on the site in Inverness once occupied by Glen Albyn, a distillery for 140 years, founded by a Provost (Mayor) of the city generally regarded as the capital of the Highlands. Before the distillery, there was a brewery on the site. There is still a small pub, The Caley. The site is alongside one of Scotland's great feats of engineering, the Caledonian Canal, the dream of James Watt and Thomas Telford. The canal links the North Sea with the Atlantic by joining Loch Ness with a series of further lochs in the Great Glen (also known in parts as Glen Albyn or Glen Mor, More, or Mhor). There is an unconnected Glen Albyn pub in the center of Inverness. Albyn is a variation on Albion or Alba, old names applied to Scotland, especially the Highlands.

The shopping strip from nowhere (or everywhere?) has not yet buried the individuality, the sensuous pleasure, and the Scottish pride afforded by a local distillery. There is still whisky, but for how long?

HOUSE STYLE Light. Fruity, nutty, dry. Aperitif.

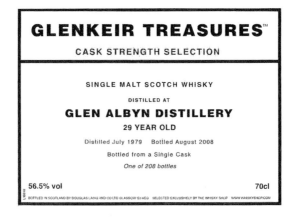

GLEN ALBYN 29-year-old,
Glenkeir Treasures, 56.5 vol

208 bottles.

COLOR Deep bronze.

NOSE Vegetal. Artichoke. Cucumber. Green.

BODY Surprisingly rich after the nose.

PALATE Rich honey. Woody spice. Some anise. Crystallized barley.
Almost syrupy. A nice balance of flavors.

FINISH Medium, pleasant, and rounded.

SCORE **85**

GLEN ALBYN 1979, 29-year-old,
Rarest of the Rare, 53.2 vol

COLOR Lemon with a green tinge.

NOSE Light. Floral. Lime. Lemon cleaner. A touch spicy.

BODY Rich, full, and creamy.

PALATE Soft and full. Sweet, rich. Very clean and rounded.
Big, full barley flavor. Sweet spices.

FINISH Medium. Sweet. Syrupy.

SCORE **83**

GLEN ALBYN 1975, Gordon & MacPhail, 46 vol

COLOR Pale gold with copper highlights.

NOSE Citrus fruit, buttery caramel, gentle smoke.

BODY Soft.

PALATE Slightly peaty, with spicy malt.

FINISH Fruity creaminess persists.

SCORE **74**

GLEN ELGIN

PRODUCER **Diageo**
REGION Highlands   DISTRICT Speyside (Lossie)
ADDRESS Longmorn, Elgin, Morayshire, IV30 3SL
TEL 01343 862000

Glen elgin has a small but passionate fan base and there are plenty who believe its whisky deserves more prominence as a single malt. The cask strength 16-year-old bottling has done much to reinforce the case. It follows a well-liked and respected "hidden malts" bottling that was released a few years ago.

The distillery itself has never been hidden, but it was for some years heavily branded with the name White Horse, in recognition of its contribution to that blend. The Glen Elgin distillery is very visible on one of the main roads into the town whose name it bears. Although it is just over a hundred years old, its façade dates from 1964, and reflects the classic DCL still-house design of the period.

Where the Lossie River approaches the town of Elgin, there are no fewer than eight distilleries within a few miles. Elgin is also worth a visit for Gordon & MacPhail's whisky shop as well as 13th-century cathedral ruins.

HOUSE STYLE Honey and tangerines.
Restorative or after dinner.

GLEN ELGIN 12 year-old, Hidden Malts, 43 vol

COLOR Deep gold.

NOSE Fruity and flowery. Heather honey.
Pears poached in spices. Hint of coffee beans.

BODY Light but firm.

PALATE Fresh and crisp, flowery, and gingery. A touch of mandarin orange.

FINISH Dry and spicy.

SCORE **77**

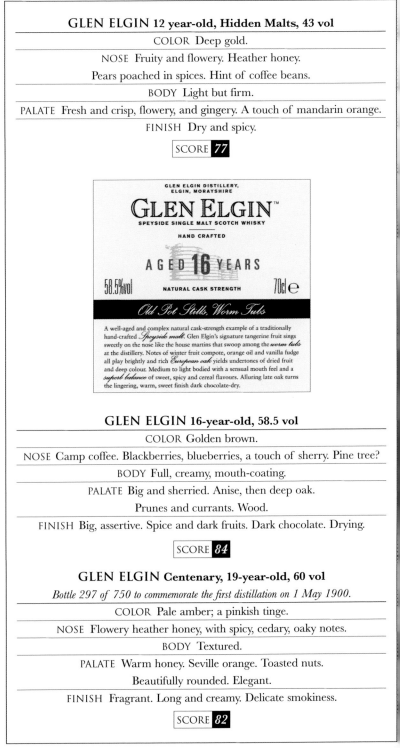

GLEN ELGIN DISTILLERY,
ELGIN, MORAYSHIRE

GLEN ELGIN™

SPEYSIDE SINGLE MALT SCOTCH WHISKY

HAND CRAFTED

A G E D **16** Y E A R S

58.5%vol   NATURAL CASK STRENGTH   70cl e

Old Pot Stills, Worm Tubs

A well-aged and complex natural cask-strength example of a traditionally hand-crafted *Speyside malt*. Glen Elgin's signature tangerine fruit sings sweetly on the nose like the house martins that swoop among the *worm tubs* at the distillery. Notes of winter fruit compote, orange oil and vanilla fudge all play brightly and rich *European oak* yields undertones of dried fruit and deep colour. Medium to light bodied with a sensual mouth feel and a *superb balance* of sweet, spicy and cereal flavours. Alluring late oak turns the lingering, warm, sweet finish dark chocolate-dry.

GLEN ELGIN 16-year-old, 58.5 vol

COLOR Golden brown.

NOSE Camp coffee. Blackberries, blueberries, a touch of sherry. Pine tree?

BODY Full, creamy, mouth-coating.

PALATE Big and sherried. Anise, then deep oak.
Prunes and currants. Wood.

FINISH Big, assertive. Spice and dark fruits. Dark chocolate. Drying.

SCORE **84**

GLEN ELGIN Centenary, 19-year-old, 60 vol

Bottle 297 of 750 to commemorate the first distillation on 1 May 1900.

COLOR Pale amber; a pinkish tinge.

NOSE Flowery heather honey, with spicy, cedary, oaky notes.

BODY Textured.

PALATE Warm honey. Seville orange. Toasted nuts.
Beautifully rounded. Elegant.

FINISH Fragrant. Long and creamy. Delicate smokiness.

SCORE **82**

GLEN ELGIN 32-year-old, Distilled 1971,
Special Release 2003, 42.3 vol

COLOR Full gold.

NOSE Fragrant. Cedary. Honeyed. Seductive.

BODY Soft, rich, tongue-coating.

PALATE Clean, sweet. A hint of Seville orange. Intense heather honey. Cereal grain. Crunchy. A lovely whisky.

FINISH Gently drying. Shortbread.

SCORE **81**

GLEN ELGIN Managers' Choice, Distilled 1998,
Bottled 2009, 61.1 vol

Matured in a rejuvenated European oak cask.

COLOR Autumn gold, with copper highlights.

NOSE Furniture polish and brittle toffee. Raisins, prunes, and spice.

BODY Smooth.

PALATE Oranges and peaches, then root ginger and black pepper.

FINISH Drying to licorice.

SCORE **79**

A COUPLE OF INDEPENDENT BOTTLINGS

GLEN ELGIN 1991, Duncan Taylor, N.C.2, 46 vol

COLOR Golden orange. NOSE Sherry, sulfur, and fruit. BODY Complex and assertive. PALATE Grungy. Smoke, intense fruit, and some sulfury smoke. Aggressive and evolving. FINISH Long and industrial. SCORE 72

GLEN ELGIN 16-year-old, Old Malt Cask, 50 vol

COLOR Brass. NOSE Toffee. Root ginger. Key lime pie. Lemon meringue. BODY Clean. Pleasant. Balanced. Sweet. PALATE Clean and sweet peach and apricot. Spice. FINISH Pleasant and sweet. Some cinnamon. SCORE 70

GLEN GARIOCH

PRODUCER Morrison Bowmore Distillers Ltd.
REGION Highlands   DISTRICT Eastern Highlands
ADDRESS Oldmeldrum, Inverurie, Aberdeenshire, AB51 0ES
TEL 01651 873450   WEBSITE www.glengarioch.com   VC

G LEN GARIOCH IS ONE OF SCOTLAND'S hidden, or even forgotten, gems. It is owned by Morrison Bowmore, whose focus has been on Bowmore and, most recently, Auchentoshan. Taste-wise Glen Garioch is confusing. Its historical peatiness has been less obvious in recent years, but peated Glen Garioch bottlings can still be found. The distillery has a delightful and relatively new visitor center and is worth a short diversion if you're heading from Aberdeen to the heart of Speyside. Certainly the distillery has a good story to tell.

First, there is the distillery's antiquity. An announcement in *The Aberdeen Journal* in 1785 refers to a licensed distillery on the same site. This makes it Scotland's oldest license holder. Then there is location. The glen grows some of Scotland's finest barley—and here is one of the few distilleries with its own malting floors. Finally, there is the question of peat. When the distillery was acquired by its present owners, in 1970, their maltster, trained on Islay, was relatively heavy-handed with the peat. The result was a whisky with the "old-fashioned," smoky flavor that the Highland/Speyside region had largely forgotten. The revival of smoky Highlander could be popular at a time when the island whiskies seem to have seized the initiative.

Production stopped in 1995, but distillation restarted in 1997. The building's stonework, decorated with a clock that might grace a municipal building, faces on to the small town of Oldmeldrum, on the road from Aberdeen to Banff.

HOUSE STYLE Lightly peaty, flowery, fragrant, spicy.
Aperitif in younger ages. Digestif when older.

GLEN GARIOCH Highland Tradition, 40 vol

COLOR Gold.

NOSE Attractive, malty. Fresh, mandarin orange zest. Simple but charming.

BODY Light.

PALATE Fresh and direct. Lively summer fruits. Malty.

FINISH Short but refreshing.

SCORE 75

GLEN GARIOCH 8-year-old, 40 vol

COLOR Full gold.

NOSE Autumn leaves, grass, a hint of peat.

BODY Medium, smooth.

PALATE Malty start. Buttery, but very clean. Then flapjack; nutty, lively flavors.

FINISH Late surge of ginger, honey, and heather.

SCORE 76

GLEN GARIOCH 10-year-old, 40 vol

COLOR Gold.

NOSE Aromatic and citric. Lemon icing, canned peach, bran. New carpets. Drier with water.

BODY Rounded but crisp.

PALATE Cereal with a creamy note playing off the firm maltiness.

FINISH Nutty. Short.

SCORE 75

GLEN GARIOCH 12 year-old, 40 vol

Mainly for Asian markets.

COLOR Bronze.

NOSE Fragrant, leafy peatiness. A touch of dry oloroso?

BODY Medium. Firm.

PALATE Interlocked heather-honey sweetness and peat-smoke dryness.

FINISH Echoes of both elements. Quick and warming.

SCORE 77

GLEN GARIOCH 15-year-old, 43 vol

COLOR Full gold.

NOSE Good whiff of earthy peat. Oily smoke. Very aromatic.

BODY Medium. Rich.

PALATE Very gradual development from malty, licorice-like, rooty notes through to heathery, flowery, perfumy smokiness. Full of character.

FINISH Very long, spicy, and warming.

SCORE 79

GLEN GARIOCH 12-year-old, 40 vol

Special bottling for the National Trust of Scotland.

COLOR Rich gold.

NOSE Tea bread, raisins, maltings, some sweetness.
Chocolate too.

BODY Medium.

PALATE Bran provides a crisp frame.
Dried fruits with some richness. Lunchtime.

FINISH Hay loft.

SCORE 75

INDEPENDENT BOTTLINGS

**GLEN GARIOCH 20-year-old, Distilled 1988, Bottled 2009
Cask No 1558, Duncan Taylor, 54.4 vol**

COLOR Mid-bronze.

NOSE Perfumed, with over-ripe melons, caramel,
new leather, and cinnamon.

BODY Full.

PALATE Full-on peppery oak, with underlying succulent fruits.

FINISH Medium in length. Relatively hot.

SCORE 76

GLEN GARIOCH 12-year-old, Provenance, 46 vol

COLOR Light lemon yellow.

NOSE Shy. Oil paint. Lemon seeds. Dusty.

BODY Medium and sweet.

PALATE Oily. Unassertive. Hints of spice. Tired.

FINISH Medium sweet.

SCORE 64

**GLEN GARIOCH 16-year-old,
Old Malt Cask, 50 vol**

COLOR Rich gold.

NOSE Spiced apple. Some peat. Sherried red fruits.

BODY Creamy and full.

PALATE Squidgy peach and apricot, then a rich and peaty underlay.

FINISH Peaty, spicy, medium-long, and fruity.

SCORE 82

GLEN GRANT

PRODUCER Campari Group
REGION Highlands   DISTRICT Speyside (Rothes)
ADDRESS Rothes, Morayshire, AB38 7BS   TEL 01340 832118   VC

A CHIC SUCCESS IN ITALY, and a Victorian classic in Scotland. Glen Grant was the lone single malt in many a bar from Glasgow to Genoa in the days when this form of whisky was scarcely known outside the Highlands. The distillery, founded in 1840 by John and James Grant, quickly gained a reputation for the quality of its whisky. James Grant, who was a prominent local politician, played a big part in bringing railroads to the area, and they in turn distributed his product. The turreted and gabled offices in the "Scottish baronial" style, and the distillery, are set around a small courtyard. James Grant's son, a military major, brought plants from his travels in India and Africa, and created a garden in the glen behind the distillery. In 1995, the garden was restored and is open to visitors.

For the greater part of its history, Glen Grant won its renown as a single malt in versions bottled by merchants. Older vintages can still be found bearing in small type the name of bottlers Gordon & MacPhail. Glen Grant is highly regarded by blenders and has long been a contributor to Chivas Regal. Indeed, the distillery and its brand were formerly owned by Chivas, but in 2006 the Italian-based company Campari acquired them, and instigated a welcome program of occasional single cask, vintage, and other limited edition releases.

HOUSE STYLE Herbal, with notes of hazelnut.
In younger ages, it works as an aperitif; with greater
age and sherry influence, it becomes an after-dinner malt.

GLEN GRANT 5-year-old, 40 vol

COLOR	Very pale; white wine.
NOSE	Light. Dry fruitiness. Spirity.
BODY	Light. Slightly sticky, almost resiny.
PALATE	Spirity. Pear brandy.
FINISH	Fruity, quick.

SCORE 65

GLEN GRANT Single Malt, No Age Statement, 40 vol

COLOR Gold.

NOSE Fruity, flowery, nutty, faintly spirity.

BODY Light but firm.

PALATE Dry. Slightly astringent at first, becoming soft and nutty.

FINISH Herbal.

SCORE **74**

GLEN GRANT 10-year-old, 43 vol

COLOR Full gold.

NOSE Still dry, but much softer, with some sweetness.

BODY Light to medium, with no obvious intervention of sherry.

PALATE Lightly sweet start, quickly becoming nutty and very dry.

FINISH Very dry, with herbal notes.

SCORE **76**

GLEN GRANT Cask Strength, 15-year-old, 59.9 vol

The first ever official, single cask, cask strength Glen Grant. 378 bottles.

COLOR Amber, with golden highlights.

NOSE Quite dry and fruity, with a hint of malt.

BODY Medium.

PALATE Rich and fruity, featuring peaches, barley sugar, ginger and pepper.

FINISH Medium to long, with persistent spice,

and lingering fresh fruit.

SCORE **83**

GLEN GRANT 1992 Cellar Reserve, 46 vol

COLOR Pale gold.

NOSE Medium-sweet, with ripening pears. Slightly heathery.

BODY Rounded.

PALATE Fresh fruit and malt, with developing nuttiness.

FINISH Medium in length, with hazelnuts and ginger.

SCORE 81

SOME INDEPENDENT BOTTLINGS

GLEN GRANT 11-year-old, Distilled 1995, Dewar Rattray, 59.9 vol

COLOR Bright gold.

NOSE Initially slightly spirity—yeast, almonds, and black pepper.

BODY Quite full.

PALATE Fairly dry, nutty, and spicy. More black pepper.

FINISH Austere.

SCORE 74

GLEN GRANT 13-year-old, Duthie's, 46 vol

COLOR Gold, with bronze highlights.

NOSE Yeast, cereal, and perfumed. Grassy notes.

BODY Light.

PALATE Delicate malt, almonds, and pears.

FINISH Short and straightforward.

SCORE 77

GLEN GRANT 1973, Berry's Own Selection, 46 vol

COLOR Bright bronze.

NOSE Honey, vanilla, sweet sherry, chocolate fondant orange.

BODY Smooth.

PALATE Very fruity: oranges, nuts, lots of spice. Slight sherried smokiness.

FINISH Lengthy, with ginger and nutty oak.

SCORE 83

GLEN GRANT 36-year-old, Distilled 1972, Bottled 2009
Cask No 8948, Duncan Taylor, 46.2 vol

COLOR Light gold.

NOSE Talcum powder, roses, and deeper Madeira notes.

BODY Silky.

PALATE Drier and nuttier than the nose; developing floral, ripe peach notes.

FINISH Medium in length, with ginger and apricots.

SCORE 82

GLEN MHOR

PRODUCER DCL
REGION Highlands   DISTRICT Speyside (Inverness)
SITE OF FORMER DISTILLERY Telford Street, Inverness, Inverness-shire, IV3 5LU

Purists pronounce it the Gaelic way, "Glen Vawr," to rhyme with "law." The distillery, built in 1892 in Inverness and demolished in 1986, was one of several at which the poet, novelist, and pioneering whisky writer, Neil Gunn, worked as an exciseman. In his book, *Scotch Missed*, Brian Townsend writes that Gunn was inspired by Glen Mhor to let slip his observation that "until a man has had the luck to chance upon a perfectly matured malt, he does not really know what whisky is." Even in Gunn's day, Glen Mhor could be found as a single malt, and casks still find their way into independent bottlings.

HOUSE STYLE Aromatic, syrupy. Quite sweet. With dessert or after dinner.

GLEN MHOR 32-year-old, 1975, Rarest of the Rare, 40.5 vol

COLOR Honey gold.
NOSE Delicate. Old lady's perfume. Talcum powder dust.
BODY Insubstantial and slight.
PALATE Soft fruit. Banana and orange pulp. But gives way to a big wave of oak and pepper.
FINISH Bitter and woody.

SCORE 65

GLEN MORAY

PRODUCER La Martiniquaise
REGION Highlands DISTRICT Speyside (Lossie)
ADDRESS Bruceland Road, Elgin, Morayshire, IV30 1YE
TEL 01343 542577 WEBSITE www.glenmoray.com

THE GRAPEY NOTE that some find in Glen Moray is a house characteristic that preceded the distillery's enthusiasm for wine finishes, such as Vallée du Rhône. The earlier Chardonnay and Chenin Blanc finishes, launched in 1999, seemed to be aimed at ladies who lunch. The use of whites was an innovation in the industry. Until its purchase in 2008 by French-based La Martiniquaise, Glen Moray shared owners with the more northerly Glenmorangie distillery, which pioneered the notion of "wine" finishes, but with reds, port, and madeira.

The two distilleries' similar names pre-date their common ownership. It is a second coincidence that both were formerly breweries. Glen Moray was converted into a distillery in 1897, acquired by Macdonald & Muir (which later became Glenmorangie plc) in the 1920s, and extended in 1958. Its whiskies are admired, but have never enjoyed great glamour. Now they sport a change of orientation: skirts instead of kilts—the distillery previously favored gift tins decorated with the liveries of Highland regiments. The smartly kept distillery is in boggy land near the Lossie River, just outside Elgin.

HOUSE STYLE Grassy, with barley notes. Aperitif.

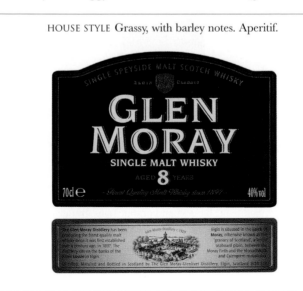

GLEN MORAY 8-year-old, 43 vol
Mainly available in Italy.

COLOR Very pale, satiny gold.

NOSE Fresh but soft. Sweet, with a late, oily hint of peat.

BODY Very light, but smooth and oily.

PALATE Very light indeed. Oily. Gin-like.

FINISH Light touch of cereal-grain firmness. Late, very light,
smoky warmth.

SCORE **71**

GLEN MORAY Single Speyside Malt, No Age Statement, 40 vol
Six to ten years in bourbon casks, then "mellowed" in Chardonnay.

COLOR Very pale gold.

NOSE Fresh, scented, fruity. Like an unpeeled dessert grape.
Perhaps a suggestion of banana. Very light hint of the sea.

BODY Very soft, textured.

PALATE Watermelon. Banana. White chocolate.
Lightly creamy. Shortbread.

FINISH Grape skins. Apple cores. Hay. Cereal grains.
Lightly dry and very crisp.

SCORE **78**

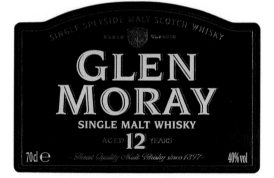

GLEN MORAY 12-year-old, 40 vol
"Mellowed" in Chenin Blanc casks.

COLOR Softer, more yellowy.

NOSE Pears. Walnuts. Fresh oak.

BODY Smooth, oily. Beeswax. Honeyed.

PALATE Pears in cream. Late, lively, peachy fruitiness. Garden mint.

FINISH Raisiny. Also resiny. Fresh oak. Soothing warmth.

SCORE **76**

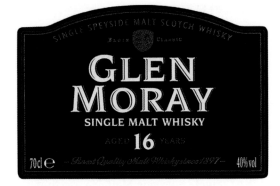

GLEN MORAY 16-year-old, 40 vol

COLOR Old gold.

NOSE Very aromatic. Hint of cloves. Apples, Tannin.

BODY Smooth and very firm.

PALATE More assertive. Toffee, apple, oak.

FINISH Long. Hints of peat. Grassy. Leafy, Resiny. Peppery.

SCORE **76**

GLEN MORAY 30-year-old, 43 vol

COLOR Bright gold.

NOSE Floral and elegant, with vanilla, nutmeg,
and a whiff of background smoke.

BODY Medium, oily.

PALATE Fruity and spicy, with lavender, eucalyptus, and nutty vanilla.

FINISH Medium to long. Elegant, with gentle oak, dates,
and creamy vanilla.

SCORE **79**

GLEN MORAY Mountain Oak Malt,
The Final Release (1991), 58.6 vol

*Matured in "A unique selection of toasted and charred mountain
oak casks from North America."*

COLOR Deep amber.

NOSE Chewy toffee, orange candies, nutmeg,
and vanilla. A hint of mint.

BODY Firm.

PALATE Pears, pineapples, soft fudge. Developing
hazelnuts, molasses, and ginger.

FINISH Lengthy, with tobacco, ginger, and a touch of pepper.

SCORE **80**

SOME VINTAGE EDITIONS OF GLEN MORAY
GLEN MORAY 1974, Port Wood Aged,
Limited Edition, Bottled 1997

COLOR Full gold.

NOSE Lovely, perfumy complexity.

BODY Far richer than other versions.

PALATE Oily cereal grain. Honey-roast nuts.

FINISH Perfumy again. Sugar-coated almonds. An after-dinner malt of extraordinary delicacy. Beautiful balance of distillery character and port.

SCORE 80

GLEN MORAY 1973, 43 vol

COLOR Pale gold, with a tinge of green.

NOSE Very sweet, but still extremely clean.

BODY Very smooth indeed.

PALATE Very complex, with lots of development of sweet (barley, malt, and chocolate) and delicately spicy notes.

FINISH Light sweetness and light peatiness. Long and lingering, with surges of flavor.

SCORE 78

GLEN MORAY 1966, 43 vol

COLOR Solid amber.

NOSE Nutty, juicy, oaky, but fresh.

BODY Smooth, soft.

PALATE Nutty dryness, malty sweetness, and a hint of grassy peatiness. Beautifully balanced and rounded. A confident, elegant malt.

FINISH Sweetness and dryness, with the latter eventually winning. Touches of sappy oakiness. A curiously spicy lift at the very end.

SCORE 80

GLEN MORAY 1959, Bottled 1999, 48.4 vol

COLOR Full amber.

NOSE Rich fruitcake steeped in sherry.

BODY Very creamy indeed.

PALATE Rich. Fruitcake. The dryness of burned currants. Intensely nutty: almondy; marzipan development.

FINISH Light, nutty dryness. Chewy. Long. Developing a touch of charred oak.

SCORE 79

GLEN ORD

PRODUCER Diageo
REGION Highlands DISTRICT Northern Highlands
ADDRESS Muir of Ord, Ross-shire, IV6 7UJ TEL 01463 872004
WEBSITE www.discovering-distilleries.com/www.malts.com VC

THE LAUNCH IN 2003 of a 12-year-old "Hidden Malt" from Glen Ord was very welcome, but begged a question. Why was it hidden in the first place? Why has this distillery been obliged to play hide-and-seek over the years? Under different managements, its whisky has occupied endless different positions in the marketing portfolio. It has even sported different names: Glenordie, Ordie, Ord, Muir of Ord. The latest addition to the list is the Singleton of Glen Ord, a version containing more sherry casks than normal and targeted at the Asian market, and particularly Taiwan, where sherry seems to appeal to the palate. The original 12-year-old is becoming increasingly hard to find in the European market.

It is at a village called Muir of Ord ("the moor by the hill"), just to the west and north of Inverness. This is the region where Ferintosh, the first famous whisky, was made. Glen Ord also has a maltings (of the drum type). The distillery and maltings look over the barley-growing country of the Black Isle.

HOUSE STYLE Flavorsome, rose-like, spicy (cinnamon?),
and malty, with a dry finish. After dinner.

GLEN ORD 12-year-old, Hidden Malt, 43 vol

COLOR Full gold.

NOSE Fresh. Turned earth, daffodils. Resiny. Golden raisins.
Malt. A hint of sulfur.

BODY Medium, firm.

PALATE Dry grass, warm cinnamon, then toffee.
A good punch.

FINISH Malt and oak.

SCORE 78

THE SINGLETON OF GLEN ORD 12-year-old, 40 vol

Matured in sherry and bourbon casks.

COLOR Rich gold.

NOSE Floral, sweet sherry, marzipan, ripe plums, and peaches.

BODY Soft and rounded.

PALATE Full, malty, approachable, with sherry, cinnamon, and hazelnuts.

FINISH Initial cough lozenges, followed by soft fruit, rose petals, and mild oak tannins.

SCORE **82**

GLEN ORD 1974, 23-year-old, Rare Malts, 60.8 vol

COLOR Very pale primrose.

NOSE Very fresh, assertive. Leafy, lightly peaty. Fragrant smoke.

BODY Big, soft, slightly syrupy.

PALATE Nutty malt, raisins, ginger, lemon peel, roses.

FINISH Spicy, flowery, peaty.

SCORE **78**

GLEN ORD 18-year-old, Old Malt Cask, 50 vol

COLOR Greeny yellow.

NOSE Banana toffee. Vanilla.

BODY Medium, soft, and sweet.

PALATE Spearmint. Sweet fluffy apple. Melon. Pleasant.

FINISH Very sweet and fruity, with some late spices.

SCORE **81**

GLEN SCOTIA

PRODUCER Loch Lomond Distillery Co. Ltd.
REGION Campbeltown
ADDRESS 12 High Street, Campbeltown, Argyll, PA28 6DS
TEL 01586 552288 *Visits by appointment only*
EMAIL mail@lochlomonddistillery.com

ALONG WITH GLENGYLE AND SPRINGBANK, Glen Scotia is one of the last survivors in the Campbeltown malt whisky region, and the distillery has suffered during the past few decades from periods of silence and lack of investment.

A major program of renovation took place between 1979 and 1982, but production has been relatively sporadic ever since. Under the ownership of the Loch Lomond company, Glen Scotia currently distills only some 100,000 liters of spirit per year, which is just a meager 15 percent of its total capacity.

In 2005 a 12-year-old bottling was released to replace the previous 14-year-old. It seems that the present owners are paying more attention to cask selection than was sometimes the case under previous regimes.

Founded around 1832, Glen Scotia is known for more than one manifestation of spirit: it is said to be haunted by the ghost of a former proprietor who drowned himself in Campbeltown Loch.

HOUSE STYLE Fresh, salty. Aperitif, or with salty foods.

GLEN SCOTIA 12-year-old, 40 vol

COLOR Gold.

NOSE Fruity peat smoke and buttery malt. Mildly maritime.

BODY Oily.

PALATE Sweet, resinous, with smoke and nuts.

FINISH Medium to long, persistent smoke and spice.

SCORE **80**

INDEPENDENT BOTTLINGS

The quality of independent bottlings has often been variable,
as good casks have been elusive.

GLEN SCOTIA 15-year-old, Old Malt Cask, 50 vol

COLOR Deep sludgey brown. NOSE Musty. Damp cricket kit.
Squelchy wet leaves. BODY Thin. sharp. Dry. PALATE Burned nut.
Tannins. Chili peppers. Dry pepper. FINISH Awkward. Bitter.
Woody. SCORE 66

GLEN SCOTIA 16-year-old,
Scotch Malt Whisky Society (93.33), 64.3 vol

COLOR Pale gold. NOSE Complex. Ripe pears, caramel,
and brine. BODY Slightly oily. PALATE Eating apples and wood smoke.
Gunpowder with the addition of water. FINISH Long, with walnuts
and ginger. SCORE 86

GLEN SCOTIA 16-year-old, 1992,
Berry's Own Selection, 55.7 vol

COLOR Dark gold. NOSE Initial heather honey, then
emerging dark syrup, damson plums, and pepper. Slightly
medicinal. BODY Syrupy. PALATE Full and lush, with summer fruits,
caramel, and a hint of cinnamon. FINISH Medium to long. Ripe peaches,
cloves, and spicy oak. SCORE 84

GLEN SCOTIA 17-year-old, Duthie's, 46 vol

COLOR Light gold. NOSE Well-mannered, with delicately
spiced malt and tangerines. BODY Slightly oily.
PALATE Fruity, with developing caramel. FINISH Spicy
and slowly drying. SCORE 80

GLEN SPEY

PRODUCER Diageo
REGION Highlands   DISTRICT Speyside (Rothes)
ADDRESS Rothes, Aberlour, Banffshire, AB38 7AU
TEL 01340 882000

DATING FROM THE 1880s, Glen Spey is in Rothes. Much of its whisky is destined for the house blend of an aristocratic wine and spirits merchant in St. James's, London. (It is coincidence that neighbor Glenrothes follows a parallel path.) In the case of Glen Spey, the merchant is Justerini & Brooks, whose house blend is J&B.

Giacomo Justerini was an Italian, from Bologna. He emigrated to Britain in pursuit of an opera singer, Margherita Bellion, in 1749. The romance does not seem to have come to fruition, but Justerini meanwhile worked in Britain as a maker of liqueurs. By 1779, he was already selling Scotch whisky. Brooks was a later partner in the firm. The business was for a time part of Gilbeys, at which point there was for a time a nutty, grassy eight-year-old Glen Spey.

HOUSE STYLE Light, grassy, nutty. Aperitif.

GLEN SPEY 12 year-old, Flora and Fauna, 43 vol

COLOR Full gold.

NOSE Maltiness (rich tea biscuits). Dusty. Kumquat. Leafy. Garden mint.

BODY Medium. Oily.

PALATE Vivacious. Starts intensely sweet, with light citrus notes, then becomes dramatically drier.

FINISH Crisp. Lemon zest. Pith.

SCORE **75**

GLEN SPEY 17-year-old, Old Malt Cask, 50 vol

COLOR Yellowy green.

NOSE Sweet. Toffee. Bourbon. Vanilla. Spearmint chewing gum.

BODY Soft and mouth-filling.

PALATE Lively. Red licorice. Peach. Soft fruit. Banana. Some spearmint. Later, tannins.

FINISH Full, firm, and sweet, with some woody and spicy notes.

SCORE **69**

GLENALLACHIE

PRODUCER Chivas Brothers (Pernod Ricard)
REGION Highlands   DISTRICT Speyside
ADDRESS Aberlour, Banffshire, AB38 9LR   TEL 01340 871315

TRUE WHISKY LOVERS LIKE TO SAMPLE EVERYTHING, and, although Glenallachie (pronounced "glen-alec-y") has only a modest reputation, it is a good example of a subtle, delicate, flowery Speysider.

The distillery was built in 1967 primarily to contribute malt to the Mackinlay blends. It was temporarily closed in the late 1980s, then acquired and reopened by Campbell Distillers at the end of the decade.

It takes its water from a spring on Ben Rinnes, just over the hill from its senior partner, Aberlour. Despite their proximity, their water is different, and so is their whisky: Glenallachie lighter, more acidic, drier, more delicate; Aberlour richer, more luscious, sweeter, maltier.

HOUSE STYLE Clean, subtle, delicate. Aperitif.

GLENALLACHIE 12-year-old, 40 vol

A Mackinlay bottling that is now difficult to find.

COLOR Very pale.

NOSE Hint of peat. Fragrant. Lightly malty.

BODY Light but firm.

PALATE Beautifully clean, smooth, and delicate.

FINISH Starts sweet and develops towards a long, perfumy finish.

A graceful pre-dinner companion.

SCORE **75**

GLENALLACHIE Cask Strength Edition, 18-year-old, Distilled 1989, Bottled 2008, Batch GA 18 005, 57.1 vol

COLOR Deep mahogany, with reddish hues.

NOSE Cloves, cardamom, leather.

BODY Full, chewy.

PALATE Rich sherry, with cloves, a Christmas plum pudding with a vast array of spices, raisins, and dates; water opens up and accents the cloves.

FINISH Long. Cloves with leather, hints of tobacco, and a not unpleasant trace of sulfur.

COMMENT Aged in first fill sherry butts, this is a wonderful dram for sherry lovers, though it does mask many of the distillery's subtle qualities.

SCORE **85**

GLENALLACHIE 12-year-old, Provenance, 46 vol

COLOR Light lemon.

NOSE Clean. Sweet Starburst fruits. Lime?

BODY Pleasant. Medium and unassertive.

PALATE Yellow fruit. Mild vanilla. Sweet and fresh.

FINISH Medium and sweet. A touch of nutmeg. Pleasant.

SCORE **69**

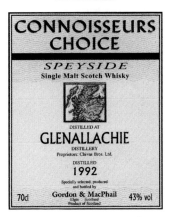

GLENALLACHIE 1992, Connoisseurs Choice, 43 vol

COLOR Pale gold.

NOSE Buttery lemon. Very peaty undertow.

BODY Medium-full.

PALATE Limp. Clean and gingery barley. Some green apple. Traces of tannin. Little depth.

FINISH Medium-long, with fluffy apple and a hint of pepper.

SCORE **63**

GLENBURGIE

PRODUCER Chivas Brothers (Pernod Ricard)
REGION Highlands   DISTRICT Speyside (Findhorn)
ADDRESS Forres, Morayshire, IV36 0QX   TEL 01343 850258

GLENBURGIE ISN'T WELL KNOWN for its whiskies and its malts rarely make it to the bottle. But the distillery has grown over the last few years and is now a sizeable powerhouse, creating whisky that is mainly destined for Ballantine's, a blend enjoying considerable success under owners Pernod Ricard. Glenburgie is a cutting edge distillery producing more than four million litres of spirit a year. A noted admirer of Glenburgie's herbal, fruity whisky was writer Maurice Walsh, whose story *The Quiet Man* was made into a movie starring John Wayne and Maureen O'Hara. Like Robert Burns and Neil Gunn, writer Walsh had a "day job" as an exciseman, in his case at Glenburgie. A less romantic, more technical claim to the noteworthiness of this distillery is its second malt whisky.

The distillery traces its history to 1810, and on its present site to 1829. It is in the watershed of the Findhorn, at Alves, between Forres and Elgin. Glenburgie was extended after World War II, at a time when many whiskies were in short supply. At that time, some Allied distilleries were being given additional stills of a different design, to extend their range. These "Lomond" stills, with a column-shaped neck, produced an oilier, fruitier malt. The whisky from Glenburgie's Lomond stills was named after Willie Craig, one of the company's senior managers. Those stills were removed in the early 1980s, but Glencraig can still be found in independent bottlings.

HOUSE STYLE Oily, fruity, herbal. Aperitif.

GLENBURGIE 15 year-old, 46 vol

COLOR Bright gold.

NOSE Attractive sweetness. Fragrant. Praline. A touch of orange peel.

BODY Medium, firm.

PALATE Round, velvety. Assertive. Fruity, toffeeish.

FINISH Dry, leafy. Hint of licorice.

SCORE **76**

GLENBURGIE Cask Strength Edition, 15-year-old, Distilled 1992, Bottled 2007, Batch GB 15 001, 58.8 vol

COLOR Dusty, antique gold.

NOSE Sweet, tangy. Allspice and pecans with a hint of orange peel. Trace of eucalyptus, coaxed out with a few drops of water. Wax beans?

BODY Chewy, mouth-coating.

PALATE Vegetation. Spices. Pine.

FINISH Long and dry, with notes of orange.

SCORE **84**

AN INDEPENDENT BOTTLING OF GLENCRAIG
GLENCRAIG 1974, 34-year-old, Rarest of the Rare, 40.3 vol

COLOR Yellow with greenish hue.

NOSE Traces of mint. Pencil eraser. Fruity jelly. Sweet. Clean.

BODY Quite light and soft.

PALATE Very clean. No blemishes or cask imperfections. Sugared barley. Traces of lemon and grapefruit.

FINISH Medium-sweet and fruity.

SCORE **82**

GLENCADAM

PRODUCER Angus Dundee Distillers plc
REGION Highlands   DISTRICT Eastern Highlands
ADDRESS Brechin, Angus, DD9 7PA   TEL 01356 622217

GLENCADAM IS A NOTABLY CREAMY MALT, using unpeated malt. Appropriately, much of the distillery's output has, over the years, gone in to "Cream of the Barley," originally blended in Dundee and now popular in Belfast.

The neat little distillery, at Brechin, was founded in 1825 and modernized in 1959. The very soft water is piped an astonishing 30 miles (48km) from Loch Lee, at the head of Glen Esk. With neighbor North Port now gone, Glencadam is a lonely survivor on this stretch of coastline. The distillery was acquired by Angus Dundee from Allied Domecq in 2003.

Glencadam uses mostly first-fill bourbon casks, and fills only a handful of sherry butts each year. This makes the new 25-year-old release an extra special bottling.

HOUSE STYLE Creamy, with a suggestion of berry fruits.
With dessert, or after dinner.

GLENCADAM 10-year-old, 46 vol

COLOR Pale gold.

NOSE Strawberries and vanilla.

BODY Moderately robust.

PALATE Creamy, with a hint of berries; perhaps cassis.

FINISH Dusting of spice.

SCORE **73**

GLENCADAM 15-year-old, 46 vol

The old-style bottling.

COLOR Old gold.

NOSE Perfumy. Floral, elegant. Ripe summer fruit. Plum pudding, peach melba.

BODY Full, silky.

PALATE Smooth, mouth-coating. So creamy. Strawberry yogurt.
Rounded and appealing.

FINISH A little shy but sweet and satisfying.

SCORE **73**

GLENCADAM 15-year-old, 46 vol

COLOR Golden.

NOSE Spicy, with hints of berries.

BODY Moderately full and smooth.

PALATE Oak and berries, with a note of coarse salt. Rich oak.
Strawberries with traces of vanilla and spice.

FINISH Long oak with spice.

SCORE **76**

GLENCADAM 25-year-old, 46 vol

COLOR Light mahogany with reddish hues.

NOSE Rich sherry, cassis, berries, cloves, leather. Complex and enticing.

BODY Mouth-coating. Warming.

PALATE Rich leather, cardamom, dark berries, dates, raisins with
a dusting of pepper. Spicy and fruity—a plum pudding.
Sherry is well balanced and complex. Wonderful.

FINISH Strawberry pie, cassis, dark vanilla, and tobacco.
Long and pleasantly lingering.

SCORE **86**

TWO INDEPENDENT BOTTLINGS
GLENCADAM 11-year-old, Provenance, 46 vol

COLOR Liquid gold.

NOSE Menthol. Peat. Plum.

BODY Thin and unassertive.

PALATE Sour. Sooty. Spicy. Sharp.

FINISH Short.

SCORE **63**

GLENCADAM 17-year-old, Dewar Rattray Cask Collection, Bourbon Cask No 5990, Distilled 2 October 1990, Bottled 17 March 2008, 58.4 vol

COLOR Pale gold.

NOSE Raw sugar, oranges.

BODY Full, slightly oily.

PALATE Oranges, butter cookies. A trace of spice and oak.

FINISH Orange peel and lots of black pepper.

SCORE **75**

GLENDRONACH

PRODUCER The Benriach Distillery Company
REGION Highlands   DISTRICT Speyside (Deveron)
ADDRESS Forgue, by Huntly, Aberdeenshire, AB54 6DB
TEL 01466 730202   VC

THE RECENT WHISKY BOOM has ensured that the potential sale of any distillery will attract a queue of possible suitors, and so it proved when Glendronach was put on the market by owners Pernod Ricard, who had inherited it after the break-up of Allied and couldn't seem to find a place for it in the company portfolio.

The new owners are the same team that has so magnificently restored the fortunes and offerings of Benriach. Fronted by the irrepressible Billy Walker, they look set to restore this distillery to all its magnificent sherried glory.

Production at Glendronach restarted in 2002 and the owners at the time announced plans for a new-style 12-year-old. Whether that will now appear in four or five years' time remains to be seen, but if it does it will add to a list of bottlings from the distillery at that age.

Over the years, Glendronach 12 has appeared in a confusion of styles. At one stage, there was a welcome choice between "The Original" (second-fill, mainly bourbon) and a version labeled "100 percent matured in sherry casks." These two were then replaced by "Traditional," which attempted to marry their virtues. Stock problems led to this being replaced by a 15-year-old, which is itself now becoming hard to find.

The distillery has good stocks and Walker has successfully traded to bring in even more. His stated intent to restore Glendronach's reputation for bold, sherried whiskies has certainly been borne out by the first releases under the new regime. He plans to re-cask some stock from bourbon casks to sherry ones, too.

The whiskies are greatly appreciated by malt lovers, but much affection is also felt for the place itself. Deep in Aberdeenshire's fertile barley-growing country, the glen of the Dronac Burn almost entirely hides the cluster of buildings that make up the distillery—though a pagoda is hard to conceal. The floor maltings have not been restarted as yet, but there have been suggestions that they might.

The distillery has its own small mansion house, flower beds, and kitchen garden, as though it were a small estate. (Domaine Dronac?)

The fifth Duke of Gordon, the man behind the legalization of distilling in the Highlands in the 1820s, is credited with having encouraged local farmers to establish this distillery. It was later run by a member of the William Grant family (owners of Glenfiddich), and in 1960 was acquired to help provide the malty background to the well-known blend Teacher's.

HOUSE STYLE Smooth and big, with a teasing sweet-and-dry maltiness. Sherry-friendly. After dinner.

GLENDRONACH 12-year-old, 40 vol

COLOR Deep tan.
NOSE Mint-flavored toffee. Vanilla. Sherry, winey notes, berries.
BODY Medium.
PALATE Fresh cranberry and blueberry juice. Peppery. No cloying sweetness, Highland peat carpet.
FINISH Medium, savory, and peaty.

SCORE **70**

GLENDRONACH 15-year-old, 40 vol

100 percent sherry maturation; being phased out.

COLOR Full amber.

NOSE Sweet, raisiny sherry, balanced by polished oak
and sweetish, fragrant peat smoke.

BODY Rich and smooth.

PALATE Oaky. Dry maltiness. Crunchy toffee. Buttery.

FINISH Licorice-toffee, sherry notes.

SCORE 79

GLENDRONACH 15-year-old, 46 vol

2009 Release.

COLOR Horse-chestnut brown.

NOSE Big. Sherry, chicory coffee, fresh figs, floral notes.
Magnificent, with wisps of sulfur.

BODY Sweet, bold, and full.

PALATE Sweet, fruit cake, followed by a pepper surge, drying tannins
and plummy smoke. Complex and intense. Evolving.

FINISH Plummy, with pepper and peat. Long.

SCORE 90

GLENDRONACH 18-year-old, 46 vol

2009 Release.

COLOR Deep bronze.

NOSE Earthy, rootsy. Sulfur. Old pantry.

BODY Creamy and soft.

PALATE Rich, deep red fruits, particularly plum. Some tannin astringency, wisps of peat, and menthol. Bold.

FINISH Sherry and a peat underlay, with gentle spice. Long and lingering.

SCORE **84**

GLENDRONACH 33-year-old, 40 vol

COLOR Deep horse-chestnut brown.

NOSE Fresh sap, apricot, raisins, dark coffee liqueur, Kahlua.

BODY Medium-full and creamy.

PALATE Very intense given the strength, with lots of sweet peach and apricot flavors. Sweet pepper, drying tannins. All gentle and rounded.

FINISH Long but soft and sweet, balanced, and very attractive.

SCORE **88**

AN INDEPENDENT BOTTLING
GLENDRONACH 1975, ECS 326, Duncan Taylor, 54.1 vol

COLOR Deep golden honey. NOSE Over-ripe blackberries, raspberries, and blackcurrants. Deep orange notes. Full and fruity. BODY Rich, full, and sherried. PALATE Anise. Spearmint. Astringent. Redcurrants. Gentle and rounded. FINISH Long fruity and dry. SCORE 87

GLENDULLAN

PRODUCER Diageo
REGION Highland   DISTRICT Speyside (Dufftown)
ADDRESS Dufftown, Banffshire, AB55 4DJ
TEL 01340 822100

THIS DISTILLERY, ESTABLISHED IN 1897–98, has had its moments of glory, notably the supply of its whisky in the early 1900s to King Edward VII, an honor that was for some years proclaimed on its casks. Today, Glendullan has the highest volume production among Diageo's distilleries, despite a name so unjustly close to "dull one." The reference is to the Dullan River, on which Dufftown stands.

HOUSE STYLE Perfumy, fruity, dry, chili-like, oily, big. Put it in a hip flask.

SINGLETON OF GLENDULLAN 12-year-old, 40 vol

COLOR Amber, with gold highlights.
NOSE Fragrant sherry, underlying cereal, apple, and subtle spice.
BODY Quite full.
PALATE Sherried, rich, caramel, brittle toffee, hazelnuts.
FINISH Medium in length. Spice, and raisins.

SCORE 77

GLENDULLAN 12-year-old, Flora and Fauna, 43 vol

COLOR Almost white, with just a tinge of gold.
NOSE Light, dry maltiness. Hint of fruit.
BODY A hard edge, then silky.
PALATE Dry start, becoming buttery, malty, nutty, perfumy, and lightly fruity.
FINISH Extraordinarily perfumy and long.

SCORE 75

GLENESK/HILLSIDE

PRODUCER DCL
REGION Highlands   DISTRICT Eastern Highlands
SITE OF FORMER DISTILLERY Kinnaber Road, Hillside, Montrose,
Angus, DD10 9EP

AT THE MOUTH OF THE South Esk River, at Montrose, lies Glenesk. Over the years, a confusion of names have been used for this establishment, employing various prefixes to the word Esk. At times it has also been known as Hillside. It began as a flax mill, converted in 1897 to become a malt distillery. At one later stage it made only grain whisky. Its career was intermittent, even by the standards of a cyclical industry.

From the mid-1960s to the mid-1980s, it contributed to the famous blend VAT 69, made by William Sanderson, part of DCL and later United Distilleries. There were, for a short time, William Sanderson bottlings of a 12-year-old Glenesk, but these are now very hard to find. They had a distinctly aromatic, clean, dry, fresh maltiness. In recent years, there have been several bottlings under the Hillside name in the Rare Malts series. The distillery closed in 1985. Its relatively modern maltings on an adjacent site was sold, but still operates.

HOUSE STYLE Fresh, clean, dry. Aperitif.

GLEN ESK 17-year-old, 1981, Duncan Taylor, 54.4 vol

COLOR Ginger orange.

NOSE Musty. Gooseberry. Citrus. Camp coffee.

BODY Sweet and creamy.

PALATE Better than the nose. Sweet. Red berry rumtopf dessert. Some sulfury notes. Canned strawberries. Peaty traces.

FINISH Sweet, earthy, and full.

SCORE **71**

GLEN ESK 24-year-old, Duncan Taylor, 52.1 vol

COLOR Deep gold.

NOSE Rich berries. Traces of sulfur and smoke. Intriguing.

BODY Creamy and soft.

PALATE Stewed apricots. Red berries. Mixed fruits. Soft but full.

FINISH Full and fruity, with a pleasant aftertaste.

SCORE **83**

GLENFARCLAS

PRODUCER J. & G. Grant
REGION Highlands   DISTRICT Speyside
ADDRESS Ballindalloch, Banffshire, AB37 9BD   TEL 01807 500257
WEBSITE www.glenfarclas.co.uk   EMAIL enquiries@glenfarclas.co.uk   VC

WITH A SIXTH GENERATION of the family now active in the business, prospects look good for this most independent of distilleries. Glenfarclas whiskies are in the top flight among Speysiders, though they are not as widely known as some similar examples from this region. From the Spey River, it is about a mile to Glenfarclas ("valley of the green grass"). The distillery is near the village of Marypark. Behind it, heather-covered hills rise toward Ben Rinnes, from which the distillery's water flows. Barley is grown in the surrounding area.

The distillery belongs to a private, family-owned company, J. & G. Grant. The family is not connected (except perhaps distantly) to any of the other whisky-making Grants, and does not own any other distilleries or bottlers. Glenfarclas traces its history to 1836, and has been in the family since 1865. Although some of the buildings date from that period, and the reception room has panelling from an ocean liner, the equipment is modern, and its stills are the biggest in Speyside.

HOUSE STYLE Big, complex, malty, sherryish. After dinner.

GLENFARCLAS 105, No Age Statement, 60 vol

Known as 105°, and 8 to 10 years old. A very youthful version for such a big malt, but it wins points for firm-muscled individuality.

COLOR Full gold to bronze.

NOSE Robust. Butterscotch and raisins.

BODY Full, heavy.

PALATE Very sweet. Rich nectar, with some honeyish dryness.

FINISH Long, and warmed by the high proof. Rounded.

SCORE **88**

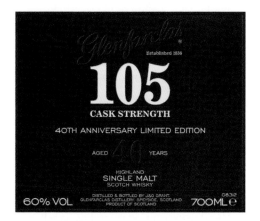

GLENFARCLAS 105 Aged 40 Years, 60 vol

COLOR Deep amber.

NOSE Big. Sherry and marzipan, with developing floral and caramel notes.

BODY Rounded.

PALATE Dry sherry, raisins, walnuts, and allspice.

FINISH Steadily drying, with spice, licorice, and hints of pipe tobacco.

SCORE **89**

GLENFARCLAS 10-year-old, 40 vol

Elegant and quite dry for a Glenfarclas.

COLOR Full gold.

NOSE Big, with some sherry sweetness and nuttiness,
but also smokiness at the back of the nose.

BODY Characteristically firm.

PALATE Crisp and dry at first, with the flavor filling out as it develops.

FINISH Sweet and long.

SCORE **86**

GLENFARCLAS 12-year-old, 43 vol

For many devotees, the most familiar face of Glenfarclas.

COLOR Bronze.

NOSE Drier than the 10-year-old, with a quick, big attack.

BODY Firm, slightly oily.

PALATE Plenty of flavor, with notes of peat smoke.

FINISH Long, with oaky notes, even at this relatively young age.

SCORE **87**

GLENFARCLAS 15-year-old, 46 vol

Many enthusiasts feel that this age most deftly demonstrates the complexity of this malt. Certainly the best-balanced Glenfarclas.

COLOR Amber.

NOSE Plenty of sherry, oak, maltiness, and a hint of smokiness—
all the elements of a lovely, mixed bouquet.

BODY Firm, rounded.

PALATE Assertive, again with all the elements beautifully melded.

FINISH Long and smooth.

SCORE **88**

GLENFARCLAS 21-year-old, 43 vol

COLOR Amber.

NOSE More sherry. Butter. Golden raisin-like fruitiness. Sweet lemon juice
on a pancake. Greater smokiness, as well as a dash of oak. All slowly emerge.

BODY Big. Firm.

PALATE Immense flavor development. Raisiny, spicy, gingery.

FINISH Remarkably long, with lots of sherry, becoming
sweetish and perfumy.

SCORE **89**

GLENFARCLAS 25-year-old, 43 vol

*More of everything. Perhaps a touch woody for purists, but a
remorselessly serious after-dinner malt for others.*

COLOR Dark amber.

NOSE Pungent, sappy.

BODY Big, with some dryness of texture.

PALATE The flavors are tightly interlocked and the whisky appears reluctant
to give up its secrets at first. Very slow, insistent flavor development.
All the components gradually emerge, but in a drier mood.

FINISH Long, oaky, sappy. Extra points out of respect for idiosyncratic age.

SCORE **88**

GLENFARCLAS 30-year-old, 43 vol

COLOR Refractive, bright amber.

NOSE Oaky, slightly woody.

BODY Very firm.

PALATE Nutty and oaky.

FINISH Oaky, sappy, and peaty.

SCORE **87**

FAMILY CASK RELEASES

In 2007 Glenfarclas released an unprecedented 43 consecutive single cask vintages, dating from 1952 to 1994, under the "Family Cask" banner. Additional bottlings have subsequently been released as initial casks from specific years sold out. Below are sampling notes for a representative selection of Family Cask releases.

From the initial release in 2007:

GLENFARCLAS 1954, Cask 444, 406 bottles, 52.6 vol

COLOR Rich, polished amber.

NOSE Soft and aromatic. Sweet, with a hint of smoke.

BODY Full and ripe.

PALATE Spicy and sherried, with drying nuts and smoke.

FINISH Dries steadily to oaky tannins.

SCORE **84**

GLENFARCLAS 1958, Cask 2245, 455 bottles, 51.6 vol

COLOR Deep amber.

NOSE Toffee apples and figs.

BODY Full and supple.

PALATE Fruity, with molasses toffee.

FINISH Long, smoky, and gently drying.

SCORE **86**

GLENFARCLAS 1964, Cask 4717, 415 bottles, 53.1 vol

COLOR Dark copper.

NOSE Rich, sweet notes. Raisins and wood polish.

BODY Medium to full.

PALATE Fruit cocktail, with a big splash of sherry.

FINISH Long and full, with dark chocolate.

SCORE **88**

GLENFARCLAS 1966, Cask 4177, 514 bottles, 51.5 vol

COLOR Dark amber.

NOSE Fresh, fragrant, and floral.

BODY Full and supple.

PALATE Big and warming, with slowly drying sherry.

FINISH Long and benign, hint of tannins.

SCORE **90**

GLENFARCLAS 1968, Cask 1316, 483 bottles, 65.1 vol

Remarkable strength for its age.

COLOR Dark amber with bronze highlights.

NOSE Complex. Smoke and spent matches. Cinnamon, figs, apricots.

BODY Full.

PALATE As complex as the nose. Gunpowder, sherry, toffee, dry spice.

FINISH Long and spicy. A whiff of smoke.

SCORE **91**

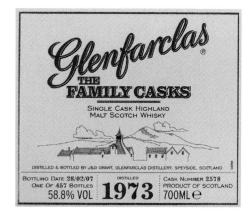

GLENFARCLAS 1973, Cask 2578, 457 bottles, 58.8 vol

COLOR Bright amber.

NOSE Quite fresh and fruity. Citrus and smoky vanilla.

BODY Medium to full.

PALATE Peaches and malt. Background sherry and smoke.

FINISH Medium. Drying to spicy oak.

SCORE 89

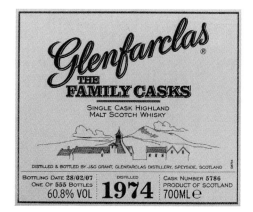

GLENFARCLAS 1974, Cask 5786, 555 bottles, 60.8 vol

COLOR Full gold.

NOSE Light for Glenfarclas.

BODY Medium. Quite firm.

PALATE Straightforward. Waxy vanilla, honey, oranges.

FINISH Medium in length, peppery, and drying.

SCORE 86

GLENFARCLAS 1977, Cask 61, 582 bottles, 59 vol

COLOR Bright gold.

NOSE Fresh and sweet. Honeyed.

BODY Smooth.

PALATE Spicy-sweet.

FINISH Short and mildly peppery.

SCORE **85**

GLENFARCLAS 1980, Cask 1942, 681 bottles, 50.1 vol

COLOR Pale gold.

NOSE Citrus fruits and well-worn leather upholstery.

BODY Medium.

PALATE Smooth and very fruity. Peaches and pineapple.

FINISH Medium to long, with lingering fresh fruits.

SCORE **88**

GLENFARCLAS 1985, Cask 2826, 329 bottles, 46.3 vol

COLOR Rich gold.

NOSE Delicate, with toffee, sherry, and sultanas.

BODY Firm.

PALATE Graceful, very drinkable. Sweet fresh fruits and walnuts.

FINISH Lengthy, with sweet sherry, raisins, and a hint of licorice.

SCORE **88**

GLENFARCLAS 1988, Cask 7033, 572 bottles, 56.3 vol

COLOR Gold with amber highlights.

NOSE Sweet. Confectionery, sherry, and vanilla.

BODY Smooth.

PALATE Balanced and buttery, with sherry and nutmeg spice.

FINISH Developing vanilla and intense fruitiness.

SCORE **89**

GLENFARCLAS 1989, Cask 11721, 600 bottles, 60 vol

COLOR Bright amber.

NOSE Powerful, with molasses toffee and a touch of smoke.
Increasingly floral.

BODY Heavy.

PALATE Intense flavors of blackcurrant, raspberry,
sherry, and licorice.

FINISH Long, drying, and nutty.

SCORE **88**

GLENFARCLAS 1992, Cask 264, 669 bottles, 55.5 vol

COLOR Pale bronze.

NOSE Initially Madeira cake, becoming fruitier,
with a whiff of smoke.

BODY Rounded.

PALATE Spicy vanilla and fruit cocktail.

FINISH Long. Quite delicate.

SCORE 88

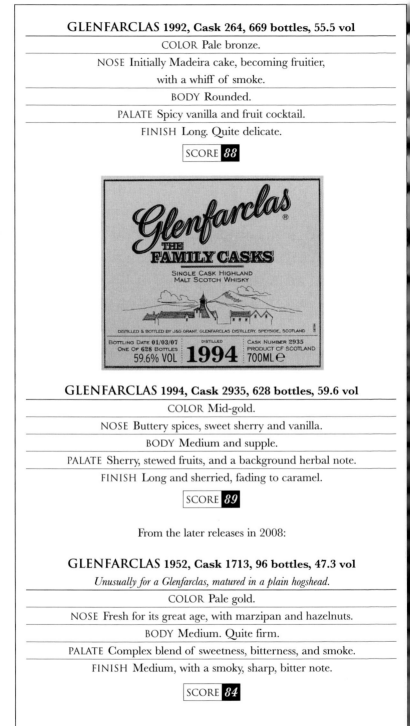

GLENFARCLAS 1994, Cask 2935, 628 bottles, 59.6 vol

COLOR Mid-gold.

NOSE Buttery spices, sweet sherry and vanilla.

BODY Medium and supple.

PALATE Sherry, stewed fruits, and a background herbal note.

FINISH Long and sherried, fading to caramel.

SCORE 89

From the later releases in 2008:

GLENFARCLAS 1952, Cask 1713, 96 bottles, 47.3 vol

Unusually for a Glenfarclas, matured in a plain hogshead.

COLOR Pale gold.

NOSE Fresh for its great age, with marzipan and hazelnuts.

BODY Medium. Quite firm.

PALATE Complex blend of sweetness, bitterness, and smoke.

FINISH Medium, with a smoky, sharp, bitter note.

SCORE 84

GLENFARCLAS 1960, Cask 1768, 152 bottles, 44.6 vol

COLOR Dark amber.

NOSE Notably fragrant, with soft leather
and sweet sherry.

BODY Luscious.

PALATE Smooth and smoky, becoming nutty and
slightly bitter.

FINISH Long. Quite tannic.

SCORE **85**

GLENFARCLAS 1961, Cask 1322, 150 bottles, 52.2 vol

COLOR Deep copper.

NOSE Gentle spices, warm leather, freshly
cracked walnuts.

BODY Medium to full.

PALATE Big sherry notes, wood smoke, and spice.

FINISH Long and subtly drying.

SCORE **86**

GLENFARCLAS 1962, Cask 2647, 161 bottles, 52 vol

COLOR Ruby.

NOSE Fruity and quite lively for its age.

BODY Rounded.

PALATE Dominant dry sherry and licorice.

FINISH Full and tannic.

SCORE **84**

GLENFARCLAS 1979, Cask 2216, 171 bottles, 50.6 vol

Matured in a plain hogshead.

COLOR Amber gold.

NOSE Fruity and floral, with lingering beeswax.

BODY Creamy.

PALATE Easy to drink. Fruit cocktail and sherry.

FINISH Medium, well-mannered.

SCORE **88**

GLENFARCLAS 1987, Cask 3826, 633 bottles, 53.2 vol

COLOR Mid-gold.

NOSE Peaches and cream. Background treacle sponge.

BODY Medium. Firm.

PALATE Quite intense, with very spicy fruit.

FINISH Gingery oak, with background melon and glacé cherries.

SCORE **86**

AN INDEPENDENT BOTTLING
GLENFARCLAS 41-year-old,
Scotch Malt Whisky Society, 1.141, 48.1 vol

COLOR Amber.

NOSE Fleshy and floral, with lavender and caramel.

BODY Rich.

PALATE Stewed fruits and spices, developing candyfloss
before becoming a little more bitter.

FINISH Short to medium. Drying oak and some smoke,
then a final buttery aftertaste.

SCORE **86**

GLENFIDDICH

PRODUCER William Grant & Sons Ltd.
REGION Highlands   DISTRICT Speyside (Dufftown)
ADDRESS Dufftown, Banffshire, AB55 4DH
TEL 01340 820373   WEBSITE www.glenfiddich.com   VC

WOE BETIDE YOU IF YOU TAKE the world's best malt distillery and its owners William Grant for (excuse the pun) granted. It's widely accepted that the quality of the whisky from this distillery has been getting better and better, and a series of vintage releases has amply demonstrated that Glenfiddich can hold its own with the very best that Scotland has to offer. Innovations such as the quite wonderful blended malt Monkey Shoulder show that the family aren't necessarily standing on tradition either.

The Glenfiddich distillery lies on the small river whose name it bears, in Dufftown. The name Fiddich indicates that the river runs through the valley of the deer. Hence the company's stag emblem.

This justifiably famous distillery was founded in 1886–87, and is still controlled by the original family. As a relatively small enterprise, it faced intense competition from bigger companies during the big economic boom after World War II. Rather than relying on supplying whisky to blenders owned by the giants, it decided in 1963 to widen the availability of its whisky as a bottled single malt. An industry dominated at the time by blended Scotches regarded this as foolishness. The widely held view was that single malts were too intense, flavorsome, or complex for the English and other foreigners.

This independent spirit was an example without which few of its rivals would have been emboldened to offer themselves as bottled single malts. Devotees of the genre owe a debt of gratitude to Glenfiddich. The early start laid the foundations for the success of Glenfiddich. Its fortunes were no doubt further assisted by its being, among malts, very easily drinkable.

Devotees of malts who are ready for a greater challenge will find much more complexity in the longer matured versions, including the one that is aged for 15 years then vatted in a solera system.

The Glenfiddich distillery is full of character. Much of the original structure, in honey-and-grey stone, remains beautifully maintained, and the style has been followed in considerable new construction.

Glenfiddich also led the way in the industry by being the first to have a visitor center. Some may argue that this is for tourists rather than purists, but no visitor to this part of the Highlands should miss it. The stills are small, and the whisky is principally aged in "plain oak" (refill bourbon), although about 10 percent goes into sherry casks. Whisky aged in different woods is married in plain oak.

Adjoining the Glenfiddich site, William Grant also owns The Balvenie (established 1892), with a small floor maltings, and the (1990) Kininvie malt distilleries. Kininvie is little more than a basic still-house. Its rich, creamy malt goes into the Grant's blends, but has not been bottled as a single. Elsewhere in Scotland, it has the Girvan grain distillery and its brand new malt distillery Ailsa Bay, which began operating in late 2008.

HOUSE STYLE When young, a dry, fruity aperitif;
when more mature, a raisiny, chocolatey, after-dinner malt.

GLENFIDDICH Special Reserve, 12-year-old, 40 vol

COLOR	Slightly fuller gold than it used to be. Faint green tinge.
NOSE	Fresh but sweet. Appetizing, fruity, pear-like. Juicy grass.
BODY	Lean. Smooth. Oily maltiness.
PALATE	Malty sweetness. White chocolate. Good flavor development. Toasted hazelnuts.
FINISH	Fragrant suggestion of peat smoke.

SCORE 77

GLENFIDDICH Caoran Reserve, 12-year-old, 40 vol

*Caoran refers in Gaelic to the embers of a peat fire. A very gently smoky,
dryish background is achieved by the use of casks that previously
contained whisky from the peaty island of Islay.*

COLOR Deep gold.

NOSE Molasses toffee, slightly burned. Sweet, cedary logs on a slow fire.

BODY Light to medium. Oily. Scented.

PALATE White chocolate. Cannoli-flavored ice cream. Strega liqueur.

FINISH Thick chocolate wafers. Dark caramel. Gently warming alcohol.

SCORE **82**

GLENFIDDICH Solera Reserve, 15-year-old, 40 vol

COLOR Bright gold.

NOSE Chocolate. Toast. Hint of peat.

BODY Light but very smooth indeed.

PALATE Suave. Silky. White chocolate. Pears in cream. Cardamom.

FINISH Cream. A hint of ginger.

SCORE **81**

GLENFIDDICH 18-year-old, 40 vol

A proportion of the whisky in this version is older than the age on the label, with a slight accent toward first-fill sherry (butts, rather than hogsheads, and made from Spanish oak rather than American), and earth-floored, traditional warehouses.

COLOR Old gold.

NOSE Rich.

BODY Soft.

PALATE Mellow and rounded, soft, and restrained.
Scores points for sophistication and sherry character.

FINISH Nutty. A flowery hint of peat.

SCORE **78**

GLENFIDDICH 21-year-old, 40 vol

COLOR Rich honey bronze.

NOSE Clean barley, boiled sweets, model adhesive, new office,
lemon cleaner on polished wood.

BODY Light, unaggressive, soft, and quite creamy.

PALATE Lemon and honey, clean sweet malt, some mint, traces of oak,
some spice and tannins.

FINISH Medium, sweet, citrusy, quite zesty, and spicy.

SCORE **76**

GLENFIDDICH 21-year-old, Gran Reserva, 40 vol

COLOR Apricot.

NOSE Toasty. Cookie-like. Petit fours. The aroma when
a box of chocolates is opened.

BODY Soft. Lightly creamy.

PALATE Vanilla flan. Sweet Cuban coffee.

FINISH Juicy. A hint of dried tropical fruits.

SCORE 86

GLENFIDDICH 30-year-old, 43 vol

COLOR Full gold, fractionally darker still.

NOSE Notes of sherry, fruit, chocolate, and ginger.

BODY Soft. Full. Some viscosity.

PALATE More sherry, raisins, chocolate, ginger. Luxurious.

FINISH Unhurried, with chocolatey notes
and gingery dryness.

SCORE 86

GLENFIDDICH Rare Collection 40-year-old, 43.6 vol

COLOR Chestnut with a green tinge.

NOSE Reticent. Chestnut, old fruit, damp.

BODY Soft, creamy, gentle.

PALATE Soft and subtle, with a big dose of anise, honey, and melon. No astringency. Incredibly dainty and polished, like a dapper old man.

FINISH Medium but very soft, rounded, and balanced. Quite a work of art.

SCORE **92**

GLENFIDDICH 50-year-old, 43 Vol

COLOR Golden amber.

NOSE Surprisingly spritely. Grapefruit marmalade. Melon. Lemon.

BODY Light and delicate.

PALATE Rich orange marmalade at first, then a wave of other citrus fruits. Clean and fresh. Sweet. Creamy vanilla. Traces of oak and peat.

FINISH Long, clean, and fruity, with a healthy dash of oak and spice.

SCORE **88**

GLENFIDDICH 1983, Cask 10888, 53.4 vol

Exclusive to Dubai.

COLOR Rich deep mahogany.

NOSE Nutty, dusty, heavily sherried. Rich fruit cake, cinnamon, and apple.

BODY Rich, creamy, and mouth-coating.

PALATE First soft, rich fruits; then anise, sweet pepper and oak.

FINISH Prune juice, sherry, tannin, and pepper.

SCORE **81**

GLENFIDDICH Vintage Reserve 1975, Cask 287, 51.1 vol

COLOR Earthy greenish-brown.

NOSE Earthy, rootsy. Artichoke, then citrus fruits.

BODY Rich, full, and oily.

PALATE Grapes, currants, prunes, anise, soft peach, and pear.

FINISH Medium and soft, with a gentle tannin burst at the very end.

SCORE **81**

GLENFIDDICH Vintage Reserve 1976, Cask 516, 52.1 vol

COLOR Pale bronze.

NOSE Beeswax polish; crystalized sweet fruits; peach, pear; vanilla.

BODY Sweet and creamy. Perfectly balanced.

PALATE Unblemished sweet barley. A pleasant mix of different fruits;
combination of sweet and sour, gentle and soft.

FINISH Gossamer soft, with a late but pleasant pepper bite.

SCORE **85**

GLENFIDDICH Vintage Reserve 1977, Cask 4414, 54.4 vol

COLOR Russet brown.

NOSE Venerable. Rich prune juice, tropical fruits. Banana, toffee, fudge.

BODY Rounded, soft, gentle.

PALATE Honeyed, with soft fruit at first, then a wave of sharp grapefruit and
lemon. Finally a burst of pepper and oakiness.

FINISH Long and lingering, with cocoa, chili peppers, and dark chocolate.

SCORE **87**

SOME VINTAGE GLENFIDDICHS

1974 In the aroma: pastry out of a hot oven. Fresh pears in butterscotch sauce. The palate suggests milk chocolate first, then dark. Chocolate limes, then mint crèmes. The finish is liqueur-ish but also slightly sharp. SCORE 83

1973 Soft, "box of chocolates" aroma. Silky smooth body. Palate suggests chocolate-coated dates. Balancing, cocoa-powder bitterness in finish. SCORE 87

1967 Touch of sweetness in the aroma. Coconut ice cream? Nougat? Garden mint in the palate. Slightly gritty. Moroccan mint tea. SCORE 82

1965 Aroma of chocolate soufflé. Syrup-sweet in the mid-palate. Remarkably chocolatey in the finish. Like eating that soufflé. SCORE 86

1961, 43.2 vol Gentle fragrance of pine needles, cypress, box trees, grass, peat, very faint smokiness. Palate has bitter chocolate, orange zest, and lemon fudge. Very deftly balanced. SCORE 92

GLENFIDDICH Classic, No Age Statement, 43 vol

This version is no longer bottled, but may still be found.

COLOR	Pale gold.
NOSE	Softer. Dry maltiness, pear skins, slight sherry, and faint smokiness.
BODY	Firm, smooth.
PALATE	Smooth. Dry maltiness balanced by restrained sweetness, with slight smokiness. Flavors tightly combined.
FINISH	Smooth, dry.

SCORE 76

GLENGLASSAUGH

PRODUCER The Scaent Group
REGION Highlands DISTRICT Speyside (Deveron)
ADDRESS Portsoy, Banffshire, AB45 2SQ

THE PURCHASE, REBUILDING, AND REOPENING of Glenglassaugh distillery after 22 years in mothballs is one of the highlights of the recent malt whisky boom, and a surprising one. The new owners are the Scaent Group, a Dutch company with substantial holdings across Scandinavia who made their name in the energy markets before diversifying in to a whole range of other markets, including consumer retail and property.

Over the years thieves, neglect, and inclement weather conditions took their toll on this pretty coastal distillery, and the new owners had their work cut out just getting the distillery running again. But they did so with great speed, and spirit was being produced by the end of 2008.

There is very little stock of old Glenglassaugh, but what there is will be released in limited batches in the coming years. In the meantime, the new production is being overseen by experienced distiller Stuart Nickerson, who has been appointed managing director.

Glenglassaugh is a coastal malt, produced near Portsoy, between the mouths of the rivers Spey and Deveron. The whisky has a distinctive taste and has contributed to highly respected blends such as The Famous Grouse and Cutty Sark in the past.

The future should be a bright and happy one. Let's hope that the new owners will use the distillery's little beach for fun events and barbecues, to fully bring this wonderful location back to life.

HOUSE STYLE Grassy maltiness. Restorative or refresher.

GLENGLASSAUGH, No Age Statement, 40 vol
This version, bottled by Highland Distillers, is labeled
12-year-old in some markets. It is now hard to find.

COLOR Gold.

NOSE Fresh linen.

BODY Light, but firm and smooth.

PALATE Grassy, sweetish.

FINISH Gentle, drying slightly.

SCORE **76**

GLENGLASSAUGH 21-year-old, 46 vol

COLOR Glowing rich warm gold.

NOSE Sweet: vanilla cake, lemon hard candies.

BODY Medium-full.

PALATE Orange and citrus. Clean barley. Sweet cinnamon. A hint of mint.
A touch of spice and oak late on. Nicely put together.

FINISH Quite short, with yellow fruit and traces of tannin and pepper.
Ordered and polite.

SCORE **82**

GLENGLASSAUGH 30-year-old, 55.1 vol

COLOR Pale honey gold.

NOSE Orange marmalade, plum, stewed fruits. Sweet.

BODY Rich, full, and mouth-filling.

PALATE Fruit sherbet. Pineapple and then sharp oak, tannin, and pepper.
All held in check and pleasant on the palate.

FINISH Rounded, long, fruity, and woody.

SCORE **90**

GLENGLASSAUGH 40-year-old, 44.8 vol

COLOR Rich brown with a reddish hue.

NOSE Rich plum, Christmas cake, dark berries.

BODY Surprisingly soft. Fudgey. Balanced.

PALATE Creamy toffee barley wrapped in nutty notes. Fruit cake, berries,
then astringent tannins and chilli pepper spice.

FINISH Very long and remarkably dignified,
with wood and plum in the mix.

SCORE **87**

GLENGLASSAUGH 1973 Vintage Reserve, The Family Silver, 40 vol

Now hard to find and of interest to collectors.

COLOR Deep, old gold.

NOSE Fresh, starched linen. Sea air.

BODY Light to medium. Firm, smooth.

PALATE Smooth, grassy. Slightly leathery and oily.

FINISH Linseed. Soothing. Warming.

SCORE **78**

AN INDEPENDENT BOTTLING
GLENGLASSAUGH 30-year-old, Single Malts of Scotland, 49.8 vol

COLOR Prune brown.

NOSE Chicory coffee. Kahlua. Musty.

BODY Medium-full.

PALATE Orange and lemon. Traces of anise. Some bubblegum notes.
Grungy wood. Intense dried fruit.

FINISH Long, tingling, plummy, and intense.

SCORE **79**

GLENGOYNE

PRODUCER Ian Macleod Distillers Ltd.
REGION Highlands   DISTRICT Highlands (Southwest)
ADDRESS Dumgoyne (by Glasgow), Stirlingshire, G63 9LV
TEL 01360 550254 WEBSITE www.glengoyne.com
EMAIL reception@glengoyne.com   VC

G LENGOYNE HAS BEEN ESTABLISHING itself as Glasgow's other distillery in recent years. Its marketing efforts have highlighted its proximity to the city, and it has made great strides in offering visitors a wide range of experiences and a growing and eclectic mix of malts. It has never been an especially well-known distillery, but it has one of the prettiest locations (complete with waterfall), and it is only a dozen miles from the center of Glasgow. The distillery is said to have been established in 1833.

It is now felt the previous emphasis on the use of unpeated malt could have been construed as a negative claim, and perhaps too technical to appeal to the lay consumer. Nor is it unique to Glengoyne. If this theme is continued in future advertising, it may be presented in a more positive context: that the lack of peat unmasks the true taste of the malt. Glengoyne does have a clean, creamy malt accent.

HOUSE STYLE Easily drinkable, but full of malty flavor.
Restorative, with dessert, or after dinner.

GLENGOYNE 10-year-old, 40 vol

COLOR Yellowy gold.

NOSE A fresh but very soft, warm fruitiness (Cox's apples?), with rich malty dryness, very light sherry, and a touch of juicy oak.

BODY Light to medium. Smooth, rounded.

PALATE Clean, grassy, fruity, with more apple notes.
Tasty and very pleasant.

FINISH Still sweet, but drying slightly. Clean, appetizing.

SCORE **74**

A Glengoyne 12-year-old, at 43 vol, now hard to find is very similar to the 10-year-old. A dash more of everything. SCORE 75

GLENGOYNE 12-year-old, Cask Strength, 57.2 vol

COLOR Soft yellowy gold.

NOSE Green apples. A touch of sulfur. Barley, a trace of almonds.

BODY Medium, oily.

PALATE Sharp spice and pepper. Abrasive but clean, with crystal barley breaking through and some sour fruits.

FINISH Medium, savory, spicy.

SCORE **68**

GLENGOYNE 15-year-old, Scottish Oak, 43 vol

COLOR Rich orange.

NOSE Tingling spices, zippy blackcurrant. Earthy, savory.

BODY Full, rich, savory.

PALATE Sweet barley, rootsy, and reedy. Unripe plum, and some strong spice notes.

FINISH Medium-long. Sugar and spice. Savory.

SCORE **74**

GLENGOYNE 16-year-old, European Hogshead, 52.3 vol

COLOR Brassy yellow.

NOSE Ginger, barley, fresh straw. Clean.

BODY Full, oily, mouth-coating.

PALATE Crystallized ginger, chunky clean barley, and then lots of oak, a licorice stick, and pepper spices.

FINISH Long and venerable, with savory and spicy notes.

SCORE **73**

GLENGOYNE 17-year-old, 43 vol

COLOR Full gold, with an orange tinge.

NOSE Warm, dry. Maltiness and fruitiness. Sherry, cedar, and fresh oak.

BODY Medium, very firm, and smooth.

PALATE Deep, rich flavors. Malt, clean fruitiness (hints of apple), nuttiness, cedar, more oak. A mature, sophisticated whisky.

FINISH Long and allusively sherryish.

SCORE **78**

GLENGOYNE Billy's Choice, 18-year-old, Amontillado, No 1202, 54.1 vol

COLOR Deep brown.

NOSE Sweet. Over-ripe peach, plums, grapes, spice, and oak.

BODY Rich, domineering, weighty.

PALATE Big sherry hit, with plum and prune notes, red berries, and an astringency from the oak tannins and spices. Puckerish.

FINISH Long and lingering, with some sherry and distinctive wood notes.

SCORE **83**

GLENGOYNE Robbie's Choice, 18-year-old, Ruby Port Hogshead, No 328, 55.1 vol

COLOR Rich sunset orangey brown.

NOSE Chestnut, moist bark, mushrooms, dates, damp leather.

BODY Rounded, full, mouth-coating.

PALATE Soft over-ripe fruit, some citrus, then wood, dark chocolate, pepper.

FINISH Long, with chili peppers, oak, plummy fruit residue, and astringency.

SCORE **79**

GLENGOYNE 19-year-old, Refill Sherry Cask, No 1227, 58.3 vol

COLOR Rich butter yellow.

NOSE Red wine, a candy jar, creamy sweet barley, grapes.
Nutty, with sherry notes.

BODY Full and balanced.

PALATE Full and astringent. Berries, licorice root,
red licorice. Chewy.

FINISH Full, mouth-coating, rich, and pleasant.

SCORE **86**

GLENGOYNE 19-year-old, Oloroso Sherry Hogshead, No 1200, 53.4 vol

COLOR Deep mahogany with green-brown hints.

NOSE Intense earthy mushroom. Chicory. Rootsy and vegetal.

BODY Mouth-coating, intense.

PALATE At first citrus fruit and plum. Dry and puckerish. Lots of tannins.
Mushrooms. Bitter orange.

FINISH Medium and unusual: savory, intense, very dry.

SCORE **78**

GLENGOYNE 21-year-old, 43 vol

A very well-balanced edition.

COLOR Full gold, with a darker orange tinge.

NOSE Fragrant. Hints of apple, oak, and earth.

BODY Firm, smooth.

PALATE Very firm maltiness. Dry creaminess.
Clean fruit (hints of orange) and oak.

FINISH Cream. Vanilla pods. Cinnamon.

SCORE **79**

GLENGOYNE 21-year-old, Sherry, 43 vol

COLOR Deep golden brown.

NOSE Juicy raisins, plum pudding, barley, grapes.

BODY Rich and full.

PALATE Fruitcake, dry fruits, grapefruit marmalade,
waves of oak, and spice.

FINISH Long. A battle between red fruits,
honey, and tannins.

SCORE **82**

GLENGOYNE 21-year-old,
Butt No 629, 53 vol

COLOR Horse-chestnut brown.

NOSE Prune, over-ripe plum, church sherry wine.

BODY Full, mouth-coating, rich.

PALATE Red fruits in the center wrapped in oak
and peppery spice. Bold. Some orange.

FINISH Long, woody, and spicy.

SCORE 76

GLENGOYNE Ronnie's Choice,
22-year-old, Bourbon, 53.6 vol

COLOR Rich auburn.

NOSE Vanilla, rock candy, strawberry cream, vanilla.

BODY Medium. Quite oily.

PALATE First sweet honey and vanilla; then canned peach and apricot;
finally gentle and pleasant woodiness.

FINISH Quite long, with soft fruit, sweet pepper,
and a distinctly puckerish quality.

SCORE 83

GLENGOYNE 30-year-old, 50 vol
An interestingly oaky interpretation.

COLOR Deep, shining gold to bronze.

NOSE Polished oak.

BODY Medium to full. Rounded.

PALATE Soft, complex. Hints of apple and orange.
Dryish spiciness.

FINISH Firm, dry. Hint of charred oak.

SCORE 79

GLENGOYNE Burnfoot, 40 vol
For travel retail outlets.

COLOR Rich flame orange.

NOSE Refined, floral, fresh sponge, light fruits.

BODY Easy and light.

PALATE Very fresh and clean. Young and zesty green fruit,
grapes, ginger barley, some savory notes.

FINISH Medium and savory.

SCORE 63

GLENGYLE

PRODUCER Mitchell's Glengyle Ltd.
REGION Campbeltown
ADDRESS Glengyle Street, Campbeltown, Argyll PA28 6EX
TEL 01586 552009   WEBSITE www.kilkerran.com
EMAIL info@kilkerran.com

THE ORIGINAL GLENGYLE DISTILLERY was established in 1872/73 by William Mitchell, previously co-owner of Springbank with his brother, John. However, the recessionary years following World War I were particularly severe for the Campbeltown distilling industry, and Glengyle closed in 1925, having changed hands six years previously.

The distillery buildings were subsequently used by Campbeltown Miniature Rifle Club, before the Bloch brothers, who owned Glen Scotia distillery, acquired the site in 1941, intending to recommence distilling. World War II prevented that from happening. In 1951, Campbell Henderson applied for planning permission to restore and reopen Glengyle as a distillery, but those plans also came to nothing.

Then, in 2000, Springbank supremo Hedley Wright—a descendant of the Mitchell family who had originally built both Springbank and Glengyle—formed Mitchell's Glengyle Ltd. to purchase the distillery site and restore it to its former glory. New equipment was commissioned, though the two stills that were adapted and installed had formerly been part of Ben Wyvis malt distillery, located within the Invergordon grain distilling complex.

Production began at Glengyle in March 2004, making it the first new distillery of the millennium and the first in Campbeltown for 125 years. The single malt produced there will be bottled as Kilkerran, as the name Glengyle is already registered for a blended malt.

KILKERRAN 4-year-old, 58.6 vol

Available from a solera cask of 2004 spirit at The Tasting Room, Springbank distillery.

COLOR	Pale gold.
NOSE	Delicate, with gentle malt, ripe peaches, and pineapples.
BODY	Medium. Slightly oily.
PALATE	Citrus fruit, cream, mixed spices.
FINISH	Lingering ginger.

SCORE **86**

GLENKINCHIE

PRODUCER Diageo
REGION Lowlands   DISTRICT Eastern Lowlands
ADDRESS Pencaitland, Tranent, East Lothian, EH34 5ET
TEL 01875 342005
WEBSITE www.discovering-distilleries.com/www.malts.com   VC

ACCORDING TO ITS LABEL, "The Edinburgh Malt." This is an eminently visitable distillery, about 15 miles (25 kilometers) from the capital, and near the village of Pencaitland. It traces its origins to at least the 1820s and 1830s, to a farm in barley-growing country in the glen of the Kinchie burn. This rises in the green Lammermuir hills, which provide medium-hard water, and flows toward the small coastal resorts where the Firth of Forth meets the sea.

In the 1940s and 1950s, the distillery manager bred prize-winning cattle, feeding them on the spent grain. Delphiniums and roses grow outside the manager's office, and the distillery has its own bowling green. The buildings resemble those of a Borders woollen mill. For much of the distillery's history, the whisky was largely used in the Haig blends. In 1988–89, it was launched as a single in the Classic Malts range, and in 1997 an amontillado finish was added. In the same year a new visitor center was opened. Among the exhibits is a 75-year-old model of the distillery which was built by the firm of Basset-Lowke, better known for their miniature steam engines.

HOUSE STYLE Flowery start, complex flavors, and a dry finish.
A restorative, especially after a walk in the hills.

GLENKINCHIE 10-year-old, 43 vol
No longer produced; replaced by the 12-year-old.

COLOR Gold.

NOSE Softly aromatic. Lemon grass. Sweet lemons. Melons.

BODY Light but rounded.

PALATE Soft, spicy. Cinnamon and demerara, then gingery dryness.
An extraordinary interplay.

FINISH Fragrant, spicy, oaky dryness.

SCORE 76

GLENKINCHIE 12-year-old, 43 vol

The new standard Glenkinchie bottling.

COLOR Pale gold.

NOSE Grassy and grainy, sustained by a discreet but present oakiness. Picks up steam with time: delicate notes of walnuts and almonds, and a whiff of wild flowers. A little honey and notes of oranges, as well as oatmeal. A breakfast malt? Very faint smokiness.

BODY Light and unassertive.

PALATE Simply sweet and fruity (apple compote) with, again, a good oakiness giving it some backbone. Balanced.

FINISH Medium-long, with a bigger grassiness now.

SCORE **79**

GLENKINCHIE 1986, Distillers Edition, Double Matured, 43 vol

Finished in amontillado sherry casks.

COLOR Full gold.

NOSE Lightly floral aroma of polished oak. Sweet lemon. Spices.

BODY Well-rounded.

PALATE The amontillado seems to heighten the interplay between sweetness and dryness. First comes brown sugar and butter, then suddenly dry nuttiness and surprising saltiness.

FINISH Sweet, astonishingly long, and soothing.

SCORE **79**

GLENKINCHIE 1989, Distillers Edition, Double Matured, 43 vol
Finished in amontillado sherry casks.

COLOR Pale amber.

NOSE Medium sherry with a herbal note; nuts, figs, and spices.

BODY Smooth and rounded.

PALATE Initially sweet, sherried, and spicy, then drying with walnuts.

FINISH Dries steadily, with delicate smoke, then a buttery aftertaste appears.

SCORE **81**

GLENKINCHIE 1991, Distillers Edition, Double Matured, 43 vol
Finished in amontillado sherry casks.

COLOR Amber, with gold highlights.

NOSE Sherried almonds, caramel, herbs, a sprinkling of pepper.

BODY Quite firm.

PALATE Spicy sherry and malt, becoming more citric.

FINISH Medium in length, nutty, and dry. Slight peat note.

SCORE **80**

GLENKINCHIE 20-year-old, 58.4 vol
Matured for 10 years in brandy casks.

COLOR Antique gold.

NOSE Rich and sweet. Red berries, brandy, and bonbons. Becoming nuttier.

BODY Medium, firm.

PALATE Oaky spices, ginger, and soft toffee. More berries.

FINISH Medium in length, very spicy, and drying, with a hint of Cognac.

SCORE **82**

THE GLENLIVET

PRODUCER Chivas Brothers (Pernod Ricard)
REGION Highlands   DISTRICT Speyside (Livet)
ADDRESS Ballindalloch, Banffshire, AB37 9DB
TEL 01340 821720   WEBSITE www.theglenlivet.com   VC

THE MOST FAMOUS WHISKY-MAKING GLEN in Scotland is that of the small Livet River, which flows into the Spey. Among the distilling districts, it is the one most deeply set into the mountains. Its water rises from granite, and frequently flows underground for many miles. The mountain setting also helps produce the weather whisky makers like. During distilling, the condensers work most effectively if cooled by very cold water, and in a climate to match. The malt whiskies made in the area are on the lighter side, very clean, flowery, subtle, and elegant.

The Livet's fame also has historical origins, in the period when Highlanders were permitted to distill only on a domestic scale. The purported justification was a shortage of grain, but there was also a question of political vindictiveness. At that time, this relatively remote mountain glen was a famous nest of illicit distillation. After legalization in 1824, the legendary spirit "from Glenlivet" was greatly in demand among merchants in the cities to the south.

Distillers absurdly far from the glen have used the geographical allusion, as if it were a synonym for Speyside in general, but this practice is now in decline as the greater interest in single malts focuses attention on the issue of origin. Braeval is the distillery highest in the glen and was previously known as Braes of Glenlivet, producing a honeyish, zesty whisky. Slightly lower is Tamnavulin, which has a notably light-bodied malt (though Tomintoul, just across the hills in adjoining Avon valley, is lighter in palate).

Only one distillery in the area is permitted to call itself The Glenlivet, however. This was the first distillery to become legal, and now possesses an international reputation. The definite article is restricted even further in that it appears on only the official distillery bottlings. These bottlings carry the legend "Distilled by George & J. G. Smith" in small type at the bottom of the label, referring to the father and son who established the original business.

The Gaelic word *gobha*, pronounced "gow" (as in typically Scottish names like McGowan) translates to Smith. It has been argued the Gow family had supported Bonnie Prince Charlie and later found it politic to change their name to Smith, but this explanation is open to question. Whatever the case, when the legalization of distillers was proposed by the Duke of Gordon, one of his tenants, George Smith, already an illicit whisky maker, was the first to apply for a license. His son, John Gordon Smith, assisted and succeeded him. After distilling on two sites nearby, in 1858 the Smiths moved to the present location, Minmore, near the point where the Livet and Avon meet. The distillery stands at a point where the grassy valley is already beginning to steepen towards the mountains. In 1880, the exclusive designation "The Glenlivet" was granted in a test case. The company remained independent until 1953, when it came under the same ownership as Glen Grant. In the 1960s, Gordon & MacPhail acquired considerable quantities of the whisky, leading to a succession of bottlings. These very old and sometimes vintage-dated expressions are identified as George & J. G. Smith's Glenlivet Whisky.

By virtue of it being the biggest-selling single malt in the large American market, The Glenlivet might be deemed commonplace, but it is a whisky of structure and complexity. It is distilled from water with a dash of hardness, and the peating of the malt is on the light side. About a third of the casks used have, at some stage, held sherry, though the proportion of first fill is considerably smaller.

HOUSE STYLE Flowery, fruity, peachy. Aperitif.

THE GLENLIVET 12-year-old, 40 vol

COLOR Pale gold.

NOSE Remarkably flowery, clean, and soft.

BODY Light to medium. Firm. Smooth.

PALATE Flowery, peachy, notes of vanilla. A delicate balance.

FINISH Restrained, long, and gently warming.

SCORE **85**

THE GLENLIVET 12-year-old,
American Oak Finish, 40 vol

COLOR Deep, refractive yellow.

NOSE The typically peachy bouquet seems to be accentuated.

BODY Firm. Medium to full. Very smooth.

PALATE Rich and fruity, with more peat smoke than usual.
Cooked peaches.

FINISH Creamy flavors. Vanilla. Some burned-grass bitterness.

SCORE **85**

THE GLENLIVET 15-year-old,
French Oak Reserve, 40 vol

COLOR Antique brass.

NOSE Sweet, rich. Honey and vanilla, with caramel.
Rich marzipan. More complex than expected.

BODY Medium. Smooth.

PALATE Oak with toasted almonds and vanilla.

FINISH Toasted almonds, assorted nuts, and oak.

SCORE **86**

THE GLENLIVET Nadurra, 16-year-old,
Batch No 0606A, Bottled 23 June, 2006, 57.2 vol

COLOR Deep gold.

NOSE Sweet malty lemon grass with a hint of caramel.

BODY Moderately hot. Buttery.

PALATE Vanilla and oak, with traces of pepper and a hint of spice. Dry.

FINISH Long and dry, with a touch of vanilla. Water brings
out sweetness and nuttiness.

SCORE 88

THE GLENLIVET Cask Strength Edition, 16-year-old,
Distilled 1990, Bottled 2006, Batch GL 16 006, 57.9 vol

COLOR Light gold.

NOSE Persimmons, vanilla, freshly cut oak. Fruity.
Water accentuates the fruit.

BODY Medium to full. Slightly oily.

PALATE Oak, vanilla, cinnamon. Water helps the balance, rounds
out the vanilla and fruit, and slightly subdues the cinnamon.

FINISH Long. Peppery.

SCORE 89

THE GLENLIVET 18-year-old, 43 vol

COLOR Deep gold to amber.

NOSE Elements beautifully combined. Deep flowery aromas,
a very light touch of fresh peatiness. Some sweetness,
and a hint of sherryish oak. Lightly appetizing.

BODY Firm. Smooth.

PALATE Flowery and sweet at first, then developing peach-stone nuttiness.

FINISH Dry, appetizing. Very long, with an interplay
of sweet and bitter flavors.

SCORE 87

THE GLENLIVET Archive, 21-year-old, 43 vol

COLOR Full gold to bronze.

NOSE Lively. Fruity. Peaty.

BODY Very firm and smooth.

PALATE Light, clean, cereal grain maltiness. Developing toastier, nuttier flavors. Orange oil. Some macaroon-like sweetness, too.

FINISH Sweet grass. Smoky fragrance.

SCORE **85**

THE GLENLIVET 25-year-old, 43 vol

COLOR Dark Amber.

NOSE Rich, fruity: waves of cooked apples, cinnamon, pecans, and orange marmalade; a hint of tobacco. Wonderful.

BODY Medium.

PALATE Red pepper, cinnamon, notes of vanilla.

FINISH Cinnamon and walnuts linger. Dry and warming.

SCORE **88**

A COUPLE OF INDEPENDENT BOTTLINGS
THE GLENLIVET 1975, Celtic Heartlands, 51.2 vol

NOSE Toffee. Fresh melon. Exotic fruits. BODY Sharp and assertive. PALATE Apple seeds. Peppery. Green leaves. Astringent. FINISH Medium, sharp, and spicy. SCORE 66

THE GLENLIVET 30-year-old, Glenkeir Treasures

NOSE Musty. Cluttered. With time and water, apple and green fruit. BODY Oily. Mouth-coating. Full. PALATE Clean and sweet. Fresh apples and pears. Juicy maltiness. FINISH Medium-sweet, with apple notes. SCORE 82

GLENLOCHY

PRODUCER **DCL/UDV**
REGION Highlands   DISTRICT Western Highlands
SITE OF FORMER DISTILLERY North Road, Fort William,
Inverness-shire, PH33 6TQ

T HE LOCHY IS A RIVER that flows through the town of Fort William, at the foot of the mountain Ben Nevis. In addition to the Ben Nevis malt distillery, which is still very much in operation, Fort William for many years had another, called Glenlochy. This was built at the end of the 19th century between 1898 and 1900, and it changed little over the decades in the first half of the 20th century. It passed to DCL in 1953, lost its railroad spur in the 1970s, and was closed in 1983. The equipment has long since gone, and the premises are now used as offices by unrelated businesses.

One sophisticated and geographically precise taster was reminded of Lebanese hashish by a Scotch Malt Whisky Society bottling of Glenlochy in the mid-1990s. The smokiness is less obvious in some bottlings, in which the wood seems tired, but more oxidation and ester notes emerge. In 1995, United Distillers released a Rare Malts edition, with a similar bottling the following year.

HOUSE STYLE Peaty, fruity, creamy. With dessert or a book at bedtime.

GLENLOCHY 27-year-old,
Rarest of the Rare, 54.8 vol

COLOR Ginger.

NOSE Chocolate lime bonbons. Pineapple candies. Camp coffee.

BODY Soft and sweet.

PALATE Barley sugar. Orange hard candies Gingersnaps.
Hints of oak late on. Vanilla.

FINISH Sweet and spicy, but rounded and well-balanced.
Impressive.

SCORE **88**

GLENLOSSIE

PRODUCER Diageo
REGION Highlands DISTRICT Speyside (Lossie)
ADDRESS By Elgin, Morayshire, IV30 3SF
TEL 01343 862000

RESPECTED IN THE INDUSTRY (its whisky was once an important element in Haig blends), this distillery has a much lower profile among lovers of malts. A Flora and Fauna edition introduced in the early 1990s has made more connoisseurs aware of it, and there have since been bottlings from Signatory and Hart.

The distillery, in the valley of the Lossie, south of Elgin, was built in 1876, reconstructed 20 years later, and extended in 1962. Next door is the Mannochmore distillery, built in 1971.

HOUSE STYLE Flowery, clean, grassy, malty. Aperitif.

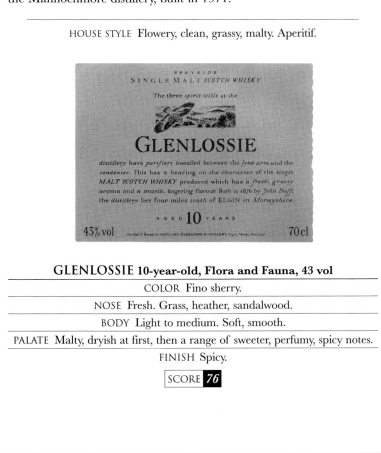

GLENLOSSIE 10-year-old, Flora and Fauna, 43 vol

COLOR Fino sherry.

NOSE Fresh. Grass, heather, sandalwood.

BODY Light to medium. Soft, smooth.

PALATE Malty, dryish at first, then a range of sweeter, perfumy, spicy notes.

FINISH Spicy.

SCORE 76

GLENMORANGIE

PRODUCER Glenmorangie plc
REGION Highlands   DISTRICT Northern Highlands
ADDRESS Tain, Ross-shire, IV19 1PZ
TEL 01862 892477   WEBSITE www.glenmorangie.com
EMAIL visitors@glenmorangieplc.co.uk   VC

STILL THE BIGGEST SELLING MALT WHISKY in Scotland; still dividing opinion by its devotion to wood finishes (which offend some whisky conservatives); still, as a company, much respected and admired.

Glenmorangie pioneered "official" cask-strength bottlings at the beginning of the 1990s. In the middle of that decade, it began introducing wood finishes, from sherry variations such as fino to madeira, port, and French wines. Subsequently it also introduced some vattings of virgin American oak.

The company selects its own trees in the Ozark mountains of Missouri, has its wood seasoned by air drying (rather than kilning), and loans its casks for four years to the Jack Daniel's distillery in Lynchburg, Tennessee. A similar arrangement existed with Heaven Hill, in Bardstown, Kentucky, until the Bourbon distillery lost substantial amounts of wood in a fire. The wood policies at Glenmorangie are some of the most highly developed in the industry. It is significant that the man who developed them, Bill Lumsden, is styled Head of Distilleries and Maturation.

Since 2004 Glenmorangie has been owned by French luxury goods company LVMH, and in 2008 production capacity was increased by 50 percent with the installation of four new stills. The distillery is near the pretty sandstone town of Tain. The town and distillery are on the coast about 40 miles (65 kilometers) north of Inverness. From the A9, the short private drive passes between an assortment of trees and a dam shaped like a millpond. Beyond can be seen the waters of the Dornocsh firth.

The distilling water rises on sandstone hills and flows over heather and clover, before emerging in a sandy pond about half a mile from the distillery. The sandstone surely contributes to the whisky's firmness of body, the flowers perhaps to its famously scenty character. (A French perfume house identified 26 aromas, from almond, bergamot, and cinnamon to verbena, vanilla, and wild mint. More recently, a New York fragrance company managed only 22).

HOUSE STYLE Creamy, leafy. Restorative or with dessert.

GLENMORANGIE Original, 10-year-old, 40 vol

Introduced in 2007, this is a replacement bottling for the previous 10-year-old.

COLOR Antique gold.

NOSE Floral, with fresh fruits, butterscotch, and toffee.

BODY Silky.

PALATE More toffee than its predecessor. Nutty,
with fresh oranges and lemons.

FINISH Medium length, progressively spicier, with ginger.

SCORE **81**

EXTRA MATURED RANGE
GLENMORANGIE Nectar d'Or, 46 vol

*Replacement for the former Sauternes Wood Finish expression. Additionally matured in
French wine barriques after a minimum of 10 years in bourbon casks.*

COLOR Lemony gold.

NOSE Dessert wine, honey, soft fruits, and spice.

BODY Medium.

PALATE Golden raisins and dates, gingerbread, and custard,
balanced by lemon notes.

FINISH Long and spicy, with developing citrus fruits.

SCORE **87**

GLENMORANGIE Quinta Ruban, 46 vol

Replacement for the former Port Wood Finish expression. Additionally matured in port pipes after at least 10 years in bourbon casks.

COLOR Coppery-pink.

NOSE Rich and fruity. Mint chocolate and walnuts.

BODY Silky smooth.

PALATE Big and slightly peppery, with hard candy and milk chocolate.

FINISH Long and comforting. Dark chocolate orange.

SCORE 86

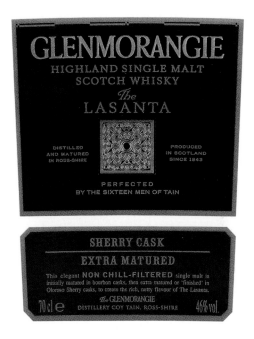

GLENMORANGIE Lasanta, 46 vol

Replacement for the former Sherry Wood Finish.
Additionally matured in Spanish oloroso sherry casks after
at least 10 years in bourbon casks.

COLOR Medium-dark gold.

NOSE Sweet and syrupy, with cinnamon and ginger.

BODY Medium and soft.

PALATE Malty and spicy, with vanilla fudge, walnuts, and raisins.

FINISH Slowly drying, with lingering, gingery oak,
and a hint of cocoa.

SCORE 86

GLENMORANGIE 18-year-old, 43 vol

COLOR Full reddish amber.

NOSE Vanilla, mint, walnuts. Sappy, oaky.

BODY Medium, smooth, fleshier.

PALATE Cookie-like and sweet at first, more walnuts,
then the whole potpourri of spiciness.

FINISH Aromatic, nutty, lightly oaky.

SCORE 81

GLENMORANGIE 25-year-old, 43 vol

Mainly for the Asian/Pacific market.

COLOR Dark polished oak.

NOSE An old shop, with fittings in polished oak, leather, and brass.

BODY Big. Slippery.

PALATE Cakey. Oily. Beeswax. A handsome whisky.

FINISH Late, gingery spiciness.

SCORE **80**

FURTHER VARIATIONS
GLENMORANGIE Astar, 57.3 vol

*Aged in casks sourced from the Ozark Mountains of Missouri and used to mature
Tennessee whiskey for four years prior to being filled with Glenmorangie new make spirit.*

COLOR Gold with green highlights.

NOSE Fresh and lively. Vanilla, newly sawn timber, and cream caramel.

BODY Rounded and smooth.

PALATE High floral, with polish notes that become richer and spicier.
Succulent peaches.

FINISH Long and creamy.

SCORE **84**

GLENMORANGIE Signet, 46 vol

*Produced using a proportion of "chocolate malt," this expression comprises whiskies that
have been matured in a variety of cask types and aged for up to 35 years.*

COLOR Copper.

NOSE Rich fruit, honey, orange marmalade, maple, sherry, sweet oak, spice.

BODY Silky.

PALATE Fruit and lively spice, with dark chocolate, vanilla,
and a hint of leather.

FINISH Medium in length. Vanilla and ginger.

SCORE **88**

GLENMORANGIE Margaux Cask Finish 1987, 46 vol

After 17 years of maturation in bourbon hogsheads, this whisky was subsequently transferred into wine barriques from the House of Margaux in the French Bordeaux region.

COLOR Amber with orange highlights.

NOSE Spicy red wine and oranges, with fragrant confectionery notes.

BODY Very smooth.

PALATE Summer berries, cinnamon, and ginger, with developing nougat.

FINISH Succulent. Spicy fruits linger.

SCORE **88**

SOME VINTAGE-DATED LIMITED BOTTLINGS
GLENMORANGIE 1979, Bottled 1995, 40 vol

COLOR Lemony gold.

NOSE Light, fragrant. A hint of peat. Faint smoke. Very appetizing.

BODY Surprisingly rich.

PALATE Beautifully balanced. Malty, with some butteriness, moving to spice and salt. Very lively flavors.

FINISH Gentle and soothing.

SCORE **84**

GLENMORANGIE 1977, 21-year-old, 43 vol

COLOR Bright, greeny gold.

NOSE A hit of oaky vanilla and spice, then grassy peat, and finally a surprisingly emphatic whiff of sea air.

BODY Light but smooth and firm. Slightly oily.

PALATE Sweet and juicy. The fresh oak character combines with the typical walnut, but somewhat overpowers the usual spiciness.

FINISH That very slight peat again, its quick, smoky, fragrant dryness adding an appetizing conclusion.

SCORE **84**

GLENMORANGIE 1975, Vintage, 54.2 vol

COLOR Full amber.

NOSE Scottish tablet. Fudge, in a gift box.

BODY Light, firm, slippery.

PALATE Firm maltiness. A very malty expression. Big flavor development. The maltiness becomes buttery, then lemon notes and burned toast. This is a confident, cerebral whisky.

FINISH Perfectly pitched, balanced dryness. Just when it all seems over, a burst of late spiciness and saltiness comes along.

SCORE **85**

GLENMORANGIE 1972, Cask No 1740, Bottle 066, 1993, 46 vol

COLOR Very full gold.

NOSE Lightly peaty, flowery, then very spicy. Lots of cinnamon.

BODY Light to medium, but smooth and textured.

PALATE Very nutty. Grassy. Dry. Full of fresh flavors.

FINISH Peaty. Grassy. Garden mint. Salty. Slightly sandy or stony.
Lightly dry. Crisp, cracker-like.

SCORE 85

SOME OLDER WOOD FINISHES
GLENMORANGIE Port Wood Finish, 43 vol

*Released without an age statement, but typically matured for 12 years in bourbon wood
and up to two in port pipes. Similar regimes for the other wood finishes.*

COLOR Orange, with pinkish blush.

NOSE Pronouncedly fruity and winey.

BODY Very soft indeed, and smooth.

PALATE The port seems to bring out butterscotch notes. It also adds sweeter,
winey notes, and melds beautifully with the spiciness of Glenmorangie.

FINISH Soothing, soporific, relaxing. In no hurry to go.

SCORE 87

GLENMORANGIE Madeira Wood Finish, 43 vol

COLOR Deep, lemony gold.

NOSE Sweet. Very spicy. Cakey.

BODY Soft, but becoming almost grainy as it dries on the tongue.

PALATE Unusually buttery. Hard-candy sweetness at first: toffeeish, chewy,
cakey. Then nutty and seed-like as it dries. Cinnamon and spices.
A teasing interplay of the madeira and the distillery character.

FINISH Short and sweet. Some rummy warmth.

SCORE 86

GLENMORANGIE Sherry Wood Finish, 43 vol

The sherry is dry oloroso.

COLOR Darkish gold.

NOSE Nutty. Dry. Faint peat. Sea air.

BODY Soft and curvaceous.

PALATE Voluptuous. Long, sustained development of hard-candy sweetness,
which almost overpowers the distillery character.

FINISH Licorice. Rooty. Late, restrained saltiness.

SCORE 85

GLENMORANGIE **Burgundy Wood Finish, 43 vol**

COLOR Warm bronze.

NOSE Toasty.

BODY Big. Soft. Syrupy.

PALATE Sweetish. Very fruity. Winey. Easily drinkable.

FINISH Lurking behind, and emerging gradually, the restrained, balancing dryness of toast and oak.

SCORE **83**

LIMITED EDITION WOOD FINISHES
(Or, where indicated, wholly matured in the wood shown.)

GLENMORANGIE **Tain L'Hermitage (Rhône Wine), Released 1995, 43 vol**

COLOR Distinctively elegant orange.

NOSE Very fruity and sweet.

BODY Creamy.

PALATE Very clean toffee and vanilla, developing to nuttiness and remarkably dry fruitiness. Great length.

FINISH Astonishingly lean and winey. Full of fruity, winey, spicy flavors. Very lively.

SCORE **88**

GLENMORANGIE **Claret Wood Finish, Released 1997, 43 vol**

COLOR Orangey amber.

NOSE Fragrant. A hint of the sea. Cedary.

BODY Firm, tongue-coating.

PALATE Dry, cedary start. Boxed dates. Becoming slightly raisiny. Long development of more spicy notes.

FINISH Dry, with a slightly cookie-like, coconut sweetness and fruity perfuminess.

SCORE **87**

AN INDEPENDENT BOTTLING
GLENMORANGIE **13-year-old, Scotch Malt Whisky Society, 125.18, 56.9 vol**

COLOR Pale amber

NOSE Orange-flavored milk chocolate. Gentle background smoke.

BODY Luscious.

PALATE More bitter chocolate than on the nose. Fruity caramel.

FINISH Long, creamy, seductive.

SCORE **85**

GLENROTHES

PRODUCER The Edrington Group
REGION Highlands   DISTRICT Speyside (Rothes)
ADDRESS Burnside Street, Rothes, Aberlour, AB38 7AA

THE MOST ARISTOCRATIC of London's wine and spirit merchants, Berry Brothers & Rudd, have in recent years showcased Glenrothes (rendered variously as one or two words) as their house malt. These are the principal bottlings of Glenrothes, and they are always vintage dated, with a partially "handwritten" label.

In 2002, the company also introduced its own range of bottlings from other distilleries, under the rubric "Berrys' Own Selection." This reflects the new appreciation of Scotland's finest whiskies. It also represents a return to tradition. Once, many respected wine merchants in England as well as Scotland offered their own bottlings of single malts, as well as combining them in house blends. Glenrothes' quietly noble whisky has traditionally been a component of Berrys' internationally known Cutty Sark, and a favourite among blenders. The distillery, established in 1878, is one of five in the small town of Rothes.

The firm of Berrys' began in the 1690s, selling tea, groceries, and wine. Cutty Sark was launched in the 1920s. It is named after the famously fast tea clipper Cutty Sark, which was built in Scotland. Both Glenrothes and Cutty Sark are sold, not only in Berrys' 1730s premises in stately St. James's, London, but also in the company's stores at London's Heathrow airport.

HOUSE STYLE Perfumy, sweet, spicy-fruity, complex. After dinner.

GLENROTHES Select Reserve, 43 vol

COLOR	Pale light straw with a slight green tinge.
NOSE	Light but complex, currants, mince pie, vanilla, a hint of orange, sherbet sweets.
BODY	Medium-full, but pleasant.
PALATE	Sherry, dried fruits, balanced with spice.
FINISH	Gentle, sweet, with prunes and spices.

SCORE 75

GLENROTHES 1998, 43 vol

COLOR Rich orange.

NOSE Toffee. Vanilla. Blood orange. Dusty lemon.

BODY Smooth and creamy.

PALATE Big orange notes. Jellied-fruit candies. Traces of oak. Some late cinnamon and nutmeg.

FINISH Medium, full and fruity, with a touch of tannin and spice.

SCORE **81**

GLENROTHES 1994, 43 vol

COLOR Rich gold.

NOSE Beeswax polish, lemon detergent, rich, sweet.

BODY Rich, sweet, oily, mouth-coating.

PALATE Clean, fresh, yellow fruit, caramel, full.

FINISH Medium-long, sweet and fruity.

SCORE **80**

GLENROTHES 1992, 43 vol

COLOR Honey golden orange.

NOSE Light and floral, sprinkled with fruit dust.

BODY Full, oily, sweet.

PALATE Licorice, melon, lemon, and pineapple.

FINISH Full, with lots of fruit and spice.

SCORE **76**

GLENROTHES 1991, 43 vol

COLOR Chestnut bronze.

NOSE Soft toffee, red fruits, cassis, vanilla ice cream.

BODY rich, soft, very pleasant.

PALATE Red fruits, caramel, some sweet fruit counter-balanced by
a hint of tannin.

FINISH Medium, rounded, very balanced and pleasant.

SCORE **86**

THE GLENROTHES DISTILLERY
SAMPLE ROOM

CHARACTER: *Mellow, oak and dried fruits*

CHECKED: *J. C. Stevens* ... DATE: *8/10/89*

APPROVED: *R.K. Fenwick* ... DATE: *26·2·00*

Distilled and Bottled in Scotland. Berry Bros. & Rudd, 3 St James's St, London
PRODUCT OF SCOTLAND

DISTILLED IN **1989** BOTTLED IN 2000

43% vol. 700ml

SCOTCH WHISKY

GLENROTHES 1989, 43 vol

COLOR Old gold.

NOSE A subtle suggestion of soft licorice, as in Pontefract cakes.

BODY Generous. Supple.

PALATE The licorice more emphatic now. Spanish root. Develops juicy,
mouthwatering flavors. Anise. Coconut.

FINISH Soothing, relaxing.

SCORE **82**

GLENROTHES 1988, 43 vol

COLOR Deep chestnut brown.

NOSE Oak. Apricot. Peach. Pepper spice. Rich and complex.

BODY Rich and creamy.

PALATE Orange. Tannin. Yellow fruits. Drying with traces of oak,
but nicely balanced.

FINISH Long, fruity and oaky.

SCORE **88**

GLENROTHES 1985, 43 vol

COLOR Clear treacle brown.

NOSE Earthy, savory, chestnut, apple pip, trace of smoke.

BODY Full, rich, soft.

PALATE Rich, chewy honeyed fruits, soft peach, burned honey, woody.

FINISH Beautifully delivered mix of flavors.
Soft, sweet, and rounded.

SCORE **87**

GLENROTHES 1984, 43 vol

COLOR Pale honey gold.

NOSE Wood sap, delicate fruits, vanilla.

COLOR Pale gold.

BODY Full, rounded and warming.

PALATE Vanilla ice cream, hard candy, and then some oak and spice.

FINISH Quite spicy but sweet, medium-long.

SCORE **83**

GLENROTHES 1981, 43 vol

COLOR Pale brown with a greenish hue

NOSE Odd. Chinese food. Stewed bean shoots. Bamboo. Sugarcane. Subtle.

BODY Wispy, quite sharp, dry.

PALATE Woody. Dried apricot. At first quite sweet but thin,

then sharp pepper.

FINISH Quite long, lots of tannins and sharp spice.

SCORE **69**

GLENROTHES 1978, 43 vol

COLOR Rich, chestnut brown.

NOSE Earthy, water chestnuts, sherbety, clean, fresh.

BODY Full, imposing, creamy.

PALATE Wonderfully sweet and rounded. with vanilla, aniseed, red licorice,

plum, peaches and then a dose of oak and spice.

FINISH Very balanced, lingering and lovely.

SCORE **90**

GLENROTHES 1973, 43 vol

COLOR Amber.

NOSE Heather and sweet fruits, spice, floral, apple, prune, nutmeg.

BODY Gentle, subtle yet rich.

PALATE Layers of orange. Vanilla, spice, and raisin flowing together.

Fine tannins.

FINISH Nutty. Everlasting. Quintessential Glenrothes.

SCORE **90**

GLENROTHES 1972, 43 vol

COLOR Rich deep brown.

NOSE Rootsy, earthy, Chinese vegetables.

BODY Creamy, full and rounded.

PALATE Sweet and fruity, with licorice and vanilla, astringent and spicy.

FINISH Long. Balanced. Lots of sweet fruit offsetting the spice and tannin.

SCORE *88*

GLENROTHES 1971, 41 vol

COLOR Copper with a greeny rim.

NOSE Sweet tobacco, licorice, chewy fruit. Berry fruits, allspice.

BODY Generous, soft. Rich, old, and elegant.

PALATE Cedar, anis, cough sweet. Gently warming.

FINISH Long, complex, sophisticated.

SCORE *87*

GLENROTHES Robur Reserve, 40 vol

COLOR Pale lemon.

NOSE Bold, honey, apricot jam, sweet lemon zest, varied.

BODY Soft, rounded, creamy.

PALATE Clean barley, melon, citrus, a touch of spice.

FINISH Quite short, with a citrus fruit flourish.

SCORE *68*

GLENROTHES 25-year-old, 43 vol

COLOR Rich full bronze.

NOSE Candied fruits, spearmint sweets, orange and lemon bits, lemonade.

BODY Full, creamy, rich and sweet.

PALATE Intense sweet tropical fruit, mango, then sweet spice and
a delicate and attractive woody finish.

FINISH Beautifully balanced and long, sweet fruit, spice with some tannin.

SCORE *93*

GLENROTHES 30-year-old, 43 vol

COLOR Rich chestnut brown.

NOSE Mushroomy, damp leaves, then opens up slowly with sherried fruits
and citrus notes.

BODY Full, creamy, and sweet.

PALATE Intense sweet spice, lemon sherbet, anise, mint cake. Astringent.

FINISH Long and intense, assertive.

SCORE *88*

GLENROTHES 1967, Berrys' Own Selection, 46.3 vol

COLOR Old gold.

NOSE Lean, light. Mushroom, dry wood, cooked fruits. Fine ash.

BODY Big, soft.

PALATE Complex. Lots of flavor development. Flowers and spices galore.

FINISH Long, floral.

SCORE **85**

GLENROTHES 1966, Berrys' Own Selection, 52.8 vol

COLOR Mahogany.

NOSE Dark, woody, fig, and walnut. Madeira cake. Coffee bean.

BODY Dry. Drying.

PALATE Slightly tannic. Good balance between savory notes and dried fruits.

FINISH Long, drying.

SCORE **82**

GLENROTHES John Ramsay Legacy 46.7 vol

COLOR Rich chestnut orange.

NOSE Old and venerable. Deep red berries. Dried fruit peel. Cocoa.

BODY Soft and velvety. Creamy.

PALATE Vanilla. Cocoa. Soft orange and yellow fruits. Late peppery spice
and oak. Beautifully balanced.

FINISH Long, spicy, and satisfying.

SCORE **91**

A COUPLE OF INDEPENDENT BOTTLINGS
GLENROTHES 1970, 38-year-old,
Cask 10577, Duncan Taylor Rare Auld series, 42.3 vol

COLOR Deep orange. NOSE Grapefruit. Tangerine. Honeyed melon.
BODY Medium, balanced. PALATE Soft apple. Pear. yellow fruit, balanced by
very gentle pepper. Very fresh for its age. FINISH Medium-fruity and drying.
Balanced and pleasant. SCORE 87

GLENROTHES 1969, 39-year-old, Lonarch, 42.7 vol

COLOR Rich orangey brown. NOSE Stewed apples and then clean and fresh
bowl of green fruit. BODY Big, full and rich. PALATE Apple. Apple seed.
Touch of nutmeg and cinnamon. Finally pepper. FINISH Rich, quite long,
and a mix of fruit and pepper. SCORE 87

GLENTAUCHERS

PRODUCER Chivas Brothers (Pernod Ricard)
REGION Highlands   DISTRICT Speyside
ADDRESS Mulben, Keith, Banffshire, AB5 2YL
TEL 01542 860272

GLENTAUCHERS WAS FOUNDED IN 1898 and rebuilt in 1965. With no visitor center and few bottlings, it has not had the attention it merits. A neighbor to Auchroisk, it is in the countryside near the village of Mulben, between the distilling towns of Rothes and Keith.

When Pernod Ricard acquired Allied Domecq in 2005, Chivas Brothers gained control of the distillery.

HOUSE STYLE Clovey dryness and malty sweetness. Soothing at its best.

GLENTAUCHERS 14-year-old, James MacArthur, 58.5 vol

COLOR Pale gold.

NOSE Intense grape. Wafts of smoke. Some sulfur. Green salad.

BODY Full and oily.

PALATE Better than the nose. Sweet, rich, soft melon.

FINISH Medium and fruity. A touch of tannin at the finish.

SCORE **69**

GLENTAUCHERS 15-year-old, Dun Bheagan, 43 vol

COLOR Pale yellow.

NOSE Banana toffee. Watermelon. Rhubarb.

BODY Sweet and medium-full.

PALATE Sweet, syrupy. Hints of tannin and astringency towards the end.

FINISH Short and sweet.

SCORE **64**

GLENTAUCHERS 1990 17-year-old, Duncan Taylor, 51.6 vol

COLOR Pale yellowy green.

NOSE Fresh and vegetal. Rhubarb. Gooseberry. Rootsy.

BODY Rich, full, and mouth-coating.

PALATE Immense, with anise and marzipan at the start, then a big green fruit and spice hit. Clean and balanced, with just the right amount of tannin.

FINISH Pleasant, rounded, and balanced, with a good length.

SCORE **88**

GLENTURRET

PRODUCER The Edrington Group
REGION Highlands DISTRICT Eastern Highlands
ADDRESS Crieff, Perthshire, PH7 4HA TEL 01764 656565
WEBSITE www.famousgrouse.co.uk VC

A DISTILLERY OR an "experience"? Glenturret is certainly a
distillery: the most visitable; one of the smallest; and a claimant
to being Scotland's oldest, tucked in a pretty glen just an hour by road
from Edinburgh or Glasgow. These attributes proved irresistible to its
owners The Edrington Group, who have made it their principal visitor
center. As their biggest selling product is The Famous Grouse, this
blend has been linked to the distillery.

A visit to Glenturret is now marketed as The Famous Grouse
Experience. The visitor is presented with a very imaginative and
entertaining range of experiences, by way of a variety of hi-tech
means, though this sits oddly in the location: one of the most rustic and
traditional distilleries. A proportion of Glenturret is said to be included
in the "recipe" for The Famous Grouse. Given the size of the distillery
and the sales of Grouse, it must be a very a small amount. Glenturret's
new role has led to a rationalization in the number of bottlings, which
was very extensive and idiosyncratic.

Glenturret also has a restaurant providing Scottish dishes
(no reservations necessary for lunch; dinner for groups only). Although
its world-famous cat Towser is now hunting mice in the heavens, he is

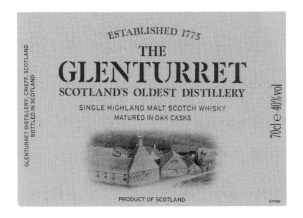

remembered in a statue. There is no monument to his alleged 28,899 victims (who documented them so precisely on behalf of Guinness World Records?).

The distillery is on the banks of the Turret River, near Crieff, in Perthshire. There are records of whisky making in the neighborhood at least as early as 1717, and some of the buildings on the present site date from 1775. The distillery itself was dismantled in the 1920s, then revived in 1959 by a noted whisky enthusiast, James Fairlie. It was acquired in 1981 by Cointreau, the French liqueur company, and became part of Highland Distillers (now Edrington) in 1990.

HOUSE STYLE Dry, nutty, fresh, flowery. Young as an aperitif; older after dinner.

GLENTURRET 10-year-old, 40 vol

COLOR Pale greeny gold.

NOSE Nasturtiums. Heavy. Sweet.

BODY Light. Seems to vanish.

PALATE Cough drops. Toffee.

FINISH Minty. Soothing.

SCORE **76**

GLENTURRET 1987, 54.8 vol

COLOR Pale gold.

NOSE Beautiful. Vanilla, freesia, fresh malt.

BODY Light.

PALATE Sweet and malty. Tangerine, cut flowers, great balance.
Wood comes through on back palate.

FINISH Clean, nutty.

SCORE **85**

AN INDEPENDENT BOTTLING
GLENTURRET 14-year-old, James MacArthur, 56.9 vol

COLOR Lemon yellow.

NOSE Pecan. Butterscotch. Over-ripe banana.

BODY Soft, sweet, and full. Creamy.

PALATE Clean sweet barley. Lemon bonbons.
Dash of pepper, touch of peppermint.

FINISH Medium and pleasant, with a dash of chili pepper at the end.

SCORE **79**

GLENUGIE

PRODUCER Whitbread/Long John
REGION Highlands   DISTRICT Eastern Highlands
SITE OF FORMER DISTILLERY Peterhead, Aberdeenshire, AB42 0XY

T HE CENTRAL STRETCH OF the East Coast has lost all its distilleries. This one was close to the remnants of a fishing village near Peterhead, where the river Ugie reaches the sea. The site incorporates the stump of a windmill. There had been distilling there since the 1830s, and the surviving buildings date from the 1870s.

The Whitbread brewing company, owners since the 1970s, gradually withdrew from the production of spirits during the 1980s, when the whisky industry was suffering one of its cyclical downturns. Industrial premises in Aberdeenshire were being snapped up by small engineering firms servicing the oil boom, and that was Glenugie's fate in 1982–83. Its whisky-making equipment was removed. There is still some stock to be found, and bottlings are still being made, though fewer as the years roll by.

HOUSE STYLE Flowery, resiny. Can be medicinal. Book-at-bedtime.

GLENUGIE 26-year-old, Old & Rare, 58 vol

COLOR Rich orange.

NOSE Dry bark. Dusty. Stewed bean shoots. Dried fruits.

BODY Full, rich, mouth-coating.

PALATE Rich sherry. Red fruits. Pleasant oakiness. Fruitcake.

FINISH Dignified. Quite smooth. Pleasant tannins. Venerable.

SCORE **76**

Douglas Laing's
Old & Rare
"A PLATINUM SELECTION"
DISTILLED: MARCH 1982   2008 A MARCH BOTTLING
SINGLE CASK · SINGLE MALT · SCOTCH WHISKY
DISTILLED AT
GLENUGIE DISTILLERY
PRODUCT OF SCOTLAND
AGED 26 YEARS
BOTTLED AT NATURAL CASK STRENGTH · TRADITIONALLY UN-CHILL FILTERED
OFFERED WITH PRIDE   THIS IS 1
58.0% alc./vol.   FROM Douglas Laing   OF 117 BOTTLES   FILLED FROM THE CASK   700ml
DISTILLED , MATURED AND BOTTLED IN SCOTLAND · DOUGLAS LAING & Co. LTD. GLASGOW G3 8EU

GLENURY ROYAL

PRODUCER DCL
REGION Highlands   DISTRICT Eastern Highlands
SITE OF FORMER DISTILLERY Stonehaven, Kincardineshire, AB3 2PY

FOUNDED IN 1825, Glenury Royal stood on the east coast of Scotland, south of Aberdeen. The water for the whisky came from the Cowie River, and the distillery's name derived from the glen that runs through the Ury district. Its founder, Captain Robert Barclay, was an athlete known for an odd achievement: he was the first man to walk 1,000 miles in as many hours without a break. He was also a local Member of Parliament. Barclay had a friend at court to whom he referred coyly as "Mrs. Windsor," and through whose influence he was given permission by King William IV to call his whisky "Royal." It was an excellent malt, judging from recent bottlings. The distillery was mothballed in 1985, and the site later sold for a housing development.

HOUSE STYLE Aromatic, spicy, fruity. Book-at-bedtime.

GLENURY 1953, 50-year-old, 42.8 vol

COLOR Dark orange.

NOSE Smoke. The burned skin of chestnuts roasting.

BODY Rich, smooth, luxurious.

PALATE A box of liqueur chocolates concentrated into a tasting glass. Dark chocolate, filled with coffee, cherry, and perhaps even peppermint liqueurs.

FINISH Sappy, oaky dryness.

SCORE 89

INDEPENDENT BOTTLINGS
GLENURY ROYAL 1984, Gordon & MacPhail, 43 vol

COLOR Bright copper. NOSE Complex. Rich, with sherry, figs, plums, smoke, and polished leather. BODY Silky. PALATE Full and fruity, lively spice, and succulent, gently smoked malt. FINISH Fruit candies. A lick of licorice with water. SCORE 84

GLENURY ROYAL 1984, 23-year-old, Rarest of the Rare, 49.3 vol

COLOR Gold. NOSE Lemon curd. Clean. Sherbety. BODY Thin. PALATE Lemon-flavored mineral water. Sweet, elegant. Faint trace of pepper. FINISH Short and citrus. Quite pleasant. SCORE 72

HIGHLAND PARK

PRODUCER The Edrington Group
REGION Highlands ISLAND Orkney
ADDRESS Kirkwall, Orkney, KW15 1SU TEL 01856 874619 VC
WEBSITE www.highlandpark.co.uk

THIS GREAT ORCADIAN DISTILLERY is now the only islander in The Edrington Group, with the sale of Bunnahabhain, on Islay. Presumably the idea was to concentrate on Highland Park as the group's island malt, and pitch the distinctiveness of Orkney against fashionable Islay. Devotees might expect a clamor of new bottlings from Highland Park: labeled to emphasize the distinctly young, heathery nature of Orkney's peat; the simple beauty of the maltings at the distillery; the big, bulbous stills; the winds that blow salt on to the shore. So far, nothing much has happened, but no doubt it will.

Highland Park is the greatest all-rounder in the world of malt whisky. It is definitely in an island style, but it combines all the elements of a classic single malt: smokiness (with its own heather-honey accent), maltiness, smoothness, roundness, fullness of flavor, and length of finish.

Interest in Scotland's northernmost distillery remains high, aided by the release of some limited edition special expressions.

HOUSE STYLE Smoky and full-flavored. At 18 or 25 years old, with dessert or a cigar. The yet older vintages with a book at bedtime.

HIGHLAND PARK 12-year-old, 40 vol

COLOR Amber.

NOSE Smoky, "garden bonfire" sweetness. Heathery,
malty, a hint of sherry.

BODY Medium, exceptionally smooth.

PALATE Succulent. Smoky dryness, heather-honey sweetness, and maltiness.

FINISH Teasing, heathery, delicious.

SCORE 90

HIGHLAND PARK 15-year-old, 40 vol

COLOR Amber.

NOSE Thick and sweet. Botrytis. Squashed apricot, over-ripe pear.
Toasted almond, beech nut.

BODY Chewy.

PALATE Great balance between caramelized fruit, honey, and heathery
smoke. Mouth-filling. Fudge. Malt.

FINISH Molasses toffee.

SCORE 87

HIGHLAND PARK 16-year-old, 40 vol

COLOR Deep gold.

NOSE Restrained, with honey, some orange, banana, and sweet citrus.

BODY Soft, sweet, and gentle; rounded and balanced.

PALATE Honey followed by a balanced peat-oak double act,
then orange sweets and traces of peat.

FINISH Like fruit juice; with orange, peat, and smoke.
Surprisingly delicate and short.

SCORE **78**

HIGHLAND PARK 18-year-old, 43 vol

COLOR Refractive, pale gold.

NOSE Warm, notably flowery. Heather honey, fresh oak, sap, peat,
smoky fragrance. Very aromatic and appetizing.

BODY Remarkably smooth; firm; rounded.

PALATE Lightly salty. Leafy (vine leaves?), pine nuts. Lots of flavor
development: nuts, honey, cinnamon, dryish ginger.

FINISH Spicy. Very dry. Oaky, smoky, and hot.

SCORE **92**

HIGHLAND PARK 25-year-old, 50.7 vol

COLOR Amber to copper.

NOSE Immense complexity. Rum and raisin, Christmas spices, dried heather, light smoke.

BODY Layered.

PALATE Mature, with perfect poise. Chocolate. Nutty oak. Fine tannins. Light smoke.

FINISH Long and subtle, with bitter orange and scented lemon.

SCORE **95**

HIGHLAND PARK 25-year-old, 48 vol

The most recent bottling at this age.

COLOR Rich deep gold.

NOSE Delicate. Grapefruit. Lemon flu powder.

BODY Soft and gentle; not too assertive.

PALATE A game of two halves: first honeyed and gentle, with orange barley and sweet fruits; then a big dose of spice, oak, and peat.

FINISH Medium, rich, and spicy, with an intriguing clash between honeyed sweet fruit and sharp spice.

SCORE **85**

HIGHLAND PARK 1977,
Bicentenary Vintage Reserve, 43 vol

COLOR Pale walnut.

NOSE Polished oak. Leather upholstery.

BODY Firm satin richness.

PALATE Minty. Creamy. Freshly peeled satsuma plums. Orange peels. Dark cherry flavors. Very bitter dark chocolate. Astonishing complexity and length. Great power. Long development of drier flavors.

FINISH Violets. Lingering flowery, scented flavors.

SCORE **94**

HIGHLAND PARK 40-year-old, 48 vol

COLOR Dark mahogany with a green tinge.

NOSE Venerable. Soft nectar, scented wax candles, sweet citrus potpourri.

BODY Silky, soft, sweet, and full.

PALATE Stunning and complex mix of stewed, syrupy, mixed exotic fruits with honey, lemon, and peat.

FINISH A classic Highland Park battle between peat, oak, fruit, and spice. Long.

SCORE **91**

AN INDEPENDENT BOTTLING
HIGHLAND PARK 21-year-old, Duncan Taylor, 53.3 vol

COLOR Rich yellow.

NOSE Lemon, citrus. Sweet melon. Pineapple chunks.

BODY Gentle, soft, and sweet.

PALATE Soft and sweet. Melon. Sweet grapefruit. Vanilla. Gentle sweet pepper. Clean.

FINISH Quite long, sweet, and fruity. Blemish-free, despite its age. Honeyed.

SCORE **90**

IMPERIAL

PRODUCER Allied Distillers Ltd.
REGION Highlands DISTRICT Speyside
ADDRESS Carron, Morayshire, AB34 7QP

MALT LOVERS THIRSTING FOR THIS underrated and rarely bottled Speysider have in recent years been permitted to satiate their desires through a number of independent bottlings.

The Imperial distillery is in Carron, just across the river from Dailuaine, with which it was historically linked. It was founded in 1897 and extended in 1965. It closed in 1985, but was reopened by Allied in 1989, then mothballed in 1998. Imperial's unusually large stills make it hard to use flexibly. "You either make a lot of Imperial or none at all," commented one observer.

HOUSE STYLE Big and (often sweetly) smoky.
After dinner or at bedtime.

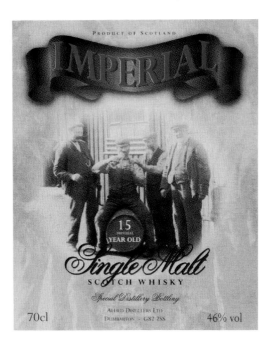

IMPERIAL 15-year-old,
Special Distillery Bottlings, 46 vol

COLOR Golden satin. Slight haze.

NOSE Lemon meringue pie. Key lime pie. Not only the fruit filling, but also the pastry. Slightly floury, dusty. Some cellar character.

BODY Thin but smooth. Falls away somewhat.

PALATE Lemon skins. Some sweet lemon, becoming quite intense, then drying. Rounds out with a little water.

FINISH Gently dry. Slight hint of smoky dryness.

SCORE **71**

IMPERIAL 13-year-old, Duncan Taylor N.C.2, 46 vol

COLOR Pale yellow.

NOSE Canned pineapple. Fruit sprinkles. Clean. Vanilla. Fresh flowers.

BODY Soft and well-balanced.

PALATE Fresh rich fruits. Some late spice.

FINISH Rich and spicy.

SCORE **80**

IMPERIAL 1990, 18-year-old, Cask No 354,
Duncan Taylor, 51.9 vol

COLOR Honey gold.

NOSE Spearmint. Lime. Refreshing and clean.

BODY Soft, pleasant, rounded.

PALATE Sweet. Grapefruit and lime. Soft and pleasant. Syrupy fruit bowl.

FINISH Short and sweet, with the merest hint of wood.

SCORE **83**

IMPERIAL 1990, 18-year-old, Duncan Taylor, 55 vol

COLOR Rich orange.

NOSE Canned melon. Exotic fruits. Glacé cherries. Vanilla. Sweet and clean.

BODY Full, sweet, balanced.

PALATE Full and fruity. Exotic fruits, as with the nose, balanced by some underlying spice.

FINISH Medium, with sugar and spice. Delightful and balanced.

SCORE **90**

INCHGOWER

PRODUCER Diageo
REGION Highlands DISTRICT Speyside
ADDRESS Buckie, Banffshire, AB56 2AB TEL 01542 836700

Tastes more like a coastal malt than a Speysider. It is both, the distillery being on the coast near the fishing town of Buckie, but not far from the mouth of the Spey River. To the palate expecting a more flowery, elegant Speyside style, this can seem assertive, or even astringent, in its saltiness. With familiarity, that can become addictive. The Inchgower distillery was built in 1871, and expanded in 1966. Its whisky is an important element in the Bell's blend.

HOUSE STYLE Dry, salty. Restorative or aperitif.

INCHGOWER 14-year-old, Fauna & Flora, 43 vol

COLOR Pale gold.

NOSE An almost chocolatey spiciness, then sweet notes like edible seaweed, and finally a whiff of saltier sea character. Overall, dry and complex.

BODY Light to medium. Smooth.

PALATE Starts sweet and malty, with lots of flavor developing, eventually becoming drier and salty.

FINISH Very salty, lingering appetizingly on the tongue.

SCORE 76

INCHGOWER 14-year-old, Old Malt Cask, 50 vol

COLOR Rich honey brown.

NOSE Maple syrup. Vanilla. Butterscotch.

BODY Rich and velvety.

PALATE Melon and other soft, yellow fruit. Some tannins.

FINISH Medium, sweet, and woody.

SCORE **67**

INCHGOWER 1992, 15-year-old, N.C.2, 46 vol

COLOR Very pale yellow.

NOSE Grass meadow. Slightly zesty citrus. Shy.

BODY Medium, clean, and sweet.

PALATE Simple, clean, and pleasant malted barley.
A touch of late pepper.

FINISH Peppery, with some fruit and a pleasant
barley aftertaste.

SCORE **69**

INCHGOWER 21-year-old, Old Malt Cask, 50 vol

COLOR Rich gold.

NOSE Mixed fruit bowl. Full. Vanilla. Honeycomb.

BODY Soft and pleasant.

PALATE Soft fruits at first. Peach. Lime. After a while, the
tannins and spices take over.

FINISH Prickly. Salt and pepper. Medium.

SCORE **74**

INCHGOWER 34-year-old,
Single Malts of Scotland, 61.2 vol

COLOR Clear gold.

NOSE Pure and clean. Spearmint. Blackcurrant. Surprisingly
zesty and fresh.

BODY Full, mouth-coating, and spicy.

PALATE Honeyed melon. Grapes. Rich, juicy barley.
Then a big wave of pepper and oak.

FINISH Long, with lots of spice and tannins.

SCORE **76**

INVERLEVEN

PRODUCER Allied Distillers Ltd.
REGION Lowlands DISTRICT Western Lowlands
ADDRESS 2 Glasgow Road, Dumbarton, Dunbartonshire, G82 1ND

A LANDMARK VANISHED when Ballantine's distillery complex at Dumbarton was demolished in 2002. The towering 1930s building had stood like a castle where the Leven River flows into the Clyde estuary. For many years, this complex operated not only a column still making grain whisky, but also two pot-still houses to produce malt for the Ballantine blends. One of the malt distilleries, called Inverleven, had conventional stills. The other produced a heavier, Lomond-still whisky. Malt production ceased in 1991–92, two more Lowlanders ceding superiority to the Highlands and Islands.

HOUSE STYLE Perfumy, fruity, oily. With a summer salad when young; with nuts at Christmas when older.

INVERLEVEN 1979 28-year-old, Rarest of the Rare, 57 vol

COLOR Full yellow.

NOSE Delightful. Banana toffee. Sweet grapefruit. Over-ripe pear, with some tobacco pipe smokiness.

BODY Full, rich, and sweet.

PALATE Anise. Canned pear. Marzipan. Stewed fruits. Clean and balanced.

FINISH Melon and pear. Pepper spice. Medium-long.

SCORE 89

JURA

PRODUCER Whyte and Mackay Ltd.
REGION Highlands   ISLAND Jura
ADDRESS Craighouse, Jura, Argyll, PA60 7XT
TEL 01496 820240   WEBSITE www.isleofjura.com   VC

EVERY VISITOR TO ISLAY also makes the crossing to Jura. The two are so close that they tend to be seen as one. While Islay has seven working distilleries, Jura has just the one. While Islay has some very assertive whiskies, Jura's is delicate—but gains power with age. Under new ownership, the distillery has been more active in introducing new products and marketing them with some vigor.

Two extraordinarily young bottlings, at three and four years old, were made for the Japanese market. Both showed considerable potential. The younger was clean, malty, and assertive, with good maritime flavors. The marginally less young version was more earthy, flowery, and fruity. In the British market, "Superstition" is a sweeter, richer, mature whisky, but seems a little confected, like its marketing story.

The first distillery on the site seems to have been founded around 1810, and rebuilt in 1876. Although a couple of buildings dating back to its early days are still in use, the present distillery was built during the late 1950s and early 1960s, and enlarged in the 1970s.

The name Jura derives from the Norse word for deer. These outnumber people, on an island 34 by 7 miles (55 by 11 kilometers). Jura has about 225 human inhabitants, among whom its most famous was George Orwell. He went there to find a healthy, peaceful place in which to write the novel *Nineteen Eighty-four*. A whisky named after him was added to the Jura range in 2003.

HOUSE STYLE Piney, lightly oily, soft, salty. Aperitif.

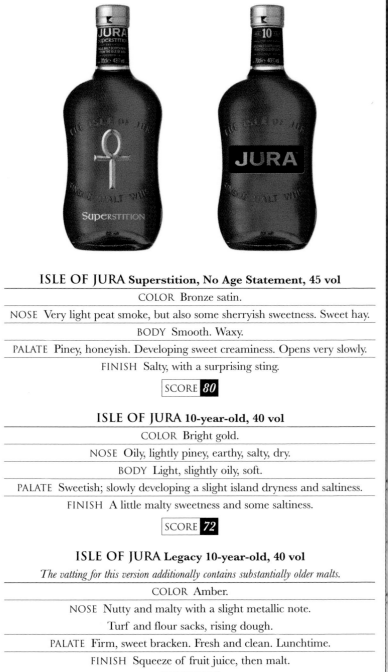

ISLE OF JURA Superstition, No Age Statement, 45 vol

COLOR Bronze satin.

NOSE Very light peat smoke, but also some sherryish sweetness. Sweet hay.

BODY Smooth. Waxy.

PALATE Piney, honeyish. Developing sweet creaminess. Opens very slowly.

FINISH Salty, with a surprising sting.

SCORE **80**

ISLE OF JURA 10-year-old, 40 vol

COLOR Bright gold.

NOSE Oily, lightly piney, earthy, salty, dry.

BODY Light, slightly oily, soft.

PALATE Sweetish; slowly developing a slight island dryness and saltiness.

FINISH A little malty sweetness and some saltiness.

SCORE **72**

ISLE OF JURA Legacy 10-year-old, 40 vol

The vatting for this version additionally contains substantially older malts.

COLOR Amber.

NOSE Nutty and malty with a slight metallic note.
Turf and flour sacks, rising dough.

PALATE Firm, sweet bracken. Fresh and clean. Lunchtime.

FINISH Squeeze of fruit juice, then malt.

SCORE **70**

ISLE OF JURA, 16-year-old, 40 vol

COLOR	Full gold to bronze.
NOSE	Freshly chopped pine trees. Ferns. Forest floor.
BODY	Light, firm, oily-creamy. Dryish.
PALATE	Ground coriander. Orange. Rhubarb jam. Buttered scones.
FINISH	Salty.

SCORE **77**

ISLE OF JURA Orwell, 42 vol

COLOR	Gold.
NOSE	Quite woody and prickly to start. Heather moor, marine. Mossy.
BODY	Dry.
PALATE	Broad with light smoke all the way playing against central tangerine-flavored sweetness. Some complexity.
FINISH	Nutty.

SCORE **78**

ISLE OF JURA 21-year-old, 43 vol

COLOR	Pale orange.
NOSE	Cedary. Then surprisingly fruity and tropical. Canned pineapple, cooked peach, papaya, melon.
BODY	Luscious.
PALATE	Oak. Fruitiness becomes more orangey. Sweet tobacco.
FINISH	Soft fruit. Refreshing acidity.

SCORE **80**

ISLE OF JURA 18-year-old

COLOR Amber honey gold.

NOSE Fresh and piney, with a hint of marzipan. Sherry and smoke.

BODY Medium.

PALATE Quite dry and nutty, with mint toffee
and developing oloroso sherry.

FINISH Fairly lengthy; subtly sherried. Licorice and
ginger at the close.

SCORE **79**

ISLE OF JURA Elements Earth

Distilled from heavily peated malt.

COLOR Mid-orange.

NOSE Soft peat, wood smoke, damp vegetation, fresh soil,
a hint of cinnamon.

BODY Waxy.

PALATE Lively and spicy, some salt, ginger, smoldering peat
and fresh citrus fruit.

FINISH Medium, fruity, insistently spicy.

SCORE **79**

ISLE OF JURA Elements Fire

Finished in fired, ex-bourbon casks.

COLOR Bronze.

NOSE Garden flowers, chewy toffee, vanilla, and citrus fruits.

BODY Quite full and silky.

PALATE Vanilla, honey, dried fruits, and gentle spices.

FINISH Spices, vanilla, and milk chocolate linger.

SCORE **81**

ISLE OF JURA Elements Air

Matured in air-seasoned, ex-Spanish manzanilla barrels.

COLOR Light gold.

NOSE Fragrant, with sherry, nuts, and fruit cake. Hints of
sea spray and citrus.

BODY Firm.

PALATE Quite dry, dark chocolate, salt, muted sherry.

FINISH Nutty, with damp oak.

SCORE **79**

ISLE OF JURA Elements Water

Made using water from Jura's ancient Loch a'Bhaile Mhargaidh,
reputed to have life-prolonging properties.

COLOR Light bronze.

NOSE Floral. Developing sherry, orange marmalade, marzipan.
A whiff of smoke.

BODY Medium, slightly oily.

PALATE Sherry, oranges, hazelnuts, coffee.

FINISH Sherry, Java coffee, drying oak.

SCORE **81**

ISLE OF JURA 1974, 44.5 vol

COLOR Copper.

NOSE Fresh, with ozone, cinnamon, and dried fruits.

BODY Medium, smooth.

PALATE Fruity, with oranges, marzipan, honey, and lively spices.

FINISH Caramel and gentle smoke.

SCORE **81**

ISLE OF JURA 40-year-old, 46 vol.

COLOR Golden amber.

NOSE Initially, pine air freshener, then heather, hazelnuts,
and marzipan.

BODY Medium, silky.

PALATE Nutty and spicy, with licorice and a hint of cinnamon.
Complex.

FINISH Drying and oaky, with oloroso sherry.

SCORE **81**

AN INDEPENDENT BOTTLING
ISLE OF JURA 1992, Gordon & MacPhail, 43 vol

COLOR Pale yellow

NOSE Initially slightly earthy, with perfume and hay aromas
coming through.

BODY Soft and light.

PALATE Fruit salad, malt and spices.

FINISH Drying and gently peppery.

SCORE **80**

KILCHOMAN

PRODUCER Kilchoman Distillery Company
REGION Islay   DISTRICT Machir Bay
ADDRESS Rockside Farm, Bruichladdich, Islay, PA49 7UT
TEL 01496 850011   WEBSITE www.kilchomandistillery.com   VC

I N THE SAME WEEK that flooding forced hundreds of people from their homes in eastern Scotland and torrential storms and gales caused mayhem in the west, Islay was blessed with sunshine as the whisky industry turned out to welcome a new member to its fold.

It's not every day that a new distillery releases its first whisky—in the case of Islay, in fact, it's the first time it has happened in more than 120 years. In traditional style, and with a degree of emotion, the malt was piped in and offered to a large group of guests, including representatives from all of Islay's other distilleries.

Kilchoman calls itself a farm distillery, and it is now officially Scotland's most westerly whisky producer, it being just a few miles northwest of Bruichladdich. It is a small, traditional distillery and uses locally grown barley and peat dug from the area. The whisky is distinctively Islay in flavor, with rich, sweet peat notes.

KILCHOMAN 3-year-old Inaugural Release, 46 vol

COLOR Pale gold.	
NOSE Peat. Wood smoke. Fresh. Vinous. Green fruit.	
BODY Rich and oily.	
PALATE Sharp citrus fruits. Fresh. Dark chocolate. Intense coal smoke. Industrial.	
FINISH Medium, clean, and very peaty.	

SCORE **84**

KNOCKANDO

PRODUCER Diageo
REGION Highlands DISTRICT Speyside
ADDRESS Knockando, Aberlour, Banffshire, AB38 7RT
TEL 01340 882000

MORE WAS HEARD OF this elegant whisky—in Britain, at least—when it was the most promoted malt in the portfolio of IDV, before the merger that created Diageo in 1997.

Knockando is among a small group of malts that are especially influential in the J&B (Justerini & Brooks) blends (*see also* Glen Spey). Knockando is a sophisticated malt, and its labelling policy is somewhat elaborate. The notion is that the malt is bottled when it is mature, rather than at a specific age.

One season does not differ dramatically from another, though there are very subtle differences. At older ages, the whisky gains greatly in complexity and sherry character.

The water with which the whisky is made rises from granite and flows over peat. The distillery's name, pronounced "knock-AN-do" (or 'du) sounds allusively comical to English speakers, but translates perfectly sensibly as "a little black hill." Knockando is hidden in a fold in the hills overlooking the Spey River at a fine spot for salmon fishing. The distillery was established in 1898.

HOUSE STYLE Elegant, with suggestions of berry fruits. Aperitif.

KNOCKANDO 12-year-old, 1996 Distillation, 43 vol

COLOR Light gold.

NOSE Subtle and complex. Quite light. Grapes. Grassy. Barley.

BODY Light and unassertive.

PALATE Sour fruit and apple seed, then sharp barley. Firm and
oily center, then a strong wave of spices.

FINISH Long and spicy.

SCORE 77

KNOCKANDO 18-year-old, 1980, 43 vol

Available mainly in the US.

COLOR Medium-gold.

NOSE More shortbread. Almonds. Nice balance of late lemon.

BODY Creamier. Rounder. Very smooth indeed.

PALATE Nuttier, spicier, drier. Tightly combined flavors.

FINISH Late fruit, lemongrass, and light peat.
Very appetizing.

SCORE 78

KNOCKANDO 1989, 43 vol

COLOR Bright gold.

NOSE Faint, grassy, sweetish, peaty. Lemon grass.
Marshmallow. Shortbread.

BODY Light but smooth.

PALATE Soft, creamy, faintly honeyed. Raspberries. Lemon zest.

FINISH Nutty, toffeeish dryness. Gently appetizing.

SCORE 76

AN INDEPENDENT BOTTLING
KNOCKANDO 1980, 28-year-old, Duncan Taylor 46.7 vol

COLOR Straw yellow.

NOSE Yellow fruit. Lime Starburst.

BODY Soft and rounded.

PALATE Subtle and evolving. Clean and sweet. Light but pleasant
fruit mix. Some late spice.

FINISH Medium and fruity, then a big spice hit.

SCORE 83

KNOCKDHU

PRODUCER Inver House Distillers Ltd.
REGION Highlands   DISTRICT Speyside (Isla/Deveron)
ADDRESS Knock by Huntly, Aberdeenshire, AB5 5LJ
WEBSITE www.inverhouse.com   EMAIL enquiries@inverhouse.com

KNOCKDHU IS THE ENGLISH VERSION of the Gaelic words for Little Black Hill, *Cnoc Dubh*. But because Diageo has a distillery with the name Knockando, Inver House was encouraged to use the name An Cnoc on its bottles to avoid confusion. It is the Gaelic for The Hill. There was probably no thought of confusion when these two distilleries were established, both in the 1890s, as their original purpose was to produce whisky for blending, rather than as single malt.

Knockdhu was built in 1894 to supply malt for the Haig blends, and closed in 1983. Only after its acquisition by the present owners, and its reopening, did official bottlings, albeit on a small scale, begin to be issued in the 1990s. These have become more common in recent years, and the brand has been repackaged, new expressions released, and the name "An Cnoc" used on bottlings.

HOUSE STYLE Creamy and fruity. A dessert malt?

12 YEARS OLD

anCnoc
HIGHLAND SINGLE MALT
SCOTCH WHISKY

PRONOUNCED: [a-nock]
The Knockdhu Distillery nestles under the black Knock Hill, known to the locals by its Gaelic name of anCnoc.

DISTILLED, MATURED AND BOTTLED IN SCOTLAND BY THE KNOCKDHU DISTILLERY COMPANY, ABERDEENSHIRE, AB54 7LJ.

Established 1894

70cle 40% Vol

16 YEARS OLD
MATURED IN AMERICAN BOURBON BARRELS

anCnoc
HIGHLAND SINGLE MALT
SCOTCH WHISKY

PRONOUNCED: [a-nock]
Wholly matured in the finest hand selected American Bourbon barrels

unchill-filtered

DISTILLED, MATURED AND BOTTLED IN SCOTLAND BY THE KNOCKDHU DISTILLERY COMPANY, ABERDEENSHIRE, AB54 7LJ.

Established 1894

70cle 46% Vol

DISTILLED
1994
BOTTLED NOVEMBER 2006

anCnoc
HIGHLAND SINGLE MALT
SCOTCH WHISKY

PRONOUNCED: [a-nock]
This fine unchill-filtered Single Malt has been carefully selected at its most optimum level.

unchill-filtered

DISTILLED, MATURED AND BOTTLED IN SCOTLAND BY THE KNOCKDHU DISTILLERY COMPANY, ABERDEENSHIRE, AB54 7LJ.

Established 1894

70cle 46% Vol

AN CNOC 12-year-old, 40 vol

COLOR Yellow with a greenish hue.

NOSE Pepper. Dusty. Coal smoke. Fresh, clean, cut barley.

BODY Medium and rich.

PALATE Sweet barley. Very clean. Herbal. Then gradually spices
and fruit, which rise to a crescendo.

FINISH Quite long, with lots of spices and a soft
melon-like fruitiness.

SCORE **80**

AN CNOC 16-year-old, 46 vol

COLOR Deep orangey yellow.

NOSE Pineapple sweets. Crystalized barley. Fresh meadow.
Confectionery. Bourbon notes.

BODY Rich full and sweet.

PALATE Sweet barley. Honeyed. Rich yellow and orange fruits.
Later a gentle and pleasant wave of oak and spice.

FINISH Long, rich, spicy, and sweet.

SCORE **85**

AN CNOC 1994, 46 vol

COLOR Rich bronze.

NOSE Clean, crystallized ginger. Hard candies. Sweet citrus.

BODY Medium, clean, and refreshing.

PALATE Very sweet and palatable. Fruity lozenges. Lots of sugary spices.
Vanilla. Very addictive.

FINISH Sweet, clean, long, and spicy.

SCORE **83**

AN CNOC 1975, 50 vol

COLOR Rich golden orange

NOSE Subtle; lemon, lime, honey, fruit zest, a bag of candies, vanilla.

BODY Rounded, medium-full; sweet and welcoming.

PALATE Soft and rounded, with honey and sweet fruits. Very balanced,
with chewy barley and a hint of wood and smoke.

FINISH Sweet, with the merest hint of age; some subtle tannin and spice.
Overall: pleasant and gentle.

SCORE **83**

LAGAVULIN

PRODUCER **Diageo**
REGION **Islay**   DISTRICT **South Shore**
ADDRESS **Port Ellen, Islay, Argyll, PA42 7DZ**   TEL **01496 302730**
WEBSITE **www.discovering-distilleries.com/www.malts.com**

I N RECENT YEARS, LAGAVULIN has lost its position as the best-selling Islay single malt, largely due to a dearth of its principal 16-year-old expression. This was a result of the distillery working for just two days per week for much of the 1980s. Today, it is operating 24 hours a day, seven days a week in order to meet demand. Consideration was given to adding a pair of stills, but it was felt that might "damage the integrity" of the beautifully kept distillery.

Lagavulin has the driest and most sustained attack of any readily available whisky, though in recent years it has seemed less brutal than it once was. The launch in 1997–98 of a version identified as being finished in Pedro Ximénez sherry casks excited great interest. How would this famously robust whisky live with the most hefty of sherries? Would each cancel out the other, so that the punch was finally restrained? Or would the two combine to produce a superpower? Neither is quite the case. The two elements are like heavyweights punching in a clinch.

The distillery's water arrives by way of a fast-flowing stream that no doubt picks up plenty of peat on the way. The maturation warehouses are battered by the sea, and they have their own jetty.

Lagavulin (pronounced "lagga-voolin") means "the hollow where the mill is." There are reputed to have been ten illicit stills on this bay in the mid-1700s. Lagavulin traces its history to 1816.

HOUSE STYLE **Dry, smoky, complex. Restorative or nightcap.**

LAGAVULIN 12-year-old, Cask Strength, Special Release 2003, 57.8 vol

COLOR Unusually pale. Vinho verde.

NOSE Delightfully gentle smokiness, but very restrained for Lagavulin. Some floweriness.

BODY Very light.

PALATE Marshmallow. Plain cookies. Assam tea.

FINISH Smoky. Some of the peatiness that might be expected in Lagavulin. Slightly fruity. Warming. Firm. Long.

SCORE 91

LAGAVULIN 12-year-old, Distilled 1995, 48 vol

Matured exclusively in European oak casks and bottled for Friends of the Classic Malts.

COLOR Orange.

NOSE Smoked fish, spices, and sweet barley notes.

BODY Rounded.

PALATE Full, fruity, and sweet, with cooked oranges, brittle toffee, and peat smoke.

FINISH Medium in length, with caramel and peat fire ash.

SCORE 91

LAGAVULIN 12-year-old, Special Releases, 2008, 56.4 vol

COLOR Pale gold with copper highlights.

NOSE Soft and buttery, with fruity peat smoke, grilled fish, and a hint of vanilla.

BODY Medium. Gently oily.

PALATE Heavily smoked. Sweet malt and hazelnuts.

FINISH Long and ashy, with lingering sweet peat.

SCORE 92

LAGAVULIN 16-year-old, 43 vol

COLOR Full amber.

NOSE Sea spray, peat smoke. Stings the back of the nose.

BODY Full, smooth, very firm.

PALATE Peaty dryness like gunpowder tea. As the palate develops, oily, grassy, and, in particular, salty notes emerge.

FINISH Peat fire. Warming. A bear hug.

SCORE 95

LAGAVULIN 1979, Double Matured, Distillers Edition, 43 vol

Finished in Pedro Ximénez sherry casks.

COLOR Orange sandstone.

NOSE Fresh attack, with hits of peat, tar, sulfur, and salt, soothed with beeswax.

BODY Full. Syrupy.

PALATE Rich and extremely sweet, then smoky, becoming medicinal, and eventually seaweedy.

FINISH Pepper, salt, sand. What it loses in distillery character, it gains in a different dimension of distinctiveness.

SCORE 95

LAGAVULIN 1989, Distillers Edition, Double Matured, Bottled 2005, 43 vol

Finished in Pedro Ximénez sherry casks.

COLOR Rich amber with orange highlights.

NOSE Smoky and mildly fishy, with big, sherried, stewed fruit and raisin notes.

BODY Full.

PALATE A textbook marriage of Islay peat smoke and Spanish sherry.

FINISH Long, softly smoky, and gently spiced. Beautifully balanced.

SCORE 95

LAPHROAIG

PRODUCER Beam Global
REGION Islay   DISTRICT South Shore
ADDRESS Port Ellen, Islay, Argyll, PA42 7DU
TEL 01496 302418   WEBSITE www.laphroaig.com   VC

T HIS IS THE MOST MEDICINAL of malts. "Love it or hate it," said one of Laphroaig's advertising slogans. Like hospital gauze? Reminiscent of mouthwash or antiseptic? Phenolic? That is the whole point: the iodine-like, seaweed character of Islay.

Many feel that the famous Laphroaig attack has diminished a little in recent years, unmasking more of the sweetness of the malt, but it is still an extremely characterful whisky, with a distinctively oily body. And a new version of the malt, partially matured in quarter-size casks, has restored some of the intensity that Laphroaig drinkers look for. Laphroaig has its own peat beds on Islay, its own dam on the Kilbride river, a floor maltings at the distillery, and relatively small stills. Its maturation warehouses face directly on to the sea.

The distillery was built in the 1820s by the Johnston family, whose name is still on the label. In 1847 the founder died after falling into a vat of partially made whisky. In the late 1950s and early 1960s, the distillery was owned by a woman, Miss Bessie Williamson—a glamorous lady, judging from a photograph on the wall. The romance of the place extends to occasional weddings at the distillery, part of which serves as the village hall. The distillery is now owned by Beam Global and watched over by a dedicated malt team, auguring well for its future.

HOUSE STYLE Medicinal. Nightcap.

LAPHROAIG Quarter Cask, 48 vol

COLOR Rich gold.

NOSE Grungey. Boat house. Industrial smoke and tar. Lemon juice. Intense.

BODY Rich, oily. Full mouth-feel.

PALATE A smoky rainbow, from sweet barley and full fruit
through to intense peat and seaweed.

FINISH Long, perfectly weighted, with rich and intense peat and smoke.
Classic Laphroaig.

SCORE *91*

LAPHROAIG 10-year-old

Versions have been marketed at 40 and 43 vol. The stronger is slightly richer.

COLOR Full, refractive gold.

NOSE Medicinal, phenolic, seaweedy, with a hint of estery
(gooseberry?) sweetness.

BODY Medium, oily.

PALATE Seaweedy, salty, oily.

FINISH Round and very dry.

SCORE *86*

LAPHROAIG 10-year-old, Cask Strength, 57.3 vol

COLOR Very full gold.

NOSE Drier, with "tarred rope" phenol.

BODY Medium, with some syrupy viscosity.

PALATE Seaweedy. Both salty and sweet. Tar-like.

FINISH Medicinal. Tar, phenol, peat, earth. A wonderfully
complex whisky.

SCORE *88*

LAPHROAIG 15-year-old, 43 vol

COLOR Pale amber.

NOSE Phenol, tar, sulfur.

BODY Medium to full, with a soothing oiliness.

PALATE A deceptive moment of sweetness and grassiness, then
an explosion of sulfur, burning peat, and Islay intensity.

FINISH Round, dry, long, warming.

SCORE 89

LAPHROAIG 18-year-old, 48 vol

COLOR Bright golden orange.

NOSE Brine and sea spray. Greasy rope. Hot road tar in the rain.

BODY Full and oily.

PALATE Industrial steam engine. Red licorice. Peppered steak cooked
on a hickory barbecue. Big and brooding.

FINISH Long, with peat coating the mouth and licorice
and hickory lingering.

SCORE 93

LAPHROAIG 25-year-old, 50.9 vol

COLOR Honey gold.

NOSE Grapey, earthy, dairy, laundry room.
Very unlike Laphroaig.

BODY Medium, quite thin, savory.

PALATE Grape. Savory. Astringency from the wood,
some citrus notes, unripe green fruit, cocoa dark chocolate,
and hints of peat.

FINISH At last a distinctive peat wave comes through—
better late than never. Cocoa and fruit.

SCORE 73

LAPHROAIG 27-year-old, 57.4 vol

COLOR Horse chestnut with plum-red hues.

NOSE Deep and rich, dark rose petals, dried fruits,
earthy, red wine.

BODY Very full and big. Venerable, enticing, teasing.

PALATE Two oral explosions for the price of one. Masses of sherry,
stewed plums, and fruit at war with intense smoke and peat. Tannins
and spices act as ringmasters.

FINISH Long, intense, pruney, and smoky. Unforgettable.

SCORE 95

LAPHROAIG 30-year-old, Bottled November 1997, 43 vol

Bottled from 123 sherry butts branded with the legend SS Great Auk, believed to be the ship in which they came from Jerez over three decades ago.

COLOR Dark orange.

NOSE Soft. Polished oak. Fragrant smoke. Roses. Lemony notes.

BODY Full, creamy.

PALATE Astonishingly fresh. Toasted almonds. Edible seaweed. Briar. Smoke.

FINISH Musky. Bittersweet. Beautifully balanced for such a great age.

SCORE **90**

LAPHROAIG 40-year-old, 42.3 vol

COLOR Old gold.

NOSE Heather and sage. Very subtle smoke in the background.

BODY Soft.

PALATE Concentrated flavors. Less iodine than usual. More pepper. Unusual, but very lively and appetizing. Flowery notes.

FINISH Very smoky. Complex.

SCORE **88**

TWO INDEPENDENT BOTTLINGS
LAPHROAIG 1987, Duncan Taylor, 53.2 vol

COLOR Rich orange.

NOSE Lots of peat. Treacle. Sweet-and-sour spare ribs.

BODY Oily and full.

PALATE Grilled trout. Whisky salt. Lemon zest. Barbecue smoke. Peat.

FINISH Medium, balanced between fruits and smoke.

SCORE **87**

LP1, Elements of Islay, Speciality Drinks, 58.8 vol

COLOR Pale brassy yellow.

NOSE Classic Laphroaig. Heavy smoked kipper. Industrial smoke. Steam engines. Grungey peat.

BODY Rich, citrusy, and mouth-coating.

PALATE Big. Citrus and peat. Lots of sour fruits. Tarry. Cocoa.

FINISH Big peat, fish, and smoke.

SCORE **88**

LINKWOOD

PRODUCER Diageo
REGION Highlands   ISLAND Speyside (Lossie)
ADDRESS Elgin, Morayshire, IV30 3RD   TEL 01343 862000

A SECRET NATURE RESERVE or a distillery? Linkwood's appropriately flowery Speyside whisky is increasingly appreciated, judging from the profusion of independent bottlings.

The dam that provides the cooling water is a port of call to tufted ducks and goldeneyes—and a seasonal home to wagtails, oyster catchers, mute swans, and otters. In the 10 acres (hectares) of the site, nettles attract red admiral and small tortoiseshell butterflies; cuckoo flowers entice the orange tip variety; bluebells seduce bees.

The distillery was founded in 1821. The older of its two still-houses, in the original buildings, continues to be used for a few months each year. It produces a slightly heavier spirit than the larger still-house built in the 1960s and extended in the 1970s.

HOUSE STYLE Floral. Rosewater? Cherries?
Delicious with a slice of fruitcake.

LINKWOOD 12-year-old, Flora and Fauna, 43 vol

COLOR Full primrose.

NOSE Remarkably flowery and petal-like. Buttercups. Grass. Fragrant.

BODY Medium, rounded, slightly syrupy.

PALATE Starts slowly, and has a long, sustained development to marzipan, roses, and fresh sweetness. One to savor.

FINISH Perfumy, dryish. Lemon zest.

SCORE 82

LINKWOOD 1975, 26-year-old, Rare Malt, 56.1 vol

A lovely whisky, as Linkwoods so often are.

COLOR Bright pale gold.

NOSE Like walking on a peaty moorland on a breezy day. Fresh, fragrant.

BODY Light to medium. Syrupy.

PALATE Starts with a faintly smoky sweetness, like the surface of a crème brûlée. Moves into a syrupy, molasses-tart sweetness.

FINISH Intensity of sweet, floral spiciness. Warming. Extraordinary length.

SCORE 84

RARE MALTS
SELECTION

Each individual vintage has been specially selected from Scotland's finest single malt stocks of rare or now silent distilleries. The limited bottlings of these scarce and unique whiskies are at natural cask strength, for the enjoyment of the true connoisseur.

NATURAL
CASK STRENGTH
SINGLE MALT
SCOTCH WHISKY

AGED **30** YEARS

DISTILLED 1974
LINKWOOD
DISTILLERY
ESTABLISHED 1825
BY ELGIN, MORAYSHIRE
54.9%vol 70cl e
PRODUCED AND BOTTLED
IN SCOTLAND
LIMITED EDITION
BOTTLE
APRIL 2005

LINKWOOD 1974, 30-year-old, Rare Malts, 54.9 vol

COLOR Gold.

NOSE Oak and hints of old roses, vanilla, and ginger. Goes on with apple skin and fresh mint leaves, getting much grassier and a little austere. Not too expressive, despite the beautiful start.

BODY Sweet and full.

PALATE A sweet and orangey start; a little more expressive now. Some custard, ripe melon, and crystallized oranges.

FINISH Gets peppery (oak) and spicy (cloves), especially at the end. Very good but not overly thrilling.

SCORE **85**

LINKWOOD Managers' Choice, Distilled 1996, Bottled 2009, 58.2 vol

COLOR Honey gold.

NOSE Soft fruits. Crunchie bar. Honey. Some floral notes and the merest trace of pepper.

BODY Soft and full.

PALATE Big peach and apricot flavors. Some milk chocolate, tannin and spice developing spice.

FINISH Sharper and spicier than the palate, but not unpleasant.

SCORE **82**

AN INDEPENDENT BOTTLING
LINKWOOD 11-year-old, Dun Bheagan, 46 vol

COLOR Deep golden brown. NOSE Fresh flowers. Spice. Honey.
BODY Medium and rich. PALATE Sweet and spicy. Green fruits.
Traces of anise and spicy-sweet peppers. All gentle and pleasant.
FINISH Medium. Sweet. Apple and pears. SCORE 82

LITTLEMILL

PRODUCER Loch Lomond Distillery Co. Ltd.
REGION Lowlands   DISTRICT Western Lowlands
ADDRESS Bowling, Dunbartonshire, G60 5BG
TEL 01389 752781   EMAIL mail@lochlomonddistillery.com

UNTIL THE NINETEEN THIRTIES, Littlemill followed the Lowland practice of triple distillation. The surviving buildings date from at least 1817, but appear to be older. Littlemill was long believed to date from 1772, but more recent evidence suggests that it was already distilling in 1750. It is thus one of the several claimants, each with a slightly different justification, to being the oldest distillery in Scotland.

HOUSE STYLE Marshmallow-soft. A restorative, or perhaps with dessert.

LITTLEMILL 16-year-old, Old Malt Cask, 50 vol

COLOR Clear honey.

NOSE Rootsy. Fresh flower cuttings. Greenery. Cucumber. Spring onions.

BODY Sweet and pleasant. Ordered.

PALATE Some citrus elements. Quite sweet and spicy. Astringent.

FINISH Short and sweet. Quite pleasant.

SCORE **65**

LOCH LOMOND

PRODUCER Loch Lomond Distillery Co. Ltd.
REGION Highlands   DISTRICT Western Highlands
ADDRESS Lomond Estate, Alexandria, Dunbartonshire, G83 0TL
TEL 01389 752781   WEBSITE www.lochlomonddistillery.com
EMAIL mail@lochlomonddistillery.com

A TRANSFORMATION IS GRADUALLY being wrought at this extraordinary establishment. The building's industrial past (as Britain's oldest car factory and a calico dyeworks) is no longer evident. It has been smartly restyled as a very functional, if complex, distillery. It has three pairs of pot stills, but with a visible difference. Two of the pairs are fitted with rectification columns. They are similar to the Lomond stills (the name is a coincidence) once used by neighbors Ballantine. By being operated in different ways, these stills can produce at least half a dozen different malts. Some of these malts are bottled as singles, but the distillery was designed to produce the components for its own blends. Loch Lomond also has a five-column continuous still.

The distillery is on an industrial estate by the Leven River, which links the Clyde and Loch Lomond. The name Loch Lomond is used on a single malt and a "single blend" (i.e., the grain and malts come from the one distillery). Other malts, such as Inchmurrin, are named after islands in the loch and other places of local interest.

Four of the malts are not usually bottled as singles. These include Glen Douglas, and the progressively more heavily peated Craiglodge, Inchmoan, and Croftengea. With the growing interest in peaty malts, the last may be bottled soon. Tasted as a work in progress, at seven years old, it had a sweet, oily, smoky aroma; a bonfire-like palate; with suggestions of fruit wood, briar, and oak smoke; and a lingering length.

Loch Lomond's unusual pattern of business dates from its acquisition in 1987 by a whisky wholesaler called Glen Catrine. This grew out of a chain of shops, which had their beginning in a licensed grocers. The Loch Lomond distillery, previously owned by the American company, Barton Brands, was established in the mid-1960s.

HOUSE STYLE Loch Lomond: Nutty. Restorative.
Inchmurrin: Fruity. Aperitif. Old Rhosdhu: Piney. Soothing.

LOCH LOMOND, No Age Statement, 40 vol

COLOR Bright gold.

NOSE Freshly made toast. Brandy snaps.

BODY Candyfloss (cotton candy).

PALATE Powdered sugar. Turkish delight. Pistachio nuts. Banana.

FINISH Light but long. Lemony, balancing dryness.

SCORE **70**

LOCH LOMOND 16-year-old,
Scotch Malt Whisky Society, No 122.19, 50.1 vol

COLOR Butter yellow.

NOSE Honey and lemon flu powder. Chalk. Vanilla.
Smoke and peat. Intriguing.

BODY Sweet and creamy.

PALATE Peaty and sweet in equal measure. Chewy and meaty.
Rich sugar barley, integrated peat, and some yellow fruits.
Unusual but very full and tasty.

FINISH Very appealing. Quite long, with peat and spice.

SCORE **88**

LOCH LOMOND 1966, 44 vol

COLOR Golden.

NOSE Sandalwood, warm hay.

BODY Light and thin.

PALATE Green. Pistachio nuts. Sugared almonds. Intense sweetness.

FINISH Gritty. Abrasive.

SCORE **66**

INCHMURRIN 10-year-old, 40 vol

COLOR Pale apricot.

NOSE Tropical fruit. Watermelons. Orange-flower water.

BODY Pleasantly oily.

PALATE Very light-tasting at first, but with some flavor development.
Honeydew melon with ginger.

FINISH Spicy, warming, long, soothing.

SCORE **70**

OLD RHOSDHU, No Age Statement, 40 vol

Minimum 5 years old.

COLOR Amber.

NOSE Scented. A luxurious malt to drink in the bathtub.

BODY Light to medium. Soft, oily.

PALATE Dry, perfumy, spicy. Powerful flavors.

FINISH Wintergreen? Perhaps not the bath—the sauna.

SCORE **65**

LONGMORN

PRODUCER Chivas Brothers (Pernod Ricard)
REGION Highlands   DISTRICT Speyside (Lossie)
ADDRESS Elgin, Morayshire, IV30 3SJ   TEL 01542 783042

Longmorn is one of the finest Speyside malts, cherished by connoisseurs but not widely known. It is admired for its complexity, its combination of smoothness and fullness of character, and from its big bouquet to its long finish. It is noted for its cereal-grain maltiness, beeswax flavors, and estery fruitiness.

The distillery was built in 1894–95, and has a disused waterwheel and a workable steam engine. Much of the equipment is very traditional, and imposing in its size and beautiful condition, including the Steel's mash mixer and some very impressive spirit safes. Alongside the distillery is the disused Longmorn railroad flag stop.

HOUSE STYLE Tongue-coating, malty, complex.
Versatile, delightful before dinner, and especially
good with dessert.

LONGMORN 15-year-old, 45 vol

COLOR Full gold.

NOSE Big, slightly oily. Barley malt, flowery-fruity notes.

BODY Smooth, rounded, medium to big.

PALATE Very emphatic, fresh, clean, cereal-grain maltiness.
Suggestion of plum skins.

FINISH Tangerines, nuts. Then peppery.
Appetizing. Very long.

SCORE 87

LONGMORN 16-year-old, 48 vol

COLOR Deep gold. Slightly greenish hue.

NOSE Full, sweet, and malt-laced, with honey and hints
of fruit—perhaps red apples. Lovely.

BODY Fiery, big, overpowering.

PALATE Big, assertive malt.

FINISH Oats, nuts. Then peppery. Long.

COMMENT A benefit can be gained from a few drops of water, which
softens the nose, allowing more fruit to emerge on the nose and palate.
The body is still full, but the water releases the inner fruits and
floral notes, and brings back the tangerines on the finish.

SCORE **85**

LONGMORN Cask Strength Edition, 17-year-old,
Distilled 1991, Bottled 2008, Batch LM 17 005, 49.4 vol

COLOR Dark, deep gold.

NOSE Big. Sweet, fruity, with notes of honey and vanilla, perhaps crème-
brûlée. Cedar and Jonathan apples. Water brings out notes of maple syrup.

BODY Full, silky, slightly oily.

PALATE Sweet honey and vanilla. The oak makes itself known,
but remains in the background.

FINISH Long, peppery.

SCORE **88**

AN INDEPENDENT BOTTLING
LONGMORN 1996, Bottled 2008, Berry's Own Selection, 56.7 vol

COLOR Pale lemon with a hint of green. NOSE Floral. Beeswax. Acacia
honey. Gooseberry. Rhubarb plants. Lime cordial. BODY Rich and
oily. PALATE Beautifully clean and sorbet-sharp. A palate cleanser. Blood
grapefruit. Green fruits. FINISH Long, with green apples lingering and a
peppery aftertaste. SCORE 86

THE MACALLAN

PRODUCER The Edrington Group
REGION Highlands DISTRICT Speyside
ADDRESS Aberlour, Banffshire, AB38 9RX
TEL 01340 872280 WEBSITE www.themacallan.com VC

As BRONZED AND MUSCULAR as a practitioner of the noble art, Macallan is Speyside's best known heavyweight—and constantly embracing a new challenge. In one such engagement, Macallan has over the years collected, and bought at auction, bottles of its own whisky from the 1800s.

An 1874 Macallan, bought by the company for $6000/£4000, inspired a bold attempt to replicate its character by making a vatting from stocks. The key seemed to be an accent toward fino sherry wood, rather than the dry oloroso currently preferred. There was sufficient fino wood in Macallan's warehouses, and a credible replica of the 1874 was produced. This appeared at the time to be a unique exercise, but a further three replica whiskies have been created since.

It is not necessary to make replicas of Macallans from the early to mid-1900s, as sufficient casks were laid down. Some of these whiskies, designated by the company as Exceptional Single Casks, have been released, one at a time, in recent years. From the 1920s, it seemed to have become pricey to lay down generous quantities. Most of the whisky was still in cask, but some had been bottled, to prevent evaporation taking it below the minimum legal strength. One hogshead yielded only 40 bottles; the most generous butt provided 548.

It was decided to create an offering of "very old" whiskies, with the criterion being that they had to have been maturing for a minimum of 30 years. Not all years were represented in the warehouses, but the chronology was surprisingly thorough. The then master distiller David Robertson and whisky maker Bob Dalgarno nosed nearly 600 casks, selecting one or two from each year for vintage bottlings. Where there was no stock for a year, Macallan bought back casks, and even cases of bottles, from the trade and collectors. The range, launched in 2003, has the rubric "Fine and Rare," with its own style of bottles, and labels highlighting vintage dates. This packaging was also applied to bottles drawn from stock, or bought back; they were all rebottled. All of the whiskies were then hand bottled at the distillery, at cask strength. Their rices range from $33,000/£20,000 for the most expensive bottle to

$110 /£65 for the cheapest miniature. The initial offering amounts to 10,000 bottles, valued at just under $23 million/£14 million. The whiskies can be bought, or a catalog obtained, from specialist retailers, through Macallan's website, or at the distillery gift shop. Some bars sell these whiskies, inevitably at very high prices.

Meanwhile, major changes in the market have affected Macallan's ability to meet worldwide demand, and owner Edrington has responded bullishly. The high cost of sherry casks and a growing demand from Asia, and particularly Taiwan, for sherried whiskies has given The Macallan a lucrative platform. In other territories, such as Europe, it responded to what it saw as a move to lighter-style whiskies by launching the Fine Oak range, a series of whiskies made using both bourbon and sherry casks. They have proved very popular, picking up many awards and bringing a new generation of malt drinkers to The Macallan. For some at least, less emphasis on sherry has allowed the high quality of The Macallan malt to shine through. But the move away from sherry in some traditional markets has not been without controversy. By 2009 Edrington was increasingly moving its sherried whiskies to the newer territories and emphasizing the Fine Oak series in Europe. It seems likely that the traditional sherried versions will be phased out of some markets altogether.

To collectors, no name has the magic of Macallan. The name derives from the Macallan church, now a ruin, on the Easter Elchies estate, which overlooks Telford's bridge over the Spey, at Craigellachie. A farmer on the hillside is believed to have made whisky from his own barley in the 1700s. Macallan became a legal distillery as soon as that was possible, in 1824. In 1998, the estate farm was put back into service to grow Golden Promise barley, albeit a token amount in relation to Macallan's requirements. The manor house from the early days has been restored as a venue for the entertaining of visitors.

Macallan has long been a renowned contributor to blends, notably including The Famous Grouse. In 1968–69, the company decided that single malts would also be an important element of the future. The character of Macallan has traditionally begun with Golden Promise barley, but this Scottish variety is becoming hard to find. Cultivation has drastically diminished because Golden Promise offers a relatively ungenerous yield of grain to farmers. Its yield to distillers in terms of spirit is also on the low side, but the nutty, oily, silky flavors produced are delicious. Until about 1994, Macallan used only Golden Promise. Since then, there has been the odd year when a good harvest and reduced whisky production has made this possible, but at other times its share of the grist has dropped to 30 or 25 percent, with more varieties such as Chariot or Optic providing the greater share.

Some distillers do not concern themselves with barley varieties, but simply set out a technical specification of performance. Many take the same view of yeasts. These arguments seem to ignore a fundamental point: what the consumer gets out of the glass must depend upon what the producer puts in. Macallan has in recent years used four yeasts, and currently employs two of them. The company believes that this particular combination enhances its fruity, spicy aromas and flavors.

Macallan's oily, creamy richness is enhanced by the use of especially small stills. When the company has expanded output to cope with demand, it has added more stills, rather than building bigger ones. The number grew from six to 21 between 1965 and 1975. The wash stills are heated by gas burners. This use of direct flame can impart a caramelization of the malt which steam heat does not. Macallan also believes it takes the narrowest cut in the industry.

When Macallan decided to market a single malt, the principals made tastings from stock and decided that their whisky tasted best from dry oloroso butts. Faced with the high cost of obtaining such casks, Macallan has been carrying out exhaustive research to establish exactly what are the influences on flavor. Given that an oak tree takes 100 years to reach maturity, and the whisky another ten or more, progress is slow. The European oak variety *Quercus robur* is rich in tannins, and imparts both the full color and the resiny, spicy (clove, cinnamon, nutmeg) fragrances and flavors so typical of Macallan.

Macallan's current view is that the reaction between wood and sherry is also of great importance. This appears to wash out the harshest tannins and help release a rich, rounded spiciness. This is felt to be far more significant than any aromas and flavors imparted by the sherry itself. One rather extreme piece of research suggested that barely a third of aromas and flavors originated from the spirit, almost 60 percent from the oak, and less than 10 percent from the sherry.

The current regime is that the butts are first filled with mosto (grape juice) for three months' primary fermentation. They then have two years with maturing sherry in a bodega. They are then shipped to Scotland. Between 70 and 80 percent of Macallan is matured in first-fill butts, the remainder in second-fill. In the principal versions of The Macallan first and second fill is vatted in broadly those proportions.

HOUSE STYLE Big, oaky, resiny sherried, flowery-fruity. Spicy.
Very long. After dinner.

THE MACALLAN Distiller's Choice, No Age Statement, 40 vol

Mainly for the Japanese market.

COLOR Bronze. Paler than most Macallans.

NOSE Especially fragrant.

BODY Medium. Very smooth.

PALATE Lightly buttery and malty. Lively, youthful flavors.
Emphasis on classic Speyside floweriness rather than sherry.

FINISH Highlights the crisp dryness of Macallan.

SCORE **81**

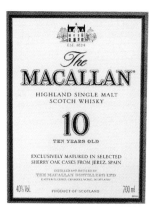

THE MACALLAN 10-year-old, 40 vol

Mainly for the UK market.

COLOR Amber.

NOSE Sherry. Butterscotch. Honeyish malt character.
Depth of aromas even at this young age.

BODY Full, without being syrupy.

PALATE Lots of sherry, without being rich. Plenty of malt.
Sweetish. Rounded.

FINISH Satisfying, malty, gingery, becoming dry, with a hint of smoke.

SCORE **87**

THE MACALLAN 12-year-old, 43 vol

Mainly for export markets.

COLOR Amber.

NOSE Sherry, honey, flowery notes.

BODY Full, smooth.

PALATE The first hints of flowering currant. Altogether more expressive.

FINISH Slightly more rounded.

SCORE **91**

THE MACALLAN 15-year-old, 43 vol

Now hard to find.

COLOR Medium-amber.

NOSE This age best expresses the estery fruitiness of Macallan.

BODY Full, very smooth.

PALATE Toffeeish. Gently fruity and spicy.
Hints of peat. A little lacking in dimension.

FINISH Grassy. Lightly peaty.

SCORE **92**

THE MACALLAN 25-year-old, 43 vol

COLOR Full amber red.

NOSE At this age, a definite smokiness manifests itself, and
embraces all the other aromas that have appeared earlier.

BODY Full, firm, round.

PALATE The smokiness greatly enhances the complexity.

FINISH Dry, complex, very long.

SCORE **95**

THE MACALLAN 30-year-old, 43 vol

COLOR Full orange.

NOSE This age best highlights the resiny contributions of the oak itself.
Reminiscent of polished oak. The faintly piney, floral aromas of
furniture polish. The waxed skin of fresh tangerines. Orange zest.

BODY Medium to full.

PALATE Despite its great age, no aggressive oakiness or overbearing
sherry. Tightly combined flavors. Its great appeal is its mellow
maturity. Complex. Just a whiff of smoke.

FINISH Dry, warming, soothing, but disappears too quickly.

SCORE **95**

MACALLAN 18-YEAR-OLDS

Most years, The Macallan has released an 18-year-old, at 43 vol, in which some malt lovers find the most robust interplay of the estery whisky and the dry oloroso maturation. These are vatted to offer continuity of character, but inevitably they vary slightly. The following five bottlings at 18 years old are each given their own score.

1984 Attractive, deep tawny color. Appetizing, yet rich, oaky, raisiny aroma. Slippery body. Flavors establish a grip nonetheless, and pace themselves. Perfumy notes. Chocolate fudge. Malty middle. Clean, crisp, gingery spiciness in finish. SCORE 94

1983 Fractionally darker and more reddish. More sappy aroma. More immediately gingery and spicy. Drier. More resiny. Harder edge. Arguably harsher, more robust. SCORE 93

1982 Deep, dark orange. Fruity, toffeeish aroma. Sweetish. More toffee and chocolate in palate. Beeswax. Leafy. Coriander? Chili-pepper finish. SCORE 94

1981 Bright, deep amber. Palest color in this flight. Aromas and flavors so melded as to be hard to unpick. Smooth, urbane. Like a person who answers questions with dismissive brevity to imply a loftier knowledge. The whisky eventually admits to some spiciness and a pleasantly oaky dryness in the finish. SCORE 93

1980 Deep bronze. Fullest color in this flight. Perfumy, spicy aroma, with cinnamon accent. Oily. Smooth. Toffeeish. Becoming spicy. SCORE 92

COLLECTABLE

1978 Solid orange-amber color; big bouquet, with some peat; medium to full, soft body; beautifully rounded and complete, with a nutty-sweet sherry accent; firm, smooth, dry, warming finish.

1977 Darker and redder; sherry and restrained fruit on the nose; buttery malt character; sweeter, more sherryish finish.

1976 Bright, full, orange color; peaty, oaky aroma; firm and smooth; lively flavors of grass, peat, and oak.

1975 More orangey color; spicy lemongrass and peat in the aroma; fresh, juicy calvados and flowering currant in the palate; fresh, oaky finish.

1974 Reddish tinge; beautifully balanced peat and malt in the aroma; malty, sherryish sweetness becoming estery and perfumy; sweetness and spice in the finish.

1973 Bright, full amber; very perfumy aroma; very full flavors; sappy oak and vanilla spiciness in a slow, long finish.

1972 Deep orange; oak and peat aroma; very smooth; good balance between peat and syrupy malt; drying, with some astringency, in finish.

1971 Shimmery orange; soft, inviting aroma; oily, perfumy; sherry sweetness.

1970 Full amber orange; assertive sherry aroma; notably complex; long, vanilla-and-oak finish.

1969 Amber, but paler than usual; peat and malt in the aroma; nutty, sweetish, syrupy; some peat in finish. A restrained edition.

1968 Apricot color; fudgey, nutty aroma; light on the tongue; slightly syrupy; toffeeish, gently spicy finish.

1967 Tawny color; very spicy, almost minty aroma; very smooth; buttery malt character; melony finish, with grassy peat.

1966 Bottled "early." This year's edition was a 17-year-old (and labeled as such, of course). Tawny color; peaty and spicy aroma; oily, nutty, smooth; very restrained peat in the finish.

1965 Tawny red; nutty, sherry aroma; anise, licorice; spicy, oily finish.

1964 Medium-orange color; good balance of peat and malt
in the aroma; lightly fruity palate, falling away in the middle;
with nutty, sherry sweetness in the finish.

1963 Refractive orange color; lightly oaky aroma; light,
sweet, and sherryish, with a cedary finish.

GRAN RESERVA

This rubric indicates 18-year-old whiskies matured
in first-fill sherry casks, at 40 vol.

1982

COLOR Chestnut.

NOSE Oaky and phenolic, but appetizingly so. A suggestion of cloves.

BODY Big, firm, smooth.

PALATE Extraordinarily powerful flavors. Initially more reminiscent
of port than sherry. Then a suggestion of Pedro Ximénez. Tar-like,
but less smoky than sweet. Cough medicine. Licorice.

FINISH Soothing. Warming. Long.

SCORE **95**

1981

COLOR Mahogany red.

NOSE Freshly cut wood. Sawmill aromas.

BODY Viscous, but lighter in body.

PALATE Similar but slightly lighter, and less complex in flavors.

FINISH Dry. Very slightly woody and astringent.

SCORE **94**

1979 Bottled 1997

COLOR Distinctively chestnut.

NOSE Rich sherry at first. Then malty nuttiness.
Raisins, dates. Finally floweriness.

BODY Big, oily.

PALATE Very dry. Thick-cut, bitter-orange and ginger marmalade on well-done toast. Then buttery, syrupy maltiness, developing to nutty, sherry sweetness. Strictly for the lover of powerfully oaked whiskies.

FINISH Richly fruity. Raisiny. Warming.

SCORE **95**

REPLICA EDITIONS

None of today's barley varieties existed in the 19th century, and malt was generally more heavily peated. The design of mash tuns and wort coolers was different, brewers' yeast was used, stills were fired with coal or coke. Sherry casks were used, but in a random fashion. The 19th century bottles that were opened to act as models for these replicas contained whiskies that, in some respects, tasted hauntingly reminiscent of today's Macallan (albeit, surprisingly, more delicate). In particular, the fruity esters seemed much the same. This seems to support the notion that a distillery's location and microclimate are formative influences on flavor. To try and replicate the individual characteristics of each bottle, large numbers of casks were nosed. To "recreate" the 1861, about 17,500 casks were sampled and 28 used.

"1876", 40.6 vol

This is the most "recent" vintage date in the series. It is also the
most recently created replica among the four reviewed here.
It seems a little thinner in body and palate than the other three.

COLOR Dark, warm gold.

NOSE Very spicy and dusty. Honeyed.

BODY Firm.

PALATE Intense sweetness at first. Then perfumy. Lemony. Anise.
A hint of quinine dryness.

FINISH A touch of oakiness.

SCORE **94**

"1874", 45 vol

The whiskies in this replica had an average age of just under 18, but included at least one
cask of 26 years. A key element was whisky with long maturation in fino sherry casks.

COLOR Orange.

NOSE Ginger cake. Caraway. Cumin seeds.

BODY Medium. Firm. Smooth.

PALATE Dry, with softly orangey notes. Spices. Anise. Lemon grass. The most
estery of the bigger Macallans. Light peat.

FINISH Powerful. Dry. Just a hint of bitterness.

SCORE **95**

"1861", 42.7 vol

The original had a pronounced oak and sherry character, and
was rich in the spicy esters that arise during maturation.

COLOR Bronze.

NOSE Spice rack. Flapjack. Syrup. Rose-water. Custard.

BODY Soothing. Syrupy.

PALATE Concentrated sweetness. Perfumy. Anise. Restrained fruitiness.
Candied orange peel. Delicious sherry character. Great depth of flavor.

FINISH Toasty dryness. Sappy oak. Long.

SCORE **95**

"1841", 41.7 vol

The original was believed to have been bottled young, at between six and ten years old, and had a remarkably fresh character when opened more than 150 years later. It may have been one of the first bottled whiskies. In 1841, most whisky was still sold by the cask.

COLOR Brilliant gold.

NOSE Very fresh. Fudge with vanilla extract and pistachio nuts.

BODY Silky.

PALATE Appetizing. Sweet but not cloying. Light, fresh,
delicate notes of orange-blossom honey.

FINISH A very gentle acidity (dessert apples?) provides a balancing dryness.

SCORE **96**

EXCEPTIONAL SINGLE CASK RANGE
1981, ESC I, Fino Sherry Butt, Bottled 1999, 56 vol

COLOR Chestnut to cherry.

NOSE Mint chocolate. Sherry. Slightly vinous. Oak.

BODY Firm, smooth. Thick. Demerara sugar.

PALATE Wafer-like. Crispy malt. Toffee. Forest berries. Oak. Some earthy notes.

FINISH Rummy. Warming. Very oaky, approaching astringency.

SCORE **92**

1980, ESC II, Sherry Butt, Cask No 4063, 59.3 vol

COLOR Dark copper.

NOSE Madeira, in the hold of a ship crossing the equator
(a hint of hot cylinder block and engine oil).

BODY Medium. Lapping on the tongue.

PALATE Hard molasses toffee. A quick gesture of sweetness, then burned
flavors, like chestnuts too long over the fire.

FINISH Warming.

SCORE **90**

1980, ESC III, Sherry Butt, Cask No 17937, 51 vol

Mainly for the Swiss market.

COLOR Distinctive pinkish amber. Palest in this flight.

NOSE Crème brûlée. Fruity. Pineapple.

BODY Medium. Luxuriously smooth.

PALATE Sweet. Sticky toffee pudding. Fruity esters. Apples. Cherries.

FINISH Coffeeish dryness. Bittersweet. Digestif.

SCORE *92*

1990, ESC IV, Sherry Butt, Cask No 24680, 57.4 vol

COLOR Dark amber. Garnet tinge.

NOSE Smoky. Toasty. Malty.

BODY Big. Firm. Smooth.

PALATE Malty and fruity, with a slightly sharp edge
of smokiness (or is it charred oak?)

FINISH Slightly medicinal.

SCORE *91*

TRAVEL RETAIL

The whiskies under this heading are available at airports and ferry terminals,
on board some aircraft and ships, and in duty-free shops.

THE MACALLAN 10-year-old, 57 vol (100° proof)

COLOR Attractive full amber.

NOSE Aromas very tightly combined and rounded, sherryish. Oaky. Resiny.
The faintest hint of peat. Flowering currants. Violets. A soft whiff of alcohol.

BODY Firm, smooth.

PALATE Sherry accent. Firm malt background.
Restrained fruitiness. Quietly intense.

FINISH Sherry, smoke, alcohol.

SCORE *89*

THE MACALLAN Elegancia 1990, 40 vol

COLOR Warm gold to pale bronze.

NOSE Crisp. Spicy. Ginger ice cream.

BODY Smooth but light.

PALATE Restrained start. Gentle flavor development. Lean. Lightly creamy.
A suggestion of malted milk. Some concentrated sweetness.

FINISH Now the ice cream is rum-raisin.

SCORE *80*

THE DECADES SERIES

Travelers with time to kill and a few shelves of whisky to browse may find the labels on this series not only eye-catching but also apposite. Like the Replica bottlings, these attempt to recall the flavors of the past, by making vattings from stock. The initial bottlings, intended to evoke the 1920–50s, are identified by social motifs of each period, based on racing. The whiskies seem to highlight the Speyside character of Macallan. All are at 40 volume.

THE MACALLAN Twenties (racing car motif). Pale walnut color. Passion fruit aroma. Notably light-bodied. Starts sweetly but quickly becomes dry. An elegant touch of oak. SCORE 92

THE MACALLAN Thirties (ocean liner motif). Pale apricot. Seville orange aroma. Smooth bodied. The sweetest and most fruity of the whiskies in this flight. SCORE 94

THE MACALLAN Forties (locomotive motif). The palest in color, primrose. Also the most flowery, grassy, herbal. Some sweetness. Playful, lively. The least complex of this flight, but deliciously drinkable. SCORE 93

THE MACALLAN Fifties (airliner motif). Deep bronze. Closest in style to The Macallan today. Well balanced and rounded. Oak, sherry, malt, light spiciness. Long, soothing. SCORE 92

THE MACALLAN Cask Strength, 58.6 vol

A new series of single-cask bottlings for the US market. The first cask was tasted in the fourth edition of Complete Guide to Single Malt Scotch, *as a work in progress. That vintage was described as "a very intense expression of a classic Macallan." So is this one, which is in the age range of 10 to 12 years.*

COLOR Distinctive reddish mahogany.

NOSE Oak. Sherry. Winey. Faint suggestion of chocolate.

BODY Big, textured. Slightly abrasive.

PALATE Robust. Dry maltiness. Hard toffee, becoming chewy. Dried fruits. Nutty. Oily. Perfumy.

FINISH Oaky dryness. Slightly astringent (less so with water).

SCORE **88**

RARE VINTAGES OF THE MACALLAN
THE MACALLAN Millennium 50-year-old, Distilled 1949, 46 vol

Offered in about 900 Caithness crystal decanters, with a copper insignia made from a retired still at Macallan. Price around $3,000/£2,000.

COLOR Very dark orange.

NOSE Peaty, smoky, almost sooty.

BODY Lean, firm, slippery.

PALATE Oily, nutty, creamy. Almond cookies. Crème brûlée. Some burned flavors. Becoming woody. Oaky. The oak is big but never quite overpowers the other elements.

FINISH Spicy. Peppermint. Smoky. Oaky.

SCORE **92**

THE MACALLAN 1961, 54.1 vol

COLOR Deep orange, with an inner glow. Sunrise.

NOSE Soft. Creamy. Fruity. Orange blancmange.

BODY Silky.

PALATE Firm. Hint of cedar. Cigar box, but it contains orange-crème pralines in very bitter chocolate. Subtle development of other citrus flavors, spices, and peppermint.

FINISH Clean, crisp, oaky bitterness.

SCORE **94**

THE MACALLAN 1951, 48.8 vol

COLOR Garnet with jade tinge.

NOSE Creamy, chocolatey, spicy.

BODY Silky.

PALATE Malt background like rich, dark fudge. Almost immediately,
sherbety explosions of fruity and spicy flavors.

FINISH Very distinctive in the interplay of sweet spiciness and
oaky dryness. Very lively and appetizing.

SCORE **93**

THE MACALLAN 1948, 46.6 vol

COLOR Old gold.

NOSE Sherry not obvious—fino? Flowery, leafy, peaty, woody.

BODY Light but firm. Smooth.

PALATE An altogether more elegant, wistful style. Some sweetness and
floweriness, but the outstanding feature is an astonishingly fresh peat-smoke
flavor. Great Speyside whiskies once tasted like this.

FINISH Gentle but lingering and warming, leaving smoky memories.

SCORE **96**

THE MACALLAN 1946, 40 vol

COLOR Bright full gold.

NOSE Much more estery-fruity.

BODY Light, smooth, almost slippery.

PALATE Firm, complex flavors. Flowery. Estery, but very
delicately balanced. Sweet lime, lemon, and orange.
A remarkably seductive whisky for its age.

FINISH Bitter orange. Grass. Peat. Again, long smokiness.

SCORE **95**

FINE & RARE VINTAGES

Most whiskies peak in their teens, but the heaviest ones can do
well in their twenties and even thirties. As the best-known heavyweight,
Macallan has made a great many outings at advanced ages.
The ticket price can be very high. Yet, given that most whiskies
do peak a decade or two earlier, it is not reasonable to expect the
performance of malts in their 30s, 40s, or 50s to be of the very best.

Some are, indeed, surprisingly good—whisky's counterparts to
Archie Moore or George Foreman—but their value is driven by their
antiquity and rarity. If a previously unknown Old Master is identified,
it may not be the painter's finest work, but it will command a great
price. If a recording of Buddy Bolden were found on a wax cylinder we
might know whether his cornet really could be heard on the far side of
Lake Ponchartrain. These tastings seem to confirm the widely held view
that Macallan was a peatier, smokier whisky until the 1950s. If it is true
of Macallan, it is probably true of other Speyside malts.

1926, 42.6 vol

Bottled as a 60-year-old in 1986. Very dark ("laburnum"
say Macallan). Medicinal, phenolic, peaty, and woody in aroma.
Surprisingly light on the tongue. Very dry and concentrated in palate.
Figs, molasses toffee. Licorice. Rooty. Finish is cedary
and oaky—dominated by the wood. SCORE 80

The vintages from 1937 to 1940 (*see p. 334*) were bought as bottled stock.
They were then rebottled for the Fine and Rare series, in 2002. The vintage
dates shown here represent the year of the original bottling.

1937, 43 vol

First bottled as a 37-year-old, in 1974. Dark gold. Green tinge.
Vanilla in the aroma. Rich, delicious, syrupy, malty middle. Sweetshop flavors.
Sufficiently soothing to calm the palate, but then somewhat abrupt
in its spicy, hot finish. Late smokiness, and some astringency. SCORE 87

1937, 43 vol

First bottled as a 32-year-old, in 1969. Bronze. Fragrant. Sweetish, spicy
aromas. Lively flavors with plenty of development. At first, bitter chocolate
pralines filled with ginger. Then with orange. Then with peppermint.
Finishes with spicy bitterness. Saffron? SCORE 85

1938, 43 vol

First bottled as a 31-year-old, in 1969. Ripe apricot color. The same fruit is
suggested by the aroma. The body is prickly, almost spiky. It all suggests
tropical fruits, but the flavor doesn't develop much more than nutty toffee.
Nice surge of orangey spiciness in the finish. SCORE 84

1938, 43 vol

First bottled as a 35-year-old, in 1973. Deep, warm bronze. Sweetly
appetizing on the nose. Lightly syrupy. Falls away in the middle.
Crispy, spicy finish. A very elegant whisky. No doubt less vigorous than
it was, but still with great charm. SCORE 86

1939, 43 vol

First bottled as a 40-year-old, in 1979. Deep bronze. Appetizing, sweetly
nutty aroma and palate. Smooth to the point of urbanity. Seduces, then slips
away. Back later, to lift the finish gracefully, as though kissing a lady's hand.
Perfumy and dry. SCORE 85

1940, 43 vol

First bottled as a 35-year-old in 1975. Pale bronze, with green tinge.
Fragrant smoke, with subtle fruit and malt. Lean, firm, elegant.
Hint of anis. Remarkable emergence of peppermint in
the finish. Aperitif. SCORE 92

1940, 43 vol

First bottled as a 37-year-old, in 1977. Slightly darker than
the earlier bottling. Considerably maltier and sweeter. Lime
zest, coriander, and garden mint. Finish very dry indeed,
but no astringency. SCORE 93

THE FOLLOWING VINTAGES WERE ALL BOTTLED IN 2002

1945, 51.5 vol

Bottled at 56 years old. Reddish orange. Peppermints and butterscotch in the aroma. A very sweet whisky. Fruity, too. Perhaps cherries, but especially green fruits. Also spicy, with lots of pepper. Somewhat erratic, crochety. SCORE 82

1946, 44.3 vol

Bottled at 56 years old. Very attractive deep yellow, tawn color. Spicy aroma, especially cinnamon. Syrupy. Lapping on the tongue. Lemony. Dry, herbal. Slightly medicinal. Phenol. Peat smoke. SCORE 92

1948, 45.3 vol

Bottled at 53 years old. Lovely, pink-tinged amber. The aroma of thick-cut orange marmalade. Lightly syrupy, sweetish palate, gently becoming drier. Orangey. Liqueur-like. Long, lively, dry, spicy finish. SCORE 85

1949, 49.8 vol

Bottled at 53 years old. Bright, reflective, deep gold. Very inviting. Sweet, flapjack aroma. Full-bodied, smooth. Appetizing, oaty, bittersweet. The trademark spicy finish. Some big whiskies are belligerent brawlers. This one floats like a butterfly and it kisses instead of stinging. SCORE 92

1949, 44.1 vol

Bottled at 52 years old. Garnet. Or morello cherry. The color suggests cherry pie, and alerts the nose to aromas of cooked fruit. Maderization, perhaps? Also some acidity. Tastes like a fruity herb bitters. SCORE 82

1950, 46.7 vol

Bottled at 52 years old. Warm, deep gold color. Clean, dessert apple aroma (a typical Macallan characteristic, making its first indisputable appearance in this flight). Big-bodied, soft, embracing. Honeyed palate. Orange flower honey? Moves to long, gingery spiciness. Some cookie-like maltiness. Light smokiness. Clean and appetizing, with plenty of flavor development. SCORE 93

1950, 51.7 vol

Bottled at 52 years old. Slightly darker color, toward bronze. Slightly sweeter and maltier aroma. Very creamy. Some vanilla. Malty. Appetizingly well-rounded peaty dryness in the finish. Over the full course of aroma, palate and finish, this rather austere expression emerges as being slightly drier than the version above, and perhaps marginally less complex. SCORE 92

1951, 52.3 vol

Bottled at 51 years old. Deep bronze. Clean, sweet, appetizing aroma, with some gingery, spicy notes. Instant hit of spiciness in the palate. As crisp as a karate chop. Then things slow to a more natural pace, and the spices present themselves one by one, against a background of malty sweetness. Finally, they meld into an endlessly soothing glow. SCORE 92

1952, 50.8 vol

Bottled at 50 years old. Deep gold. Floral, lemony aroma. Straight into a firm, malty base. The top notes are spicy from start to finish. Flowery and fruity characteristics persistently try to take over but never quite manage it. Nice touch of oak in the finish. SCORE 91

1952, 48 vol

Bottled at 49 years old. Deep copper red color. Sherry, charred oak and anis in the nose. Rich, syrupy body. Licorice and chewy malt in the palate. Woody finish, with some astringency. SCORE 84

1953, 52 vol

Bottled at 49 years old. Extraordinary garnet-to-ruby color. Iron and passion fruit in the aroma. Dark, deep flavors. Alcohol-soaked fruitcake, studded with cherries, topped with marzipan and toasted sliced almonds. Warm, clovey spiciness and toasted oak in the finish. SCORE 86.

1954, 50.2 vol

Bottled at 47 years old. An even fuller ruby color and a gently smoky aroma seem promising. The palate is intensely sweet. This whisky may have been drinkable when it was bottled. Now it is strictly collectable. NOT SCORED

1955, 45.9 vol

Bottled at 46 years old. Almost opaque. Black, with red tinges. Clovey aromas. Syrupy. Herbal. Fruity (prunes?). A wintry dram, but lacking in vigor. Toward the end of its life. SCORE 83

No stocks of 1956 or 1957 have been traced.

1958, 53.7 vol

Bottled at 43 years old. Sauternes-like color. Earthy aroma, with suggestion of apples (a boxful, not peeled). Syrupy maltiness in the palate. Sugary, toffee-like. Toffee apples? Finishes with dusty spiciness. SCORE 85

1959, 47 vol

Bottled at 43 years old. Very dark orangey amber color. Nutty, sugary, and deeply malty aromas. Like a spiced cake glazed with sugar and studded with cloves. Similarly wintry flavors: nutty, crystal sugar, ginger. Spicy, bittersweet finish. SCORE 84

No stocks of 1960, 1961, 1962, or 1963.

1964, 58.6 vol

Bottled at 37 years old. Pale, greeny gold color. Very unusual for a Macallan. Fruity, creamy aroma, with some vanilla, and woody dryness. Syrupy body. Palate is sweet, with suggestions of green fruits—or chili peppers. Finishes with the burning sensation of having bitten into a chili pepper. An interesting whisky, but not very Macallan-like. SCORE 76

1965, 56.2 vol

Bottled at 36 years old. Cerise. The color suggests cherries and the aroma seems to follow suit. The palate is sweet, fruity, and toffeeish. Cherries, again, in the finish. Reminiscent of cherry "brandy" (the liqueur type, as famously made in Denmark). SCORE 79

1966, 55.5 vol

Bottled at 35 years old. Claret color. Instant spicy, bittersweet attack. Peppery. Dry. Drying. Some astringency in the finish. Not very Macallan-like. Not very whisky-like. SCORE 77

1967, 56.3 vol

Bottled at 35 years old. Mahogany red. Sherry and malt in the aroma. Very sweet and toffeeish in the palate. Good wood extract. Spicy. Dusty. Lively, long finish, with slight astringency. SCORE 87

1968, 51 vol

Bottled at 34 years old. Bright yellow gold. Sweet and fruity in the aroma. Pineapple. Banana. Syrupy. Spicy. Vanilla. Creamy. Beautifully balanced between sweetness and dryness. A playful, refreshing demonstration of Macallan's fruity esters. Otherwise not at all typical. SCORE 80

1968, 46.6 vol

Bottled at 33 years old. Pale gold, faint green tinge. Oily, cereal-grain aroma. Sweet at first, then a dusty dryness. Finally, a huge, sweet fruitiness. Pineapple. Papaya. Custard apple. SCORE 78

1969, 52.7 vol

Bottled at 32 years old. Dark oak color. Deep, malty aroma. Palate starts with sweet maltiness, developing chocolatey flavors, becoming rooty, resiny, and fruity. Very slight oaky astringency in the palate. SCORE 92

1969, 59 vol

Bottled at 32 years. Deep, refractive, gold to bronze. Lemony aroma. Fresh, lemony palate. Orange blossom. Flowery. Scenty. Delicate. Lively finish. SCORE 84

1970, 54.9 vol

Bottled at 32 years old. Dark claret color. Oaky aroma, but Macallan spiciness and apple esters come through. Chewy, malty, sweet, rum-butter flavors. Sherryish. The finish is peppery and very long, with some woody astringency. SCORE 85

1970, 52.4 vol

Bottled at 31 years old. Dark chestnut. Sweet, fruity plum pudding aroma. Very smooth body. Sweetish palate. Malty, rooty, garden mint, resiny, fruity. Slight woody astringency in the finish. SCORE 89

1971, 56.4 vol

Bottled at 30 years old. Dark, tawny. Palate starts malty and very sweet. Becomes drier, with cocoa-like flavors. Long, lively, spicy. Reminiscent of root ginger. SCORE 90

1971, 55.9 vol

Bottled at 30 years old. Very dark oak color. A surprisingly soft, gentle expression. Lightly syrupy. Brown sugar and cherry brandy flavors. Perfectly pitched spicy finish. SCORE 89

1972, 49.2 vol

Bottled at 29 years. Rosewood. Almost opaque. Passion fruit aroma. Palate has violets, bitter chocolate, fudge, and espresso. Bitterness of finish rather aggressive. SCORE 88

1972, 58.4 vol

Bottled at 29 years. Very dark mahogany. Fruity, calvados-like aroma. Fruity, resiny, spicy palate. Very lively. Slightly abrasive. Sappy, oaky finish. SCORE 89

THE FINE OAK RANGE
THE MACALLAN Fine Oak 10-year-old, 40 vol

COLOR Rich golden honey.

NOSE Fresh orange, clean barley, hints of cedarwood. Honeyed, gentle.

BODY Full, soft, and rounded.

PALATE Vibrant razor-sharp barley. Fresh, clean, citrus fruit and spice.

FINISH Medium but perfectly balanced, with more citrus fruit and spice.

SCORE **75**

THE MACALLAN Fine Oak 12-year-old, 40 vol

COLOR Rich, golden honey.

NOSE Vanilla, butterscotch, satsumas, orange chews.

BODY Medium-full, assertive, very pleasant.

PALATE Mixed fruits, including grapefruit and orange, then a big dash
of spices.

FINISH Quite long, spicy, and fruity, in equal measure.

SCORE **77**

THE MACALLAN Fine Oak 15-year-old, 43 vol

COLOR Rich golden honey.

NOSE Soft, honeyed. Peaches and apricots.

BODY Full and rich; mouth-coating.

PALATE Rich fruits, including melon and peach, ginger barley, a wave of
sweet spice, and some oakiness.

FINISH Spice, tannins, and fruits in balance. Excellently made.

SCORE **85**

THE MACALLAN Fine Oak 18-year-old, 43 vol

COLOR Rich golden honey.

NOSE Soft and shy. Vegetal. Not assertive; mushy.

BODY Full. Quite oily. Rich, soft, and rounded.

PALATE Better than the nose. Very balanced, with rich sweet fruit, clean
barley, intense pepper, and some wood tannins.

FINISH Medium, soft, honeyed, and rounded.

SCORE **81**

THE MACALLAN Fine Oak 21-year-old, 43 vol

COLOR Rich golden honey.

NOSE Quite light. Orange and other citrus fruits. Sweet barley.

BODY Medium, rounded, soft, and sweet.

PALATE Summery, clean, and refreshing. Orange and lemons, some spice,
but not as much depth as other expressions.

FINISH Orangeade, icing sugar. Medium-long.

SCORE **74**

THE MACALLAN Fine Oak 25-year-old, 43 vol

COLOR Rich golden honey.

NOSE Bold. Some red berries, dark chocolate, stewed apple. Rich,
with a trace of smoke.

BODY Medium, spikey, and spicy.

PALATE Assorted sweet and exotic fruits, a trace of red licorice,
then late sweet spice and gentle, pleasant oakiness.

FINISH Quite long. Mannered and pleasant, with some sweet
spice and wood.

SCORE **89**

THE MACALLAN Fine Oak 30-year-old, 43 vol

COLOR Rich golden honey.

NOSE Orange and pineapple. Grapefruit. Rich, venerable. Red berries.

BODY Full and mouth-coating; creamy.

PALATE Orange marmalade dominates, with softer and supportive spice and oak. Drying.

FINISH Big on all fronts, with the fruit holding out above the oaky tannins and spiciness. Excellent balance and wonderful, long aftertaste.

SCORE **91**

THE 1824 COLLECTION
THE MACALLAN Whisky Maker's Edition, 42.8 vol

COLOR Orange gold.

NOSE A hint of sherry and sulfur, but pleasant. Orange and grapefruit zest. Sweet spices. Wax polish.

BODY Creamy. Soft.

PALATE Gossamer-like. Refreshing. Fresh orange juice. Spice. Some oak. Very balanced.

FINISH Medium. Fruity. Soft, with gentle tannins and full fruit.

SCORE **86**

THE MACALLAN Select Oak, 40 vol

COLOR Honey gold.

NOSE Butterscotch. Vanilla. Beeswax. Toffee. Traces of cocoa.

BODY Medium-full.

PALATE Honeyed peach. Tangerine. Vanilla. Clean barley. Soft spices.

FINISH Medium length, medium-sweet. Pleasant.

SCORE **83**

THE MACALLAN Estate Reserve, 45.5 vol

COLOR Deep gold.

NOSE Complex and evolving. Big citrus fruits. Red berries. Hints of sherry, sulfur, spearmint, vanilla, and cherry.

BODY Quite rich and creamy, but not aggressive.

PALATE Delicious vanilla and orange fruit mix. Soft and rounded. Canned fruit and cream. Then gentle pepper and traces of oak.

FINISH Cocoa. Milk chocolate. Orange jellybeans. Gentle and sweet. The cocoa lingers.

SCORE **92**

THE MACALLAN 1824 Limited Edition, 48 vol

COLOR Deep golden amber.

NOSE Venerable. Rich sherry fruits. Dried orange peel and red berries. Traces of smoke and oak. Molasses toffee.

BODY Full, creamy, and mouth-coating.

PALATE Orange marmalade. Honeycomb. Red berry fruits. Both clean and complex.

FINISH Long and impressive. Fresh fruit salad. Oak, spice, some astringency.

SCORE **93**

TWO INDEPENDENT BOTTLINGS

THE MACALLAN 17-year-old, Single Malts of Scotland, 46 vol

COLOR Pale gold.

NOSE Shy. Mandarin. Orange fruit.

BODY Medium, sweet, and pleasant.

PALATE Some anise. Sweet barley. Honeycomb. Toffee fudge. Stewed fruits.

FINISH Medium-sweet and quite spicy, reflecting its age.

SCORE **83**

THE MACALLAN 18-year-old, Glenkeir Treasures, 54.8 vol

216 bottles released.

COLOR Pale gold.

NOSE Odd. Rootsy. Musty. Doughball. Then some berry and citrus notes.

BODY Full and creamy.

PALATE Orange pips. Stewed fruits. Tannin. Apple core. Almonds.

FINISH Medium-long. Sweet, but with fruit and spice nicely balanced.

SCORE **79**

MACDUFF

PRODUCER John Dewar & Sons Ltd. (Bacardi)
REGION Highlands   DISTRICT Speyside (Deveron)
ADDRESS Macduff Distillery, Banff, Banffshire, AB45 3JT
TEL 01261 812612

A LTHOUGH THE DISTILLERY claims whisky production dating back centuries, citing "church records from the 1700s [that] describe the local whisky as excellent," Macduff was built during the optimistic 1960s, when distillers could not keep up with demand. It has a workaday appearance compared to some of the more architecturally refined distilleries built around that time. Its clean, uncluttered interior has in general been mirrored in the character of its whiskies. They, too, have been clean and uncluttered—whiskies that tasted of malt. They still do, but a 10-year-old, repackaged in 2002 and now the distillery's principal product, has a strong wood influence too.

The distillery is in the old fishing town and former spa of Macduff at a point where the glen of the Deveron reaches the sea (the reason why the whiskies are now marketed with the name Glen Deveron). On the other side of the river is the town of Banff. At a stretch, this is the western edge of Speyside. Not only is it a fringe location geographically—Macduff was for years somewhat lonely as the sole distillery of the William Lawson company. The distillery's output has largely gone into the Lawson blends. Since 1992, Macduff has been part of Bacardi, which also owns Dewars.

HOUSE STYLE Malty. Sweet limes in older versions.
Restorative or after dinner.

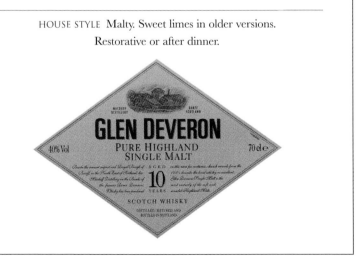

GLEN DEVERON 10-year-old, 40 vol

COLOR Deep gold.

NOSE Freshly cut wood. Cedar-like. Surprisingly assertive.

BODY Light to medium. Notably smooth.

PALATE Malted milk. Condensed milk. Fig toffee. Butterscotch. Thick yogurt. Slightly sour. Lemony.

FINISH Crisp. "Sea foam" toffee.

SCORE **72**

GLEN DEVERON 12-year-old, 40 vol

COLOR Gold.

NOSE Faint hint of sherry. Rich, sweet, fresh maltiness.

BODY Light to medium, but notably smooth.

PALATE Full. Very clean delicious maltiness.

FINISH Malty dryness. Quick but pleasantly warming.

SCORE **75**

GLEN DEVERON 15-year-old, 40 vol

COLOR Deep gold.

NOSE Sweet, butterscotch, with notes of sherry.

BODY Rich, full, spicy, well-rounded.

PALATE Oak, with traces of cinnamon and a whisper of lemon.

FINISH Short, clean, crisp.

SCORE **76**

SOME INDEPENDENT BOTTLINGS
MACDUFF 17-year-old, Old Malt Cask, 50 vol

COLOR Buttery yellow.

NOSE Dusty office. Polished desk. Treacle toffee.

BODY Soft. Sweet. Unassuming.

PALATE Lemon. Zesty. Talcum powder. Drying. Peat bed.

FINISH Short and polite. Surprisingly gentle. Little trace of wood.

SCORE **67**

MACDUFF 1989, Connoisseurs Choice, 43 vol

COLOR Bronze.

NOSE Rootsy. Green salad.

BODY Sweet, creamy, and full.

PALATE Sweet barley. Gentle spice. Unassuming. Some fruits. Pleasant.

FINISH Medium, with sugar and spice.

SCORE **73**

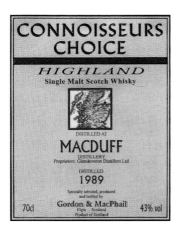

CONNOISSEURS CHOICE

HIGHLAND
Single Malt Scotch Whisky

DISTILLED AT
MACDUFF
DISTILLERY
Proprietors: Glendeveron Distillers Ltd.

DISTILLED
1989

Specially selected, produced
and bottled by
Gordon & MacPhail
Elgin . Scotland
Product of Scotland

70cl   43% vol

MACDUFF 1968, 38-year-old, Duncan Taylor, 49.1 vol

COLOR Golden.

NOSE Sharp grape. Almond extract. Anise. Deep, vinous. Bourbon and vanilla notes.

BODY Medium and sharp.

PALATE Old. Some citrus and barley notes, but they have to battle to survive intense pepper and tannin.

FINISH Some fruity melon holds on, but mainly it is a medium finish of oak and spice.

SCORE **76**

MACDUFF 1969, 38-year-old, Lonarch, 40.3 vol

COLOR Gingery yellow.

NOSE Lemon cupcake. Pastry. Dairy custard. Lime sherbet.

BODY Sweet and mouth-coating. Intense.

PALATE Sugar and spice. Vanilla. Some citrus. chili peppers.

FINISH Medium. Lemon sherbet. Traces of almond. Slightly bitter at the death.

SCORE **80**

MACDUFF 40-year-old, Old Malt Cask, 50 vol

COLOR Mahogany.

NOSE Rich sherry. Church altar wine. Red fruit trifle. Some oaky tannins.

BODY Full. Rich. Mouth-coating.

PALATE Sherry trifle. Red fruits. Honeyed. Prunes. Some astringency from the wood. Still quite soft.

FINISH Long. Drying as tannins kick in. Soft, smooth, and fruity.

SCORE **85**

MANNOCHMORE

PRODUCER Diageo
REGION Highlands   DISTRICT Speyside (Lossie)
ADDRESS By Elgin, Morayshire, IV30 3SF   TEL 01343 862000
WEBSITE www.malts.com

T HE BLACK WHISKY Loch Dhu was produced here. This curious
product was aimed at "image-conscious young men." Given the
fashionability of black among young women, they may have felt
excluded. Diageo insists that the color of the whisky derived from "a
secret preparation, involving the double charring of selected bourbon
barrels." The best guess is that the "preparation"—perhaps first a
spraying and then a charring—involved caramelization.

The distillery is quite young itself, having been established in
1971–72. Its original role was to provide malt whisky as a component
of the Haig blends, augmenting the production of its older neighbor,
Glenlossie. The two are south of Elgin, and take their water from the
Mannoch hills. With the same raw materials and location, the two
make similar malts. Mannochmore's seems slightly less complex, but it
is very enjoyable nonetheless.

HOUSE STYLE Fresh, flowery, dry. Aperitif.

LOCH DHU The Black Whisky, 10-year-old, 40 vol

COLOR Ebony, with a mahogany tinge.

NOSE Licorice, medicinal. Fruity, flowery. Whisky aromas very evident.

BODY Medium. Softly syrupy.

PALATE Light, dryish. Licorice. Hint of cough drops. Fruit.
Scores for initiative, but not for the whisky lover.

FINISH Whisky flavors gently emerge. Licorice root. Dryish. Hint of warmth.

SCORE **70**

MANNOCHMORE 1996, Bottled in 2007,
Berry's Own Selection, 46 vol

COLOR Very pale yellow.

NOSE Marzipan. Buttery fudge. Lemon drizzle cake. Crystalized fruit.

BODY Soft and sweet.

PALATE Fresh barley. Sweet yellow fruits. Refreshing. A touch of spice.

FINISH Quite short and sweet, with some spice.

SCORE **70**

MANNOCHMORE 1984, Scotch Malt Whisky Society,
No 64.18, Cask 4588, 56.3 vol

COLOR Lemon yellow.

NOSE Chinese food. Stewed vegetables.

BODY Full and creamy. Mouth-coating.

PALATE Anise. Peat and oak prominent, but also sweet fruit. Peach?

FINISH Sweet barley nicely balanced with oak and spice.

SCORE **76**

MANNOCHMORE 18-year-old, Old Malt Cask, 50 vol

COLOR Clear honey.

NOSE Freshly cut barley field. Unripe pear. Dry grass.

BODY Sweet and creamy.

PALATE Sweet. Honey. Rich barley. Boiled sweets. Vanilla.

FINISH Medium-rich and full.

SCORE **80**

MILLBURN

PRODUCER DCL
REGION Highlands DISTRICT Speyside (Inverness)
SITE OF FORMER DISTILLERY Millburn Road, Inverness,
Inverness-shire, IV2 3QX

As the train from London finishes its 11-hour journey to Inverness, it glides by recognizable distillery buildings that are now a pub-steakhouse. At least there is still drink on the premises.

Millburn is believed to have dated from 1807, and its buildings from 1876 and 1922. It was owned for a time by Haig's. The distillery closed in 1985. Whiskies distilled a decade earlier have been released at 18 years and now 25, as Rare Malts.

HOUSE STYLE Smoky, aromatic. Nightcap.

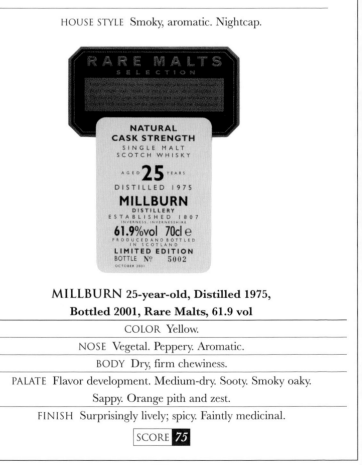

MILLBURN 25-year-old, Distilled 1975, Bottled 2001, Rare Malts, 61.9 vol

COLOR Yellow.
NOSE Vegetal. Peppery. Aromatic.
BODY Dry, firm chewiness.
PALATE Flavor development. Medium-dry. Sooty. Smoky oaky. Sappy. Orange pith and zest.
FINISH Surprisingly lively; spicy. Faintly medicinal.

SCORE 75

MILLBURN 18-year-old, Distilled 1975, Rare Malts, 58.5 vol

COLOR Greeny gold.

NOSE Oaky and aromatic.

BODY Lightly smooth.

PALATE Dryish, perfumy, smoky.

FINISH Oaky, sappy.

SCORE **74**

MILLBURN 1978, Gordon & MacPhail, 46 vol

COLOR Pale gold with amber highlights.

NOSE Fragrant, fruity, with mildly smoked malt.

BODY Smooth.

PALATE Malt and peat, plus background ginger.

FINISH Drying quite swiftly to oak.

SCORE **75**

MILTONDUFF

PRODUCER Chivas Brothers (Pernod Ricard)
REGION Highlands   DISTRICT Speyside (Lossie)
ADDRESS Elgin, Morayshire, IV30 3TQ
TEL 01343 547433

THE BENEDICTINE PRIORY OF PLUSCARDEN, which still exists, was once a brewery—and provided the land on which the Miltonduff distillery stands. Although there is no other connection, the name of the Priory is invoked on the box that houses the Miltonduff bottle. The distillery, established in 1824, south of Elgin, was extensively modernized in the 1930s, and again in the 1970s. Its whisky is very important in the Ballantine blends. Formerly owned by Allied Distillers, Miltonduff was acquired by Pernod Ricard in 2005.

For a time, the company also had a Lomond still on the site. This produced a malt with similar characteristics to Miltonduff, but heavier, oilier, and smokier, identified as Mosstowie. That still has been dismantled, but the malt can occasionally be found in independent bottlings. The Miltonduff malt is well regarded by blenders, and makes a pleasant single.

HOUSE STYLE Flowery, scenty, clean, firm, elegant. Aperitif.

MILTONDUFF 10-year-old, 40 vol

COLOR Honeyed gold.

NOSE Fragrant, flowery. Very faint peat.

BODY Light to medium. Firm. Smooth.

PALATE Sweetish, firm, clean.

FINISH Firm. Lightly nutty. Soothing.

SCORE **75**

MILTONDUFF 15-year-old, Special Distillery Bottling, 46 vol

COLOR Gold.

NOSE Very soft fruits. Toffee. Pigskin. Viennese whirls.

BODY Velvety.

PALATE Aromatic herbs: rosemary, thyme. Toffee.

Soft and gentle. A demure dram.

FINISH Almond and chocolate.

SCORE **78**

AN INDEPENDENT BOTTLING OF THE MOSSTOWIE MALT FROM MILTONDUFF'S FORMER LOMOND STILL
MOSSTOWIE 33-year-old, 1975, Rarest of the Rare, 47.7 vol

COLOR Pale yellow.

NOSE Lemon and lime. Clean and fresh.

BODY Soft and pleasant.

PALATE Minty. Lime and citrus fruit. Some pepper. Gentle tannins.

FINISH Medium, fruity, and surprisingly clean. Some peppery spice.

SCORE **70**

MORTLACH

PRODUCER Diageo

REGION Highlands DISTRICT Speyside (Dufftown)

ADDRESS Dufftown, Banffshire, AB55 4AQ

TEL 01340 822100 WEBSITE www.malts.com

ALL THE PLEASURES OF A GOOD SPEYSIDE single malt are found in Mortlach: floweriness, peatiness, smokiness, maltiness, and fruitiness. Its complexity may well arise from its extraordinary miscellany of stills. In the course of a history stretching from the earliest days of legal distilling, successive managers seem to have been heretics: fiddling with the shape, size, and design of stills to achieve the result they desired. It seems that they strayed so far from the orthodoxies of the industry that they were never corralled, and the whisky was so good that no one wanted to risk changing it. Nor does anyone wholly understand how the combination of stills achieves its particular result. The whisky has such individuality that its character is not overwhelmed by sherry maturation. While UDV/Diageo has over the years moved away from sherry, and argued for "distillery character," Mortlach has not been bound by that orthodoxy, either.

HOUSE STYLE A Speyside classic: elegant and flowery yet supple and muscular. Immensely complex, with great length. After dinner or bedtime.

SPEYSIDE
SINGLE MALT
SCOTCH WHISKY

MORTLACH

was the first of seven distilleries in Dufftown. In the 19th farm animals kept in adjoining byres were fed on barley left over from processing Today water from springs in the CONVAL HILLS is used to produce this delightful smooth fruity single MALT SCOTCH WHISKY.

AGED 16 YEARS

Distilled & Bottled at SCOTLAND
MORTLACH DISTILLERY
Dufftown, Keith, Banffshire, Scotland

43% vol 70 cl

MⓄRTLACH

SPEYSIDE SINGLE MALT
SCOTCH WHISKY

YEARS 32 OLD

A complex expression of a rich after-dinner malt from one of the most picturesque distilleries on Speyside, this tantalising natural cask-strength 1971 Mortlach has a freshness that belies its 32 years.

First of seven distilleries built here at the heart of Speyside, Mortlach was the original DUFFTOWN malt.

It is uniquely distilled in a Byzantine configuration of ...three wash and ...three spirit stills to make it a firm, elegant, long-finishing malt.

NATURAL CASK STRENGTH

||| UNIQUELY
||| DISTILLED

50.1% vol 70cl

Bottled in 2004
Limited Edition

BOTTLE: Nº
6000

Distilled & bottled in Scotland Mortlach Distillery
Dufftown, Keith, Banffshire AB55 4AQ, SCOTLAND

MORTLACH 16-year-old, Flora and Fauna, 43 vol

COLOR Profound, rich amber.

NOSE Dry oloroso sherry. Smoky, peaty.

BODY Medium to full, firm, and smooth.

PALATE Sherryish, smoky, peaty, sappy.
Some fruitiness. Assertive.

FINISH Long and dry.

SCORE **81**

MORTLACH 22-year-old, Distilled 1972, Rare Malts, 65.3 vol

COLOR Very full gold.

NOSE Cereal grains. Fresh baked bread. Some smoky peat.

BODY Remarkably smooth; layered.

PALATE Hugely nutty. Developing from dryness to sweeter
juiciness. Then sweet smokiness.

FINISH Complex, with candy-sugar nuttiness and surging warmth.
Tremendous length.

SCORE **85**

MORTLACH 32-year-old, 50.1 vol

COLOR Light gold with a greenish tinge.

NOSE Surprisingly zingy and citrusy. Clean. Fresh grapefruit.

BODY Oily. Full. Assertive.

PALATE Lovely balance between fresh lemon and zesty fruits,
on the one hand, and engaging sweet spice and oak, on the other.
Rounded and full.

FINISH Long. Sweet and spicy.

SCORE **90**

MORTLACH Managers' Choice, Distilled 1997, Bottled 2009, 57.1 vol

COLOR Pale gold.

NOSE Peach. Stewed fruits. Sweet.

BODY Rich and sweet.

PALATE Lots of fruit—some orange, some peach,
and some over-ripe apple.

FINISH Medium and fruity. Like crystallized fruit jellies.

SCORE **80**

NORTH PORT

PRODUCER DCL/UDV
REGION Highlands   DISTRICT Eastern Highlands
SITE OF FORMER DISTILLERY Brechin, Angus, DD9 6BE

T HE NAME INDICATES THE NORTH GATE of the small, once-walled
city of Brechin. The distillery was built in 1820. The pioneering
whisky writer Alfred Barnard, who toured Scotland's distilleries in the
1880s, recorded that this one obtained its barley from the farmers
around Brechin, and its peat and water from the Grampian
mountains. The writer Derek Cooper reports that the condensers were
cooled in a stream that ran through the distillery. North Port was
modernized in the 1970s, and closed in 1983. It was subsequently
demolished, and a supermarket now occupies the site. Some bottlings
of this malt appear under the name Brechin.

HOUSE STYLE Dry, fruity, gin-like. Aperitif.

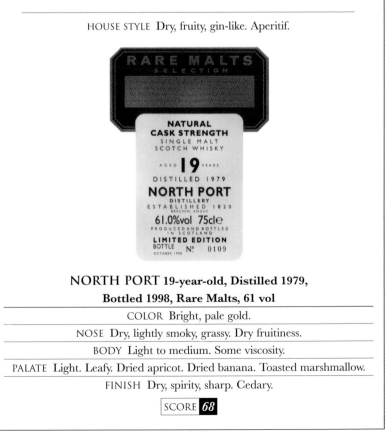

NORTH PORT 19-year-old, Distilled 1979,
Bottled 1998, Rare Malts, 61 vol

COLOR Bright, pale gold.

NOSE Dry, lightly smoky, grassy. Dry fruitiness.

BODY Light to medium. Some viscosity.

PALATE Light. Leafy. Dried apricot. Dried banana. Toasted marshmallow.

FINISH Dry, spirity, sharp. Cedary.

SCORE 68

NORTH PORT 23-year-old, Distilled 1971, Bottled 1995, Rare Malts, 54.7 vol

COLOR Bright gold.

NOSE Aromatic, dry, almost sharp.

BODY Very light, smooth.

PALATE Light, with suggestions of mints, crystallized fruit, and pineapple.

FINISH Sharp.

SCORE **67**

BRECHIN 28-year-old, Special Releases 2005, 53.3 vol

COLOR Pale straw.

NOSE Soft and rich. Peaches in brandy.

BODY Firm.

PALATE Quite thin and austere, with dried fruits and lemony oak.

FINISH Drying oak and mild spice.

SCORE **73**

NORTH PORT BRECHIN 1982, Connoisseurs Choice, 43 vol

COLOR Honey gold.

NOSE Gooseberry and grape. Lime sorbet.

BODY Sweet and creamy.

PALATE Refreshing. Sherbety. Kiwi fruit. Mixed fruit sweets.

FINISH Lots of exotic fruit. Fudge. A touch of peat.

SCORE **82**

NORTH PORT 26-year-old, Distilled 1981, Bottled 2007, Cask No 775, Duncan Taylor, Rarest of the Rare, 52.9 vol

COLOR Very pale gold, with copper highlights.

NOSE Distinctive. Coal tar, licorice, and a hint of violets.

BODY Full and slightly oily.

PALATE Cough syrup, hazelnuts, salt. Progressively drying.

FINISH Holds its dryness with walnuts and licorice, plus a little peat.

SCORE **76**

NORTH PORT 27-year-old, 1981, Rarest of the Rare, 56.5 vol

COLOR Golden honey.

NOSE Evolving: stewed vegetables, sherry, roasted nuts, red berries, cocoa.

BODY Warm, soft, and sweet.

PALATE Anise. Cherry liqueur. Red berries. Sherry notes. Dark chocolate.

FINISH Long, sweet, sherried, and pleasant.

SCORE **79**

OBAN

PRODUCER Diageo
REGION Highlands   DISTRICT Western Highlands
ADDRESS Stafford Street, Oban, Argyll, PA34 5NH
TEL 01631 572004   WEBSITE www.malts.com   VC

ENTHUSIASTS FOR THE WESTERN HIGHLAND malts sometimes dismiss Oban as being too restrained. With the 14-year-old augmented not only by the Montilla fino, but also by a 2002 Limited Release, there is now enough of an oeuvre to prove otherwise.

Oban is one of the few Western Highland distilleries on the mainland. It is a small distillery in a small town, but has a commanding position. Oban is regarded as the capital of the Western Highlands, and the distillery has a central site on the main street, facing the sea.

The principal expression of its whisky, the 14-year-old, has a label design incorporating a summary of the town's history: settled by Mesolithic cave dwellers before 5000BC; later by Celts, Picts, and Vikings. It was a fishing village, and in the era of trains and steamships became a gateway to the islands of the wests. Travelers following the muses of Mendelssohn, Turner, Keats, or Wordsworth to Mull, Iona, or Fingal's Cave, return to see a harborfront centered on the distillery—backed by mossy, peaty hills from where its water flows.

A family of merchants in the town became brewers and distillers in 1794, though the present buildings probably date from the 1880s. The still-house was rebuilt in the late 1960s and early 1970s.

HOUSE STYLE Medium, with fresh peat and a whiff of the sea.
With seafood or game, or after dinner.

OBAN 14-year-old, 43 vol

COLOR Full gold to amber.

NOSE "Pebbles on the beach," said one taster. A whiff of the sea,
but also a touch of fresh peat, and some maltiness.

BODY Firm, smooth, slightly viscous.

PALATE Deceptively delicate at first. Perfumy. Faint hint of fruity seaweed.
Then lightly waxy, becoming smoky. Dry.

FINISH Aromatic, smooth, appetizing.

SCORE **79**

OBAN 1980, Double Matured, Distillers Edition, 43 vol

Finished in Montilla fino wood.

COLOR Amber.

NOSE Fragrant. Edible seaweed. Peaches. Very complex.

BODY Smooth, bigger.

PALATE Salty, nutty, peachy. Sweet in the middle, developing
notes of tobacco and seaweed.

FINISH The salt comes rolling back like an incoming tide.

SCORE **80**

OBAN 32-year-old, Limited Release of 6000, Bottled 2002, 55.1 vol

COLOR Greeny gold. Ripe pears.

NOSE Sweet, sandy. A walk on the beach.

BODY Soft, oily, soothing.

PALATE Silky, teasing. Tightly combined flavors.
Oily creaminess. Sweet, edible seaweed.

FINISH Surprisingly assertive. Sandy. Almost gritty.
Stinging, salty.

SCORE **83**

OBAN Managers' Choice, Distilled 2000, Bottled 2009, 58.7 vol

Matured in a European oak sherry cask.

COLOR Burnished gold.

NOSE Maple syrup, toffee bonbons, spicy salt,
and delicate smoke.

BODY Relatively full.

PALATE Fresh citrus fruits, hazelnuts, and a tang of sea salt.

FINISH Dries steadily to dark chocolate.

SCORE **80**

OLD PULTENEY

PRODUCER Inver House Distillers Ltd.
REGION Highlands   DISTRICT Northern Highlands
ADDRESS Huddart Street, Wick, Caithness, KW1 5BD
WEBSITE www.inverhouse.com/www.oldpulteney.com
EMAIL enquiries@inverhouse.com

ONE OF WHISKY'S GREAT DEBATES (or was it a storm in a copita?) began here, and went public in 2003: do coastal whiskies really taste of salt? The debate surfaced in *Whisky Magazine*, but the salty suggestion had first been made in respect of Old Pulteney 25 years earlier, in the wine magazine *Decanter*.

Not only is the Pulteney distillery on the coast, it is the northernmost distillery on the Scottish mainland, at the town of Wick, in the famously peaty, rock-faced county of Caithness. Part of the town was designed by Thomas Telford and built by Sir William Pulteney in 1810 as a model fishing port. The distillery, founded in 1826, is in "Pulteneytown." It is thus one of the few urban distilleries, albeit only 250 yards from the nearest part of the harbor front. Even that walk can be sufficiently windy to demand a dram. "Caithness is a bare county, and needs a good whisky to warm it up," observed an early writer on the water of life, Professor R. J. S. McDowall. He was referring to Old Pulteney.

HOUSE STYLE Fresh, salty, appetizing. Pre-dinner.

OLD PULTENEY 12-year-old, 40 vol

COLOR Deep yellow.

NOSE Dry. Peat, grass, sweet broom.

BODY Light, oily.

PALATE Light. Still honey and nuts, but oilier.

FINISH Oily. Soothing. Very salty.

SCORE **79**

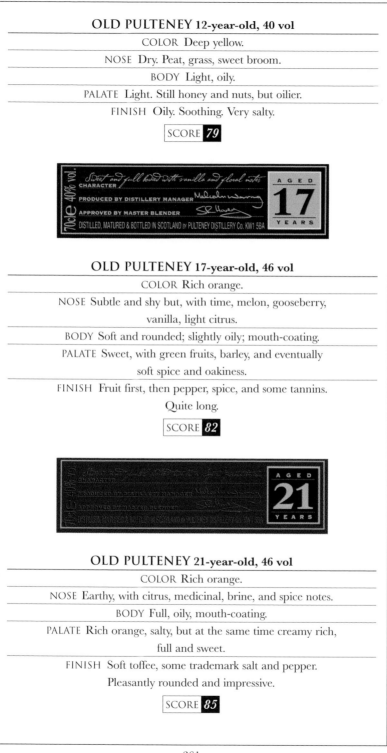

OLD PULTENEY 17-year-old, 46 vol

COLOR Rich orange.

NOSE Subtle and shy but, with time, melon, gooseberry,
vanilla, light citrus.

BODY Soft and rounded; slightly oily; mouth-coating.

PALATE Sweet, with green fruits, barley, and eventually
soft spice and oakiness.

FINISH Fruit first, then pepper, spice, and some tannins.
Quite long.

SCORE **82**

OLD PULTENEY 21-year-old, 46 vol

COLOR Rich orange.

NOSE Earthy, with citrus, medicinal, brine, and spice notes.

BODY Full, oily, mouth-coating.

PALATE Rich orange, salty, but at the same time creamy rich,
full and sweet.

FINISH Soft toffee, some trademark salt and pepper.
Pleasantly rounded and impressive.

SCORE **85**

OLD PULTENEY 30-year-old, 44 vol

COLOR Rich gold.

NOSE Summer flowers. Lemon rind. Wood shavings. Vanilla.

BODY Firm and full.

PALATE Lemon and honey lozenges. Exotic fruits. Pineapple. Pleasant and unobtrusive oak and spices. Sweet.

FINISH Clean and long, with fruit, spice, and oak in harmony.

SCORE **84**

OLD PULTENEY 32-year-old,
Highland Selection Limited Edition, 56.2 vol

COLOR Mahogany.

NOSE Full sherry. Rich dried fruit, figs, raisins. Cherry liqueur chocolates. Tobacco. A balsamic touch (eucalyptus?).

BODY Full, syrupy.

PALATE A sherry burst-out. The distillery character is buried under assertive oak and punchy spices. Burned wood. Bitter chocolate. Not typical of Old Pulteney.

FINISH Muscular. Dry.

SCORE **75**

AN INDEPENDENT BOTTLING
OLD PULTENEY 8-year-old, Gordon & MacPhail, 40 vol

COLOR Pale gold.

NOSE Fresh, lively, spicy, and honeyed.

BODY Light to medium. Slightly oily.

PALATE Quite dry, with a discreet sprinkling of salt and emerging citrus flavors.

FINISH Drying. Mild oak. A tang of distant peat.

SCORE **81**

PITTYVAICH

PRODUCER Diageo
REGION Highlands   DISTRICT Speyside (Dufftown)
SITE OF FORMER DISTILLERY
Dufftown, Banffshire, AB55 4BR

Bulldozed in 2002, after a short and unglamorous life, the industrial-looking distillery was built by Bell's in 1975. In the late 1980s, enthusiasts for single malts began to wonder whether the product would become available to them. Then independent bottler James MacArthur released a 12-year-old, revealing a perfumy, soft-pear house character. The same bottler then added a 14-year-old that more assertively pronounced its dry finish. A bottling of the same age from the Scotch Malt Whisky Society was similar, but seemed to have more spicy dryness on the nose. In 1991 there was finally an official bottling, at 12 years old, in the Flora and Fauna series. This had all the other characteristics, plus a hefty dose of sherry.

HOUSE STYLE Fruity, oily, spicy, spirity.
After dinner—a Scottish grappa, so to speak.

PITTYVAICH 21-year-old, Cadenhead, 54.3 vol

168 bottles released.

COLOR Rich gold.

NOSE Lemon. Linament. Medicine cabinet.

BODY Medium-full and soft.

PALATE Fiery. Peach. Sugar beet and sugar barley. The merest hint of oak and spice. Not much depth.

FINISH Medium-long and undramatic.

SCORE **64**

PITTYVAICH 29-year-old, Rarest of the Rare, 50 vol

COLOR Yellow with a green hue.

NOSE Lime Starburst. Sweet barley.

BODY Sweet and creamy.

PALATE Sweet citrus. Rootsy. Melon skin. Pleasant but two-dimensional.

FINISH Short, sweet, and citrusy.

SCORE **67**

PORT ELLEN

PRODUCER Diageo
REGION Islay   DISTRICT South Shore
SITE OF FORMER DISTILLERY Port Ellen, Isle of Islay, PA42 7AH
WEBSITE www.malts.com

WHICH WILL BE THE FINAL VINTAGE of this cult whisky? As stocks at the distillery diminish, and the fashionability of Islay soars, speculation mounts. Port Ellen is the rarest of Islay malts, despite a surprising number of independent bottlings. The distillery, near the island's main ferry port, was founded in 1825, substantially rebuilt and expanded during the boom years of the 1960s, then closed during the downturn in the 1980s. In the last two or three years, the modern parts of the distillery have been demolished, but the original pair of malt kilns have been preserved, complete with pagodas.

Adjoining the distillery is a modern maltings. The malt is supplied, in varying levels of peatiness, to many of the other Islay distilleries, including those that make a proportion of their own.

In 1995, Diageo started marketing whiskies from silent distilleries as The Rare Malts. These are vintage dated, so the number of bottles is determined by the amount of whisky held from a single year. In 1998, a 20-year-old Port Ellen was included in the range. In 2000, there was a further bottling of the same vintage at 22 years old. In order to vary the offerings, The Rare Malts had made it a rule not to feature the same distillery two years running. Such was the interest in the Port Ellen that it was decided to circumvent the rule. The Rare Malts selection ceased to include Port Ellen, which became a stand-alone Limited Edition. In 2008, a 29-year-old Port Ellen became the eighth such Limited Edition bottling.

HOUSE STYLE Oily, peppery, salty, smoky, herbal. With smoked fish.

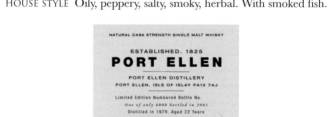

PORT ELLEN 1979, 22-year-old, Limited Edition Numbered Bottles, First Release 2001, 56.2 vol

COLOR Solid, greeny gold. Bright, refractive.

NOSE Fresh. Bison grass. Cereal grain. Oily.

BODY Firm, nutty, malty.

PALATE Earthy. Peaty. Salty. Quite hard. Austere.

FINISH Pronounced salt. Dry smokiness. Intensely appetizing.

SCORE **92**

PORT ELLEN 1978, 24-year-old, Limited Edition Numbered Bottles, Second Release 2002, 59.35 vol

COLOR Lemony with golden hues.

NOSE Grassy and herbal. Dill, angelica, camomile.
A pleasant earthiness comes through.

BODY Tender.

PALATE Surprisingly smooth and sweet. A refreshing coolness.
Smokiness slowly emerges and hovers on menthol and vanilla.

FINISH Pleasantly dry and slowly dying.

SCORE **90**

PORT ELLEN 1979, 24-year-old, Limited Edition Numbered Bottles, Third Release 2003, 56.2 vol

COLOR Pale gold. Faint green tinge.

NOSE Herbal. Slightly sour. Seaweedy. Sea breezes.

BODY Soft, textured.

PALATE Edible seaweed. Salty flavors reminiscent of
some vermouths. Developing spicy notes.

FINISH Powerful, peppery, warming.

SCORE **91**

PORT ELLEN 21-year-old, Anniversary Bottling, 58.4 vol

A rare "official" bottling, to celebrate 25 years of the maltings at Port Ellen.

COLOR Bright gold.

NOSE Very medicinal, but clean and firm.

BODY Exceptionally oily. Creamy.

PALATE Smooth and deceptively restrained at first, then the tightly
combined flavors emerge: bay leaves, parsley, peppercorns.

FINISH Slowly unfolding. Salty, smoky, oaky. Very warming. A subtlety and
complexity to which no aquavit or pepper vodka could quite aspire.

SCORE **83**

PORT ELLEN 20-year-old, Distilled 1978, Rare Malts, 60.9 vol

COLOR Gold.

NOSE More assertive. Appetizing and arousing. Bay trees. Seaweed.

BODY Lightly oily.

PALATE More expressive, fruity, dryish flavors. Fruity olive oil. Parsley.

FINISH Salty. Smoky. Oaky. Extremely peppery.

SCORE **82**

PORT ELLEN 22-year-old, Distilled 1978, Rare Malts, 60.5 vol

COLOR Pale yellow.

BODY Big, textured.

NOSE Fruity, seaweed, bay leaves, olive oil.

PALATE Big-bodied. Slightly sticky. Chewy. Edible seaweed. Parsley.

FINISH Hugely salty and equally peppery.

SCORE **85**

PORT ELLEN 1978, Limited Edition Numbered Bottles, Fourth Release, 2004, 56.2 vol

COLOR Straw.

NOSE Bold, slightly spirity, smoky oak.

BODY Quite dry.

PALATE Powerful, complex, salty-sweet. Brittle toffee and a hint of licorice.

FINISH Long and smoky, slightly woody, dark chocolate and dry fruits.

SCORE **90**

AN INDEPENDENT BOTTLING

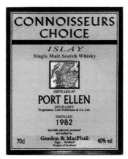

PORT ELLEN 1982, Connoisseurs Choice, 40 vol

COLOR Pale gold. NOSE Ozone and citric peat.
BODY Medium. PALATE Fresh fruit, damped-down bonfires and
developing maritime salt. FINISH Peat ash and ginger. Finally old-fashioned
hospital dressings. SCORE 82

ROSEBANK

PRODUCER **Diageo**
REGION Lowland DISTRICT Central Lowlands
SITE OF FORMER DISTILLERY Falkirk, Stirlingshire, FK1 5BW
WEBSITE www.malts.com

In 2002, the queen opened The Falkirk Wheel, a rotating lift to hoist boats between the Union canal and the restored Forth-Clyde canal. There had been hopes that the development of the canalside at Falkirk would include a tourist distillery to replace the silent Rosebank, but this prospect has so far not materialized.

Roses once bloomed on the banks of the Forth-Clyde canal, and a great deal of very early industry grew there. The Rosebank distillery may have had its origins as early as the 1790s. From the moment the canals lost business to the roads, the distillery's location turned from asset to liability. The road awkwardly bisected the distillery and as the traffic grew, it was difficult for trucks to drive in and out of the distillery. Rosebank was closed in 1993.

Rosebank's whisky at its best (i.e., not too woody) is as flowery as its name. It was the finest example of a Lowland malt, and was produced by triple distillation, in the Lowland tradition. It is a grievous loss.

HOUSE STYLE Aromatic, with suggestions of clover and camomile.
Romantic. A whisky for lovers.

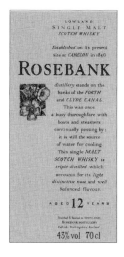

ROSEBANK 12-year-old, Flora and Fauna, 43 vol

This bottling was released in 2003.

COLOR Limey yellow.

NOSE Rosebank's typical camomile.

BODY Lightly creamy.

PALATE Flowery sweetness.

FINISH Mint imperials.

COMMENT Beginning to tire. Snatch a kiss while you can.

SCORE **76**

ROSEBANK 12-year-old Flora and Fauna, 43 vol

A limited release, bottled in 2007.

COLOR Pale gold.

NOSE Pure and clean. Honeyed barley with green fruit underneath.

BODY Light, creamy, and soft.

PALATE Gossamer-like. Honey. Fresh barley. Hints of green fruits.
Traces of mint. Balanced and rounded.

FINISH Minty and fruity in equal measure. Some subtle spices.

SCORE **90**

ROSEBANK 1981, Bottled 1997,
Cask Strength Limited Bottling, 63.9 vol

COLOR Lemony yellow.

NOSE Seductively aromatic. Clover. Camomile. Dry.

BODY Soft, caressing.

PALATE Creamy, lemony, flowery—buttercups? Potpourri.

FINISH Fragrant, faintly smoky.

SCORE **78**

ROSEBANK 20-year-old, Distilled 1981, Rare Malts, 62.3 vol

COLOR Pale straw.

NOSE Floral, with lemon, cut grass, spices, delicate oak.

BODY Firm.

PALATE Initial sweetness gives way to drier,
spicy, citric notes.

FINISH Medium to long, with nuts and lemons.

SCORE **80**

ROSEBANK 18-year-old Chieftain's, 48 vol

COLOR Pale gold with a greenish hue.

NOSE Zingy and subtle. Fruit sherbets.
Crushed gooseberries.

BODY Grape skin. Medium-full. Prickly. Sharp.

PALATE The grape and gooseberry notes coat the mouth.
Oak and pepper follow and wash over them.

FINISH Long and complex.

SCORE **80**

ROSEBANK 17-year-old, Single Malts of Scotland, 55.2 vol

COLOR Rich golden yellow.

NOSE Stewed apple. Cinnamon. Vanilla. A touch of star anise.

BODY Rich and creamy.

PALATE Apple-flavored candy. Toffee apple.
Hints of applewood. Strudel.

FINISH Thick and rich fruits, with a long finish.

SCORE **87**

ROSEBANK 18-year-old, Glenkeir Treasures, 55.4 vol

180 bottles released.

COLOR Pale lemon.

NOSE Shy and needs water. Fresh grass. Spring meadow.
Clean. A hint of fresh herbs and spices.

BODY Soft, creamy, and gentle.

PALATE Apple seeds. Apples and pears. Sweet barley.
Lime sorbet. Gentle spices. Varnished wood.

FINISH Medium, complex, and with some late tannins.

SCORE **80**

ROSEBANK 18 year old, Chieftain's, 48 vol

COLOR Honey gold.

NOSE Banana toffee. Rock candy. Make-up box.

BODY Rich. Oily. Full.

PALATE Spearmint. Intense honey. Citrus. Restrained spice and oak.
Apple. Almond. Subtle and complex.

FINISH Long, rounded, and gentle.

SCORE **88**

ROSEBANK 16-year-old, Cadenheads, 55.7 vol

COLOR Honey gold.

NOSE Jellybeans. Spring meadow. Buttercups.

BODY Full and creamy.

PALATE Beautifully honeyed. Soft peach. A touch of mint. With water,
traces of apple.

FINISH Gentle, soothing, and very pleasant.

SCORE **86**

ROSEBANK 16-year-old,
Single Malts of Scotland, 55.2 vol

COLOR Pale lemon.

NOSE Light. Gooseberry. Summer meadow. Fresh polished wood.

BODY Medium-full. Quite sharp.

PALATE One trick, but a good one: a solid sugar surge of barley
then some spice. With water, hints of apple and pear.

FINISH Soft, with some tannins and spice coming through.
A certain Irishness about this.

SCORE **79**

ROSEBANK 18-year-old, Distilled 1990, Bottled 2008,
Cask No D113286, Duncan Taylor, 47.4 vol

COLOR Pale gold.

NOSE Tinned pears, fresh sawdust, mildly herbal.

BODY Medium.

PALATE Initially intensely syrupy fruits, then spice and fudge.
A hint of nutmeg.

FINISH Medium in length. Hazelnuts and pepper.

SCORE **78**

ROYAL BRACKLA

PRODUCER John Dewar & Sons Ltd. (Bacardi)
REGION Highlands   ISLAND Arran   DISTRICT Speyside (Findhorn Valley)
ADDRESS Royal Brackla Distillery Cawdor, Nairn,
Inverness-shire, IV12 5QY   TEL 01667 402002   VC

THE DISTILLERY WAS FOUNDED in 1812, on the estate of Cawdor, not far from Nairn, on the western fringes of Speyside. In 1835, Brackla became the first distillery to receive the royal warrant, granted by King James IV. Brackla has twice been rebuilt, and was extended in 1970. A 10-year-old Flora and Fauna bottling was produced in the 1990s and, under the current management, the distillery launched a new 10-year-old in 2004.

HOUSE STYLE Fruity, cleansing, sometimes with a dry, hot finish.
A refresher or a pousse-café.

ROYAL BRACKLA 10-year-old, Flora and Fauna, 43 vol

COLOR Pale gold.

NOSE Smoky, slightly sulfurous, burned, molasses.

BODY Medium, drying on the tongue.

PALATE Starts malty and sweet, becomes robustly fruity; then spicy notes.

FINISH Cedary, smoky.

SCORE **74**

ROYAL BRACKLA 1993, WG, 46 vol

COLOR Ginger.

NOSE Fresh. Grapefruit. Diced apple. Grapeskin.

BODY Soft, gentle, and rounded.

PALATE Clean and sweet, with fresh zesty fruit and a dash of chili pepper.

FINISH Medium, clean, and sweet.

SCORE **72**

ROYAL LOCHNAGAR

PRODUCER Diageo
REGION Highlands   DISTRICT Eastern Highlands
ADDRESS Crathie, Ballater, Aberdeenshire, AB35 5TB
TEL 01339 742705
WEBSITE www.discovering-distilleries.com/www.malts.com   VC

QUEEN VICTORIA'S FAVORITE DISTILLERY was once on the tourist route, but has recently been used by Diageo as a place in which to educate its own staff and customers on the subject of malt whisky. The process of making whisky can best be understood in a small, traditional distillery, and Lochnagar qualifies on both counts. It is Diageo's smallest. It is also very pretty—and makes delicious whisky.

The distillery is at the foot of the mountain of Lochnagar, near the river Dee, not far from Aberdeen. A man believed originally to have been an illicit whisky maker established the first legal Lochnagar distillery in 1826, and the present premises were built in 1845. Three years later, the royal family acquired nearby Balmoral as their Scottish country home. The then owner, John Begg, wrote a note inviting Prince Albert to visit. The Prince and Queen Victoria arrived the very next day. Soon afterwards, the distillery began to supply the Queen, and became known as Royal Lochnagar. Her Majesty is said to have laced her claret with the whisky, perhaps anticipating wood finishes. There is no claret finish at Lochnagar as yet. The 12-year-old is aged in second-fill casks, while the Selected Reserve has 50 percent sherry.

HOUSE STYLE Malty, fruity, spicy, cake-like. After dinner.

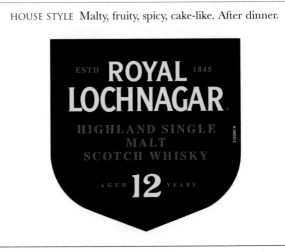

ROYAL LOCHNAGAR 12-year-old, 40 vol

COLOR Full gold.

NOSE Big, with some smokiness.

BODY Medium to full. Smooth.

PALATE Light smokiness, restrained fruitiness, and malty sweetness.

FINISH Again, dry smokiness and malty sweetness. The first impression is of dryness, then comes the sweet, malty counterpoint.

SCORE 80

ROYAL LOCHNAGAR Selected Reserve,
No Age Statement, 43 vol

COLOR Amber red.

NOSE Very sherryish indeed. Spices, ginger cake.

BODY Big, smooth.

PALATE Lots of sherry, malty sweetness, spiced bread, ginger cake. Obviously contains some very well matured whisky.

FINISH Smoky.

SCORE 83

ROYAL LOCHNAGAR Rare Malts, 30-year-old,
Distilled 1974, 56.2 vol

COLOR Pale gold.

NOSE Cut grass, slightly spirity.

BODY Medium.

PALATE Eating apples and a sprinkling of pepper and ginger.

FINISH Long, dry, astringent.

SCORE 80

AN INDEPENDENT BOTTLING
ROYAL LOCHNAGAR 22-year-old, Distilled 1986, Bottled 2009,
Cask No 942, Duncan Taylor, 56.4 vol

COLOR Bright gold.

NOSE Rose petals, green wood, gentle spices.

BODY Firm.

PALATE Nutty and spicy, fresh oak sawdust, and linseed.

FINISH Medium, with ginger, delicate smoke, and slightly assertive oak.

SCORE 79

ST. MAGDALENE

PRODUCER DCL
REGION Lowland   DISTRICT Central Lowlands
SITE OF FORMER DISTILLERY Linlithgow, West Lothian, EH49 6AQ

THIS SITE ACCOMMODATED a leper colony in the 12th century, and later a convent, before a distillery was established, possibly in 1765. Production ceased in 1983 and some of the buildings have since been converted into apartments. The distillery has sometimes been known by the name of its hometown, Linlithgow, which lies west of Edinburgh, close to the Forth River.

HOUSE STYLE Perfumy, grassy, smooth. Restorative.

ST. MAGDALENE 26-year-old, Glenkeir Treasures, 59.1 vol

144 bottles released.

COLOR Rich yellow.

NOSE Delicatessen. Vegetal. Grass cuttings.

BODY Rich and creamy.

PALATE Soft and gentle barley. Honey. Stewed fruits. Lovely and rounded.

FINISH Short. Soft. Very pleasant.

SCORE **82**

ST. MAGDALENE 1975 Rare Old, Gordon & MacPhail, 43 vol

COLOR Brass.

NOSE Evolves quickly. Raspberry sherbet. Wall garden. Primrose. Pachouli oil.

BODY Medium. Sweet.

PALATE Maple syrup. Clear honey. Citrus. Zesty. Some spice. Balanced.

FINISH Some fruit, but wrapped in oak and spice.

SCORE **83**

LINLITHGOW 26-year-old, Single Malts of Scotland, 63.7 vol

COLOR Pale gold.

NOSE Damp straw. Melon. Grassy.

BODY Oily. Sweet. Soft.

PALATE Sweet and soft. Banana skin. Sharp and peppery.

FINISH Medium, sharp, and spicy.

SCORE **69**

SCAPA

PRODUCER Chivas Brothers (Pernod Ricard)
REGION Highlands   ISLAND Orkney
ADDRESS St. Ola, Kirkwall, Orkney, KW15 1SE
TEL 01856 872071   WEBSITE www.scapamalt.com

FORMERLY OWNED BY ALLIED DISTILLERS, Scapa was acquired by Pernod Ricard in 2005. The distillery had been operated intermittently, and marketed sporadically, but, nearing its 120th anniversary, it underwent a complete renovation and reopened in 2004. It retains its two stills, and the restored water wheel, which once powered the distillery in the early 19th century.

Scapa's greatest asset is its evocative location. Scapa Flow, a stretch of water linking the North Sea to the Atlantic, is famous for its role in both World Wars.

The water for the distillery's mash tun is from springs that feed a stream called the Lingro Burn. The water is very peaty, though the distillery uses wholly unpeated malt. Scapa has a Lomond wash still, which may contribute to the slight oiliness of the whisky. Maturation is in bourbon casks. Although the whisky is quite light in flavor, it has a distinctive complex of vanilla notes, sometimes suggesting very spicy chocolate, and nutty, rooty saltiness.

HOUSE STYLE Salt, hay. Oily, spicy chocolate.
After a hearty walk, before dinner.

SCAPA 12-year-old, 40 vol

COLOR Bright, full gold.

NOSE Softer. Hay. Warm.

BODY Light, smooth, salty.

PALATE Clean, sweetish. Vanilla, nuts, salt.

FINISH Late salt and pepper, with a hint of peat.

SCORE **76**

SCAPA Cask Strength Edition, 14-year-old,
Distilled 1992, Bottled 2006, Batch SC 14001, 60.6 vol

COLOR Deep gold.

NOSE Menthol, minty straw with a hint of grapefruit.
Chocolate-covered cherries.

BODY Sinewy, silkily smooth, mouth-coating, slightly oily.

PALATE More minty straw, with vanilla and a hint of citrus.
Water brings out oak.

FINISH Long, peppery, dry, with a return of menthol.

SCORE **85**

SCAPA 16-year-old, 40 vol

COLOR Full gold. Brass.

NOSE Sweet, inviting. Peaches and custard, with a trace of ocean air,
as if near a beach.

BODY Slippery, slightly oily, smooth, salty.

PALATE Clean, sweet custard with floral notes; vanilla with a hint of coconut.

FINISH Late salt and pepper, with a hint of peat.

SCORE **79**

SPEYBURN

PRODUCER Inver House Distillers Ltd.
REGION Highlands   DISTRICT Speyside (Rothes)
ADDRESS Rothes, Aberlour, Morayshire, AB38 7AG
WEBSITE www.inverhouse.com   EMAIL enquiries@inverhouse.com

Pretty as a picture: both the growing range of whiskies (flowery and fruity) and the distillery (a much photographed Victorian classic, masked by trees in a deep, sweeping valley). Speyburn makes a spectacular sight on the road out of Rothes, heading towards Elgin. It was built in 1897 and, despite various modernizations over the years, has not undergone dramatic change. In the early 1990s, Speyburn was acquired by Inver House.

HOUSE STYLE Flowery, herbal, heathery. Aperitif.

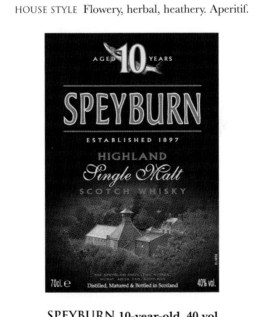

SPEYBURN 10-year-old, 40 vol

COLOR Solid gold.

NOSE Flowery.

BODY Medium, gentle.

PALATE Clean, lightly malty. Developing fresh, herbal, heathery notes.

FINISH Fresh, very sweet, lightly syrupy.

SCORE 71

SPEYBURN 16-year-old, Highland Selection Limited Edition, 46 vol

COLOR Shimmery greeny gold.

NOSE Sweet and fruity.

BODY Light. Very smooth.

PALATE Lots of flowers and fruit. Raspberry? Strawberry?
One of the most assertive, flavorsome expressions of Speyburn.

FINISH Long. Echoing.

SCORE **78**

SPEYBURN 25-year-old Solera, 46 vol

COLOR Rich brassy yellow.

NOSE A slight off note, but then rich barley, some citrus fruits,
and a hint of wood, reflecting the age.

BODY Rich, full, sweet, and mouth-coating.

PALATE Honeyed, soft, sweet, and rounded, with some fruit held
in check by a wave of oak and spice.

FINISH Medium, with sweet fruit giving way to late spice and tannin.

SCORE **82**

AN INDEPENDENT BOTTLING
SPEYBURN 1974, Connoisseurs Choice, 43 vol

COLOR Honey with a greenish hue.

NOSE Dusty. Sulfur. Gooseberry. Cocoa.

BODY Sugary. Full. Oily.

PALATE Rootsy. Fresh green salad. Sharp tannins.

FINISH Quite long and spicy.

SCORE **66**

SPEYSIDE

PRODUCER Speyside Distillers Co. Ltd.
REGION Highlands   DISTRICT Speyside
ADDRESS Tromie Mills, Glentromie, Kingussie, PH21 1HS
TEL 01540 661060
WEBSITE www.speysidedistillers.co.uk   VC By appointment

SPEYSIDE IS A SMALL DISTILLERY which made its first spirit in late 1990. In recent years, it has been developing a portfolio of more mature whiskies, initially under other names and more recently as Speyside. The handsome, gabled stone building is intended to look old and traditional. Its opening was the realization of a dream for its original owner, whisky blender George Christie, who had planned it for three or four decades. His progress on the project ebbed and flowed with the fortunes of the industry. One of his earlier essays was a vatted malt, popular in the United States under the name Glentromie.

The distillery is in the small town of Drumguish, where the tiny river Tromie flows into the highest reaches of the Spey, and hence the name for some of the whiskies that issue from the distillery. The company, Speyside, takes its name, not only from its location but also from a distillery by that name which operated in nearby Kingussie between 1895 and 1910.

HOUSE STYLE Oily, nutty, lightly peaty. Aperitif.

DRUMGUISH Single Malt, No Age Statement, 40 vol

COLOR Full gold.

NOSE Flowery. Jasmine. Passion fruit.

BODY Medium, soft.

PALATE Cashew nuts and a sweetish, dried-grass note that recalls great Scotch whiskies of the past. Cookies. Toasted marshmallows.

FINISH Faintly kirsch-like; dry fruitiness. A bit abrupt.

SCORE **73**

SPEYSIDE 10-year-old, 43 vol

COLOR Golden satin.

NOSE Pronounced oily nuttiness.

BODY Very light and soft.

PALATE Sweet, buttery, rich. Some cream toffee,
cookies, and caramel.

FINISH Lightly dry. Leafy. Grain mustard. Long.

SCORE

SPEYSIDE 12-year old, 43 vol

COLOR Orange Amber.

NOSE Orange zest, touch of cloves, oak.

BODY Moderate. Slightly oily. Chewy.

PALATE Orange oil on oak.

FINISH Dry, lingering, warming. Orange oil polish.

SCORE

SPRINGBANK

PRODUCER Springbank Distillers Ltd.
REGION Campbeltown DISTRICT Argyll
ADDRESS Well Close, Campbeltown, Argyll, PA28 6ET
TEL 01586 552085 VC Summer only by appointment

WITH THE OPENING OF SPRINGBANK'S new "sister" distillery of Glengyle in 2004, Scotland's one-time whisky capital of Campbeltown gained renewed credibility as an autonomous malt whisky region. The production at Springbank, from 1997 onwards, of a triple-distilled, unpeated single malt under the Hazelburn name has added even more momentum. As an 8-year-old, Hazelburn is now a fully-fledged member of the Springbank core range of whiskies. The original Hazelburn distillery, which closed in 1925, having existed since 1796, was an immediate neighbor of Springbank.

Springbank's own whisky is made from medium-peated malt, with a trajectory that amounts to two-and-a-half times distillation. With its brineyness, its oily, coconut-like flavors, and its great complexity, Springbank features in almost every whisky lover's top ten malts.

Springbank dates from the 1820s, and even earlier as an illicit still. Its present proprietor, and tireless revivalist of Campbeltown distilling, Hedley Wright, is a member of the founding Mitchell family.

In the early 1990s, Springbank revived its own floor maltings. It now uses only its own malt. (Among other distilleries with their own floor maltings, none is self-sufficient.) This has been of particular benefit in the production of another revivalist malt, Longrow, first released in 1985. Springbank first distilled Longrow in 1973–74.

Longrow is double distilled from heavily peated malt. With its own maltings, the distillery can achieve exactly the character of peatiness it requires. In their peatiness, oiliness, brineyness, and sense of restrained power, the Longrows are becoming cult whiskies. The original Longrow distillery closed in 1896. It adjoined the Springbank site.

Over the centuries, the town has had about 30 distilleries, some of which ruined their reputations by producing hurried whiskies for the US during Prohibition, and closed soon afterward. Vestiges of them remain in a bus garage, a business park, and other manifestations. These sites have been diligently mapped by Frank McHardy, who manages Springbank. Campbeltown was the great whisky region in the age of coastal steamers, before the railroads made Speyside more accessible.

As an isolated independent with its own underutilized bottling line, in 1969, J. & A. Mitchell bought the century-old firm of Cadenhead. This company, formerly based in Aberdeen, has always been an independent bottler. Both Springbank and Cadenhead use the same bottling line, in Campbeltown, but they are run as separate enterprises.

Neither company chill filters its whiskies, or adds caramel to balance the color. Being long-established enterprises, they have a considerable inventory of casks. Some Springbank once even found its way into a couple of casks of acacia wood. As awareness of woods has increased in the industry, Springbank has mainly acquired bourbon barrels, to highlight the character of the whisky itself, but most bottlings are vatted to give a touch of color and sweetness from sherry wood.

With a maltings, two distilleries, four single malts, an independent bottlings business, and a chain of shops (Eaglesome's in Campbeltown and Cadenhead's in Edinburgh and London), J. & A. Mitchell has ensured that Campbeltown remains a whisky center. This surge of activity was the response of Hedley Wright to a suggestion that Springbank and its local rival, Glen Scotia, were insufficient justification for the town retaining its status (along with Islay, the Highlands, and the Lowlands) as one of the whisky regions. Mr. Wright can be famously taciturn, but his actions are stentorian.

The geography itself is tenuous. Hanging from the coast by a neck of land only 1 mile (1.6 kilometers) wide, Kintyre looks like an island, but is actually a peninsula, stretching 40 miles (65 kilometers) south. Physically, either an island or a peninsula might better qualify as a region, but there are no distilleries until the town itself, which is near the southern extremity. At this point, the peninsula is at its broadest, but still less than 10 miles (16 kilometers) wide. Drive and climb to Crosshill Loch, and the sea is visible to both east and west, as are Islay and Arran on a clear day.

This loch has provided water for all the Campbeltown distilleries: an unusual situation that perhaps accounts for some similarities of character. To the immediate south of the town, the land narrows at the tip, or "mull" of the peninsula. This is the mull of Kintyre, where the mist rolls in from the sea just as Paul McCartney promised it would. It hangs over the back-street warehouses of the curiously urban distilleries, and entraps the ghosts of all those whiskies past. No wonder Springbank and Longrow have so much character.

HOUSE STYLE Springbank: salty, oily, coconut. Aperitif.
Longrow: piney, oily, damp earth. Nightcap.

SPRINGBANK 10-year-old, 46 vol

COLOR Gold.

NOSE Light brine, spice, rounded malt, pear. Elegant for a youngster.

BODY Rich and oily. Mouth-coating.

PALATE Fantastic mix of dry and sweet. Tinned pear. Citrus.
A suggestion of smoke.

FINISH Melon.

SCORE **83**

SPRINGBANK 10-year-old, 100 Proof, 57 vol

COLOR Amber with golden highlights.

NOSE Fresh, slightly briny. Toffee.

BODY Mouth-coating.

PALATE Relatively sweet, honeyed, and fruity, with salty,
maritime notes developing.

FINISH Long, with more salt and a hint of sweet peat.

SCORE **90**

SPRINGBANK Vintage 1997, 54.9 Vol

COLOR Full gold.

NOSE Floral, with beeswax and tangerines.
Discreet, background earthy smoke.

BODY Generous.

PALATE Powerful ginger and pepper notes. Nuts and smoke.

FINISH Long, with chocolate ginger and vanilla.

SCORE **89**

SPRINGBANK 15-year-old, 46 vol

COLOR Light amber.

NOSE Sophisticated. Dundee cake, vanilla, new leather, pipe tobacco, dried apricot, peat, tea.

BODY Full and rich. Mouth-coating.

PALATE European oak is there, but doesn't dominate. Sweet tobacco, nut, smoke in the background. Complex.

FINISH Soot. Malt.

SCORE **90**

SPRINGBANK 16-year-old, Rum Wood Expression, 54.2 vol

COLOR Greeny gold.

NOSE Tropical fruits and sweet spices. Ozone.

BODY Medium to full.

PALATE Sweet, spicy, fruity rum notes. Smoke, hazelnuts, and salt.

FINISH Rum sweetness, with developing citrus fruit and chilli peppers.

SCORE **87**

SPRINGBANK 25-year-old, Limited Edition, 46 vol

COLOR Apricot.

NOSE Sea air. Sherry oak. Very clean.

BODY Creamy.

PALATE Excellent sherry, but held in balance. Walnuts. Restrained esters. Very faint suggestion of banana. Coconut. Salt. Brine. A magnificently complex whisky.

FINISH Salty. Some peat. Dry.

SCORE **95**

SPRINGBANK Frank McHardy Anniversary, 1975, 46 vol

COLOR Rich gold.

NOSE Nutty, spicy oak, mandarin/curaçao, macadamia, herbs, light smoke.
Oakiest of current expressions, but understated.

BODY Creamy and soft.

PALATE Coconut, pine, citrus, coffee. Spices to the finish.

FINISH Nutty, sooty.

SCORE **90**

LONGROW
LONGROW 10-year-old, 1991, 46 vol

COLOR Antique gold.

NOSE Fresh, with salt, smoke, and sweeter notes of toffee and peat.

BODY Robust.

PALATE Medium-sweet, with peaches and peat.

FINISH Medium to long, becoming nutty, with persistent smoke.

SCORE **85**

LONGROW 10 year-old, 1992, 46 vol

COLOR Light gold.

NOSE Medium-full, sweet, and a little floral. But also
slightly medicinal and earthy.

BODY Robust, succulent.

PALATE Peaches and soft fruit under the peat. Good, nutty depth.

FINISH Dry, peaty.

SCORE **83**

LONGROW 10-year-old, 100 Proof, 57 vol

COLOR Pale gold.

NOSE Lavender, ripe oranges, subtle peat.

BODY Medium.

PALATE Initially dry and smoky, sweetening with more orange.

FINISH Long, with peppery peat.

SCORE **84**

LONGROW 13-year-old, Sherry Cask, 53.2 vol

COLOR Old gold.

NOSE Fruitcake, raisins, pecans, smoke. More sherry than smoke.

BODY Gentle and soft.

PALATE The peat bedded down in the rich fruit cake character
given by the sherry cask. Subtle, rich, and weighty.

FINISH Oily.

SCORE **80**

LONGROW 14-year-old, 46 vol

COLOR Straw.

NOSE Barley, fresh cream, apples. Subdued peat.

BODY Textured and oily.

PALATE Sweet and fruity, with malt, pepper, and smoke.

FINISH Peat, pepper, and brine.

SCORE **87**

LONGROW CV, 46 vol

Comprises vattings of 6, 10, and 14-year-old whiskies.

COLOR Straw.

NOSE Brine and fat peat notes, followed by vanilla fudge and smoky malt.

BODY Mildly oily.

PALATE Lively brine and bonfire smoke. Spicy.
Background vanilla and ginger.

FINISH Medium, with peat and persistent, oaky ginger and pepper.

SCORE **87**

LONGROW Gaja Barola Finish, 7-year-old, 55.8 vol

COLOR Reddish bronze.

NOSE Initially bonfire smoke, then rosewater and
marshmallow notes develop.

BODY Quite full-bodied.

PALATE Big and fruity, with dried grapes and subtle, oak tannins.

FINISH Long and drying, with fading fruit and lingering peat smoke.

SCORE **85**

LONGROW Tokaji Finish, 10-year-old, 55.6 vol

COLOR Gold to amber.

NOSE Sweet, with wood adhesive, dark treacle, and peat.

BODY Soft and rounded.

PALATE Big and bold. Oily. Early gummy sweetness; a hint of Cointreau.

FINISH Drying peat and soot notes linger long.

SCORE **84**

HAZELBURN
HAZELBURN Triple-distilled 8-year-old, 46 vol

COLOR	Pale gold.
NOSE	Light, fruity, faintly resinous.
BODY	Medium.
PALATE	Lively, with malt, banana, a touch of sherry, and vanilla essence.
FINISH	Caramel, pear drops, and spicy oak.

SCORE **85**

SOME INDEPENDENT BOTTLINGS
SPRINGBANK 11-year-old,
Scotch Malt Whisky Society (27.71), 59.4 vol

COLOR Gold with copper highlights. NOSE Soft caramel, fresh sawdust, and a whiff of the sea. BODY Firm. PALATE Aggressively peppery, tamed to something sweeter and nuttier with water. FINISH Medium in length, slightly bitter, spicy oak. SCORE 83

SPRINGBANK 40-year-old, Distilled 1967, bottled 2007,
Cask No 1945, Duncan Taylor, Peerless Range, 44.1 vol

COLOR Mid-gold. NOSE Pipe tobacco, brine, doused bonfires, cinnamon. BODY Rich. PALATE Nutty, spicy, dried fruits, and mild peat, becoming smokier. FINISH Sweetens to buttered fruit malt loaf. SCORE 88

HAZELBURN 7-year-old, Cadenhead, 49.4 vol

COLOR Mid-gold. NOSE Fresh, softly fruity, cereal, and a hint of yeast. BODY Rounded. PALATE Sweet, with developing peach, spice, caramel, and vanilla. FINISH Vibrant, with slow-burning pepper. SCORE 86

STRATHISLA

PRODUCER Chivas Brothers (Pernod Ricard)
REGION Highland   DISTRICT Speyside (Strathisla)
ADDRESS Seafield Avenue, Keith, Banffshire, AB55 3BS
TEL 01542 783044   VC

THE OLDEST DISTILLERY in the north of Scotland has its roots in the 13th century, when Dominican monks used a nearby spring to provide water for brewing beer. The same water, with a touch of calcium hardness and scarcely any peat character, has been used in the distillation of whisky since at least 1786.

Strathisla, which has also at times been known as Milltown, began its life as a farm distillery. It was rebuilt after a fire in 1876, and, over the years, has been restored and added to, creating a somewhat idealized traditional distillery. Chivas bought it in the 1950s.

Lightly peated malt is used, as well as wooden washbacks and small stills. Although wooden washbacks are by no means unusual, Strathisla believes that fermentation characteristics play a very important part in the character of its dry, fruity, oaky malt whisky.

HOUSE STYLE Dry, fruity. After dinner.

STRATHISLA 12-year-old, 43 vol

COLOR Full, deep gold.

NOSE Apricot. Cereal grains. Fresh, juicy oak.

BODY Medium, rounded.

PALATE Sherryish, fruity. Mouth-coating. Teasing sweet-and-dry character.

FINISH Smooth and soothing. Violets and vanilla.

SCORE **80**

STRATHISLA Cask Strength Edition 14-year-old,
Distilled 1993, Bottled 2008, Batch SI 14 006, 54.9 vol

COLOR Deep, golden amber.

NOSE Layers of syrupy sweet notes of vanilla, layered upon honey and apricots. Water brings out apricot notes.

BODY Full, very thick, mouth-coating, slightly hot.

PALATE Rich malty, vanilla, honey, and fruit.

FINISH Lingering notes of oak and honey.

SCORE **85**

STRATHMILL

PRODUCER Diageo
REGION Highlands   DISTRICT Speyside (Strathisla)
ADDRESS Keith, Banffshire, AB55 5DQ
TEL 01542 885000   WEBSITE www.malts.com

GRAPES HAVE TO BE CRUSHED; grain has to be milled. The town of Keith must once have been a considerable grain-milling center. The Glen Keith distillery was built on the site of a grain mill. Strathmill, as its name suggests, went one better. It was rebuilt from a grain mill, in 1891, when the whisky industry was having one of its periodic upswings. Three years later, it was acquired by Gilbey, of which Justerini & Brooks became a subsidiary through IDV (Diageo). Arguably, it has been in the same ownership for more than a century. Its whisky was for many years central to the Dunhill/Old Master blends, but does not seem to have been available as a single until a 1980 bottling by the wine merchant chain Oddbins in 1993.

HOUSE STYLE The whisky world's answer to orange muscat. With dessert.

STRATHMILL 18-year-old, Old Malt Cask, 50 vol

COLOR Pale lemon.

NOSE Sherbet. Lemon. Crystal barley. Clean and fresh.

BODY Medium and unassertive.

PALATE Bitter lemon. Barley. Some astringency. Peppery notes.

FINISH Short and spicy.

SCORE 66

TALISKER

PRODUCER Diageo
REGION Highlands ISLAND Skye
ADDRESS Carbost, Isle of Skye, IV47 8SR
TEL 01478 614308
WEBSITE www.discovering-distilleries.com/www.malts.com VC

ALREADY VOLCANICALLY POWERFUL, Talisker has boosted its impact in recent years by adding new expressions. However many versions there may be, it remains a singular malt. It has a distinctively peppery character, so hot as to make one taster's temples steam. The phrase "explodes on the palate" is among the descriptions used for certain whiskies by blenders at UDV; surely they had Talisker in mind when they composed this. "The lava of the Cuillins" was another taster's response. The Cuillins are the dramatic hills of Skye, the island home of Talisker. The distillery is on the west coast of the island, on the shores of Loch Harport, in an area where Gaelic is still spoken. The local industry was once tweed.

After a number of false starts on other sites, the distillery was established in 1831 and expanded in 1900. For much of its life, it used triple distillation, and in those days Robert Louis Stevenson ranked Talisker as a style on its own, comparable with the Islay and Livet whiskies. It switched to double distillation in 1928, and was partly rebuilt in 1960. The distillery uses traditional cooling coils—"worm tubs"—which can make for a fuller flavor than a modern condenser.

Some malt lovers still mourn the youthfully dry assertiveness of the eight-year-old version that was replaced by the current, more rounded version a couple of summers older. For a time, this was the only expression, but official bottlings have multiplied. As if to balance an equation, independent bottlings seem to have vanished.

The island is also home to an unrelated company making a vatted malt called Poit Dubh, and a blend, Te Bheag. Both are said to contain some Talisker, and their hearty palates appear to support this suggestion. A dry, perfumy, blended whisky called Isle of Skye is made by the Edinburgh merchants Ian Macleod & Co. The style of whisky liqueur represented by Drambuie is also said to have been created on the Isle of Skye, though its origins actually remain somewhat clouded in Scotch mist.

HOUSE STYLE Volcanic. A winter warmer.

TALISKER 10-year-old, 45.8 vol

COLOR Bright amber red.

NOSE Pungent, smoke-accented, rounded.

BODY Full, slightly syrupy.

PALATE Smoky, malty sweet, with sourness and a very big
pepperiness developing.

FINISH Very peppery. Huge, long.

SCORE **90**

TALISKER Distillers Edition, 12-year-old, 1996, 45.8 vol

Finished in an amoroso sherry cask.

COLOR Rich orange.

NOSE Distinctly unlike Talisker. Savory fruit sauce. Soft peach. Smoky
and perfumed like a hussy's handbag. Tingling pepper.

BODY Oily, sharp. Intense.

PALATE Far better than the nose. A mix of peaty earth, tangy seaside notes,
and a rich and oily fruitness.

FINISH Big. Rich. Spicy. Fruit liqueur.

SCORE **85**

TALISKER 57 Degrees North, 57 vol

COLOR Rich orange.

NOSE Seaweed. Damp boathouse. Islay-like peat and seaweed.

BODY Mouth-coating. Oily. Full.

PALATE Sweet and peaty. Very smoky, but with peach and apricot and apple seeds. Oily and spicy. Fatter and fuller than most Taliskers. Aggressive and masculine.

FINISH Long and peaty; the trademark pepper appears at the end.

SCORE **86**

TALISKER 18-year-old, 45.8 vol

COLOR Rich orange.

NOSE Seaside. Peat, seaweed, rich pepper.

BODY Full, rich, and creamy.

PALATE Immense and rich. Classic Talisker, but richer than the 10-year-old. Lots of rich fruit, with oak and peat arriving later.

FINISH Perfectly balanced. Pleasant and long, with pepper and peat in the conclusion.

SCORE **94**

TALISKER 1982, 20-year-old, 58.8 vol

COLOR Gold, with a green tinge.

NOSE Scorched earth. Harbor aromas. Seaweed.

BODY Medium to full. Firm.

PALATE Distant thunder. Seems to rumble and reverberate as the volcanic heat builds ever so slowly. Hot, slightly sour, and peppery. Very tightly combined flavors, reluctant to unfurl. When they do, the earth moves.

FINISH Quite quick and sharp. A thunderflash.

SCORE **93**

TALISKER 25-year-old, Bottled 2001, 59.9 vol

COLOR Peachy, tan.

NOSE Warm. Minerally. A hint of sulfur.

BODY Quite rich.

PALATE Nutty, with a suggestion of artichoke. A touch of salt,
then a burst of freshly milled pepper.

FINISH Volcanic. Reverberating.

SCORE **92**

TALISKER 25-year-old, Bottled 2006, 56.9 vol

COLOR Full gold.

NOSE Soft peachy fruits. Hints of chili pepper and oak.

BODY Full. Syrupy. Spicy.

PALATE Bang! A big hit of chili pepper. Oily citrus fruits. Lemon and lime
sours. Big and powerful.

FINISH Delicious, rich, sour fruits and peat in the mix. Long and special.

SCORE **92**

TALISKER 30-year-old, 51.9 vol

COLOR Golden brown.

NOSE Lots of peat. Musty sleeping bag. Big stewed fruit.

BODY Full. Rich. Sweet.

PALATE Chili-lemon chicken. Oaky tannins, pepper, peat.

FINISH Long, powerful, impressive, with oak, pepper, and fruit in the mix.

SCORE **93**

TAMDHU

PRODUCER The Edrington Group
REGION Highlands   DISTRICT Speyside
ADDRESS Knockando, Morayshire, AB38 7RP

THIS DISTILLERY IS STILL somewhat overshadowed by its charismatic neighbor, Macallan, six or seven miles downriver. Both malts are significant contributors to The Famous Grouse, the biggest selling blend in Scotland. As singles, their fortunes differ. Since Macallan and Tamdhu came under the same ownership, the former has been promoted as the group's Speyside malt at the expense of the latter.

Like several Speyside distilleries, Tamdhu shares its name with a station on the railroad that ran up and down the valley. Tamdhu station is more elaborate than most, with two full-length platforms and a signal box. The distillery was founded in 1896, and largely rebuilt in the 1970s. Water comes from the Tamdhu burn, which flows through woodland into the Spey.

Tamdhu has a sizeable and impressive Saladin maltings, providing for all its own needs and those of several other whisky makers. A modest reminder of this is the stylized ear of barley that appears on the label of the principal version of Tamdhu. The distillery is impeccably well kept, and has its own touches of tradition, notably its enthusiasm for wooden fermenting vessels.

HOUSE STYLE Mild, urbane. Sometimes toffee-nosed. Versatile.

TAMDHU Single Malt, No Age Statement, 40 vol

COLOR Bright gold.

NOSE Flowery. Faintly lemony. Cereal grain.

BODY Light, soft.

PALATE Clean, sweet. Very slightly toffeeish. An easily drinkable, malt-accented introduction to singles.

FINISH Flowery. Very faint hint of peat.

SCORE **74**

SOME INDEPENDENT BOTTLINGS
TAMDHU 15-year-old, James MacArthur, 58.2 vol

COLOR Pale orange.

NOSE Zingy. Lemon- and lime-flavored sherbet. Cake icing.

BODY Full and sweet.

PALATE Very sweet. Fruit in syrup. Canned pear. Marzipan.

FINISH More syrupy fruit and then some late spices.

SCORE **79**

TAMDHU 17-year-old, Old Malt Cask, 50 vol

COLOR Brassy yellow.

NOSE Quite shy. Stewed vegetables. Cut bamboo.

BODY Rich, sweet, and creamy.

PALATE Rich and full. Better than the nose. Creamy barley. Some gentle peat underneath. Rock candy. Traces of wood. A balanced mix of sweet and sour.

FINISH Quite long, spicy, and peaty.

SCORE **80**

TAMDHU 39-year-old, Lonarch, 40 vol

COLOR Golden orange.

NOSE Rich and full. Citrus fruits. Summer flowers. Scented wax polish.

BODY Full and intense.

PALATE Fruit sherbet. Intense apricot and peach, and then big oakiness, peppers, and tannins.

FINISH Medium, dry, and peppery.

SCORE **84**

TAMNAVULIN

PRODUCER Whyte and MacKay Ltd.
REGION Highlands   DISTRICT Speyside (Livet)
ADDRESS Ballindalloch, Banffshire, AB37 9JA

ON THE STEEP SIDE OF THE GLEN of the Livet, the river is joined by one of its tributaries, a stream called Allt a Choire (in English, "Corrie"). This is the site of the Tamnavulin distillery, taking its name from "mill on the hill." The location is more often spelled Tomnavoulin, but such discrepancies are hardly unusual in Scotland.

Part of the premises was formerly used for the carding of wool. The distillery, built in the 1960s, has a rather industrial look. Tamnavulin was mothballed in 1996, but was somewhat surprisingly reopened after the UB Group bought Whyte & Mackay in 2006.

Among the malts produced in and around the glen of the Livet River, the elegant Tamnavulin is the lightest in body, although not in palate. In taste, it is a little more assertive than Tomintoul, with which it might be most closely compared.

HOUSE STYLE Aromatic, herbal. Aperitif.

TAMNAVULIN 12-year-old, 40 vol

COLOR	Vinho verde.
NOSE	Very aromatic. A touch of peat, hay, heather, herbal notes. Slightly medicinal.
BODY	Very light indeed, but smooth.
PALATE	Lemon, flowering currant. Winey. Vermouth-like.
FINISH	Aromatic. Juniper?

SCORE 76

TEANINICH

PRODUCER Diageo
REGION Highlands   DISTRICT Northern Highlands
ADDRESS Alness, Ross-Shire, IV17 0XB
TEL 01463 872004   WEBSITE www.malts.com

T HIS LESSER-KNOWN NEIGHBOR of Glenmorangie and Dalmore is
beginning to develop a following for its big, malty, fruity, spicy
whisky: not before time. Teaninich was founded in 1817, as an estate
distillery, and later provided whisky for such well-known blends as
VAT 69 and Haig Dimple. It gained a classic DCL still-house in the
1970s. The tongue-twisting name Teaninich (usually pronounced
"tee-ninick," but some say "chee-ninick") began to be heard more
widely in the 1990s, when the malt was bottled in the Flora and Fauna
series. Three Rare Malts bottlings followed.

HOUSE STYLE Robust, toffeeish, spicy, leafy. Restorative or after dinner.

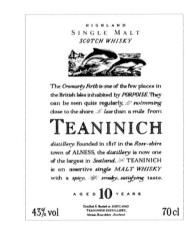

TEANINICH 10-year-old, Flora and Fauna, 43 vol

COLOR Pale gold.

NOSE Big, fresh aroma. Fruity. Hints of apple. Smoky.

BODY Medium, rich.

PALATE Sweet and dry. Chocolate limes. Fruity. Remarkably leafy. Lightly
peaty. Gradually warms up until it fairly sparks with flavor. Very appetizing.

FINISH Coriander. Herbal. Rounded.

SCORE 74

TEANINICH 1972, 27-year-old, Bottled 2000,
The Rare Malts, 64.2 vol

COLOR Full, bright gold.

NOSE Very perfumy. Incense, sandalwood, vanilla.

BODY Big.

PALATE Intense sugar-coated almonds, but big and profound.

FINISH Powerful, explosive. Gunpowder tea.

SCORE **77**

TEANINICH Managers' Choice, Distilled 1996, Bottled 2009, 55.3 vol

Matured in a rejuvenated American oak cask.

COLOR Bright gold.

NOSE Rounded and sweet. Melon and ripe bananas.
Background violet-flavored candies.

BODY Soft.

PALATE Banana-toffee pie with a sprinkling of ginger.

FINISH Medium length, spicy, with oak and black bananas.

SCORE **78**

AN INDEPENDENT BOTTLING
TEANINICH 12-year-old, Duncan Taylor, NC2, 46 vol

COLOR Gold.

NOSE Brittle toffee, slight oil, nutty, becoming spicier.

BODY Quite full.

PALATE Rich, with soft fudge and hazelnuts; gently spiced.

FINISH Spicy toffee.

SCORE **76**

TOBERMORY

PRODUCER Burn Stewart Distillers plc
REGION Highlands   DISTRICT Mull
ADDRESS Tobermory, Isle of Mull, Argyllshire, PA75 6NR
TEL 01688 302645   WEBSITE www.burnstewartdistillers.com
EMAIL enquiries@burnstewartdistillers.com   VC

IF THE ART OF DISTILLATION was brought from Ireland over the Giant's Causeway to Scotland, it must have arrived in Fingal's Cave, on the tiny island of Staffa. A later immigrant from Ireland, St. Columba, founded an abbey on nearby Iona and urged the community to grow barley. One and a half thousand years later, a whisky called Iona was launched.

Both Staffa and Iona are off the island of Mull, where the harbor village of Tobermory gives a home and a name to the local distillery. (Lovers of trivia, albeit literary trivia, may know that this name was also given to a talking cat by the Edwardian author Hector Hugh Munro, better known by his pen-name Saki). The village was once known as Ledaig (sometimes pronounced "ledchig," and meaning "safe haven" in Gaelic). The distillery traces its origins to 1795, but has a much interrupted history, peppered with many owners.

Those in charge of the distillery have at times used the name Tobermory on a blended whisky and a vatted (blended) malt, but it now appears on a clearly labeled single malt, produced after the distillery reopened in 1989–90. This version has a peatiness, albeit light, derived entirely from the water. The barley-malt is not peated. The name Ledaig was for some years used for older versions of the whisky, employing peated malt. Ledaig is now being made again, and its peatiness gradually being increased.

The maritime character of the whiskies was diminished when the warehouses were sold by previous owners during a financial crisis to make room for apartments. However, in 2007, a small warehouse facility was created at the distillery, so that some spirit could mature on its native island.

HOUSE STYLE Faint peat, minty, sweet. Restorative.

TOBERMORY 10-year-old, 40 vol

COLOR Light amber.

NOSE Fresh and nutty. Citrus fruit and brittle toffee. A whiff of peat.

BODY Medium.

PALATE Quite dry, with delicate peat, malt, and nuts.

FINISH Medium to long, with a hint of mint and
a slight citric tang.

SCORE **73**

Born in Mull's only distillery, this jewel-like malt is aged for almost 15-years before our Master Blender performs the finale of his rare dual-location-maturation; transferring it into Gonzàlez Byass Oloroso Sherry casks, then moving them from the mainland, through the swirling mists, back to the island to absorb the subtle sea influence for its final year. The superb fleeting spiciness and delicate, fruity, chocolatiness that this un-chillfiltered dram captures is to be cherished. A hidden gem.

Matured and Bottled in Scotland
PRODUCT OF SCOTLAND

TOBERMORY EST. LIMITED 1798 EDITION
AGED 15 YEARS
ISLAND SINGLE MALT SCOTCH WHISKY
Tobermory Distillers Limited

46.3% vol 70cle UN-CHILLFILTERED
Tobermory Distillery, Isle Of Mull, Scotland
www.tobermorymalt.com

TOBERMORY 15-year-old, 46.3 vol

COLOR Gold to bronze.

NOSE Fruit pudding, with sherry, spicy milk chocolate, and a whiff of smoke.

BODY Medium to full.

PALATE Rich, with sherry, fruitcake,
toffee, and a sprinkling of pepper.

FINISH Long and luxurious, with coffee and
chocolate-coated raisins.

SCORE **81**

TOBERMORY 32-year-old, 49.7 vol

COLOR Dark amber.

NOSE Rich and fragrant, with dry sherry, raisins, and peat smoke.

BODY Full and rounded.

PALATE Powerful sherry, smoke, chocolate, stewed fruit, and some tannins.

FINISH Medium in length. Drying, with coffee.

SCORE **85**

THE LEDAIG BOTTLINGS
LEDAIG Single Malt, No Age Statement, 42 vol

COLOR Lemon gold.

NOSE Fruit, brine, and sweet peat.

BODY Medium, oily.

PALATE Smoky peat, with a hint of seaweed, ginger, and milk chocolate.

FINISH Quite long, warming, and gingery.

SCORE **73**

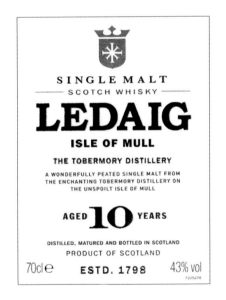

LEDAIG 10-year-old, 43 vol

COLOR Pale gold.

NOSE Peaty and sweet, with notes of roasted nuts, butter, and smoked fish.

BODY Medium, firm.

PALATE Bold yet sweet. Soft peat, heather, fresh fruit, a hint of iodine.

FINISH Medium in length, with pepper, ginger, licorice, and peat.

SCORE **74**

LEDAIG Sherry Finish, No Age Statement, 42 vol

COLOR Bright gold.

NOSE Sweet. Custardy, with an appetizing fruitiness.
Sherry enhances the oak. Toffeeish.

BODY Medium and smooth.

PALATE Mellow roundness. Elegant combination of fruit and oak.
Good balance. A hint of peat in the back.

FINISH Drying, with soft spices. Satisfying.

SCORE **74**

LEDAIG Over 15 Years, 43 vol

The preposition is superfluous; all ages on labels represent the youngest whisky in the bottle.

COLOR Gold to bronze.

NOSE Soft, full peatiness.

BODY Light but smooth.

PALATE Slightly thin. Toffeeish, then spicy.

FINISH Sweet, smoky, full peatiness. A hint of the sea in this one.

SCORE **73**

LEDAIG 32-year-old, 48.5 vol

COLOR Deep amber.

NOSE Sweet, with smoked mackerel, rich fruity sherry, and roasted nuts.

BODY Full and slightly oily.

PALATE Peat and sherry dominate, with coffee, dark chocolate, spicy barley.

FINISH Medium to long. Drying.

SCORE **84**

THE IONA BOTTLING
IONA Single Malt, 4-year-old, 40 vol

Created for sale only at the distillery.

COLOR Almost white. NOSE Lichen. Moss on the rocks. Cockles and
mussels. BODY Lightly oily. PALATE Broth-like. Miso. Hot-smoked
salmon. FINISH Wintergreen. Iron. SCORE 78

AN INDEPENDENT BOTTLING OF TOBERMORY
TOBERMORY 12-year-old, Duncan Taylor, Whisky Galore, 46 vol

COLOR White wine. NOSE Pear drops and deeper notes of cocoa. A little
smokiness. BODY Slightly waxy. PALATE Citrus fruits, spices, a hint of peat;
drying, becoming nuttier. FINISH Fruit and nut chocolate, stem
ginger. SCORE 73

TOMATIN

PRODUCER The Tomatin Distillery Co. Ltd.
REGION Highlands   DISTRICT Speyside (Findhorn)
ADDRESS Tomatin, Inverness-shire, IV13 7YT
TEL 01808 511444   WEBSITE www.tomatin.com
EMAIL info@tomatin.co.uk   VC

STANDING BY THE UPPER REACHES of the Findhorn, Tomatin distillery was established in 1897, but saw its great years of expansion between the 1950s and 1970s. During this period, it became the biggest malt distillery in Scotland and was just a little smaller than Suntory's Hakushu distillery in Japan. Both these distilleries have scaled down volume since those heady days: Tomatin by removing almost half of its stills, Hakushu by mothballing its biggest still-house. Tomatin might just remain the largest in Scotland; though it is pretty much neck-and-neck with Glenfiddich.

As a large distillery, Tomatin developed a broad-shouldered malt as a filler for countless blends during the boom years. It is neither the most complex, nor the most assertive of malts, but it is far tastier than is widely realized. For the novice wishing to move from lighter single malts to something a little more imposing, the climb to Tomatin will be very worthwhile.

HOUSE STYLE Malty, spicy, rich. Restorative or after dinner.

TOMATIN 12-year-old, 40 vol

COLOR Bright, greeny gold.

NOSE Cookie-like sweetness. Vanilla. Soft mints.

BODY Smooth, velvety.

PALATE Mellow and round. Toffeeish. Pine nuts. Apples and pears.

FINISH Sweet, with a pleasant, refreshing mintiness.

SCORE 75

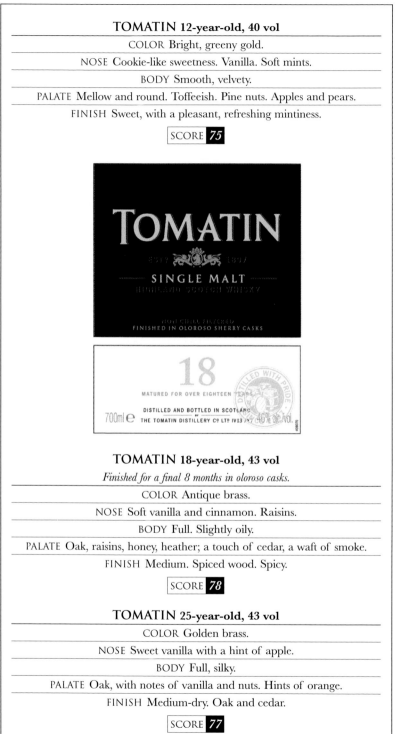

TOMATIN 18-year-old, 43 vol

Finished for a final 8 months in oloroso casks.

COLOR Antique brass.

NOSE Soft vanilla and cinnamon. Raisins.

BODY Full. Slightly oily.

PALATE Oak, raisins, honey, heather; a touch of cedar, a waft of smoke.

FINISH Medium. Spiced wood. Spicy.

SCORE 78

TOMATIN 25-year-old, 43 vol

COLOR Golden brass.

NOSE Sweet vanilla with a hint of apple.

BODY Full, silky.

PALATE Oak, with notes of vanilla and nuts. Hints of orange.

FINISH Medium-dry. Oak and cedar.

SCORE 77

TOMATIN 30-year-old,
Distilled November 22, 1976 Bottled October 22, 2007 49.3 vol

*Matured in hogsheads, then finished for three years in two
oloroso sherry butts; 1500 bottles released.*

COLOR Dark gold.

NOSE Rich, spiced red apples, vanilla, cinnamon, cloves, and caramel.
Very complex.

BODY Full, rich.

PALATE Spicy, oak, oranges, and embers. Nuts.

FINISH Lingering and spicy, like the aftertaste of mulled wine.

SCORE **82**

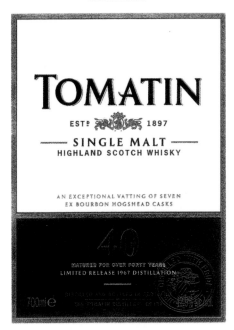

TOMATIN 40-year-old,
Distilled May 17, 1967 Bottled October 2 2007, 42.9 vol

Matured in bourbon hogsheads; 1614 bottles released.

COLOR Tarnished brass.

NOSE Unique menthol, spearmint, and apples. A hint of eucalyptus,
evolving into marzipan. Amazing.

BODY Silky. Light.

PALATE Spicy: spiced apples, cloves, with a hint of leather.

FINISH Long spicy finish, like the aftertaste of strong cider.

SCORE **84**

TOMATIN 1970, Bourbon Barrel Cask 12267, Bottled August 2007, 51.2 vol

COLOR Solid gold.

NOSE Fiery. Vibrant orange zest with notes of cinnamon.

BODY Full, slightly oily.

PALATE Orange, apples with a dusting of cinnamon. Cedar and apricots.

FINISH Lingering orange peel and warm cedar.

SCORE **81**

TOMATIN 1976, Bourbon Barrel Cask 19090, 47.2 vol

COLOR Deep brass.

NOSE Sweet orange, tangerines with a trace of pipe tobacco.

BODY Full, slightly oily.

PALATE Sweet oranges with light vanilla and hints of cinnamon.

FINISH Lengthy. Orange aftertaste with a return of pipe tobacco.

SCORE **81**

TOMATIN 1980, Bourbon Barrel Cask 994, 47.4 vol

COLOR Pale gold, straw.

NOSE Apricots, kumquats, vanilla.

BODY Medium. Full.

PALATE Slightly astringent. Apricots, tangerines, grapefruits.

FINISH Moderate, but very fruity, with notes of citrus.

SCORE **77**

TOMATIN 1990, Hogshead Cask 7738, 54 vol

COLOR Light brass.

NOSE Bright grapefruit with hints of spearmint and eucalyptus (like a younger sibling of the 40-year-old).

BODY Lively. Full.

PALATE Bright citrus. Spearmint with apples and almonds.

FINISH Lingering. Medicinal mints.

SCORE **82**

TOMATIN 1967, Celtic Heartlands, 47.7 vol

COLOR Pale gold.

NOSE Sage-and-onion stuffing. Mushy. Cereal.

BODY Soft. Medium-full. Pleasant.

PALATE Honeycomb. Sugar and spice. Peach. Tannins.

FINISH Long, spicy, and oaky.

SCORE **78**

TOMINTOUL

PRODUCER Angus Dundee Distillers plc.
REGION Highlands   DISTRICT Speyside (Livet)
ADDRESS Ballindalloch, Banffshire, AB37 9AQ
TEL 01261 812612   WEBSITE www.tomintouldistillery.co.uk

THE VILLAGE OF TOMINTOUL (pronounced "tom in t'owl") is the base camp for climbers and hikers in the area around the rivers Avon and Livet. Nearby, Cromdale and the Ladder Hills foreshadow the Cairngorm Mountains. It is about 8 miles (13 kilometers) from the village to the distillery, which is on the edge of a forest, close to the Avon River.

The distillery was built in the 1960s and is modern in appearance, with large warehouses and no pagoda roofline. The wildness of the surroundings contrasts with the delicacy of the district's malts. Tomintoul has traditionally seemed the lightest among them in flavor, although it has a little more body than its neighbor Tamnavulin.

HOUSE STYLE Delicate, grassy, perfumy. Aperitif.

TOMINTOUL 10-year-old, 40 vol

COLOR Full, sunny gold.

NOSE Grassy. Lemon grass. Orange-flower water.

BODY Light, smooth, slippery.

PALATE Sweetish. Crushed barley. Potpourri.

FINISH Lively and lingering gently. Nutty. Lemon grass.

SCORE 77

TOMINTOUL 12-year-old Oloroso Sherry Cask Finish, Limited Edition, 40 vol

Finished for 18 months in oloroso casks.

COLOR Pale to mid-amber.

NOSE Orange peel and rinds. Rhubarb, vegetal spice, hints of sherry.

BODY Light, approaching medium. Smooth.

PALATE Malt with traces of oak and vanilla, and a touch of orange oil.

FINISH Spicy dryness. Lingering and warming.

SCORE 78

TOMINTOUL "With a Peaty Tang," No Age Statement, 40 vol

COLOR Dark straw with greenish tint.

NOSE Peat, with notes of barley mash. Malty.

BODY Light to medium. Smooth.

PALATE Full, very clean. Delicious maltiness.

FINISH Clean. Lingering moderately. Complexity develops in the finish.

SCORE **80**

TOMINTOUL 16-year-old, 40 vol

COLOR Pale bright orange.

NOSE Orange-cream icing on a cheesecake.

BODY Silky.

PALATE Finely grated, zesty citrus peel. Syllabub. Zabaglione. Nougat.

FINISH Refreshing but also warming, like the sherry in a trifle.

SCORE **78**

TOMINTOUL 27-year-old, 40 vol

COLOR Amber, with orange hues.

NOSE Oranges—lots of oranges, and a hint of vanilla.

BODY Medium, smooth.

PALATE Rich. Oranges; traces of oak. Green apples, brown sugar, and honey.

FINISH Clean and short, with traces of orange.

SCORE **81**

TOMINTOUL 31-year-old Reserve, 1976, Bottle 270/1200, 40 vol

COLOR Orange amber.

NOSE Silky. Orange cream swirl. Rich.

BODY Rich. Slightly oily. Full.

PALATE Vanilla, raisins, with hints of lemon grass and orange. Complex.

FINISH Dry and lingering.

SCORE **82**

OLD BALLANTRUAN, 50 vol

COLOR Pale gold.

NOSE Almost non-existent. Wafts of peat and a hint of rubber.

BODY Full, slightly oily.

PALATE Strong peat—a sneak attack, as the nose belies the palate. The peat fire rages.

FINISH Lingering, very pleasant, and warming.

SCORE **82**

TORMORE

PRODUCER Chivas Brothers (Pernod Ricard)
REGION Highlands DISTRICT Speyside
ADDRESS Advie by Grantown-on-Spey, Morayshire, PH26 3LR
TEL 01807 510244

THE MOST ARCHITECTURALLY ELEGANT of all whisky distilleries, Tormore stands among the Cromdale Hills, overlooking the Spey. It was designed by Sir Albert Richardson, president of the Royal Academy, and erected as a showpiece in 1958–60, during a boom in the Scotch whisky industry. It looks somewhat like a spa.

The whisky was originally intended as a component of Long John, and later became an element of Ballantine's. Admirers find it aromatic, sweet, and easily drinkable, but the more cautious deem its firmness "metallic." The distillery does not have tours, which seems a wasteful denial of its original purpose as a visual celebration.

When Pernod Ricard acquired Allied Domecq in 2005, Chivas Brothers gained control of the distillery.

HOUSE STYLE Dry, fruity. After dinner.

TORMORE 12-year-old, 40 vol

COLOR Bright, sunny gold.

NOSE Nutty. Hint of barley sugar. Soft pear in a fudgey sauce.

BODY Medium, smooth.

PALATE Sweet, soft. Caramelized walnuts. Braised artichokes.

FINISH Rounded.

SCORE 73

TULLIBARDINE

PRODUCER Tullibardine Ltd.
REGION Highlands DISTRICT Midlands
ADDRESS Stirling Street, Blackford, Perthshire, PH4 1QG
TEL 01764 682252 WEBSITE www.tullibardine.com

TULLIBARDINE IS AMONG THE GROUP of distilleries that could be bracketed as new-millennium success stories. It reopened in 2003 under new management and began launching a range of different malts. By 2009, there were rumors of a possible sale.

Tullibardine Moor is in the Ochil hills. In this area, the village of Blackford is the source of Highland Spring bottled water. The hills and their springs have provided water for brewing since at least the 12th century. In 1488, a Tullibardine brewery brewed the ale for the coronation of King James IV at Scone. It is a former brewery site that accommodates the distillery.

There may have been whisky making there in the late 1700s, but it was not until 1949 that the present distillery was built. It was the work of Delmé-Evans, a noted designer of distilleries, whose functional styling can also be seen at Glenallachie and Jura. Evans was fascinated by breweries and distilleries. One of his enthusiasms was the "tower" brewery design, popular in the late 1800s. In this system, a water tank on the roof and a malt loft disgorge their contents, which flow by gravity, without pumps, through the processes that lead to a cellar full of beer. At Tullibardine, he sought to incorporate gravity-flow into a distillery. Delmé-Evans died just before the distillery reopened.

HOUSE STYLE Winey, fragrant. With pre-dinner pistachios. More sherried versions with a honeyish dessert (baklava?).

TULLIBARDINE 1993, 10-year-old, 40 vol

COLOR Bright gold.

NOSE Soft, lemony, malty, sweetish.

BODY Medium, firm, oily, smooth.

PALATE Full, with clean, grassy-malty, buttery sweetness. Only medium-sweet. Develops to a fruity, almost Chardonnay-like wineyness.

FINISH Sweetish, fragrant, appetizing, big. Vanilla-pod spiciness.

SCORE 76

TULLIBARDINE 1992 Vintage, 46 vol

COLOR Pale gold.

NOSE Sweet, licorice, marjoram.

BODY Light to medium. Slightly oily.

PALATE Very inviting. Refreshing citrus mingles with unique spice and licorice.

FINISH Long and spicy, with dry licorice as after a pastis.

SCORE 79

TULLIBARDINE 1993, Sauterne Wood Finish, 46 vol

COLOR Deep gold.

NOSE Sweet, the Sauterne really shows through. Light fruits: apples, apricots.

BODY Fuller than the 1992, slightly oily.

PALATE Hints of spiced fruit, mulled apples, and poached pears, but the distillery qualities are still present.

FINISH Malty, dry, almost hoppy, like in a brewery.

SCORE 81

TULLIBARDINE 1993, Moscatel Wood Finish, 46 vol

COLOR Pale gold.

NOSE Sweet, syrupy. Grapes, figs.

BODY Medium.

PALATE The wine is more pronounced, but complements the distillery standard; licorice and spiced apples remain, but as if seen through wine-colored glasses.

FINISH Sweet, winey; shorter than other distillery expressions.

SCORE 82

TULLIBARDINE 1993, Port Wood Finish, 46 vol

The final 11 months of maturation are in port wood.

COLOR Light pinkish amber.

NOSE Wonderfully complex. Grapes, raisins, spice.

BODY Rich, well-balanced.

PALATE Grape-flavored vitamins and wine. Raisins. The distillery qualities shine through the grape flavor, and the underlying malt is not overpowered.

FINISH Moderate. Grape vitamin lingers.

SCORE 81

SHERRY WOOD FINISH

Tullibardine™
SINGLE HIGHLAND MALT

Scotch Whisky

BEST PROCURABLE

YEAR DISTILLED	YEAR BOTTLED	CHECKED BY
1993	2007	CW

Tullibardine
Distillery
PERTHSHIRE

MATURED
IN
SHERRY BUTTS

70cl
700ml ℮   DISTILLED AND BOTTLED IN SCOTLAND

46% vol
46% alc./vol.

NON CHILL-FILTERED

TULLIBARDINE 1993, Sherry Wood Finish, 46 vol

COLOR Pale brownish amber.

NOSE Sherry nose initially, then notes of apples, cinnamon, and leather.

BODY Full, robust.

PALATE Rich, traditional sherry (above average sherry butts). Leather,
cloves, with hints of toffee, dates, and chocolate.

FINISH Long and spicy. Leather with traces of cloves. Warming.

SCORE **83**

TULLIBARDINE 1988 Vintage, 46 vol

Celebrating the 500th anniversary of King James IV's Coronation.

COLOR Bright gold.

NOSE Hot, bright citrus, with notes of vanilla.

BODY Light to medium.

PALATE Bright citrus lemons, and traces of vanilla and custard.

FINISH White pepper. Dry.

SCORE **77**

TULLIBARDINE 1975 Vintage, Cask 1010,
Distilled March 4, 1975, Bottled August 3, 2007, 52.5 vol

COLOR Deep gold.

NOSE Complex. Butterscotch, orange peel, vanilla, caramel, crème brûlée.

BODY Rich, chewy.

PALATE Layers of vanilla, butterscotch, toffee, and oak; hints of orange peel.

FINISH Long. Mostly oak, with notes of orange.

SCORE **85**

1975 VINTAGE

Tullibardine
SINGLE HIGHLAND MALT
Scotch Whisky
BEST PROCURABLE
NON CHILL-FILTERED

| CASK NUMBER | CASK TYPE | BOTTLE NUMBER | DATE BOTTLED |

Tullibardine Distillery
PERTHSHIRE SCOTLAND

70cl
700ml ℮

Fine, rare, smooth & mellow
DISTILLED AND BOTTLED
IN SCOTLAND

% vol
% alc./vol.

VINTAGE EDITION

TULLIBARDINE 1966 Vintage, Sherry Butt 1112, Distilled March 1, 1966 Bottled April 28, 2006 49.8 vol

COLOR Brownish amber.

NOSE Subtle. Leather. Notes of dark vanilla and demerara rum emerge when coaxed. Wonderful.

BODY Oily, coats your mouth and dries it.

PALATE Sumptuous. Leather, tobacco, cloves, cardamom, and dark sherry. Rich notes of chocolate, demerara rum, and vanilla beans, with a trace of black pepper. Big and complex.

FINISH Long and drying; cloves linger.

SCORE 89

TULLIBARDINE 1965 Vintage, Hogshead 949, Distilled March 25, 1965 Bottled July 8, 2005 48.3 vol

COLOR Brownish amber.

NOSE Rich, spicy, Madagascan vanilla, sweet pipe tobacco, leather. Complex.

BODY Moderate, smooth, slightly tannic. Not nearly as heavy as the 1966.

PALATE Complex blend of pipe tobacco, cloves, and leather. Better balanced than the 1966.

FINISH Lingering spices. Cloves and tobacco.

SCORE 87

UNSPECIFIED MALTS

A LIMITED NUMBER of bottlings do not carry the name of the distillery. It may be because an independent bottler has an arrangement with the distillery or, conversely, does not want a dispute with them. It may also be because the bottler wants to promote the flavor of the particular malt rather than the distillery per se. And some companies have used this approach to appeal to consumers put off by traditional labeling, as with Burnfoot, from Glengoyne.

A VERY SPECIAL SPEYSIDE 40-year-old
Glenkeir Treasures, 56.7 vol

COLOR Deep orange.

NOSE Fruitcake. Rich berry fruits. Cake mix. Sherry.

BODY Intense, oily and mouth-coating.

PALATE Balanced and outstanding mix of sherried red fruits, chocolate orange, some spice and a gentle peat carpet.

FINISH Long, sweet, fruity, venerable and balanced.

SCORE **87**

A VERY SPECIAL SPEYSIDE 17-year-old
Old Malt Cask, 50 vol

COLOR Rich clear honey.

NOSE Grapefruit. Orange and lemon zest. Some vanilla.

BODY Full and mouth-coating.

PALATE Confectionery. Pineapple, range and citrus. Very gentle. Soft spice.

FINISH Quite short but beautiful, a touch of spice rounding off a balanced and stylish malt.

SCORE **87**

AS WE GET IT Cask Strength Islay 8-year-old
Ian Macleod, 58 vol

COLOR Very pale yellow.

NOSE Intense coal smoke. Creamy, with some sweet soft fruits.

BODY Oily. Rich. Full.

PALATE Green fruits. Gooseberry. Grapefruit. Peat and then pepper spice arrive midway.

FINISH Pepper and peat. Long, full, with fruits among the smoke.

SCORE **83**

BARBECUE SAUCE SPEYSIDE CASK Vintage 1990
Wemyss, 55 vol

576 bottles released.

COLOR Rich golden brown.

NOSE Welcoming. Honeyed. Sweet. Over-ripe melon. Vine tomato.

BODY Full and mouth coating but quite gentle.

PALATE Robust but very rounded. some anisette, Honey. Orange fruits.
Traces of peat. Vanilla. Mild spice.

FINISH Medium-long. tangy and spicy.

SCORE **82**

FRUIT AND NUT FUDGE Vintage 1989, Wemyss, 46 vol

345 bottles released.

COLOR Yellowy gold.

NOSE Peat fire embers. Some lemon and vanilla. Gooseberries.

BODY Full, spicy, oily.

PALATE Rich cocoa. Peat. Vanilla. Green fruits—perhaps kiwi fruit and
gooseberry. Grungy.

FINISH Peppery and medium-long. some nuttiness. Spicy nuts. Peaty.

SCORE **83**

GLACE FRUIT Vintage 1994, Wemyss, 46 vol

367 bottles released.

COLOR Liquid gold.

NOSE Very subtle but very pleasant. Tutti frutti ice cream topped with
cherry. Fruit sherbet.

BODY Full and creamy.

PALATE Nice balance of sweet fruits, drying tannins, and cake-icing spice.

FINISH Medium, very soft, gossamer-like. Delightful.

SCORE **83**

HONEYCOMB VINTAGE HIGHLAND CASK 1994,
Wemyss, 46 vol

COLOR Pale yellow.

NOSE Honeycomb is spot on. Gorse bush. Gentle citrus notes.

BODY Soft. Sweet. Creamy.

PALATE Delicate and honeyed. Apricot. Yellow plum.
Some tannic touches.

FINISH Long, with sweet spice at the end.

SCORE **85**

ISLAY 2000 Dun Bheagan Limited Edition, 43 vol

Distilled 2000 and bottled exclusively for Canada.

COLOR Rich orange. Very unlike Islay.

NOSE Again not very Islay-like. Some peat smoke, but subdued. Orange fruit. Trace of ginger. An oddball sulfury note, but not unpleasant.

BODY Medium-full, sweet, and spicy.

PALATE Restrained but nicely balanced. Some peat smoke, some spice. Yellow and orange fruits.

FINISH Medium, balanced, and with a peaty aftertaste. Islay for beginners?

SCORE **78**

SEA SMOKE Islay Vintage 1984, Wemyss, 55 vol

248 bottles released.

COLOR Deep yellow.

NOSE As described—industrial smoke, salty seaweed, and smoked meat.

BODY Full, oily, mouth-coating, sharp.

PALATE Nicely balanced. Peat and smoke. Rich fruits, including gooseberry and unripe pear.

FINISH Medium-long with smoke, sea salt, and grapey fruit.

SCORE **84**

SMOKEHEAD, Ian Macleod, 43 vol

COLOR Rich yellow.

NOSE Blackened trout with lemon juice. Engine oil. Industrial smoke.

BODY Oily and mouth-coating.

PALATE Smoked haddock. Rich. Peat. Salt and pepper. Some citrus. Full and assertive.

FINISH Long and smoky, but soft and rounded.

SCORE **86**

SMOKEHEAD Extra Black 18-year-old, Ian Macleod, 46 vol

COLOR Lemon yellow.

NOSE Extremely dense. Coal smoke and phenols. Licorice. Lemon. Molasses.

BODY Medium and sweet.

PALATE In three parts: thick dense peat; green melon and citrus fruits; salt and pepper.

FINISH Chili powder; green fruit; peat smoke—in that order. Cigar-like aftertaste.

SCORE **90**

BLENDED MALTS

Dominic Roskrow

THE CONCEPT OF MIXING MALTS from different distilleries together to create a whisky with a different taste is not new. Malts have been mixed together since the early 1800s and were recognised in law as early as 1853. Even before Andrew Usher's earliest forays in to the science of blending he sought to achieve balance and quality with the use of malted whisky only, and his first big success—Usher's Old Vatted Glenlivet—combined different malts.

In more recent times there has been a steady flow of vatted malt products. In the early part of the millennium, though, it looked like the category could be resurrected and given a new role—that of bringing a new generation of drinker to the world of Scotch by ridding it of its historical baggage and presenting it in a new and modern way. If malt whisky was the solo musician of the whisky world, it was argued, and a good blended whisky like an orchestra, then vatted malts could be the modern rock group, bringing excitement and vitality to the category.

Jon Mark and Robbo's Easy Drinking Whisky Company replaced weighty writing and age statements with modern and stylish labeling and attempted to sell its whiskies around flavor, with considerable success. The company's founders eschewed the normal whisky festival circuit and traditional magazine route and promoted their whiskies at skiing, cycling, climbing and sailing exhibitions instead. John Glaser's Compass Box, meanwhile, created a new category of "boutique whiskies" and continues to combine the very highest quality malts with an innovative approach to whisky making.

And when William Grant maintained its reputation for staying close to the cutting edge of the industry and launched Monkey Shoulder, a mix of three malts dressed in fashionable and stylish packaging but actually named after a traditional distillery affliction caused by turning malt, it looked like the vatted malt sector would break wide open.

It hasn't happened, and probably the reason it hasn't is because of an unsightly row several years ago and the debate over terminology and brand definitions that followed it. The dispute flared over Cardhu, a Diageo malt that performs extremely well in Spain. In order to meet burgeoning demand for the malt, its owners decided to mix it with the malts of two lesser known distilleries and to rename it Cardhu Pure

Malt rather than Cardhu Single Malt. Some minor changes were made to the packaging. But William Grant, which has used the word "pure" on its Glenfiddich single malt packaging, was not happy and launched a campaign in the media to point out what it saw as Diageo's deception. Diageo backed down.

That was not the end of the matter, however. The Scotch Whisky Association, a body set up and controlled by the leading distilling companies, followed the row by making three main declarations: one, that the name of a distillery could only be used on labeling if the whisky inside was only from that distillery; two, that the word "pure" should not be used; and three, and most controversially, that the term "vatted malt" should be replaced by the term "blended malt."

Opponents of this terminology argue that the word "blend" should never be used in a description of a drink containing only malted whisky and no grain, and that the general public, still in the main confused by whisky terminology, would not be able to distinguish between "blended whisky" and "blended malt whisky." Nevertheless, the new terminology has been adopted.

It does perhaps explain why many new whisky drinkers, convinced that malts are better than blends, have been reluctant to try a blended malt. If that's the case it is a real pity, because there are some excellent whiskies in the category. Perhaps, as the industry puts more emphasis on flavor over age, it will change in the future. Here is a selection of the best vatted/blended malt whiskies.

DUNCAN TAYLOR Vatted Malt 12-year-old, 56.6 vol

COLOR	Rich lemon.
NOSE	Zingy. Grapefruit and lemon zest. Clean and fruity.
BODY	Pleasant. Medium. Sweet.
PALATE	Very fresh and fruity. Yellow fruit. Crystallized pineapple cubes.
FINISH	Lots of fruit, with the gentlest touch of spice to give it depth.

SCORE **80**

DUNCAN TAYLOR Vatted Malt 20-year-old, 53.4 vol

COLOR	Brass.
NOSE	Vanilla ice cream. Milk chocolate. Lemon sherbet. Lime sorbet.
BODY	Creamy and full.
PALATE	Earthier than the nose suggests. Some peat and salt in the mix. Some citrus. Bitter lemon.
FINISH	Medium. Sour fruit, spice, peat.

SCORE **79**

DUNCAN TAYLOR Vatted Malt 30-year-old, 47.5 vol

COLOR Rich gold.

NOSE Sherried berries. Redcurrants. Over-ripe peach and pineapple.

BODY Soft, rounded, and pleasant.

PALATE Orange marmalade. Red berries. Dark chocolate.
Late tannins. Touch of pepper.

FINISH Lemon and orange fruits. Long and spicy.

SCORE **85**

DUNCAN TAYLOR Vatted Malt 40-year-old, 44.6 vol

COLOR Deep orange.

NOSE Orange jellybean. Trace of cherry. Cocoa powder.
Dusty sofa. Used leather.

BODY Syrupy and full.

PALATE Tangerine and mandarin. Barley fruits. Eventually
sweet chili peppers and oakiness, but soft and balanced.

FINISH Long. Orange fruits. Spice.

SCORE **87**

FAMOUS GROUSE Blended Malt, 40 vol

COLOR Orange.

NOSE Mix of honey, citrus fruit, and a chemistry set. Some orange.

BODY Smooth, soft, and rounded.

PALATE Clementine. Honey. Given depth by late peat and spice.

FINISH Medium and spicy.

SCORE **72**

FLAMING HEART FH16MMVII,
Compass Box, 48.9 vol

COLOR Pale gold.

NOSE Port Ellen ferry. Oil and smoke. Lemon. Intense.

BODY Rich, sweet, and oily, but very gentle.

PALATE Rootsy, then smoky, with a big fruit compote fightback.
A syrupy contest between smoke and plummy fruits.

FINISH A score draw. Perfectly balanced between strawberry and
blackcurrant jam and a steam engine festival.

SCORE **93**

MONKEY SHOULDER
William Grant & Sons, 40 vol

COLOR Honey gold.

NOSE Apples. Fresh and zesty. Grapefruit. Young.

BODY Light, soft, and rounded.

PALATE Green apples. Citrus fruit. Refreshing, with clean barley.
Very rounded and balanced.

FINISH Medium and fruity, with some late fruit.

SCORE **88**

OAK CROSS, Compass Box, 43 vol

COLOR Brassy yellow.

NOSE Orange squash. Tangerine zest. Anise.
Nail polish.

BODY Medium. Soft. Full.

PALATE A tour de force. Gentle citrus fruits, sandalwood spice,
then pepper takes over. Sweet and sour citrus.

FINISH Sweet chili spice. Sour lemon and lime.
A delightful aftertaste.

SCORE **90**

OPTIMISM, Compass Box, 44 vol

COLOR Pale gold.

NOSE Toffee apples. Fresh. Summer fair.
Butterscotch sauce on vanilla ice cream.

BODY Rich, full, soft, and creamy.

PALATE Peatier than the nose suggests. Fresh. Lemon and lime sorbet.
Apples and pears. Refreshing.

FINISH Quite short, gentle, and clean. Palate-cleansing.

SCORE **90**

THE PEAT CHIMNEY, Wemyss, 43 vol

COLOR Golden honey.

NOSE Rich oily smoke. Beach barbecue. Enticing.

BODY Full, rich, and creamy.

PALATE Sweet, peat, over-ripe pear. Almonds.
Some dark chocolate.

FINISH Quite long, with pepper and peat notes.

SCORE **83**

THE PEAT MONSTER, Compass Box, 46 vol

COLOR Lemon yellow.

NOSE Rootsy. Lemon zest. Wafting smoke.

BODY Creamy and peaty.

PALATE Sweet and balanced, with sugar fruits, kipper smoke, and sea notes.

FINISH Medium, balanced, and peaty.

SCORE **85**

THE SIX ISLES, 43 vol

COLOR Light gold.

NOSE Lime, lemon, grapefruit. Honeyed. Gentle wafts of peat and smoke.

BODY Quite full and assertive.

PALATE Much peatier and smokier than the nose suggests. Some fruit notes.

FINISH Medium-full and peaty, with some peppery notes.

SCORE **80**

THE SMOOTH GENTLEMAN, Wemyss, 43 vol

COLOR Golden honey.

NOSE Honey. Slightly musty. Vegetal. Something vaguely fishy?

BODY Soft. Light and smooth.

PALATE Clean sweet barley. Green fruit. Two-dimensional, but pleasant.

FINISH Quite short and enjoyable, but relatively insubstantial.

SCORE **69**

THE SPICE KING, Wemyss, 43 vol

COLOR Golden honey.

NOSE Musty. Oily fish. Soy. Tingling.

BODY Oily and creamy.

PALATE Sweet, with gentle smoke and peat. Balanced and engaging.

FINISH Medium, with late pepper and a rounded peat and fruit finish.

SCORE **75**

THE SPICE TREE, Compass Box, 46 vol

COLOR Orangey gold.

NOSE Vanilla. Soft golden fruit. Orange.

BODY Rich and full.

PALATE Complex. Tingling orange and citrus. Zesty. Oak spices. Tannins.

FINISH Long, fruity, and beautifully spicy.

SCORE **92**

JAPANESE MALTS

Gavin D. Smith

WHEN FOCUSING ON JAPANESE SINGLE MALTS in the fifth edition of this book, Michael Jackson wrote that "fourteen malts from Japan were reviewed in the fourth edition of *Complete Guide to Single Malt Scotch*. Since then, releases from Japan's malt distilleries have swollen from a trickle into a torrent." To continue the aquatic metaphor, that torrent has now become a positive deluge; hence this significantly enlarged section devoted to Japanese malt whiskies.

For many years, most malt whisky produced in Japan was blended with grain spirit for the domestic market, but as that market began to decline during the 1990s, distillers started to place a greater emphasis on single malts, specifically for the export trade. Today, Japan is the second-largest producer of single malt whisky after Scotland.

The ultimate accolade for Japanese whisky came in 2008 when Yoichi 20-year-old won *Whisky Magazine's* coveted "World's Best Single Malt Whisky" award, while Suntory Hibiki landed the comparable blended whisky prize. The announcement of this prestigious double provided a brief media frenzy, and provoked headlines about alleged "consternation" in the Scotch whisky industry.

Certainly, it made good copy for newspapers, but for anyone who had been monitoring Japanese whiskies over the previous few years it would not have come as a great surprise. The award would certainly not have astounded Michael Jackson, whose respect for the product of Japan's stills was apparent by the award of high scores to a number of expressions.

The growth of interest in premium Japanese whiskies has also been encouraged by the English-based Number One Drinks Company, which, since 2006, has imported and distributed throughout Europe mainly single cask bottlings, principally from silent stills in Japan.

Compared to Scotland, Ireland, and the US, the Japanese whisky industry is youthful, tracing its roots back to the years immediately after the end of World War I, when a number of indigenous spirits producers tried their hand at emulating Scotch whisky.

However, the first real commercial success came as result of a collaboration between Shinjiro Torii, founder of Kotobukiya—ultimately renamed Suntory in 1963—and Masataka Taketsuru.

Taketsuru was the son of a sake distiller. He enrolled as a student of organic chemistry at Glasgow University in 1918 and subsequently married a Scot and worked at distilleries in Campbeltown and on Speyside before returning to his native Japan.

In conjunction with Torii, Taketsuru was responsible for the creation of Japan's first dedicated whisky distillery, which was established near Kyoto in 1923 and named Yamazaki. Taketsuru went on to found the Nikka distilling company (now owned by Asahi Breweries Ltd.) and create his own Yoichi whisky distillery, near Sapporo city on the island of Hokkaido in 1934.

Yoichi bears a resemblance to many distilleries in Scotland, and its location was chosen due to its similarity with Scotland in terms of humidity levels and water supply. There is even a nearby peat moor. Yoichi can turn out five million liters of spirit a year and continues to use direct-fired stills, fueled by coal. Some commentators claim that this factor adds to the character and quality of the whisky.

Today, Suntory and Nikka dominate the Japanese whisky industry, and Suntory's Yamazaki distillery was supplemented in 1973 by Hakushu, constructed in a spectacular forest setting at Yamanashi, west of Mount Fuji. In 1981 a second distillery, known as Hakushu East, was built on the site. The original "West" plant is currently used only as a product test bed for new whiskies.

Hakushu East can produce three million liters of spirit per year and is notable for its diversity of stills, which vary significantly in terms of size, shape, and lyne arm angle. Some are direct-fired by gas, while others are steam-heated. One wash still operates with a worm tub, and the rest are fitted with modern condensers.

Yamazaki now echoes Hakushu East: three of its six pairs of stills were replaced in 2006 to bring in a greater variety of shapes and sizes. Its maximum annual output is 3.5 million liters.

Before Suntory branched out with Hakushu, Nikka had already constructed a second distillery in 1969, naming it Miyagikyo, though it is also known as Sendai. As well as four pairs of pot stills, the five million liters capacity Miyagikyo plant is additionally equipped with Coffey stills, which are sometimes used to distill malted barley, principally destined for blending with malt spirit from pot stills.

In addition to the more mainstream releases of Suntory and Nikka, single malts are offered by the Kirin Holdings-owned duo of Fuji-Gotemba and Karuizawa. Much of the spirit made using Golden Promise barley at the currently mothballed Karuizawa distillery, situated near Mount Asama, in the Japanese Alps, is very close in style to traditional single malt Scotch and is matured in sherry wood before being released as single cask bottlings.

Other notable single cask releases were produced in the Hanyu distillery, located in the Saitama prefecture. Hanyu was dismantled in 2004, but single cask bottlings are offered by Ichiro Akuto, grandson of Hanyu's founder, under his "Ichiro's Malt Card Series." Akuto is also the founder of Japan's newest distillery, Chichibu, which came on stream in spring 2008 and is located northwest of Tokyo, some 30 miles (50 km) from Hanyu. It is the first new distillery to be built in Japan since 1973. Samples of its new make and very young spirit are receiving extremely positive reviews.

CHICHIBU Newborn Bourbon Barrel, 2008, Cask 127, 62.5 vol
Very briefly matured in a bourbon cask prior to release.

COLOR Very pale straw. NOSE Crisp and clean. Fresh fruits and mild spice. BODY Light. PALATE Full and spicy, notes of melon. FINISH Lengthy, with a tang of ginger. SCORE 79

HANYU Japanese Oak Cask, 17-year-old, Distilled 1990, Bottled 2007, Cask 9511, 55.5 vol

COLOR Pale amber. NOSE Floral, with malt and fresh fruits, plus a hint of sandalwood. BODY Lush. PALATE Apple pie and custard. Spicy and more citric with water. FINISH Lengthy and pleasantly dry. Ultimately, slightly herbal. SCORE 82

HANYU, Ichiro's Malt Card Series, Ace of Diamonds, Cask 9023, Distilled 1986, Bottled 2008, 56.4 vol
Finished in a cream sherry butt.

COLOR Deep amber. NOSE Very fruity. Soft nose. Ripe peaches with a whiff of caramel. Smoky, fresh fruit, with the addition of water. BODY Rich. PALATE Mouth-coating and fruity, with spice and fudge notes. FINISH Dries quite rapidly through spices. SCORE 83

HANYU, Ichiro's Malt Card Series, Ten of Clubs, Cask 9032. Distilled 1990, Bottled 2008, 52.4 vol.
Finished in a Pedro Ximénez sherry butt.

COLOR Russian gold. NOSE Slightly tobacco-like, with developing white chocolate and maraschino cherry notes. BODY Muscular. PALATE Reminiscent of eating canned peaches by a campfire. FINISH Long, succulent, spicy and deliciously fruity. SCORE 85

HANYU, Ichiro's Malt Card Series, Eight of Hearts, Cask 9303, Distilled 1991, Bottled 2008, 56.8 vol

Finished in a Spanish oak oloroso sherry butt.

COLOR Deep copper. NOSE Rich, antique leather, with background notes of gunpowder tea and plasticine. BODY Medium to full. PALATE Spicy and quite lively. FINISH Medium-length, with raisins, ginger, and more gunpowder tea. SCORE 84

HANYU, Ichiro's Malt Card Series, Five of Spades, Cask 9601, Distilled 2000, Bottled 2008, 60.5 vol

Finished in an American oak refill sherry butt.

COLOR Bright gold. NOSE Floral, with sherry trifle. BODY Creamy. PALATE Confident, with pepper, spice, leather. FINISH Lengthy, with fresh sherry fading to almonds. SCORE 85

KARUIZAWA Noh Series, 13-year-old, Distilled 1995, Bottled 2008, Cask 5004, 63 vol

Matured in a Japanese wine cask.

COLOR Rich orange. NOSE Sherry, oak, potted plants, and cooked oranges. BODY Medium to full. PALATE Initially astringent, fragrant, and sherried. FINISH Long, with lingering chocolate ginger and chocolate-coated Turkish Delight. SCORE 82

KARUIZAWA 1992, Bottled 2007, Cask 3300, 61.5 vol

Matured in an American white oak cask.

COLOR Rich gold. NOSE Spice, vanilla, almonds, and milk chocolate. With time, darker cocoa and syrup aromas develop. BODY Full. PALATE Quite dry, with tangy, citrus fruits. FINISH Long and drying, with a touch of soot. Gingery oak, a hint of chili pepper at the close. SCORE 83

KARUIZAWA 1991, Bottled 2007, Cask 3318, 62.5 vol
Matured in a sherry butt.

COLOR Antique gold. NOSE Initially quite restrained. Delicately floral and gently sherried, with a suggestion of plum pudding.
BODY Rich. PALATE Sophisticated, with malt and sherry merging nicely, with an undertone of well-mannered spice.
FINISH Persistent sherry and polished oak. SCORE 85

KARUIZAWA 1988, Bottled 2007, Cask 3397, 59.8 vol
Matured in an ex-sherry butt.

COLOR Full amber. NOSE Floral, sweet sherry, honey, ginger, and raspberries. Orange marmalade notes develop with exposure to air.
BODY Full. PALATE Fruitcake, rich spices, and licorice. Much drier with the addition of water, when licorice dominates, with a hint of pepper. FINISH Medium to long, drying, and spicy to the end. SCORE 86

SUNTORY MALTS
HAKUSHU 10-year-old, 40 vol

COLOR Pale to mid-gold. NOSE Grassy, leafy, floral. Developing cinder toffee. BODY Delicate. PALATE Floral, mildly fruity, gentle spice, and vanilla fudge. FINISH The short side of medium. Citrus fruit and nuts. SCORE 82

HAKUSHU 12-year-old, 43 vol

COLOR Mid-gold. NOSE Puff candy (cinder toffee), cut grass, toffee apples. BODY Soft. PALATE Fruity, slightly smoky, with honey and a hint of pepper. FINISH Medium length, Steadily drying, with spicy lemon. SCORE 84

HAKUSHU 18-year-old, 43 vol

COLOR Antique gold. NOSE Initially fresh. Hay. Nougat. Then sherried fruitcake, cherries, oranges, and bitter chocolate emerge. BODY Silky. PALATE Fruit and nut milk chocolate, slightly perfumed, gentle oak. FINISH Medium to long. Drying, smoky, some bitter oak. SCORE 85

HAKUSHU 25-year-old, 43 vol

COLOR Amber. NOSE Polite, with fresh fruit, sherry, oak, and peat. BODY Rounded. PALATE Rich and full, with summer berries, chocolate, malt, and vanilla. FINISH Long and mildly smoky. SCORE 86

YAMAZAKI 10-year-old, 40 vol

COLOR Mid-gold. NOSE Orange blossom, ginger, almonds, and fudge. BODY Smooth. PALATE Slightly herbal, floral; malt and toffee. FINISH Medium, drying, spicy cereal notes. SCORE 83

YAMAZAKI 12-year-old, 43 vol

COLOR Mid-gold with amber highlights. NOSE Lavender, cinnamon, root ginger. BODY Creamy. PALATE Initially, quite dry and herbal, but becoming fruitier; with some smoke. FINISH Quite long, with sultanas, and caramel. SCORE 85

YAMAZAKI 18-year-old, 43 vol

COLOR Deep amber. NOSE Profound sherry, fresh leather, freshly squeezed oranges. Becoming smokier. BODY Luscious. PALATE Smoky, citrus fruit, figs, and oloroso sherry. FINISH Very long, fruity; drying with silky smooth oak. SCORE 87

YAMAZAKI 25-year-old, 43 vol

COLOR Full amber. NOSE Sweet sherry, plum jam, bitter chocolate. BODY Full. PALATE Dry sherry, smoke, tannic oak, treacle. FINISH Long and drying. SCORE 88

NIKKA MALTS
MIYAGIKYO 10-year-old, 45 vol

COLOR Amber. NOSE Quite light and floral, with eating apples, gentle oak, and brittle toffee. BODY Smooth. PALATE Tropical fruits, vanilla. Spicy and rounded. FINISH Medium length. Fruit, spice, and a note of peat. SCORE 82

MIYAGIKO 12-year-old, 45 vol

COLOR Mid-amber. NOSE Rich and full; sherried, with soft toffee, oak and some smoke. BODY Medium to full. PALATE Sherry, honey, cereal. Sweet peat, with spicy oak. FINISH Honey and lemon, with lively oak making its presence felt. SCORE 83

MIYAGIKO 15-year-old, 45 vol

COLOR Amber and gold. NOSE Complex, with spicy orange, hazelnuts, honey, and sherry. BODY Slightly oily. PALATE The complexity continues: citrus fruits, sherry richness, spicy peat. FINISH Long, with sherry and oak tannins. Citric, with a hint of licorice. SCORE 84

YOICHI 10-year-old, 45 vol

COLOR Amber with gold highlights. NOSE Mild smokiness, leafy, with citrus fruits. BODY Soft, slightly oily. PALATE Peat smoke and spice; oranges and vanilla. FINISH Comparatively short, with fruity oak and delicate smokiness. SCORE 82

YOICHI 12-year-old, 45 vol

COLOR Burned amber. NOSE Smoke, spicy sherry, and dried fruits. BODY Creamy. PALATE Rich and luxurious, with sherry, walnuts, malt, and peat smoke. FINISH Long, with oak tannins. SCORE 83

YOICHI 15-year-old, 45 vol

COLOR Rich amber. NOSE Pipe tobacco, chocolate-coated almonds, cinnamon, and vanilla. BODY Oily. PALATE Spicy, with cloves, ginger, and dark chocolate. FINISH Nutty, spicy, dried fruits. A little smoke and oak. Complex. SCORE 84

US MICRODISTILLERIES

O NE OF THE MOST INTRIGUING and potentially exciting trends in recent years has been the growth of American microdistilleries. Encouraged by the success of American beer microbreweries, which have thrown away the rule book and revolutionized beer production in recent years, the microdistilleries have been thinking outside the box when it comes to making malt. In Europe, the rules are clearly laid down as to what you can and can not do when making single malt whisky, and failure to adhere to them means that you are unable to sell your product in Europe under the name "whisky." But the Americans are bound by a different set of laws and have started to show some admirable initiative when it comes to using American barrels and production techniques.

American whiskey makers have started to explore what happens when you make single malt whiskey using some of the techniques more common to bourbon. For instance, new oak barrels would destroy the flavor of malt if left for the European minimum maturation period of three years, but not if the malt is taken out after a few months. If the beer sector is anything to go by, where extreme and original flavors are now the norm, then microdistilling is likely to be a major story for the future. Here are a few of the best US micromalts.

CLEAR CREEK DISTILLERY
MCCARTHY'S Oregon Single Malt 3-year-old, 2005
Batch #W08-02, 42.5 vol

This expression was bottled on July 15, 2008.

COLOR Brassy gold. NOSE Clean peat. Dry. Like inhaling a peat brick; not smoky. Hints of apple try to peek out. BODY Medium; well-rounded. PALATE Well-balanced. Peat with notes of sweetness and tar. The peat complements without overpowering the malt. FINISH The peat, which began on the nose, continues on the palate, builds into a grand crescendo, and crashes on the finish, like a fireball exploding when it hits a wall. An interesting peat: lacking the seaside characteristics of an Islay, it likes to show itself on the nose and palate, building to the finish. SCORE 87

COPPER FOX DISTILLERY
WASMUND'S Single Malt, Batch 27, 4-month-old, 48 vol

COLOR Reddish amber. NOSE Fruity. Ripe red apples, cherries, pears, and caramel, with notes of cinnamon red hots. After decanting, red-hot cinnamon becomes more prominent. BODY Rough, fiery, full-bodied. PALATE Maple syrup. Apples. FINISH Dry. Apples, and spices linger. More refined, better balanced, than previous editions—much improved! Water tames the palate, but mutes some flavors. SCORE 71

ST GEORGE Single Malt Whiskey, Lot 7, 43 vol

COLOR Deep gold. NOSE Sweet nose of apples, almost like a calvados, with notes of pear and wafts of nail polish. Water releases heavier notes of cider. BODY Vibrant, slightly rough for some. PALATE Sweet waves of calvados. Extremely fruity, as huge notes of pears and apples leap from the glass. Water smooths the edges but tones down the apple notes. FINISH Long and spicy, with vibrant notes of pears and cinnamon. SCORE 82

TUTHILLTOWN SPIRITS
HUDSON Single Malt Whiskey, 46 vol
Bottled in 2008, Batch #6, petit charred American Oak casks.

COLOR Reddish Mahogany. NOSE Apples, root beer, dark vanilla. BODY Vibrant. Slightly rough, but full-bodied. PALATE Intriguing. Perhaps the missing link between bourbon and scotch. Lovely notes of vanilla and hints of apple. Similar to bourbon, but lacking the cherry flavor note. Rich and flavorful, with notes of oak and spice. A drop of water softens the nose and releases cinnamon on the palate. FINISH Spicy and dry. SCORE 81

WHISKY WORLDWIDE

Dominic Roskrow

"Australian wine … fine wine that really opens the sluices at both ends"

Those of us old enough to remember Monty Python's disparaging remarks about Australia's early attempts at wine making still laugh at the memory. The sketch was funny because the whole idea of Australians making fine wine was.

And yet, within 15 years, wine makers in the Antipodes were picking up awards for their wines, and, within 20, were competing for top honors with the very best of the "Old World." Today it is hard to imagine that Australia was ever away from the top table, and the same can be said of New Zealand, South Africa, and Chile. It's not just the quality of the drink, either—the emerging nations have brought a refreshing and novel approach to packaging and have trampled all over the snobbishness of the old school.

So could it happen with malt whisky? The answer, unequivocally, is yes. Indeed, it already is. Given the nature of whisky and the time it takes to mature, progress in emerging markets may be slower. But everything is relative, and in terms of the world of whisky, the speed of change is remarkable. Since the last edition of this book, there has been an explosion in quality whisky. In just four years, a number of whiskies from around the world have gone from being "me-too" malts, with as much depth as an imitation after-shave, to malts capable of winning international awards, which is what they have started to do. Scotland will dominate the world of malt whisky for decades to come, but New World whiskies will play an increasing role in the future.

This shouldn't come as a total surprise. Ireland and America have produced styles of whisky every bit the equal of a great many Scottish malts. And, in recent years, some Japanese whiskies have outperformed in competitions the very best from Scotland. What should excite broad-minded malt lovers, though, is the scale and breadth of the world whiskies revolution, and the speed of improvement in the quality of malts from distilleries outside traditional whisky-producing countries.

Much of this has happened under the radar of the established whisky world, at least in part because most British whisky journalists have shown little interest in seeking out malts in new territories. The exception is leading whisky expert Jim Murray, who for many years has supported emerging distilleries from every part of the world, making the effort to visit them, writing about them, and giving their whiskies the same level of respect as he has to the Ardbegs and the Macallans. His faith and loyalty is being vindicated by the progress being made by many of them.

By anyone's standards, some of the malts from Bakery Hill and Lark in Australia, Mackmyra in Sweden, Penderyn in Wales, Slyrs in Germany, Cooley in Ireland (producers of Connemara, Locke's, and The Tyrconnell), and Uberach in Alsace need to be taken seriously. Bushmill's in Northern Ireland has long been distinguished for quality, and the new distilleries in France (Glann ar Mor) and England (St. George's) suggest there is plenty more to come.

It would be impossible to provide a comprehensive guide to world malts. Many are made in small quantities, available only within a stone's throw of the distillery, and sell out on release. But here is a round-up of the best world malt whiskies currently on offer.

AUSTRALIAN MALTS

BAKERY HILL Classic Malt, 2008 bottling, 46 vol

COLOR Lemon yellow. NOSE Buttercups. Sweet clean barley. Honey. Traces of orange and apple. BODY Gossamer light. Quite unassuming. PALATE Apple seed, then apple. Barley. Clean citrus fruit. Traces of vanilla. Young, vibrant, refreshing. FINISH Medium, with a some peppery spice. SCORE 77

BAKERY HILL Peated Malt, 46 vol

COLOR Deep orange. NOSE Different to most peated whiskies. Rich. Melon. Wafts of dry peat. Clean and fresh. BODY Soft, sweet, and rounded. PALATE: Sophisticated. Apple. Some citrus notes. Homemade cookies. Smoky peat. Vanilla. Soft. FINISH Reasonably long. Sweet pepper mixing with fruit and a peaty carpet underlay. SCORE 82

BAKERY HILL Classic Malt, Cask Strength, 60.2 vol

COLOR Rich gold. NOSE Needs time and water. Then blood orange and rich fruit. BODY Soft, sweet, slightly oily. PALATE Sweet apple and pear. Hot chocolate drinking powder. Hints of anise and pepper. Clean and refreshing. FINISH Medium, sweet, and pleasant. Very balanced and well-structured. SCORE 82

BAKERY HILL Peated Malt, Cask Strength, 59.8 vol

COLOR Deep orange. NOSE Greenhouse. Intense green vegetable.
Unripe tomatoes. Wafts of peat smoke. BODY Sweet and soft.
PALATE Intense version of the standard malt. Green fruits,
big bursts of flavor. Restrained but noticeable earthy peat.
FINISH Fresh. Quite long. Peaty. SCORE 86

BAKERY HILL Double Wood, 46 vol

COLOR Rich yellow. NOSE Fragrant. Canned fruit in syrup.
Sweet melon. BODY Medium-full. PALATE Clean exotic fruits.
Refreshing. Canned pear. Honeyed. FINISH Medium, very
soft, sweet, and pleasant. SCORE 83

LARK Cask Strength, Cask LD31, 58 vol

COLOR Chestnut. NOSE Fine pepper dust. Savory. Furniture varnish.
Unusual. BODY Sweet, soft, rich. PALATE Soft, thick honey.
Over-ripe plum and pepper. Touches of salt and pepper. FINISH Gentle
and rounded. Different, but balanced and impressive. SCORE 83

LARK Distiller's Select Cask, 46 vol

COLOR Deep gold. NOSE Sweet lemon and honey cough sweet.
Fruity boiled sweets. Complex. BODY Oily. Very soft. Mouth-coating.
PALATE Gooseberries. Plums. Lots of other fruits. Complex but gentle.
A trace of pepper. FINISH Quite long. Graceful, honeyed,
and soft. SCORE 85

ENGLISH MALTS

ST GEORGE'S DISTILLERY Chapter 3, Cask 32/2007, 46 vol
English malt at least 18 months old.

COLOR Very pale yellow. NOSE Confused mix of green fruit and vegetables. Sweet and clean. No plasticine or sulfur traces at all. BODY Oily, sweet, and full. PALATE Confused adolescent. Still pudgy and green, but developing muscle. Pleasant and sweet. Clean. Intriguing. FINISH Short and sweet, like the trailer for a big blockbuster. Okay, you have our attention. SCORE 74

ST GEORGE'S DISTILLERY Chapter 4, Peated, 46 vol
English malt at least 18 months old.

COLOR Pale yellow. NOSE Peat. Citrus fruit. Apple. BODY Creamy and full. PALATE Rounded. Almonds. Spices. Peat. Not much depth. FINISH Medium-hot and spicy. SCORE 74

FRENCH MALTS

GLANN AR MOR 3-year-old, 46 vol

COLOR Pale lemon. NOSE Lemon puff biscuits. Buttery pastry. Citrus. Stewed rhubarb. BODY Soft, sweet, and gentle. PALATE Young, earthy, and spicy. Traces of apple and yellow fruits. Some peat and pepper. Fairly one-dimensional, but pleasant and promising. No negatives. FINISH Medium, peppery, pleasant. SCORE 80

UBERACH Single Cask 00116, 43.8 vol

COLOR Dark chestnut brown. NOSE Nutty. Chestnuts. Musty. Vegetal. Noticeable sulfur. Toffee. BODY Sweet, full, and mouth-coating. PALATE Fruitcake. Pleasant sulfury notes. Plums. Sweet. Some spice. FINISH Quite short. Salt and pepper. Some sweetness too. Very different and intriguing. SCORE 80

GERMAN MALTS

SLYRS Bavaria Single Malt, 43 vol

COLOR Pale orange. NOSE Pastry, doughball. With time, jasmine. Fresh flowers. Fudge. BODY Pleasant, medium, soft. PALATE Cherry lozenge. Canned fruit. Candy sweets. Sweet cake mix, then some late spices. FINISH Medium-sweet, with a very different but enjoyable cough-drop conclusion. SCORE 83

SLYRS Bavaria Single Malt, 2005, 43 vol

COLOR Orangey gold. NOSE Thai spice. Meadowland. Spring flowers.
BODY Pleasant. Rounded. PALATE Clean barley. Melon. Sweet fruit. Nutty.
FINISH Medium and sweet, with some spice. SCORE 77

INDIAN MALTS

AMRUT Single Malt, 46 vol

COLOR Golden honey. NOSE Creamy toffee. Lemon vanilla drops. Ripe
grape. Fresh barley. BODY Medium-full. PALATE Waldorf salad. Apple and
pear slices. Some nuttiness. Licorice stick. Some spice. Very
gentle. FINISH Medium, fruity, and spicy. Razor sharp. SCORE 78

AMRUT Cask Strength Single Malt, 59.1 vol

COLOR Golden orange. NOSE Spicy orange marmalade. Intense. Mandarin
jellybeans. BODY Rich and mouth-coating. PALATE Intense, clean barley.
Honey and vanilla, bourbon wood. Wafts of tannin and spice. All refined
and balanced. FINISH Soft, honeyed, rounded.
Medium length. SCORE 85

AMRUT Peated, 46 vol

COLOR Golden NOSE Fish. Smoke. Scottish breakfast room.
Thai crab cake. BODY Medium-full and pleasant. PALATE Kippers. Savory.
Earthy barley. Salt and pepper. FINISH Balanced, long, and smoky, with
savory aftertaste. SCORE 79

AMRUT Peated Cask Strength, 62.78 vol

COLOR Rich gold. NOSE Wafting smoke. Some vanilla. Some fruit.
Restrained. BODY Full, oily, peaty. PALATE Peppermint, then squelchy fruit,
some peat smoke. Soft, honeyed. Reserved but evolving. FINISH Slow, but
fruit, spice, and peat all come through in excellent balance. SCORE 90

IRISH MALTS

BUSHMILLS 10-year-old, 40 vol

COLOR Pale gold. NOSE Fresh fruit. Peach. Juicy berries.
Honey. BODY Gossamer soft. PALATE In two parts: initially sweet grape,
over-ripe red apples, pleasant summer fruits; then bitter chocolate and
pepper spice, giving the overall taste definition. FINISH Rounded and
structured, with a nice balance of sweetness and spice. Impressive
assertiveness. SCORE 84

CONNEMARA Single Malt, No Age Statement, 40 vol

COLOR Yellow gold. NOSE Prickly. Twig fire. Gentle smoke.
Earthy. BODY Creamy and smoky. PALATE Oral battle between apple pip,
molasses, green fruit, and gentle wafting smoke. FINISH Peat and earth
at their strongest at the end. SCORE 75

CONNEMARA 12-year-old, 46 vol

COLOR Pale yellow. NOSE Gentle. Reeds. Clean barley. Very light traces of
smoke. BODY Sweet, soft, gentle, and rounded. PALATE Gooseberry. Grape.
Unripe pear. All very gentle, then some tannins from the
wood. FINISH Long and peppery. Quite dry. SCORE 79

CONNEMARA 10-year-old, Sherry Finish, 46 vol

COLOR Rich brown. NOSE Musty. Rootsy. Some peat. Embers. BODY Full
and intense. Mouth-coating. PALATE Strange conflict between peat and fruit.
Smoky grapes. Plums in fire embers. Sherry trifle. Earthy. FINISH Battle
between sweet fruit and peatiness, with peat winning out. Quite long, with a
sherry trifle aftertaste. SCORE 76

CONNEMARA Cask Strength, 60 vol

COLOR Pale lemon. NOSE Old Hornby train set. Burned dust.
Engine oil. Metal polish. BODY Oily, rich, and full.
PALATE Canned pear smoked over a wood fire. Hot chocolate powder.
Soft. FINISH Long, sweet, gentle, and smoky. SCORE 83

LOCKE'S 8-year-old, 40 vol

COLOR Pale gold. NOSE Fresh straw. Cereal.
Gentle citrus. BODY Soft and gentle. PALATE Sharp. Astringent.
Pepper spice. Sour fruit. Abrasive. FINISH Medium, with pepper
and some tannins. SCORE 70

THE TYRCONNELL, No Age Statement, 40 vol

COLOR Honey gold NOSE Zesty. Sherbet. Lemon and lime
Starburst. BODY Soft and rounded. Quite thin.
PALATE Nice balance of green and orange fruits. Not too sweet.
Refreshing and summery. FINISH Medium and fairly sweet, with a dash
of oak holding the fruitiness in check. SCORE 78

THE TYRCONNELL 15-year-old, Single Cask 1850/52, 46 vol

COLOR Pale yellow with a greenish hue. NOSE Honeyed.
Melon. Vanilla. Barley. Demerara sugar.
BODY Medium, soft, and sweet. PALATE Initially spearmint.
Then toffee apple, green fruits, and pepper.
FINISH Nice balance between apple, toffee, and pepper. SCORE 82

THE TYRCONNELL 15-year-old, Single Cask 957/92, 46 vol

COLOR Pale gold. NOSE Sweet grape. Some citrus.
Melon. Light and sweet. BODY Sweet, full, rich.
PALATE Intense. Brown sugar. Sweet melon. Lots of
oaky spice. Almond. Green apple core.
FINISH Medium, sweet and peppery. SCORE 82

THE TYRCONNELL 10-year-old, Sherry Finish, 46 vol

COLOR Honey gold. NOSE Dusty old office.
Polished leather. Air freshener. BODY Slight and soft.
PALATE Completely dominated by sherry fruits. Blackcurrants. Red berries.
Little trace of the core Tyrconnell malt. Some tannin notes.
FINISH Earthy rich, medium, and sherried. Pleasant enough,
but not distinctive. SCORE 70

THE TYRCONNELL 10-year-old, Madeira Finish, 46 vol

COLOR Gold. NOSE Soft and zesty. Exotic fruits. Guava. Sweet lime. Gorgeous. BODY Soft, full, and sweet. PALATE Strawberry jelly. Soft but appetising mix of orange and red fruits. Exotic fruits. Vanilla. FINISH Tutti frutti ice cream over canned pear, melon, and other rich fruits. SCORE 90

THE TYRCONNELL 10-year-old, Port Finish, 46 vol

COLOR Rich gold. NOSE Rum and raisin. Red fruits. Cherry ice cream. BODY Oily. Creamy. Full. PALATE Sweet and fruity. Bakewell tart. Dark chilli chocolate. Intense. Complex. FINISH Plummy. Cocoa. Soft, long, and delightful. SCORE 88

WILD GEESE Single Malt, 43 vol

COLOR Orangey yellow. NOSE Old brewery. Some odd notes. But then saved by pleasant toffee. Fresh apple orchard. BODY Gossamer-like. Soft. Rounded. PALATE Delicate. Sweet. Gentle. Apple and pear. Touches of spice. Ragged. FINISH Pleasant. Soft and sweet, with a trace of late spice. SCORE 79

A SPANISH MALT

DYC 8-year-old Single Malt, 65.7 vol

COLOR Rich orange. NOSE Strange mix of wood varnish, carpenter's workshop, baking powder, and some floral notes. BODY Sweet and oily. PALATE Very sweet. Not much depth, but very clean. Youthful barley, some green fruit battling through, and some fiery Spanish pepper. FINISH Quite short. Hot. Some pepper. SCORE 70

SWEDISH MALTS

MACKMYRA Preludium 04, 53.3 vol

COLOR Light gold. NOSE Shy. Citrus fruits. Some orange. Woodshavings. Carpenter's workshop. BODY Oily. Full. PALATE Soft yellow fruit at first, then oily, smoky center. Some pepper. FINISH Prickly. Rich. Some smoke and spice. SCORE 70

MACKMYRA Preludium 05, 48.4 vol

COLOR Pale yellow. NOSE Pine needles. Fresh and clean barley. Hints of flowers and polish. BODY Full and creamy. PALATE Soft. Quite peaty. Pine needles. Sour apples. Earthy. FINISH Peat and earth. Salt and spice. SCORE 74

MACKMYRA First Edition, 46.1 vol

COLOR Rich butter yellow. NOSE Tingly. Rich tangerine liqueur.
Sweet ginger. Mandarin. BODY Pleasant.
Creamy. Full. PALATE Cinnamon. Orange. Tangerine.
Children's cough medicine. Delightful clash between orangey
fruits and a peaty underlay. Sweet and savory.
Swathes of spice. FINISH Rounded and sweet, then drying with
gentle peat. A roller coaster ride, ending with a fruit
lozenge aftertaste. SCORE 83

MACKMYRA Special, 51.6 vol

COLOR Greeny yellow. NOSE A now distinctive
Mackmyra nose: orange liqueur; concentrated canned fruit.
Melon. BODY Soft and full. PALATE Sweet fruit.
Squishy melon. Del Monte canned fruit. Then a mix of
oiliness, a big burst of tannins, peat, and pepper.
FINISH Long, sweet, peppery. SCORE 86

WELSH MALTS

PENDERYN Single Malt, 46 vol

COLOR Rich gold NOSE Lemon and lime sherbet sweets.
Light toffee. BODY Quite light. Gentle. PALATE Wispy.
Light and floral. Vanilla. Perhaps a trace of apricot.
Later, lime liqueur. FINISH Surprisingly long, with gentle
Starburst lime and sweet spice. SCORE 82

PENDERYN Peated, 46 vol

COLOR Greeny brown. NOSE Distinctive, but not heavy on the peat.
Youthful cereal and hay. Vegetal. BODY Medium-full.
PALATE Gentle peat. Almost flowery. Root vegetable. Spice.
FINISH Smoky and rootsy. Not much complexity. SCORE 75

PENDERYN Sherrywood, 46 vol

COLOR Rich golden brown. NOSE Prickly. Redcurrant
and berries. Rich sherry. BODY Quite full.
PALATE Red fruits. Pear drops. With water, green apples.
Hard pear. Fruit zest. Refreshing. FINISH Clean and fruity. Crisp,
with a delightful sweetness. SCORE 80

FURTHER READING & RESOURCES

BOOKS

The Whisky Distilleries of the United Kingdom, Alfred Barnard. (1887 classic, reprinted 2008)

The Making of Scotch Whisky, John R. Hume and Michael S. Moss. Canongate, 1981. Updated 2000. (Standard work)

The Scotch Whisky Industry Record, Charles Craig. Index Publishing Limited, 1994. (Includes a year-by-year chronology of whisky making from 1494)

Scotch Whisky: A Liquid History, Charles MacLean. Cassell, 2003. (Social history and commentary by a whisky specialist)

Malt Whisky, Charles MacLean. Mitchell Beazley, 1997, revised edition 2006

Eyewitness Companion to Whisky, Editor-in-Chief Charles MacLean. Dorling Kindersley, 2008

Handbook of Whisky, Dave Broom. Hamlyn, 2001

Jim Murray's Complete Book of Whisky, Jim Murray. Carlton, 1997

The Whisky Bible, Jim Murray. Dram Good Books, published annually

The Malt Whisky Yearbook, Editor: Ingvar Ronde. MagDig Media, published annually

The Scotch Whisky Industry Review (annual), Alan S. Gray. Sutherlands, Edinburgh. (Industry statistics, financial analysis and commentary)

The Scottish Whisky Distilleries, Misako Udo. Black and White Publishing, 2006

The Whisk(e)y Treasury, Walter Schobert. Neil Wilson Publishing, 2002. (A–Z lexicon of owners, distilleries, industry terms)

The World Guide to Whisky, Michael Jackson. Dorling Kindersley, 1987, reprinted 2005. (Scotch, Japanese, US, and Irish whiskies.)

Scotland and its Whiskies, Michael Jackson. Duncan Baird, 2001. (Photography: Harry Cory Wright)

Whisky: the Definitive World Guide, Michael Jackson. Dorling Kindersley, 2005

Appreciating Whisky, Phillip Hills. HarperCollins, 2000, reprinted 2002. (Physiology and chemistry of taste)

Collins Gems: Whiskies, Dominic Roskrow. Harper Collins, 2009

Need To Know? Whiskies: from Confused to Connoisseur, Dominic Roskrow. Harper Collins, 2008

The Connoisseur's Guide to Whisky, Helen Arthur. Apple Press, 2002

MAGAZINES & WEBSITES

Whisky Magazine (Published in the United Kingdom) www.whiskymag.com

Malt Advocate (Published in the United States) www.maltadvocate.com

Celtic Malts (International news, issues and debates, among devotees. Online magazine) www.celticmalts.com/default.htm

Ulf Buxrud's and the Malt Maniacs' websites are both extraordinary sources of information and inspiration for whisky lovers. www.buxrud.se www.maltmaniacs.org

Single Malt TV offers entertaining short features on aspects of whisky making and appreciation. www.singlemalt.tv

SPECIALIST MALT RETAILERS IN THE UK & US

D&M, Fillmore St., San Francisco dwandm.com

Milroy's, Greek Street, London www.milroys.co.uk

Park Avenue Liquor Store, New York City www.parkaveliquor.com

The Vintage House, Old Compton Street, London www.sohowhisky.com

The Whisky Exchange at Vinopolis, London www.thewhiskyexchange.com

Royal Mile Whiskies, London and Edinburgh www.royalmilewhiskies.com

Sam's, Marcey St., Chicago www.samswines.com

The Whisky Shop, 15 outlets across England and Scotland www.whiskyshop.com

Whisky Shop, Dufftown www.thewsd.co.uk

AUTHORS' ACKNOWLEDGMENTS

For their generous time and effort in helping with this and past editions of the book, the authors would like to thank the following.

Pauline Agnew, Rob Allanson, Rolf Andersen, Nick Andrews, Raymond Armstrong, Bridget Arthur, Elaine Bailey, Sarah Bailey, David Baker, Duncan Baldwin, Ian Bankier, Liselle Barnsley, Rachel Barrie, Pat Barrow, Owen D. L. Barstow, Michael Barton, Sonia Bastian, Micheal Beamish, Paul Beevis, Thierry Benitah, Bill Bergius, Jérôme Bordenave, David Boyd, Neil Boyd, Stephen Bremner, Dave Broom, Derek Brown, Lew Bryson, Emily Butcher, Ian Buxton, Alec Carnie, Ian Chapman, Karen Christie, Rick Christie, Neil Clapperton, Paula Cormack, Isabel Coughlin, Simon Coughlin, David Cox, Ronnie Cox, Jason Craig, Katherine Crisp, Andrew Crook, Jim Cryle, Peter Currie, Bob Dalgarno, Stephen Davies, Jancis Davis, Jürgen Deibel, Jean Donnay, Lucy Drake, Jonathan Driver, Gavin J. P. Durnin, Anthony Edwards, Hans-Jürgen Ehmke, Joel Elder, Kate Enis, Gable and Ralph Erenzo, Amy Felmeister, Robert Fleming, John Glaser, John Glass, Alan Gordon, Jim Gordon, Steve Gorton, Lesley Gracie, Heather Graham, George Grant, Alan S. Gray, Peter Greve, Natalie Guerin, Anna Hall, Nick Harris, Donald Hart, Ian Henderson, Dennis Hendry, Stuart Hendry, Robert Hicks, Sandy Hislop, David Hume, Brigid James, Richard Jones, Caitriona Kavanagh, Frances Kelly, Sheila Kennedy, Edward Kinsey, Ed Kohl, Kiran Kuma, Mari Laidlaw, Fred Laing, Stewart Laing, Bill Lark, Christine Logan, Lars Lindberger, Richard Lombard-Chibnall, Jim Long, Bill Lumsden, Neil Macdonald, Lorne Mackillop, Dennis Malcolm, Lauren Mayer, Fritz Maytag, Anthony McCallum-Caron, Stephen McCarthy, Jim McEwan, Frank McHardy, Douglas McIvor, Ian Macmillan, Stephen Marshall, Carla Masson, Annabel Meikle, Claire Meikle, Marcin Miller, Keita Minari, Euan Mitchell, Matthew Mitchell, Shuna Mitchell, Mike Miyamoto, Glen Moore, Lindsay Morgan, Nicholas Morgan, Malcolm Mullin, Stuart Nickerson, Margaret Nicol, B.A. Nimmo, Martine Nouet, Rebecca Painter, The Patel Family, Richard Paterson, Lucy Pritchard, Annie Pugh, John Ramsay, Stuart Ramsay, Kevin Ramsden, Robert Ransom, Kirsty Reid, Mark Reynier, Rebecca Richardson, Damian Riley-Smith, Pat Roberts, Dave Robertson, Pamela Robertson, Amy Robson, Geraldine Roche, Chris Rodden, Colin Ross, Fabio Rossi, Imogen Russell-Taylor, Colin Scott, Jacqui Seargeant, Catherine Service, Euan Shand, Rubyna Sheikh, Raj Singh, Sukhinder Singh, David Smith, Rory Steel, David Stewart, David Stirk, Elizabeth Stubbs, Kier Sword, Andrew Symington, Jack Teeling, Elodie Teissedre, Jens Tholstrup, Graeme Thomson, Pippa Thomson, Margaret Mary Timpson, Hide Tokuda, Robin Torrie, Gerry Tosh, Rich Trachtenberg, Robin Tucek, Cathy Turner, The Urquhart Family, Alistair Walker, Billy Walker, Karen Walker, Rick Wasmund, Ian Weir, Amy Westlake, Cristina Wilkie, Michelle Williams, Alan Winchester, Arthur Winning, Lance Winters, Gordon Wright, Kate Wright, Vanessa Wright, Ken Young, Ron Zussman.

Thameside Media and Dorling Kindersley would like to thank the following distilleries and drinks companies for supplying their images, labels or bottles for use as illustrations in this book: Isle of Arran, Beam Global, Bladnoch, Bruichladdich, Burn Stewart, Chivas Brothers, John Dewar & Sons, Diageo, Duncan Taylor, Edradour, Edrington Group, Glenfarclas, Gordon & MacPhail, Inver House, Kilchoman, Morrison Bowmore, Speciality Drinks, Springbank, Tomatin, Whyte & Mackay, William Grant & Sons.

Photography: pp1–3 Michael Ellis; pp6–69 Ian O'Leary (except p12 Chivas Brothers, p32 Diageo, p43 Edrington Group, p13 Cathy Turner); p72 Paul Harris.

INDEX